Fascist Modernities

STUDIES ON THE HISTORY OF SOCIETY AND CULTURE

Victoria E. Bonnell and Lynn Hunt, Editors

Fascist Modernities

Italy, 1922–1945

RUTH BEN-GHIAT

University of California Press

BERKELEY   LOS ANGELES   LONDON

University of California Press
Berkeley and Los Angeles, California

University of California Press, Ltd.
London, England

Library of Congress Cataloging-in-Publication Data

Ben-Ghiat, Ruth.
    Fascist modernities : Italy, 1922–1945 / Ruth Ben-Ghiat.
        p.   cm.
    Includes bibliographical references and index.
    ISBN 0-520-22363-2 (cloth : alk. paper).
        1. Fascism and culture—Italy—History.   2. Fascism—Italy—
    History.   3. Italy—Politics and government—1922–1945.
    4. Italy—Intellectual life—20th century.   I. Title.
    DG571.B4376   2001
    945.091—dc21   99-087279
                                                                CIP

Manufactured in the United States of America

09 08 07 06 05 04 03 02 01 00
10 9 8 7 6 5 4 3 2 1

The paper used in this publication meets the minimum requirements
of ANSI/NISO z39.48-1992 (R 1997) (*Permanence of Paper*). ♾

Contents

Illustrations

Acknowledgments

This book could not have been written without the generous support of many institutions and individuals. I am indebted to the American Philosophical Society, the Fulbright Commission, the Getty Research Institute, the University of North Carolina at Charlotte, and Fordham University for grants and leave time for research and writing, and to the University Seminars at Columbia University for assistance in preparing the manuscript for publication. I also wish to thank Lynn Hunt for her support of the project, as well as Sheila Levine of the University of California Press. In Rome, my work was facilitated by Giuseppe d'Errico of the Biblioteca Nazionale, Mario Serio and the staff of Archivio Centrale dello Stato, Tonino Cilenti of the Accademia dei Lincei, Luigi Oggianu of the Istituto LUCE, Carlo Chiarenza of the Italian Fulbright Commission, and Paola Castagna and the staff of the Centro Sperimentale di Cinematografia.

Ernesto Treccani, Mara Blasetti, Luciano Anceschi, and the Granata family generously shared their papers and experiences with me. I am also grateful to Omer Bartov, Emily Braun, and Carl Ipsen for their comments on portions of the manuscript, and to Alexander De Grand for years of encouragement and for the example of his own pioneering work on Italian fascist culture. Lisa Tiersten read several drafts of the manuscript; her humor, intelligence, and camaraderie are much appreciated. A great many other friends and colleagues provided support over the years. I would like to remember the late Nicola Gallerano and Niccolò Zapponi and express my heartfelt thanks to Corin Asti, Mario Biagioli, Richard Bosworth, Bill Bowman, Sande Cohen, Diane Coyle, Angela Dalle Vacche, Mia Fuller, Bruce Gardner, Emilio Gentile, Glenda Gilmore, Frances Glenn, Nita Juneja, MacGregor Knox, Linda Kroff, Charlie Lee, Paolo Macry, Cinzia Mulé,

Franco Pirone, Tip Ragan, Kriss Ravetto, Magdalena Sanchez, Bette Talvacchia, Curt Welty, and Jeanne Willette. Alice Kelikian has been an important presence all along, as a dissertation advisor, mentor, and friend. My family has also offered much encouragement, and my brother, Michael Benghiat, is a continuing source of inspiration. My husband, Elliot Jurist, gave the manuscript the benefit of his critical and psychological acumen and showed great patience during the long process of writing and revision. I am grateful for the gift of his love and for his wonderful cooking.

Introduction

In 1934, the young art critic Renato Poggioli asked his peers: "What is this Europe in dissolution that wants to drag us into the abyss as well? Should we Italians become more European, or should Europe become more Italian? . . . Are we merely an eccentric peninsula on the continent, or are we still and always the garden of the Empire? To defend ourselves spiritually, should our culture turn its back on Europe, or should we be open to that which comes from outside?"[1] Poggioli's concerns over national identity and the future of Europe were shared by intellectuals throughout the continent after World War I. The expansion of consumer capitalism and mass culture raised fears of eroded national and social boundaries, giving rise to protectionist measures in both democracies and dictatorships. The economic crisis, political turmoil, and decreases in fertility also heightened fears of a generalized European decline. To many intellectuals, the ruin of the bourgeois-capitalist order that had secured for Europe colonies, markets, and cultural authority in the world seemed imminent.[2] In this climate, new political movements developed that combined seemingly contradictory agendas: the defense of national traditions and the establishment of new supranational empires based on antiliberal principles. In Italy, Germany, and France, intellectuals lent their support to ideologies that promised to transform the existing political, economic, social, and cultural order as a means of reversing Europe's supposed degeneration.[3]

The belief that identities of every sort would be compromised by mass society had structured the experience of modernity for European intellectuals since the fin de siècle years. Urbanization and the growth of industrial capitalism, feminism, and mass politics conjoined to democratize societies by weakening traditional barriers to the circulation of goods, people, and information. Following a central paradox of modernity, technological advance

1

and the conquest of space and time heightened fears of regression: colonial expansion and the cinema brought greater awareness of extra-European peoples but also increased anxieties about degeneration and the preservation of cultural and genetic patrimonies. Race, along with gender, emerged as a primary category through which intellectuals articulated mass society's challenge to the established political and social order.[4] For Gustave Le Bon and other fin de siècle social scientists, Europe's "dangerous classes" (women, workers, the poor, criminals) were atavistic beings who threatened social order by seeming to breach the boundary between colony and metropole.[5]

World War I further diffused the belief that modernity might cause Europe to "slip back into barbarism" by subverting hierarchies of power and taste. The stark revelation of the machine's capacity to maim and murder millions lent a new urgency to ongoing reflections about the human costs of industrial advance. In the twenties, many intellectuals and artists had embraced machine aesthetics and the rationalization of industrial and cultural production as evidence of mass society's transformative potential.[6] By the thirties, though, the economic crisis and the perception of an insidious leveling of manners and identities led even those who championed continued modernization to ponder modernity's regressive social effects.[7] Among European males, the war also set off a collective crisis of authority that formed the subtext of the burgeoning literature on continental decline. Antonio Gramsci observed shrewdly that the contemporary "crisis of civilization" was partly a projection of elites' fears over the loss of hegemony; and the "symptoms" of Europe's fatal illness as described in one 1929 analysis—"tiredness, psychic imbalances, and a striking arrest of productive and reproductive powers"—tellingly converge with those displayed by many traumatized European men after World War I.[8] In this context, perceived shifts in gender and racial hierarchies became metaphors for social decay and the demise of civilization itself. Ultimately, the perception of a crisis of authority brought on by the war and the advent of mass society created support for political movements that promised to discipline all those "vertical invaders," who, as José Ortega y Gasset put it in 1930, had "appeared on the stage [of civilization] through a trapdoor."[9]

This cultural history examines how one project of national regeneration and international conquest developed in Italy in the decades following World War I. I argue that fascism appealed to many Italian intellectuals as a new model of modernity that would resolve both the contemporary European crisis and long-standing problems of the national past. For those who believed that both capitalism and communism led to social and economic leveling, fascism offered the fantasy of a mass society that allowed economic development without harm to social boundaries and national traditions. Many different models of modernity competed for legitimacy under the dictatorship, but all of them presented fascism as a movement that would forestall the spread of standardization and degeneration while bringing to Italians the benefits of contemporary life. In this scheme, the spaces of modernity (such as cinemas, colonies, and mass political gatherings) would lose their associations with social anarchy and instead function as sites that reinforced order and hierarchy. As one Italian boasted in an article on the regime's new "mass life," the genius of fascism lay in its development of a system "that allows each personality to retain its perfect contours, because we assign each person in the social scale a specific place."[10] At a time of fears about European hegemony and shifting social identities, then, the fascists proposed a model of modern existence that foresaw a comforting continuity of master narratives of privilege and domination.

Yet the fascists did not seek simply to protect traditional interests in the face of mass society. Rather, fascism represented an attempt to modernize under authoritarian premises by placing new technologies of information, mass mobilization, and reproduction at the service of the regime. Mussolini intended not only to "make Italians," fulfilling the promise of liberal nationalization schemes, but to remake them in ways that would facilitate his projects of conquest and colonization. Through a combination of indoctrination, legislation, and punitive action, he and his followers aimed to remold behaviors and bodies to combat domestic decadence and achieve international prestige.

Fascism certainly contained many "reactionary" elements. Under the dictatorship, women, workers, and Jews lost the privileges they had won since Unification. Moreover, the regime's "return to traditions," which valorized peasant and artisanal culture, clearly constituted a rejection of urban and cosmopolitan visions of modern life. Fascist policies may also be seen, however, as outgrowths of an agenda of social engineering that aimed to refashion Italians and establish a new civilization. The "return to traditions," for example, which involved peasants in folklore festivals and costume exhibitions, appealed to the makers of fascist policy and to fascist intellectuals less as a nostalgic revisitation of history than as an opportunity to create a peculiarly Italian and fascist mass culture that celebrated order and hierarchy. In the same vein, the 1938 anti-Jewish laws and "reform of custom," which formed part of a campaign to "Aryanize" Italians, were not merely the result of the German alliance. These measures also answered long-standing anxieties about "primitive" elements within the national population who had supposedly hindered Italy's path to modernity and status as a Great Power. Rather than constituting a departure from previous policies, they were the culmination of a decade of efforts designed to create a more "civilized" Italian who, Mussolini claimed, would "speak little, gesticulate less, and seem driven by a single will."[11] From this perspective, the fascist regime looks less like an incoherent mix of modern and antimodern impulses than an ambitious totalitarian plan to remake Italy and the Italians in the service of a utopian vision of international hegemony.[12]

The concept of *bonifica*, or reclamation, was central to many discourses of fascist modernity. Initially, the term referred to the conversion of swampland into arable soil and New Towns along the Latium coast and in Sicily and Sardegna. Yet land reclamation merely constituted the most concrete manifestation of the fascists' desire to purify the nation of all social and cultural pathology. The campaigns for agricultural reclamation *(bonifica agricola)*, human reclamation *(bonifica umana)*, and cultural reclamation *(bonifica della cultura)*, together with the anti-Jewish laws, are seen here as different facets and phases of a comprehensive project to combat degeneration and radically renew Italian society by "pulling up the bad weeds and cleaning up the soil."[13]

Several different traditions of thought informed this attempt to mandate a totalizing national transformation. First, modernism had always proclaimed the world as malleable to the will of individuals whose work could alter moral and political climates as well as aesthetic ones. Italian avant-gardists envisioned spiritual and cultural renewals that would facilitate the realization of expansionist political agendas. After World War I, Mussolini put his own twist on this celebration of the power of the creative urge, proclaiming himself an artist who would mold and style the national body as a sculptor did a lump of clay.[14] Second, the belief in war as a means of national regeneration was a common theme of avant-garde culture in the fin de siècle years. This myth grew even more powerful after World War I as a means of staving off the feelings of impotence and disorientation that overtook many Europeans. Those veterans who joined groups such as the Freikorps, the Croix de Feu, and the *fasci di combattimento* had come away from the conflict with a desire to extend war's "purificatory violence" into the domestic arena.[15] Throughout the two decades of dictatorship, war was considered the privileged motor of collective transformations that would allow Italy to assume a leadership role in a new international order. Indeed, fascist propagandists presented the regime's domestic and colonial campaigns as moments in an ongoing process of national regeneration that had commenced with World War I. The experience of conquest in Africa would generate a "new type of human being" whose toughness and discipline would guarantee the continuation of white racial hegemony. Thus Mussolini characterized his country's 1935 invasion of Ethiopia as a continuation of the "most gigantic work of agricultural, social, and human *bonifica* of our times."[16]

Third, the fascist urge to *bonificare* expressed technocratic social planning impulses and a mode of scientific thinking that, as Omer Bartov has observed, approached human society as "an organism to be manipulated by means of a vast surgical operation."[17] As in Nazi Germany, engineering, medicine, and science provided the paradigms and lexicon of this approach to governance, which offered comfort and an illusion of control to those racked by fears of Europe's imminent decline. In fact, Mussolini referred to himself not just as an artist but also as a "clinician" who would intervene to combat symptoms of degeneracy and decline. In the early thirties, before Hitler had come to power, he and officials such as Giuseppe Bottai advocated what they called a "therapeutic" approach to governance. The state would intervene to "cure" *(curare)* deviant and decadent impulses, creating positive energies that could be channeled and coordinated to fulfill fascism's goals. Over the next decade, this idea translated into an array of social, scientific, and cultural policies designed to encourage the "regeneration" of the national body. The regime's anti-Semitic policies, in this light, merely constituted the most radical of these "therapeutic" measures: as one official publication reasoned in 1938, anti-Jewish provisions, "like any other surgical operation," temporarily disturbed the organism in the name of long-term health and stability.[18] Although the Italians never engaged in the kind of racial eugenics that this mode of thinking produced in Nazi Germany, social and natural scientists were mobilized to manage and redesign the population in Rome as in Berlin.[19]

If the Italian and German dictatorships shared a vision of the state as a laboratory for the creation of a "new man," important differences did separate the two regimes. In Hitler's Germany, where racial concerns predominated, reclamation efforts focused on reengineering the bloodline of the Volkskörper (the body of the nation) through the eradication of impure and "foreign" genetic material. In contrast, the Italian regime preferred to segregate and rehabilitate, rather than physically eliminate, those who were labeled as delinquents or worse. This was less a function of differences in national character or behaviors—the squadrists had had no difficulty killing opponents of fascism, and in the colonies and during World War II Italians often acted as barbarously as the Nazis—than of divergent national issues and goals. Concerns about prestige and form weighed heaviest in Italy, where reclamation represented above all a chance to reverse the nation's perceived subaltern status with respect to other foreign powers and to all things modern. Since Unification, discourses of Italian nationalization and modernization had been tied to the desire to "catch up" to other nations and shed the stigma of perennially being, in Francesco De Sanctis's rueful words, "at the end of the line, or in the second-class seats." For many fascists, the dictatorship offered an opportunity to bring all of Italy's natural and human resources to bear on the task of escaping a liminal position as "the least of the great powers" and emerging as a respected international force.[20]

Thus, while "perfecting man" certainly figured in fascist strategies of social engineering, improving Italy's image and international position proved to be a more compelling goal for many who subscribed to Mussolini's movement. Totalitarian treatments would toughen and discipline a population that, the Duce claimed, had been "feminized" and "disarmed" by centuries of foreign occupation. State-mandated reforms of custom and language would temper tendencies toward servility and regional fragmentation, and eugenics and military training would produce hardy conquerors who would refute Bismarck's scornful comment (made in reference to Italy's colonial ambitions) that the country had a big appetite but very poor teeth. In the Italian context, then, *bonifica* formed a central component of a comprehensive modernization strategy designed, as Mussolini boasted in 1927, to "make Italy unrecognizable to itself and to foreigners in ten years."[21]

This book explores culture's role in diffusing these ideals of modernity and national regeneration. Many fascist intellectuals viewed culture as a carrier of values and moral norms and endowed it with the power to transform as well as represent: both practitioners and audiences, these Italians believed, could be reborn and renewed by contact with Art. The aestheticized politics that characterized the regime's mass culture applied this modernist principle on a collective level with the intent of creating new communities of feeling and faith.[22] This intertwining of ethics and aesthetics gave cultural creation an important function in fascist schemes of collective change. For many fascist critics, "becoming modern" was a learned behavior, since modernity implied not only a set of aesthetic choices but the adoption of a hierarchy of values that translated into a distinct way of approaching the world and acting in it.[23] Culture was also assigned a key role in the regime's projects for international expansion. Italy's formidable cultural patrimony made many fascists acutely aware of the role aesthetic prestige could play in the arrogation of international influence. A regenerated Italian culture would advertise national creative genius throughout the world, much as it had during the Renaissance. From the inception of the regime, then, fascist culture was to aid external as well as internal colonization schemes, supplementing military conquest with a work of "spiritual penetration."[24]

For many intellectuals, the advent of dictatorship in Italy represented an opportunity to redress an issue that had nagged at elites since the Risorgimento: the lack of a national culture. The absence of a cohesive Italian taste and style, fascists felt, had allowed the country to become a cultural colony of more dominant nations. Internalizing foreign views of themselves as "insignificant imitators," Italians had become a people who believed that "everything foreigners do is great, everything we do is awful."[25] Such status anxieties resulted, in part, from the different path taken by the Italian cultural industries with respect to those of France and Germany. Since the late nineteenth century, low literacy rates and a high percentage of dialect speakers had kept production of Italian-language newspapers, periodicals, and books small—even under market demand. World War I had only intensified this trend, since book production fell and the formerly prestigious Italian film industry nearly ceased to operate. Throughout the liberal period, therefore, Italian consumption of foreign culture, both popular and elite, was among the highest in Europe. The fascists won followers by promising to reverse this situation of "foreigner-worship" and create a national culture that would be well received abroad.[26]

This project, no less than other fascist nationalization schemes, involved the mobilization of state resources to remold the social collective. Culture was envisioned as an integrative device that would create a shared set of values to bind Italians to the state and reaffirm the normative behaviors envisioned by fascist reclamation schemes. Especially after 1936, when Mussolini accelerated his campaigns of collective transformation, culture became an important site for the articulation of autarchic and racist sentiments by those who wished to replace the "voice of the ghetto and the amusement park" with "the voice of blood and the spirit."[27] Considering cultural developments in the context of the regime's social and foreign policies, this book seeks to problematize the distinctions between "moderate" and "extremist" movements and individuals that have long been used to plot the dictatorship's cultural map.[28] Openness to the latest foreign trends, as we will see, was not incompatible with racism of the most virulent sort: the officials Giuseppe Bottai and Roberto Farinacci were both anti-Semites, despite their famously different attitudes with respect to modern art.[29] In the years of the Axis alliance, though, culture also served as a sphere through which Italians asserted their autonomy and opposition to Nazi agendas of cultural imperialism.

A premise of this book is that fascism found support among the majority of Italian intellectuals because it addressed both the hopes and the fears of the modern age. Defined by Mussolini as a "revolution of reaction," fascism expressed tensions within modernity between the push toward progress and the fear of degeneration, the demand for emancipation and the impulse to preserve order, the frisson of impermanence and the desire for stable identities. Its ideologies gave political voice to the cult of youth, the primacy of myth, and the modernist idea of history as malleable, but also represented a response to long-standing anxieties about modernity that escalated in the interwar years. Natalist measures, for example, answered fears about unstable racial and gender hierarchies, and the mass organizing undertaken by the *Opera Nazionale Dopolavoro* (OND, or National Leisure Time Organization) aimed to break down class and regional allegiances and protect local traditions of culture and craft. For still other Italians, fascism appeared to counter the dangers posed by globalization, which were summed up by one commentator as the "yellow peril, the red peril, and the danger of the American standard."[30]

At the level of doctrine, the fascist claim to protect the individual from the excesses of technology and mass society found expression in several ways. Whereas capitalism and communism valorized only *homo economicus*, supporters claimed, the fascist model of modern existence catered to "real man in all his historic and psychological complexity" by promoting spiritual as well as social development.[31] As theorized by party philosopher Giovanni Gentile, the dictatorship was an "ethical state" that embodied moral values and offered the individual protection and community without suppressing individual initiative. Fascism, accordingly, was defined as a "spiritual revolution" that, unlike socialism or communism, would improve the moral as well as material climate of Europe. The left might offer a worker's paradise of "wine, women, chicken, and cinema," Mussolini declared, but only fascism would generate new values to underpin innovations in the social and economic spheres.[32]

To fascism's opponents, the idea that it constituted a spiritualistic "return to man" contrasted ludicrously with the repressive and dehumanizing reality of life under blackshirt rule. Yet the notion of fascism as an ethical force proved to be a valuable consensus-building device among Italians. First, it underwrote the production of a sacralized political culture and public sphere that used religious symbols and rites as integrative devices.[33] Second, it allowed Catholics to discover points of convergence between the

ideas of fascism and those of the Roman Church, facilitating their participation in the life of the dictatorship.[34] Third, it enabled the blackshirts to
distinguish themselves from the Bolsheviks even as they made use of leftist language to advance a competing program of "revolutionary" change.
Fourth, it helped intellectuals to sustain their understanding that fascism
respected personal conscience and will. This notion also informed distinctions Italians drew in the thirties between Mussolini's "humane" regime
and the brutal dictatorships set up by Stalin and Hitler. The ideologue
Camillo Pellizzi spoke for many of his peers when he characterized fascism
in 1936 as "the last trench in the modern world where one fights for the defense of *Man.*"[35]

As a study of how culture contributed to the diffusion of fascist models
of modernity, this book necessarily addresses the relationship of Italian
intellectuals and Mussolini's regime. To succeed in creating a culture that
would underwrite the transformation of the Italian nation, the fascists
needed the support of the intellectual class. Over two decades, they developed a complex patronage structure that was designed to contain dissent
and draw creative individuals into collaborative relationships with the state.
Like other regimes of the twentieth century, the fascist dictatorship used
intimidation and flattery in ways that tested each individual's capacity for
idealism and opportunism. Unlike the rulers of state socialist regimes,
though, Mussolini never prescribed an official aesthetic style; nor did he go
out of his way to prevent the production of certain kinds of art, as did Hitler
from the inception of Nazi rule. Rather, he and some of his functionaries
adopted an ostentatiously "tolerant" stance on the subject of which styles
and themes would best represent fascism.

This proved to be a shrewd strategy, as it encouraged intellectuals of diverse tendencies to compete for legitimacy and recognition by the government and allowed those who did not openly identify themselves as fascists
to participate in the public initiatives of the regime. It also ensured that far
fewer intellectuals emigrated from fascist Italy than from Nazi Germany,
and some of the few who did leave Italy even decided to return. Such policies have led some scholars to speak of fascism's "pluralist" tendencies, but
the use of this term is questionable in reference to a state that was contin-
uously purging its cultural field, forcing antifascist intellectuals to choose
between silence, imprisonment, and exile.[36] Moreover, although Mussolini
may have placed fewer overt controls on artistic content than did other dictators, a web of tacit regulations kept intellectuals in check and encouraged
them to practice self-censorship. Even as the Duce declared his respect for
creative freedom, he tapped intellectuals' telephones, intercepted their mail,

and spied on them through a web of specialized police informers culled from the universities, the cinema, the theater, and journalism.[37]

To better explore the dynamics of the relationship between Italian intellectuals and the dictatorship, this book relates parallel histories of identity construction. As I examine the elaboration of visions of fascist culture and modernity, I also seek to reconstruct how Italian intellectuals crafted new identities for themselves as men and women working within the regime's reward and punishment structures. This double narrative extends to my analysis of texts, which I view as moments in an ongoing process of negotiation and positioning by their authors with respect to the state and to the works of other intellectuals. Following both creative development and career trajectories, I elucidate the process by which Italian intellectuals came to terms with Mussolini's regime. My emphasis here is on the dynamic between cultural policy and cultural production: how intellectuals responded to and interpreted official goals and ideologies and how, in turn, the regime reacted to their efforts, determining the conditions (studio resources, censorship requirements, funding) under which future works would be created.

At the same time, I emphasize the ties that bound intellectuals and cultural policy makers, and highlight their roles in diffusing the causes of the regime's domestic and foreign policy campaigns. Complex networks of influence and patronage linked censors and other officials to cultural producers, and it was not uncommon for one person to fulfill several roles simultaneously. Moreover, authority was often masked in fascist Italy. Intellectuals authored government textbooks and propaganda pamphlets anonymously or pseudonymously, and officials asked intellectuals to publicize their own private causes.[38] After two decades of dictatorship, few intellectuals had not become entangled in fascist cultural enterprises and institutions. This collective complicity made it difficult to defascistize Italian culture after World War II, and made it difficult for intellectuals to come to terms with their role in legitimating the myriad causes of the dictatorship.

Through the lens of culture, this book also examines the factors that complicated and ultimately bedeviled fascism's goal of remaking Italians. First, the adulation shown Mussolini did not, in many cases, extend to the policies and representatives of his regime, and it rarely inspired the transformation of mental habits and bodily practices envisioned in official circles. As the government knew from a steady stream of informer's reports, certain groups, such as workers in northern and central Italy and university students, greeted its populist promises with great skepticism.[39] And while the OND and the *fasci femminili* (women's organizations) could boast a mass membership and a high level of activism, participation in the collective activities of these organizations sometimes fostered the development of those very values that the regime wished to extirpate.[40] As we will see, Italians supported the regime for over twenty years in numbers sufficient to sustain the destruction of socialism, the subjugation of Ethiopia, the persecution of the Jews, and, after September 1943, the armies of the Republic of Salò. But a wide range of variables, including class, geography, gender, family traditions, and religious beliefs, mediated Italians' relationships with the regime and influenced how and to what extent fascism affected their thoughts and behavior.

Ironically, social and economic developments related to modernization also hampered the development of a distinctly fascist modernity that would foster economic development without harm to social and national boundaries. After World War I, urbanization, consumerism, and improvements in transportation and information technologies created more cosmopolitan tastes and allegiances.[41] Like the Germans and the French, the Italians responded by promoting artisans, celebrating local customs, and developing advertising cultures that highlighted recognizably "national" symbols and aesthetic styles. One French observer thus noted in 1927 that "[national] particularities and peculiarities are appearing everywhere . . . at the very moment they are being denied."[42] These tensions between protectionism and internationalization were exacerbated rather than resolved by the fascist regime, whose policies and ideologies formed part of a broader impulse to rethink the nation-state after World War I. Like the Nazis, the fascists combined autarchic agendas with programs for territorial aggrandizement. For Mussolini, as for Hitler, the creation of a unified nation was a first step in the realization of a supranational empire that would implement a new political and economic order.[43] Thus admonitions to "keep Italy Italian" coexisted with incitements to adopt an "imperial" consciousness founded on a belief in fascism as a universal rather than a national phenomenon. As one publicist asserted, being Italian was a fact of civil status; being fascist was a matter of thinking and acting in a particular way.[44]

The conflicts created by these oppositional impulses became particularly evident in the course of the dictatorship's attempts to realize a national culture. While studies of fascism have traditionally focused on the regime's use of culture for purposes of internal consensus-building, I argue that the desire to expand Italian influence abroad also shaped the evolution of cultural policy and cultural production under Mussolini. If national cultures are constructions that serve agendas of internal order, they also operate in a larger context, as products that compete for audiences on an international scale. The convergence of fascist imperial pretensions and the arrival of American mass culture on the continent meant that debates over which styles would best represent the Italian nation were conducted with one eye trained on the foreign market. The concern to produce works that would have a "universal" appeal worked at cross-purposes with the government's aims to homogenize and unify Italians and tempered tendencies to mandate recognizably "fascist" styles or themes for Italian culture.

The Italian fascists were hardly unusual in their impulse to look abroad as they sought to build a new national culture. In nineteenth-century Greece and Germany, as in twentieth-century Spain, China, and Thailand, intellectuals who engaged in the fashioning of national aesthetics turned to foreign cultures for ideas and practices that could then be filtered, assimilated, and recontextualized.[45] Italy was no different. Cross-cultural borrowings had been prized since the Risorgimento by intellectuals who associated *aggiornamento* (becoming up to date) with the absorption and adaptation of elements from foreign countries.[46] Such sentiments took on a more overtly imperialist cast by World War I, preparing the way for the fascist view that taking the best that other peoples had to offer was one step on the road to conquering them. As the young militant Giulio Santangelo would write in 1928,

> Do we want to make this empire? Then we must leave our beautiful little towns and go out into the world to get to know those whom we intend to dominate. We need to rid ourselves of all that suits us alone, and highlight the things we possess that are suitable for others as well. We must ruthlessly take the good wherever we find it and make it ours, Italian, and serve ourselves of it for our own ends.[47]

Starting in the early 1930s, the regime translated this concept into cultural policy, creating an array of institutions that facilitated the selective appropriation of foreign ideas. Although the German alliance changed the direction of fascist cultural exchanges and restricted their scope, the desire to "master" cultural modernity as articulated by others never really abated. As late as February 1943, the official Fernando Mezzasoma—who would soon become the head of Salò's Ministry of Popular Culture—upheld the utility of such foreign explorations. Although he supported bans on works that might "influence our new generations to develop tendencies that are outside our own," he recognized that familiarity with foreign "customs, movements, and manners" was necessary knowledge for any modern power.[48] Such policies ultimately worked against the fulfillment of purists' fantasies of a uniquely Italian and fascist culture and society, and ensured the failure of the regime's designs to shape a national collective that was free of all "unhealthy" cultural tendencies.

The contradictions I have outlined here also complicated the fascists' plans to create a new ruling elite that would perpetuate their models of modernity. Billing itself as a "regime of youth," the dictatorship spared no resources to attract the best youth into its orbit. Italians born between roughly 1905 and 1915—contemporaries of Simone de Beauvoir and Hans Werner Richter—were known collectively as "the favorite child of fascism," the one upon whom the greatest expectations were placed, and the one who, accordingly, had the greatest potential to delude.[49] Too young to have participated in World War I or the March on Rome, the most militant felt a kind of status anxiety in a regime that made combat experience a measure of political faith and masculinity. "We twenty-year-olds feel irremediably *parvenus*," complained the journalist Indro Montanelli in 1933. "We are spiritually equipped to be assault squads, but fate has given us the role of Swiss Guards of the constituted order."[50] Young women shared these feelings of impatience but had to negotiate additional restrictions on their activities by fearful parents, a natalism-obsessed government, and their often misogynistic male peers.

Culture served this generation of intellectuals as a compensatory sphere within the fascist state. Through subsidies and lenient censorship laws, the regime made it possible for younger Italians to give voice to their own visions of a fascist modernity. Taking to heart Mussolini's promises to bring social justice to Italy, younger men and women produced blueprints for antibourgeois mass societies that would embody the principles of gender equality, corporativist economics, and social revolution. This brought them into direct conflict with many older intellectuals and regime officials, whose own visions of fascist mass society foresaw the strengthening, rather than the erosion, of hierarchies of gender and class. Although the liberties of younger Italians were further restricted after 1936, and corporativism's main patron, Bottai, transferred his energies to racial causes, the promulgation of new aesthetic codes that would underwrite a uniquely fascist modernity remained this cohort's primary project. During World War II, though, the regime lost the support of many young intellectuals, including those of a newer generation—born around 1920—who had come of age entirely under the regime. As in Franco's Spain, official youth organizations would become one recruiting ground for dissidents; state-sponsored journals such as *Cinema* and *La Ruota* would be another. Whatever their provenance and formation, in the final war-torn years of the dictatorship young intellectuals began to utilize their positions within fascist cultural institutions to advance models of national culture divorced from Mussolini's state. In the end, the military enterprises that were central to official schemes of national reclamation turned many in their twenties and thirties against the fascist regime.

This study utilizes a wide range of sources—documents from public and private archives, the official and independent press, memoirs, and interviews—and makes reference to architecture, music, and painting. Novels and films, however, serve as my primary representations of fascist cultural production. Cinema and literature have always been closely related in Italy, through the frequency of screen adaptations of novels and the habit of many writers to act as screenwriters on occasion.[51] These practices were consolidated during the 1930s, creating a considerable interchange between Italian filmic and literary cultures that would continue long after the fall of the dictatorship.

The first half of the book is organized thematically and concentrates on the early 1930s. Chapter 1 discusses the evolution of the regime's patronage structure and examines how Italians' critiques of foreign mass societies played a role in the definition of fascist models of modernity. Chapters 2 and 3 explore the ways in which literature and film participated in the regime's reclamation enterprises. Chapter 4 discusses the regime's attempts to apply its "therapeutic" politics to young intellectuals and explores how generational tensions within the dictatorship found expression in conflicting visions of fascist modernity. The book's second half takes the narrative from the invasion of Ethiopia to the fall of the regime in 1943. Chapter 5 discusses how the regime's colonial enterprise and racial measures were received by the intellectual class, and looks at the cultural effects of the Rome-Berlin Axis. Chapter 6, which focuses on World War II, looks at how the regime counted on culture in order to assert itself as an international power after military debacles ended fascist hopes for political domination. Against this backdrop, I show how young intellectuals such as Luchino Visconti and Alba De Céspedes utilized literature and film as vehicles for the expression of antifascist sentiments. The epilogue looks at the period 1943–45. It explores how the traumatic events of those years led many Italian intellectuals to see themselves as victims rather than perpetrators, complicating the process of collective reckoning with their engagement with the dictatorship.

The fascist desire to remake Italians was no isolated dream. In the interwar period, the disciplinary imperatives of nationalism and consumer capitalism combined with the reformist urges of social-planning schemes to produce states that intervened more strenuously in the governance of everyday life. Under Mussolini, though, the state also emerged as a laboratory for the creation of a new civilization that would impose social, sexual, and racial order at a time of widespread uncertainty and change. How the world of culture participated in the making and unmaking of this project forms the subject of this book.

1   Toward a Fascist Culture

Six months before taking power, Mussolini asked readers of his new review *Gerarchia*, "Does fascism aim at restoring the State, or subverting it? Is it order or disorder? . . . Is it possible to be conservatives and subversives at the same time? How does fascism intend to escape this vicious circle of paradoxical contradictions?"[1] With an impossibly heterogeneous coalition of supporters, which included Nationalists, monarchists, national syndicalists, squadrists, and conservative clericals, Mussolini did not really intend to clarify his movement's ideological identity. The fascist leader had initially marketed himself as a radical populist, using antibourgeois rhetoric and promises of access to land and voting rights to attract women, veterans, workers, and underemployed university graduates. Once he became prime minister in October 1922, though, this stance was all but jettisoned for a realpolitik approach that allowed for compromises with industrialists, the Church, and other major interest groups. Working in tandem with the fascist government, these elites recast political and economic institutions, adopting new strategies of compromise and coercion to maintain old privileges.[2] By 1926, it seemed that conservative interests had been secured. Organized labor had been neutralized and negotiations had begun with Church officials that would lead to the 1929 Lateran Accords Concordat.

Yet it would be wrong to reduce fascism to a movement of bourgeois restoration. The "return to order" planned by Mussolini and his officials was merely the initial step of a comprehensive program of domestic transformation that would allow the country to emerge as an international and colonial power. The fascists' projects for collective change drew upon various liberal-era strains of thinking about Italian development, all of which envisioned the nation as a body whose individual parts had meaning only insofar as they ensured the harmonious functioning of the whole. In the

17

years preceding World War I, Positivists such as the criminal anthropologist Cesare Lombroso had utilized an organic model of the nation to justify interventions against those who complicated Italy's achievement of social harmony. Modernity, in this scheme, became a means of managing societal development by facilitating the detection and segregation of criminals, political rebels, prostitutes, and other "atavistic" elements.[3] The Italian Nationalist movement had also postulated the nation as an organic entity whose productive and reproductive energies were to be regulated and channeled to fulfill state goals. Nationalist thinkers such as Scipio Sighele, Alfredo Rocco, and Enrico Corradini had called for "order and collective discipline at home" to heal the "congenital Italian illness" of excessive individualism that had supposedly hindered Italy's progress as an imperial force. The demographer Corrado Gini added his own concerns about degeneration to the Nationalist project, arguing that the key to Italy's future as a modern and international power lay in the qualitative and quantitative amelioration of its population. As with the Positivists, emphasis was placed on the links between internal unity and foreign expansion.[4]

All these ideas about the state's role in the management of the modernization and nationalization processes found a place under fascism. For Gini and Rocco, who stood among the regime's leading policy makers, the advent of dictatorship provided the opportunity to pursue a politics of expansionism without obstructions from organized labor and the political opposition. The new fascist rulers also intended to mobilize state resources to discipline social groups whose presence was thought to obstruct the efficient functioning of the national body. The managerial and normalizing aspects of this vision of governance are evident in a speech Rocco made soon after his 1925 appointment as minister of justice: "Fascism, too, believes that it is necessary to guarantee the individual the conditions required for the free development of his faculties. . . . it is clear that a normal development of the individual life is necessary to social development. Necessary, provided that it is normal: an enormous and disordered development of some individuals and groups would be for society what an enormous and disordered development of cells is for an animal organism: a fatal disease."[5]

What this meant in practical terms became all too clear over the next years. From 1925 to 1929, a series of laws drafted by Rocco and other members of Mussolini's government transformed Italy into a police state with extensive powers of surveillance and detention. Groups with autonomist tendencies (the Mafia, former squadrists, regionalists) were coerced to coordinate their interests with those of the state; ethnic minorities in border regions such as the Val d'Aosta and the Alto Adige, for example, were labeled as "anti-Italian and antifascist" and forced to adopt new "national" surnames. Other disciplinary measures punished "nonproductive" members of the national collective (single men and women, criminals, dissidents, homosexuals, vagrants) and provided for the confinement *(confino)* of problematic persons in remote areas.[6] At the same time, the Central Institute of Statistics (ISTAT) was established under Gini's direction to manage and manipulate the national population pool. For the next seventeen years, mass population transfers to *bonifica* sites, eugenics research, and other demographic policy initiatives formed the cornerstones of the regime's policies of national transformation. Concurrently, the government created the OND as a vehicle for the indoctrination of peasants and the working class, who would learn the martial virtues of order and discipline through participation in collective cultural, tourist, and sporting events. Some of these initiatives certainly stemmed from the government's designs to domesticate the Fascist National Party (PNF). Taken collectively, though, they also point to an attempt to actuate a program of social engineering *(bonifica umana)* that, Mussolini hoped, would transform "the character, mentality, habits, and customs of the Italian people" and "fascistize the Nation, until Italian and fascist, almost like Italian and Catholic, are one and the same thing."[7]

Mussolini's 1927 Ascension Day speech clarified the larger goals that inspired such visions of collective change in Italy, presenting domestic and foreign policy measures as two sides of one totalitarian vision of national regeneration. Fascism's modernity, in this speech, is linked to its supposed capacity to utilize the tools of science to reclaim and transform Italy and the Italians in ways that would facilitate international expansion. Natalist programs would not only combat internal decadence by curtailing female emancipation but would close the demographic gap with dominant European nations and allow Italy to emerge as a leader on the continent. The government would undertake "necessary hygienic actions" to cure the "plagues" caused by southern "delinquents" and their "diseased" surroundings. As in Rocco's speech, politics takes on a therapeutic cast: the state emerges as a rehabilitative institute, with Mussolini as its chief clinician. Tellingly, the fascist leader used a medical metaphor to let Italians know what would happen to those who persisted in "unhealthy" behaviors: "We remove them from circulation as a doctor would an infected person," the Duce concluded.[8]

The concern with degeneration that pervades this speech also stemmed from Mussolini's fears of a subversion of racial hierarchies. That same year, the Duce wrote a preface for the Italian translation of Richard Kohrerr's Spenglerian tract *Decline of Births: Death of Peoples*, which warned that decreases in European fertility endangered the global racial balance of power. In his preface, Mussolini warned that "the entire white race, the Western race, could be submerged by races of color that multiply with a rhythm unknown to our own."[9] The Ascension Day speech addressed such concerns by offering a blueprint for a revolution in reproductive habits that would preserve white European hegemony. Demographic increase would not only make Italy a leader on the continent but would also solve Italy's land-hunger problem by permitting mass population transfers to Libya (held by Italy since 1911) and to future African colonies. For Mussolini, then, fascist modernity did not merely imply the defeat of degenerative influences within Italy, but also the neutralization of nonwhite races whose continued growth would bring about an era of "senseless disorder and unfathomable despair."[10]

POLITICS AND PATRONAGE IN ITALIAN FASCIST CULTURE

Since the squadrist years, the fascists had taken Mussolini's ideal of "surgical violence" to heart as they cut short the lives of those at home and abroad whom they felt would obstruct the process of Italian regeneration. Concluding in 1923 that consensus was "as changeable as the sand formations at the edge of the sea," the Duce relied on force and intimidation rather than popular consent to sustain him as he transformed Italy from a democracy to a dictatorship.[11] Yet, fascist officials recognized that brutality and coercion would prove counterproductive with the intellectual class. They lost no time in formulating "a special disciplinary system" for those whom they hoped would generate a fascist culture for domestic and foreign consumption. From the inception of the regime, promises of creative autonomy and state subsidies formed the parameters of a cultural policy that aimed to domesticate and normalize intellectuals while giving them the illusion that they worked within a pluralist system.[12]

Two factors determined this "magnanimous" approach to aesthetic affairs. First was the desire to give fascism an air of respectability at a time of ongoing squadrist violence and illegal imprisonment of opposition leaders. Second was Mussolini's need to keep fascism inclusive enough to accommodate the agendas of his disparate group of supporters. The movement thus emerged in the press as an antidogmatic authoritarianism, and the Duce reiterated his commitment to creative autonomy when pressed to give an opinion on the function of art in his state. The repressive policy measures that accompanied this rhetoric, however, made clear that Mussolini's "tolerance" was the fruit of political pragmatism. In 1923–24, the fascists expanded press censorship and created a government press office, a state radio company (the *Unione Radiografia Italiana*), and a production center for newsreels and documentary films (the Istituto LUCE), establishing a foundation for later initiatives of mass indoctrination.[13]

The efficacy of these instruments of propaganda control was tested late in 1924, when the fascists' murder of the popular Socialist politician Giacomo Matteotti provoked intense public hostility to Mussolini and his government. The Duce "resolved" the crisis with a political crackdown that mandated a heightened level of image control. Along with increasing censorship, the regime made its first serious attempts to recruit a corps of public intellectuals. At the inauguration of the National Institute of Fascist Culture (INCF) in March, Gentile asked attendees to sign a "Manifesto of Fascist Intellectuals," which would be circulated in the press to prove that fascism was not incompatible with culture and civility. This initiative prompted the philosopher Benedetto Croce and others to produce a countermanifesto, which appeared in the opposition daily *Il Mondo*. Croce had supported fascism even during the Matteotti crisis, seeing it as a buffer against mass society and leftist collectivism, but now became the regime's most prestigious dissident. The government quickly dismissed the Croce manifesto, but those who had signed it, such as the writer Marino Moretti, found themselves excluded from patronage networks for the years to come. Those who instead stuck by the fascists or chose this moment to declare their allegiance—as did the playwright Luigi Pirandello—increased their chances of official rewards, such as election to the Italian Academy.[14]

The declaration of dictatorship in 1925 also led to the first attempts to create an infrastructure that would support the development of a fascist culture. The esprit de corps that had bound together members of the avant-garde now came under attack as the remnants of a decadent bohemianism; although café society remained strong during the dictatorship, allegiances and affiliations of a public and statist nature increasingly structured Italian cultural life. No less than other social groups, intellectuals were subjected to *bonifica* policies meant to expurgate "unhealthy" tendencies from Italian culture and create disciplined cadres who would serve the state. Instead of liberal eclecticism and pluralism, which dissipated creative energies, the fascist intellectual should espouse "an effective intolerance[,] which is at the base of every constructive culture." Reclamation, here, aimed to produce a new totalitarian mentality among intellectuals that favored a militaristic "decisiveness and cleanliness in our thoughts and our positions."[15]

Organizations such as the National Confederation of Fascist Syndicates of Professionals and Artists emerged as the primary motors of this political-aesthetic "coordination." In theory, only PNF adherents could join a syndicate, and only those listed in the registers *(albi)* of that syndicate were eligible for employment. The fascists claimed that the syndical system would stimulate quality cultural production by fostering peer competition for state subsidies. In practice, though, the syndicates were hardly meritocratic. Building on clientalistic traditions among Italian elites that predated fascism, syndical officials commandeered positions of authority in fascist cultural institutions. Influencing job offers, juries, and examining commissions, they shaped power and patronage networks based on party membership, habituating generations of intellectuals to practices and attitudes that would characterize the Italian cultural world long after the fall of the regime.[16]

The openly coercive character of fascist cultural policy did not stop officials from describing fascism as a "regime of liberty" that respected the autonomy of conscience. Along with the philosopher Gentile, the official Giuseppe Bottai played a crucial role in the formulation of this party line. Bottai had come to fascism via the *arditi* assault troops and Futurism, and quickly staked out a role within the dictatorship as the premier patron of all that was modern: corporativism, some forms of artistic modernism, youth, and, later, also anti-Semitism—which he understood as a salutary cure of degenerate influences on the national body. In 1923, as a means of attracting "that class which is most reluctant to join the party—the intellectuals," he had created *Critica fascista* as a forum for "open, serene, and responsible discussion." Naturally, "fascist criticism" did not mean "criticism of fascism"; the achievement of ideological unity, rather than the cultivation of pluralism, remained the official goal. As one writer argued in the review, through the practice of fascist criticism "dissent is manifested, clarified, and eliminated dialectically, leading to a granite-block synthesis that represents the new civilization."[17] Indeed, for Bottai, as for many other rightists in interwar Europe, unregulated individual agency and civil liberties were among the legacies of the French revolution that had led Europe to a situation of social, political, and cultural crisis. Freedom, in this view, came through submission to a collective that regulated individual rights and duties, preventing both anarchy and atomization. Even as they restricted intellectual liberties, then, officials presented themselves as the protectors of individual spirituality and personhood. As Bottai wrote, fascism was the "last defense of Man" against the twin evils of "democratic leveling and communist annihilation."[18]

While this vision of a highly stratified society undoubtedly assuaged anxieties over the eclipse of transcendence and tradition within modernity, one might wonder how many Italian intellectuals truly believed that fascism constituted a force for freedom. In one sense it is a secondary question. As in other patronage situations, clients who wished to improve their positions were expected to make statements that confirmed their outward acceptance of the worldview of those who exercised power, regardless of their private beliefs. In this light, interventions in the fascist press constituted linguistic performances designed to demonstrate fidelity and a willingness to stay in a game that all the players knew was fixed.[19] For their part, Italian officials made it as easy as possible for intellectuals to participate by continually emphasizing fascism's commitment to freedom of conscience and opinion. In a 1928 speech to the directors of sixty daily newspapers, the Duce reiterated his will to maintain "a diversity of artists and temperaments" within the dictatorship, reasoning that overly politicized cultural criticism and cultural production would cause fascism to cut a *brutta figura* (bad figure) at home and abroad:

> In the fields of art, science, and philosophy, the party card cannot create a situation of privilege or immunity. Just as it must be permissible to say that Mussolini, as a violin player, is a very modest dilettante, it must also be permissible to advance objective judgments on art, prose, poetry, and theater without the threat of a veto due to an irregular party card. Here party discipline has no place. Here the revolution does not enter. . . . A fellow may be a valorous fascist, even of the first hour, but an idiot [*deficiente*] as a poet. The public must not be put in the position of having to choose between looking like antifascists for booing, or looking stupid and vile for applauding literary failures, poetic babblings, and housepainters' art. The party card does not give talent to those who don't already possess it.[20]

Such assurances of creative autonomy gave Italians something to work with. Over the next years, some intellectuals developed discursive strategies that may have minimized what Francesco Flora would later refer to as a collective sense of "habitual guilt." In discussions of cultural affairs, many came to favor an elliptical linguistic style that discouraged open political references and supported the comforting collective myth that the world of ideas ran on a strictly parallel course with that of the dictatorship. While such elusiveness angered party militants who wished for a more overt "fascistization" of Italian culture, several factors encouraged its diffusion. First was the influence of Crocean ideas of artistic autonomy, which made many intellectuals pause before the prospect of an openly propagandistic art. Second was the regime's goal of increasing its approval ratings abroad, which mandated the use of a "neutral" language at events that attracted high-profile foreigners. Third was the desire to involve as many Italian intellectuals as possible in public cultural initiatives, even those who may have wished to reap the rewards of participation with a minimum of compromise. When the painter Ardengo Soffici urged his peers to produce works "inspired by the reality surrounding us," was the referent for this reality fascism or simply contemporary society?[21] It was far shrewder not to say.

The regime's efforts to win over the intellectual class and create a mechanism for the continuous renewal of its authority also hinged on the promise of something much more tangible than creative autonomy: material aid. At the popular level, the dictatorship involved peasants and other Italians in spectacles that proclaimed its ability to orchestrate the population. Among intellectuals, though, gift giving emerged as the most effective medium for the circulation of state power. The profferal and acceptance of countless subsidies, grants, and prizes ceaselessly renewed the ties that bound culture and the regime and occasioned public declarations of support that, even if insincere, legitimated fascism and added to its symbolic authority.

The policies of the Italian Academy, one of the regime's principal patronage institutions, clarify how the task of creating a national culture became intertwined with the desire to draw intellectuals into cliental relationships with the government. Inaugurated in 1929, the Academy's official goals were to "promote and coordinate Italian intellectual movement in the fields of science, literature and the arts, keep the national character pure in accordance with the genius and traditions of the stock, and favor the expansion and influence [of this national spirit] outside the confines of the state."[22] To this end, the Academy financed an unsuccessful campaign for linguistic autarchy and established a State Record Library (*Discoteca dello Stato*) for the preservation of traditional songs and dialects. The Academicians, who included the Nobel Prize winners Enrico Fermi and Pirandello, were supposed to bring the body prestige, but informers' reports relate that most nominations aroused contempt among Italians and the resident foreign community. "The Academy is an institution devoid of content and lacking any reason for being," one Roman spy wrote in 1930, conveying the current café consensus on the subject.[23]

This scornful attitude did not stop thousands of intellectuals from applying for Academy grants to fund their creative and scholarly endeavors. Well-known Italians like the writers Ada Negri and Emilio Cecchi each received the lucrative Mussolini Prize, which was funded by the proprietors of the newspaper *Corriere della sera*. The painter Mario Mafai and the writers Anna Maria Ortese and Elio Vittorini were among the many members of Italy's postwar elite who won the much smaller "encouragement prizes" *(premi d'incoraggiamento)* aimed at younger, relatively unknown intellectuals. Like all ritual gifts, these came with strings attached: good intentions mingled with a desire to co-opt and control. While the Academy did promote culture under the dictatorship, its primary function, as stated in *Critica fascista,* was to check the "excessive individualism of our intellectuals" and prevent "the formation of literary and artistic hierarchies that might act against the State."[24]

If the regime's new institutional framework for culture allowed officials to monitor and "coordinate" the activities of intellectuals, it did little to stimulate the development of a specifically fascist culture. To redress this problem, in 1926–27 *Critica fascista* asked prominent intellectuals for their opinions on "fascist art," starting a public debate about the relationship of politics and culture that continued until the fall of the regime. Although all the participants echoed Mino Maccari's contention that fascist art would have to be "intimately and unmistakably Italian," no consensus could be reached on what that might mean. For the conservative critic Cipriano Efisio Oppo, *italianità* (Italianness) stood for order, discipline, and the classical heritage, while the Futurist Filippo Tommaso Marinetti interpreted it as a penchant for the spontaneous and the original. The most politic associated Italy with beatific equilibrium in all things: the country was at once spiritual and temporal, classical and Romantic, traditional and modern. It was a place whose culture, Soffici asserted, "unites the experience of the past with the promise of the future."[25]

Although these intellectuals proved reluctant to enunciate positive guidelines for fascist art, they did not hesitate to declare what that art must not be. Soffici denounced artists whose works showed "anti-Italian, liberal, Judaic, Masonic, and democratic" tendencies, and Bottai launched a not-so-veiled attack on modernism, labeling "psychoanalytic, fragmentary, syncopated" works as "rebellions against the great Italian artistic tradition." The official Alessandro Pavolini, who would later help to deport Jews to Nazi death camps during the period of the Republic of Salò, contributed a vitriolic, if coded, attack on Jews and other "cosmopolitan elements." He decried "recluses in ivory towers who speak to each other in their latest jargon, above the fray and beyond national borders[,] . . . critics who speak a mysterious tongue, editors of unfindable and unreadable journals, frauds and perverts, lazy intellectuals and idiotic wheelers and dealers, merchants who buy for five and resell for a thousand after the death of the 'misunderstood artist.'"[26] The practices inaugurated in the course of Bottai's initiative would be followed by much of the fascist intellectual community until the fall of the regime. Although it remained bad form to mandate the style or content of the new national culture, the public naming of negative and undesirable traits was encouraged as a way of steering Italians away from certain tastes. Fascist anti-Semitism, which received no political or legal expression until the late thirties, found its earliest and most congenial home in the cultural press, where "Judaic" soon came to stand for the foreign and the pathological. The stated desire to cleanse Italian culture of Jews and others who acted as agents of decadent foreign modernities would find official support after 1936 in the campaigns for cultural autarchy and cultural reclamation.[27]

As Bottai's survey came to a close, two factions of intellectuals vied for the right to stand as the leading expression of fascist art. Both Strapaese (Supervillage) and Novecento (Twentieth Century) claimed to be the supreme interpreters of *italianità* but held contrasting conceptions of the meaning of Italian modernity and national identity. Yet both movements expressed a desire to fashion an Italian mass culture that would meet the challenges posed by Americanization. Led by the artist Mino Maccari, a former squadrist, Strapaese took shape in the midst of the Matteotti crisis as a lobby for intellectuals who opposed the abandonment of fascism's revolutionary politics. These same autonomist tendencies doomed it to an early death as a political project, and Maccari decided to shift the group's field of struggle to the plane of aesthetics: "We have well understood that today not everyone is allowed to engage in politics. For fascism, politics is the art of the government, not the party. . . . thus *Selvaggio* [the group's journal] . . . has closed its squadrist period and has chosen a new existence centered on the cultivation of art."[28] Over the next fifteen years, under the guise of cultural politics, Maccari and his colleagues protested the transformations being produced in Italy by the convergence of consumer capitalism and the centralizing tendencies of the fascist state. Against a threatening culture of "fads, foreign ideas, and modernist civilization," the intellectuals of Strapaese proposed a model of community based on ethnic identity. Here, the local stood as a synecdoche for the national, and the village as a repository of national tradition. Of course, local identities had long served to filter the experience of national belonging in Europe; the slipperiness between the two allegiances is expressed in the double meaning of the words *Heimat, paese,* and *pays,* which can refer to both a national and a provincial homeland. In Italy, though, where regionalist sentiments had continued to form an integral, if contested, component of national identities, the Strapaese movement offered a way to build a national culture on autochtho-

Figure 1. "Collectivism," modernity as seen by Strapaese. *Il Selvaggio,* May 15, 1931. Reprinted with permission of the Biblioteca Nazionale, Rome.

nous models. The *paese* became a formative agent for what Maccari called "a modernity of our own, an Italian modernity," one that would preserve local actions and allegiances within the modern mass state (fig. 1).[29]

The intellectuals of the Novecento movement took a different route to the construction of a national culture. As an architectural and artistic trend, Novecentism took shape as an attempt to create a modern aesthetic with visible roots in Italy's rich cultural past.[30] Literary Novecentism's patriotic profile was less evident at first. Its journal, *'900,* was published entirely in French for the first two years, it featured works by André Malraux and D. H. Lawrence, and its editorial board included James Joyce, Georg Kaiser, and Ilya Ehrenburg. The review met with hostility from the editors of the

Strapaese-allied review *L'Italiano,* who accused Bontempelli of diffusing a modernist culture designed for and by "Jews and pederasts." Yet *'900's* cosmopolitan ethos was founded on impeccable imperialist principles, as the statements of its editors Massimo Bontempelli and Curzio Malaparte make clear. Bontempelli believed that Italians could dominate Europe and compete with America for cultural hegemony only if they became "rapidly and conscientiously acquainted with all of the developments that the rest of Europe has achieved on its own." Like the Futurists, who launched their hypernationalistic movement in the pages of a French newspaper, the editors of *'900* chose to publish in French after making a pragmatic assessment of the realities of the international cultural marketplace. As the former diplomat Malaparte maintained, it was the most "tactful and tasteful" way to publicize the values of fascism abroad.[31]

Imperial pretensions also shaped the aesthetics of literary Novecentism, which aimed to develop a corpus of national texts with a transnational and transhistorical significance. Liberal-era solipsism and materialism would give way to a collectivist and mythopoetic sensibility that would "infuse daily things with a sense of mystery," transforming local and quotidian realities and truths into universal ones. This "magic realism," as Bontempelli called it, placed writers in the role of bards of the fascist national community and invested them with the task of "inventing myths and fables that then distance themselves from the writer to the point of losing all contact with his pen. In this way they become the common patrimony of men and almost things of nature." The will to transmute chronicle into epic and history into nature has often accompanied the fashioning of national cultures. In fascist Italy, it underwrote an intertwined agenda of domestic consolidation and imperial expansion.[32]

As the thirties began, the existence of new cultural movements and organizations did not prevent Italians from complaining that, in cultural affairs, fascism remained a *révolution manqué.* The editor Gherardo Casini lamented that the dictatorship enjoyed only a "superficial consensus" among intellectuals: although everything had a fascist label on it, nothing was "really and substantially" fascist.[33] Younger intellectuals emerged as the most vociferous critics of a fascist culture that seemed merely to perpetuate liberal-era aesthetics, authorities, and ideas. The twenty-seven-year-old journalist Berto Ricci identified two of the factors that most hindered the development of a uniquely Italian and fascist modernity. First, he charged, many older intellectuals fetishized the past, remaining too dazzled by Italy's artistic heritage to conceive of a true break with tradition. Second, a national inferiority complex, inherited from the liberal period, led many Italians to associate modernity with the achievements of more dominant nations. Taken together, these attitudes ensured that, ten years after the March on Rome, Italian modernity still consisted largely of "following the trends of German, French, or American modernity, ten years later: doing what is done abroad, but a bit later, a bit less, and (to use our much-loved adverb) moderately. . . . so [we end up with] the contemporaneous triumph of the museum and America: and what gets screwed is the famous Italian modernity."[34] In the early thirties, Ricci's complaints were echoed by many intellectuals his age who wished to create a culture that would reflect the regime's "revolutionary" achievements in the political and social spheres. They also found an attentive audience in regime officials, who hoped to market fascism abroad as an antidote to the European crisis and realize culture's potential as an instrument of diplomacy. The convergence of these factors produced a new round of debates and policies designed to clarify the components and boundaries of fascist models of modernity.

TASTE WARS I: GENERATIONAL POLITICS AND FASCIST AESTHETICS

In a 1933 novella, the twenty-six-year-old writer Vitaliano Brancati articulated the dilemma of the first generation to come of age under Italian fascism: "We are brimming over with vital energies. They've fired us up from all sides. . . . But what are we supposed to do with these energies[?] . . . we conserve them, putting them aside in silence. . . . Just what is it we're doing here? What do they want from us?" Celebrated in the press as fascism's next political and cultural elite, young intellectuals such as Brancati began their careers under a cloud of frustration. Born between 1905 and 1915, too late to have participated in World War I or the March on Rome, they felt out of place in a society that valorized martial virtues and conquest fantasies. Excluded from the collective memory of fascism's past, they claimed a central place for themselves in the fashioning of fascism's future. Yet, as the young art critic Nino Bertocchi charged, the government and the intellectual establishment cast them in a quite different role, as "those who look on[,] . . . those who, for good or ill, merely obey."[35]

Such complaints unsettled officials who considered one of fascism's central tasks to be the creation of a future political and intellectual elite. Yet as we will see in chapter 4, the fascists themselves had created the conditions for the production of separatist discourses. Generational thinking had always been integral to Mussolini's movement, and the construct of "youth" performed for the fascists in the same way that class and race had for the Bolsheviks and National Socialists—as a mobilizing and integrating national myth. Bottai and his *Critica fascista* group, in particular, had long argued that fascism's survival depended on its ability to have younger Italians identify their interests with those of the state. Starting in the late twenties, under Bottai's guidance, the regime began a public campaign to favor youth for positions and patronage over Italians of the war and prewar generation.[36]

If the strategy of "making way for youth" *(far largo ai giovani)* did not lead to any significant changes in administrative personnel, it did restructure the field of fascist cultural debate. Starting in 1930, the government authorized the publication of a slew of independent youth reviews that denounced the continued hegemony of liberal-era arts and letters and advanced sincere, if often incoherent, programs for cultural modernization in Italy. The editors and contributors to publications such as *Saggiatore, Orpheus,* and *L'Universale* were an overwhelmingly male and middle-class group who lived in central and northern Italian cities. While their journals normally lasted only a few years and had a rather limited readership, they hold interest as laboratories for the formulation of ideas about politics and aesthetics that would have influence in Italy long after the fall of the dictatorship. Romano Bilenchi, Mario Pannunzio, Indro Montanelli, and many others who would occupy prominent positions in postwar culture got their first experiences as journalists and public intellectuals in these reviews, which were read with interest and sometimes suspicion by government officials. Although each group worked in isolation at first, and each had its own particular attitudes and agenda, their shared goal of getting rid of the "old men and ideas that continue to reign undisturbed on the political and cultural stage" drew them into an alliance that, as one youth wrote, aimed to bring about "the birth of a new *Weltanschauung*" in Italy.[37]

Several causes united this generation and would influence its activities in the coming years. First and foremost was the embrace of cultural politics as a solution to and compensation for limitations on political activities. Culture became a surrogate sphere of operation and the primary means of expressing enthusiasms and animosities that otherwise could not be voiced. Lambasting their elders for their "lack of commitment," writers in Milan, Bologna, Florence, and Rome advanced a vision of culture as "an arm, a means of action, an instrument on the same plane as other instruments in life," and claimed for their own purposes the regime's theme of intellectual mobilization. Voicing sentiments held by many his age, twenty-two-year-old *Orpheus* editor Luciano Anceschi characterized his cohort's mission in

1933 as "the search for a new interpretation of the world rooted in the concrete needs of the masses. He who still wastes time dreaming of artificial literary paradises, who tries to evade the concrete with enchanting *'invitations au voyage'* and reduces the world to his own experience, does not live in our climate, which requires the adoption of a nongeneric position with regard to all problems of life."[38]

Second was the creation of a modern code of values that would allow Italians to rise to the challenges posed by mass society. As the university student Domenico Carella contended in his journal, *Saggiatore,* only by operating an "internal revolution" could individuals adapt to modernity's new political forms, social practices, and mentalities. For Carella and his peers, the arbitration of taste contained a moral as well as aesthetic mandate: it implied a series of choices in how to organize society. Thus they criticized the continued hold of liberal-era philosophies and aesthetics in Mussolini's Italy as a primary obstacle to the realization of fascism's ethical revolution. "If culture remains completely disinterested in all that is 'new' in contemporary life," Carella wondered, "who will be able to form a conscience for modern man?"[39] Over the next decade, the definition of the styles and values of fascist modernity would constitute one of this generation's primary political projects.

The collective desire for *engagement* created support in the early 1930s for an aesthetic that, as one put it, would be "more direct and immediate in its effects." Associating decorativism with democratic decadence and self-indulgence, young intellectuals such as Leo Longanesi argued for a "post-crisis aesthetic" that would be "poor, without much 'artistic appeal,' bare, crude, and very direct." This new style would hold little appeal for "those who prefer theatrics, papier-mâché constructions and rhetorical garlands," another warned, but would "represent man as an active force who engages with his society." What was needed, as summed up by the philosophy student Giorgio Granata, was a "a work of integral reclamation" *(un opera di bonifica integrale)* in this realm as well.[40] This taste for the concrete was advanced by Rationalist architects who touted their streamlined designs as the embodiment of fascism's constructive and anti-ideological ethos. Concurrently, young film critics championed a "cinematography of real life," and their peers in music and literature called for "antirhetorical" compositional and writing styles. The moral connotations ascribed to this bare-bones aesthetic disposition were conveyed by the twenty-eight-year-old historian Delio Cantimori, who informed older Italians that "what counts for us is to be sincere and serious, to refuse to mystify our surroundings with beautiful words, to look at reality as it is, without fictions or hypocrisy, without resorting to such cowardly cover-ups as blue skies, pink clouds, thrones, dominations, and little cherubs: beautiful but false. Reality means man, his life, his association with other men; with them, and for them, we live. Nothing else matters."[41]

This culture of "concreteness" and commitment was by no means restricted to Italy, however, nor to those on the right. In both communist and capitalist Europe, realism became a keyword of interwar cultural discourse, as intellectuals and artists experimented with narrative techniques and modes of analysis that would allow a more direct relationship between the observation and representation of mass society. In Weimar Germany, the new ethos found expression under the rubric of the amorphous *Neue Sachlichkeit* (New Objectivity) movement, which sought to represent reality without the distorting filters of individual emotion. A documentarist aesthetic took hold in film, painting, photography, and literature, and Logical Positivists joined Bauhaus architects in a campaign for a culture born, in Walter Gropius's words, of "sober calculation and the precise analysis of practical experience."[42] The *Neue Sachlichkeit's* credo of impersonality found few followers in France, but intellectuals there also sought to replace the culture of "pretense and plaster" that supposedly characterized the Third Republic. Young philosophers such as Jean-Paul Sartre gravitated to phenomenology and psychology, and aesthetic agendas took on an ethical significance. As Emmanuel Mounier explained in his journal, *Esprit,* "honest" art inspired by surrounding reality rather than subjective sentiment could help to resolve the crisis of values by offering "a complete vision of man."[43]

Then, as always, realism was a slippery term that invoked a variety of representational modes and ideological positions. Although social realism, socialist realism, magic realism, *Neue Sachlichkeit,* and neorealism all flourished between the wars and used similar lexicons, they had radically different political implications. Moreover, those who embraced the cult of objectivity were hardly objective. More often than not, the discourse of neutrality masked a desire to naturalize a politically derived worldview. In a sense, realism became a handy vessel that served parties and individuals in purveying their agendas as they competed for control of the social and ideological spaces opened up by the crisis of bourgeois democracy.[44]

In Italy, in fact, the new outlook became closely associated with fascism, which had been advertised as an anti-ideological ideology even before the March on Rome. Depicting communism as a prisoner of rigid planning schemes, blackshirt propagandists pronounced fascism to be a dynamic, pragmatic, and quintessentially modern movement whose policies were dictated by the needs of the present. Fascism signified "clarity, simplicity of method, linearity of application, rectitude, and honesty," one supporter wrote in a typical paean to totalitarian "transparency."[45] Thus, if in France and Weimar Germany the call for antirhetorical aesthetics and philosophies often formed part of an oppositional political agenda, Italian intellectuals often identified their interests with those of the government. As the editors of *Saggiatore* argued, this convergence of attitudes put Italians in a privileged position with respect to other countries, since diffused aspirations could be transformed into concrete policies: "Decadence of the democracies, intolerance of all old ideologies, the creation of new ethics, calls for new realisms . . . are by now common terms in the vocabulary of young intellectuals in all countries. But it is Italy's task to take these symptoms and themes and form from them a new culture."[46]

TASTE WARS II: ANXIETIES OF INFLUENCE

If fascism provided a political point of reference for this culture as it developed over the early thirties, foreign institutions and ideas also proved inspirational to those who wished to modernize Italy's aesthetic identity. Temperament, rather than age, often determined the position one took on the question of foreign influence, and no strict generational divide can be drawn between those who built on the paradigms for national culture set up by the Strapaese and Novecento groups. Nonetheless, cultural debates took on a generational tinge in the early thirties, as younger Italians who sought stylistic suggestions abroad came into conflict with members of the fascist cultural establishment who feared that uncontrolled foreign influence might bring about the loss of national cultural traditions.[47] To win them over, some younger intellectuals argued that borrowing from other cultures was itself a hallowed practice in Italian history. Refuting criticism from older architects that his movement's buildings were anti-Italian, the Rationalist architect Carlo Enrico Rava contended that "Italy has always absorbed, assimilated, and recreated that which it has received from other races, making it something entirely ours." Their intent was not to imitate other nations, Rava argued, but to learn from them as a means of creating superior cultural products that would expand Italian influence abroad.[48]

Although some fascist cultural authorities never accepted this line of reasoning, several factors pushed Mussolini and many officials to promote a form of cultural internationalism in the early thirties. First, Nazi Germany and Stalinist Russia emerged as rivals in the race to establish an antidemocratic new order. Faced with regimes that, like fascism, offered supranationalist solutions to the crisis of the nation-state, Mussolini sought to cultivate a more international image. He acted as senior statesman during the negotiation of the 1933 Four Power Pact and patronized "universal fascist" currents that sought to realize his movement's transnational potential. Second, Italy was in the midst of a tourist crisis brought on by the revaluation of the lira and the depression, and Mussolini needed to improve fascism's standing abroad to lure foreigners back into the country.[49]

These concerns created support for a politics of cultural "openness" with two intertwined goals: to expose Italian intellectuals to the latest foreign trends, allowing them to fashion a modern culture that could be exported to other countries, and to attract foreign intellectuals into Italy in the hope of converting them to the fascist cause. To this end, cultural bureaucrats such as Bottai and Luigi Chiarini mobilized state resources to manage processes of exchange and appropriation that had gone on informally in the liberal period. Writing in 1932 in his Ministry of Education–linked review *Educazione fascista*, Chiarini proposed a three-point strategy for the development and marketing of a new national culture. First, Italians must become informed about the latest trends abroad, since "knowing other peoples also means knowing what they think of us[,] . . . how they reject or accept fascism." Second, "discussions and clarifications" were necessary before deciding on which innovations might be "absorbed" and "assimilated" into Italian traditions. This state-of-the-art national culture would then facilitate "the penetration and diffusion abroad of the doctrine and ideals of fascism."[50]

The new policy orientation gave rise to a variety of mechanisms that facilitated the examination and selective appropriation of foreign cultures. *Educazione fascista* inaugurated a column entitled "Ideas beyond the Borders" to expose Italians to "the most diverse and extreme tendencies" of foreign avant-garde culture. Literary reviews such as *Circoli*, which translated foreign authors, received government subsidies, and official institutions such as the School for Corporative Sciences sponsored book series that examined how other peoples sought to "resolve questions that preoccupy us as well." As one author asserted in a INCF-sponsored study on the international treatment of ethnic minorities, "Fascism gives just weight to the experiences of other nations. . . . their experiments are precious to us as sources of information and comparison."[51] Daily newspapers devoted more space to foreign trends and reportage from abroad, while *L'Architettura,* the journal of the architects' syndicate, announced that it would give more space to foreign design trends. "It is necessary to have a thorough knowledge of what others are doing in order to surpass them," one editor wrote in explaining the change to the journal's conservative readership.[52]

Bringing a managerial mentality to bear upon the old national ideal of *aggiornamento*, the regime also invested in international congresses and study centers that would attract high-profile foreign intellectuals into fascist Italy. The Institute for International Film Education hosted Rudolph Arnheim, who wrote *Film als Kunst (Film as Art)* during his tenure in Rome, and big-budget conferences sponsored by the Italian Academy and other official entities brought Le Corbusier, Stefan Zweig, Alban Berg, Werner Sombart, Nadia Boulanger, and dozens of other luminaries onto Italian soil. While these encounters surely stimulated Italians, they were also designed to convince foreign elites that fascism cared about culture. As the composer and government functionary Mario Labroca reminded his peers in *Critica fascista*, "We do propaganda work not only when we export our ideas abroad, but also when we invite foreigners here so they can come into contact with our lifestyle and our way of thinking."[53]

As it turned out, conferences were only one component of a comprehensive politics of exhibition(ism) that, as the critic Ugo Ojetti termed it, placed fascist Italy "on display" in order to cultivate tourism, foreign currency holdings, and the cult of *bella figura*.[54] Exhibitions had long been used by governments to communicate particular visions of social organization and substantiate their power to their citizens and to other states. Under Mussolini, exhibitions took on a central importance as agents of indoctrination and mass mobilization. Yet foreigners, as much as Italians, were the target audience of the festivals and other public offerings (including the infamous punctual trains) that proclaimed the end of Italy's historic inefficiency and cultural backwardness. The regime soon imposed a sort of *Gleichschaltung* on these spectacles, scheduling them in clusters to maximize their touristic and propagandistic potential. Following complaints from the prefect of Venice that foreigners "of class" were increasingly abandoning the city, an International Music Festival was added to the Venice Biennale art exhibition in 1930.[55] The success of this initiative, which premiered works by Ernest Bloch, Darius Milhaud, and Paul Hindemith, who also performed as a violinist, led administrators to add film to the program as well. The first Biennale Film Show opened in 1932 in time to coincide with the Grape Festivals *(Feste dell'Uva)* held in September throughout Italy, and with the opening of the blockbuster Exhibition of the Fascist Revolution in Rome.[56] In 1933, the coordination of such events became even more complete, with the Triennale architectural and design exhibition serving as linchpin of a season of spectacle that included the Milan Trade Fair and international music and architectural congresses.[57] In the midst of these events, the novelist Corrado Alvaro noted in his diary that fascism seemed less a nationalistic movement than "an attempt to Europeanize Italy[,] . . . to conform to other countries[,] . . . to open a window on Europe, but in a provincial way. It is the manifestation of the inferiority complex of the Italian middle class."[58]

This politics of display and appropriation proved successful for the regime in several ways. First, as Alvaro correctly perceived, it helped to assuage ingrained anxieties about modern Italy's marginal status as a cultural power. The plethora of exhibitions also enabled the fascists to consolidate patronage relations, since writers, architects, scenographers, and artists of every type could compete for high-profile commissions. These "ensnaring enticements," as Flora later termed them, proved especially effective in drawing younger intellectuals into the regime's reward system. Giuseppe Pagano, Mario Mafai, Franco Albini, and Carlo Emilio Gadda were among the emerging talents who provided texts and images for government-generated displays.[59]

Fascism's new internationalist orientation did not please everyone. The intellectuals of Strapaese protested that "it is simply ridiculous to bring false foreign novelties among us—even with the intention of absorbing them and using them for our own goals." Even those who were involved in the implementation of these policies specified that the regime's openness to foreign trends did not entail any relaxation of censorship or cultural controls. Commenting on the cosmopolitan program he had approved for the 1930 International Music Festival in Venice, the composer and fascist deputy Adriano Lualdi warned that government officials had no intention of becoming "accomplices in the importation of certain artistic poisons and drugs that have wreaked havoc beyond the Alps."[60]

The critic Ugo Ojetti, who organized the 1933 music congress, reacted with particular alarm to this internationalist orientation. An Academician and president of the High Council for Antiquities and Fine Arts, the conservative Ojetti had long advocated Italy's autonomy in cultural affairs. In 1929, he had argued arrogantly that Italians did not need to look to other countries for inspiration because their culture represented an ideal synthesis of the world's civilizations. In 1932, even as he issued invitations to foreign music celebrities, he accused Bottai of modernizing at the expense of Italy's national identity and aesthetic patrimony. "For you it is important that Italy is not 'out of date,' for me it is important that Italy remain Italian," Ojetti declared polemically in his journal *Pègaso*. Bottai responded by reprinting Ojetti's attack in *Critica fascista* and appending a rebuttal so that he could have the last word. "Knowing something does not necessarily mean accepting it," Bottai reminded his critic. "It can also signify rejecting it, reacting to it, and gathering force for our own critique of it." Learning how nations like Germany, Russia, and America "face and resolve the contradictions of modern civilization" was essential if Italy intended to play a hegemonic role in a rapidly changing world.[61] Whether or not Ojetti agreed with this reasoning, by the end of 1933 he seemed to have acquiesced. The initial editorial of his new journal, *Pan*, promised to "keep readers informed of new developments, including those beyond the Alps and overseas, which will be measured against our own character and civilization."[62]

IN SEARCH OF MODERNITY: ITALIANS ABROAD, 1929–34

In the early thirties, as the regime intensified its efforts to define a specifically Italian and fascist model of modernity, critiques of foreign cultures on Italian soil were complemented by the firsthand perspectives provided by intellectuals who traveled abroad. Anxieties over the social and economic crisis and the desire to increase exports created a ready market in Italy for information on foreign models of modernity. Reportage from New York, Berlin, and Moscow appeared regularly in *La Stampa*, *Il Lavoro*, *Il Popolo d'Italia*, and other newspapers.

Those who produced travel literature under the dictatorship differed widely in their motives, outlooks, and occupations. Novelists, former diplomats, engineers, psychologists, and architects joined journalists in turning their impressions of life abroad into print. Some authors swathed themselves in the mantle of journalistic objectivity, claiming that they had crossed the Alps "with the sole desire of looking and observing." Others, like the engineer Gaetano Ciocca, whose 1933 account of his experiences in setting up a Fiat ball-bearings plant in Moscow went through six printings in five months, felt that reportages should "propose [solutions,] . . . not as a way of playing diplomat, but to aid the One who makes the decisions."[63] Indeed, while the works of this genre teem with facts about life abroad, they also convey the dominant political and ideological discourses of fascist Italy. More often than not, their comparisons between foreigners and Italians reaffirm the superiority of national tastes and social mores. Taken collectively, they helped to articulate visions of a mass society that would differ from American and Soviet models of modernity.

Italians had many fellow travelers as they pursued their purposeful peregrinations after World War I. As Mary Nolan and other scholars have shown, the interest in rationalization and new models of industrial production led managers, academics, and labor leaders from western Europe to America and Russia in the twenties and early thirties, while technicians and specialists from Britain and other countries helped to run the hydro-electric plants and factories of Stalin's Five-Year Plan. Italy attracted its share of foreign visitors who were curious about corporativism and fascist social planning schemes. European governments faced similar problems in the twenties and thirties, and looked beyond their borders to learn how allies and enemies implemented the public works programs, social welfare measures, and managed economies that composed the landscape of the new state-interventionist capitalism.[64]

As a model of mass society and modernity, Soviet Russia caused the most curiosity in Italians. In the years 1928–35, more than fifty books appeared on the place that one writer called "the grandest laboratory of social experience in existence."[65] As the Italian government knew, the communist dictatorship exerted a special fascination in a country whose own leftist political culture had been persecuted out of existence. Disgruntled former socialists and idealistic young fascists were allowed to show their admiration for the Bolshevik state by depicting it as fascism's "enemy twin"—another mass regime with a flair for propaganda and mass mobilization. But wariness increased with the onset of the depression, when debates began all over Western Europe about which revolution—the red or the black—would guide the world in the future. As one blackshirt worried, "The decline of nineteenth-century civilization has left only two roads to follow: ours and theirs. And we can be sure that in time these two roads will meet. But will we end up on their path, or they on ours? The serious person must ask himself: will it be Rome or Moscow?" The degree to which officials still worried about communism's attraction for Italians also came through clearly in Chiarini's journal, *Educazione fascista*, which reminded those who might be setting off for Russia to avoid ideological "confusions" by looking at Moscow "with the eyes of Rome."[66]

Whether out of conformism or self-censorship, most Italians did exactly that on their trips East. As a place where collectivization appeared to be proceeding "without any brakes or restraints," the Stalinist state played on ingrained fears about modernity's leveling effects. To many Italians, communism stood as an example of modernity's potential to forge a civilization that, by privileging uniformity and quantity over creativity and quality, would turn human beings into "automatic puppets." While other foreign visitors to Russia came to similar conclusions, in the Italian context such critiques of communism helped to create a consensus for the fascists' goal of actuating a mass society that preserved the spiritual realm.[67]

While economists and industrial planners focused on the mechanics of the Five-Year Plan, many writers and journalists concentrated on the social, psychological, and cultural effects provoked by Russia's "idolatry of the machine." Alvaro, who toured the country on assignment for *La Stampa*, evoked the image of a country selling off its cultural patrimony to pay for machines, while Luigi Barzini denounced the sacrifice of humanism at the altar of a "religion of technology."[68] The transformation of churches into restaurants, workers' circles, and party headquarters provoked equal horror in Italian travelers. A visit to the antireligious museum in Leningrad only strengthened the Catholic faith of the young novelist Enrico Emanuelli, who confessed that he "now believed more than ever."[69]

For many Italians, the reaction against religion in Russia constituted but one aspect of communism's abandonment of all things spiritual and natural—the family, the home, maternal and conjugal love, and private property. Collective kitchens and shared living spaces discomfited Italians who associated the hearth (*focolare*) and the dinner table with a private, familial space. Male travelers saw the "masculinized" Soviet woman as a symbol of this social disintegration and found communism's gender relations disorienting. "One suspects that a matriarchy is in the offing," wrote a disconsolate Alvaro from Moscow in 1934.[70] Some Italians stressed Mother Russia's racial as well as sexual otherness, emphasizing the country's Asiatic and Jewish nature. The literary scholar Ettore Lo Gatto and the art critic Pier Maria Bardi presented the Soviet state as a place where Jews occupied positions of enormous economic and political authority.[71] For visitors from fascist Italy, then, Russia represented a world that confirmed modernity's potential to undermine "natural" social and sexual hierarchies. Even Ciocca, who looked with sympathy upon many aspects of Soviet life, lambasted Russia for "renouncing thousand-year-old norms and habits and trying to destroy all vestiges of the past, confusing good and evil, tempting fate and the very dictates of nature." Moscow, he concluded, was to be studied, understood, and negated.[72]

For many other intellectuals, though, capitalist America, not communist Russia, formed the biggest threat to the survival of Italian institutions and ways of life. As Maccari warned his peers in *Il Selvaggio*, Americans relied not on political propaganda but on the insidious lures of mass culture to convince other nations to follow their path: "Today's enemy is unarmed. . . . He enters into your house via newspapers, photographs, and books that diffuse his mentality. Look around you, Italians: and you'll see Americanism all around you. . . . we call a poor fool who sings a Communist song a sub-versive, and we smile, exalt, and honor those who are introducing among us things that will destroy our spiritual health."[73] Maccari's alarmist tone reflected the enormous popular appeal America had in fascist Italy as a symbol of glamour and freedom from tradition. Known above all for its cinema, America functioned in the interwar period as a giant screen upon which Italians projected their fears and fantasies about consumerism, sex-ual emancipation, and other developments associated with mass society. The ambivalence that most Italian intellectuals showed toward America is captured in Barzini's 1931 remark that the country was both "the most stu-pendous and powerful phenomenon of modernity in the world" and "a place where all the deviations of the spirit bear fruit."[74] Other Europeans felt similarly divided. Many French intellectuals saw America's faults—disrespect for (French) traditions, small-scale economies, and individual eccentricities—as the source of its strength as a financial power, and few refused to see the films of Charlot, no matter what they said publicly about American cinematic imperialism. In both Italy and France, the thirties saw the formation of attitudes toward America that would continue, often un-der different political guises, long after 1945.[75]

Still, America occupied a special place in the Italian imagination. Emi-grations of the late nineteenth and early twentieth centuries had brought millions from the old world to the new, and letters and contact with those who made reverse migrations gave many Italians some familiarity, how-ever mediated, with American culture. This sense of connectedness was en-couraged by the fascist government, which labeled emigrants as "Italians abroad" and established free summer camps for emigrants' children to nur-ture their sense of Italian identity. Moreover, Mussolini adopted a friendly stance toward America in his first decade of rule, partly to guarantee Italy's receipt of monies from the J. P. Morgan loan and encourage exports. In this period, with the help of his eager admirer William Randolph Hearst, Mus-solini wrote many articles for the American press that highlighted the putative similarities between the two countries—both were young, both were forging new ground, and both, at least in Hearst's papers, were anti-communist.[76]

While pro-American attitudes found public expression until the out-break of World War II, the Wall Street crash created a ready audience for anti-American messages as well. In the years of the depression, a flood of books and articles appeared whose depictions of the country ranged from ambivalent to hostile. Far from being the land of the free, America increasingly appeared as a "dictatorship" of capital that enslaved its citizens to a materialistic lifestyle. Returning from the States, the critic Margherita Sarfatti reported that Americans had created a "modern, efficient, and rational hell" where the "roar of riches in the making" had replaced church bells and birdsong.[77] Many accounts placed the blame on unregulated consumer capitalism, which standardized bodies and souls in its push to forge national markets. The journalist Valentino Piccoli likened the American socialization process to a Fordist assembly line: "The standard mentality is like an enormous octopus whose tentacles extend over all of life, imprisoning the mind and the spirit, forcing ideas and attitudes to conform to one type, in the same way that the great mechanized factories produce the different pieces of an auto according to a uniform model."[78]

Paradoxically, the most modern people on earth also seemed to be the most primitive. Adriana Dotterelli and other Italian visitors took the popularity of jazz, spy novels, comic books, and mass-produced trinkets as proof of Americans' infantility and lack of taste.[79] As the writer Emilio Cecchi reported after he returned from a year-long lectureship at the University of California at Berkeley in 1931, in matters of culture America was truly a blank slate. Describing a student's inability to pick out the Madonna figure in a Renaissance painting, Cecchi recalled, "I was ecstatic. I really was in the desert." As for French intellectuals, the notion of taste among Italians implied some internalization of cultural norms that, in turn, were indicative of shared moral and social discourses. The failure to provide for the education of the senses signified that, after 150 years, America had remained "prenational" and primitive.[80]

The New World served as a repository for Italians' fears over the shifting of racial hierarchies as well. Cecchi characterized the San Francisco Bay Area's black communities as "disturbing and swarming breeding grounds of that savagery to which America is still profoundly tied," and the painter Renato Paresce looked askance at the "animalesque" aspects of Hispanic culture. Even religious practices appeared to be showcases of regressive behavior. From New York, the writer Mario Soldati recorded the activities of black-influenced "carnal and colorful cults," and Paresce reported on the self-mutilation and crucifixion supposedly practiced by deviant Hispanic Catholic sects. "The American conscience is a ferment of barbaric and panicked energies," Cecchi concluded.[81]

The "shockingly amoral" nature of American life also struck Italian observers who investigated gender relations and the family. Like their counterparts from France and Weimar Germany, Italians castigated American women whose lifestyles confirmed the outcome of modern trends that had begun to manifest themselves at home: female emancipation, the supposed neglect of maternal duties, the eclipse of traditional patterns of seduction and courtship. American wives dominated their husbands, they claimed, and their focus on careers meant that, as in Stalinist Russia, the hearth and the home-cooked meal were things of the past. As one reporter observed, American homes consisted of "cold radiators, iron, cement, glass, and aluminum, all without history, beauty, or dreams. One has instead levers, buttons, floodlights, and bare bulbs. Everything is standardized." [82]

Taken collectively, such texts created support for models of modernity that might maintain patriarchal traditions and strong family identities. By underscoring the tyranny of democratic models of modernity and social life, they also aided Italian intellectuals in sidestepping the issue of fascism's own violence and inhumanity. The case of the writer Soldati and his book *America primo amore* (*America First Love*, 1935) holds interest in this regard. In 1929, at the age of twenty-three, Soldati came to America to do graduate work in art history at Columbia University. A friend of Carlo Levi and student of Lionello Venturi, the Turin native was no fan of the regime, and he viewed his sojourn abroad as a step toward a possible emigration. After just two years, though, he returned voluntarily to live under the Italian dictatorship, and made peace with fascism in the interests of career ambitions and family obligations.[83] He published several literary reportages drawn from his American experiences in the daily and periodical press, and in 1935 reprinted most of them in *America primo amore*, earning a reputation as a preeminent Italian commentator on America that persisted well into the postwar period.

Despite his book's title, Soldati depicts America as a violent and pathological place that stands as a warning against unchecked modernization. Unregulated consumer capitalism had created a new type of standardized mass-subject devoid of all taste and humanity. Emitting strange metallic odors, "like certain high-voltage electric machines," Americans were heartless automatons who thought nothing of throwing their relatives out on the street and who pursued their own interests at whatever cost.[84] The random violence that plagued America was further evidence of American barbarism for Soldati. New World criminals did not fit Lombrosian stereotypes of degeneracy; assassins there were "blond and handsome, with sweet eyes and serene expressions," driven to the criminal life by "inner emptiness" rather than defective genes. Every American was thus a potential killer (including Soldati's knife-brandishing Midwestern girlfriend), and crime formed part of the fabric of everyday life. "Violent and moral passions, kidnappings, evasions, lynchings, murders, and suicides[:] . . . there are more crimes in one day in America than in a whole year in Italy," Soldati wrote in a 1933 article that typified the unwillingness of many Italian intellectuals living under fascism to come to terms with their own government's state-sponsored brutality.[85]

Discourses of gender and race also perform in *America primo amore* to underscore America's status as an emblem of deviant modernity. Like the mass culture and mass politics with which it was so closely associated, America was often likened by Italians to a woman for its primitivity, venality, and capacity to seduce. As the writer Alberto Moravia reflected on the way home from his own sojourn in America, there "one is continually tempted, violated by things to eat things to buy things to enjoy, and all these things can be had for the asking. . . . it is a bit like the temptation of the bazaar, and of the brothel."[86] In Soldati's book, America's "cosmopolitan and suffocating embrace" is embodied in the figure of a woman "as black as coal," whom he meets in a Harlem nightclub. He experiences the club's jazz music and dancing bodies with a "sense of strange freshness, almost of perversion," and wonders if his "fantastically sensual" dancing partner might be a prostitute. His adventure ends when he flees to the "sweet company" of his all-male Columbia dormitory, his "love of exoticism" temporarily sated.[87]

What a prude!

At a broader level, Soldati's entire American stay is characterized as an unwholesome period of absorption into a very "un-Italian" sphere of decadence and femininity. In a preface that would be removed from most postwar editions of *America primo amore*, the writer foregrounds his desire for America as pathological:

> Many men, for a period in their lives, that is, during their first love, believe that it is possible to exist totally outside of oneself, and dedicate oneself exclusively to another person. In the same manner, during my American stay, I believed it was possible to evade: to change one's country, one's religion, one's memories and one's conscience. And for more than a year I lived with the morbid conviction that I had succeeded. The first love and the first journey are sicknesses that resemble one another.[88]

His decision to return to Mussolini's Italy thus appears to be a therapeutic act, an event that marks his return to his senses as a man and as an Italian. In the year following the publication of this book, Soldati demonstrated his commitment to completing his rehabilitation by scripting the colonial film *Il grande appello* (*A Call to Arms,* Mario Camerini, 1936), which, tellingly, recounts the transformation of a cynical Italian emigrant into a duty-bound patriot who sacrifices his life in the Ethiopian War.

America was not the only country that Italians routinely described in gendered terms. Fickle, faddish, and feminized in its compulsory disarmament, Weimar Germany came across in Italian writings as another example of modernity's potential to erode identities. With its Russian-inspired architecture and American-influenced films and factories, Germany offered the frightening example of how a nation could lose its sense of collective purpose and make the imitation of foreign trends into a way of life. During a six-month stay in Berlin, the writer Alvaro identified two elements of Weimar culture that facilitated this denationalization: the modernist scorn for the autochthonous and the traditional, and the influence of a cosmopolitan "Hebraism." "Italy, Russia, or America? Which of these *new* countries should we take as a model?" wrote another Italian critic, scornfully summing up the country's current disorientation.[89] Nowhere more than in the Weimar Republic did male travelers feel the weight of those shifts in gender relations that, in contemporary cultural discourse, often stood as the most visible sign of the crisis of "civilization." Italians reported that the triumph of female habits and logic in Germany had turned the country into a shrine to feminine consumer and erotic desire. Even in the bedroom, the New Woman had disrupted old patterns of life: by privileging performance over preliminaries, she had made sex into an "anonymous and indifferent act," depriving males of the "control and devotion" that made intimacy possible.[90]

An autobiographical story by Alvaro based on his stay in Berlin in 1929–30 shows the extent to which changing sexual dynamics stood for modernity's threat to the established social order. Like the famous movie *The Blue Angel* (Josef von Sternberg, 1930) that preceded it, "Solitudine" recounts a saga of female domination. An Italian visitor to Berlin becomes involved with Elfrida, whose shaved neck, managerial position, and *sachlich* manner mark her as the quintessential New Woman. When he visits her workplace, he feels like "an exotic fruit placed there as an ornament" and muses that he'd like to "give her a small humiliation." Yet he is the one who wakes up feeling ashamed and degraded after a night spent together.[91] A dinner party Elfrida takes him to clarifies the political referent of this world turned upside down, as we learn that all the guests are leftists, including a doctor who performs in drag at the end of the evening. Elfrida finally drives Alvaro's character to a hotel and abandons him there after a bout of lovemaking. As the story ends, he learns that her aim was to become pregnant and then raise the child on her own. In the Weimar Republic, Alvaro warns, men have become instruments of female ambitions and desires.

Russia, America, Germany: three dystopias whose fates Italians hoped to avoid. In the travel writings of this period, Russia, America, and Weimar Germany emerge as laboratories of a dangerous modernity that exploited the body, suffocated the spirit, and ultimately led to degeneration. Reportage on these countries functioned as a sort of border patrol, identifying which elements of contemporary existence would have no place in Italian modernity. It also gave intellectuals an opportunity to improve their political standing by affirming the superior freedoms that distinguished Italy under Mussolini. The journalist Giuseppe Lombrassa surely spoke both to his peers and to his patrons when he asserted that "we fascists have earned a great privilege: that of finally being able to look foreigners in the face without rancor or envy and tell the truth as it appears to us, without the need to exaggerate the bad or conceal the good for propagandistic reasons." [92] Among Italians who returned voluntarily to live under the dictatorship, the need to emphasize fascism's respect for personhood and humanity proved especially compelling. Alvaro argued after his return from Berlin that the only liberty that mattered was "the interior liberty of the individual." Paresce proclaimed that American liberty consisted mainly of the right to make money and "the right to kill oneself and, naturally, to be killed," and Soldati assured his compatriots upon his return from New York that Italy was "more civil, more solid, [and] more humane." [93] Such statements worked together with fascist officials' continual assurances of artistic autonomy, allowing intellectuals to deny or disavow the regime's everyday repression and remain in Italy to realize their own cultural ambitions and those of the government. The next chapters will examine how two generations of intellectuals articulated their visions of Italian and fascist modernity in the realms of literature and film.

ELABORATION, EXAMPLES ?

2   Narrating the Nation

In a 1928 article entitled "Invitation to the Novel," the Italian literary critic Giovanni Titta Rosa remarked,

> It is commonly said that there is no modern Italian life, and the little that exists does not offer material for the writer. The truth is the opposite. Modern Italian life exists, and is rich with passions, with content. The war and postwar—for those who have known how to understand them—offer the most varied and vast panorama of passions imaginable. I dare say that even the Napoleonic era did not produce such an outburst of expression.

Rather than remaining "in an ivory tower" in the face of such dramatic material, the critic concluded, Italian writers must "feel contemporary life in the most intimate and committed way."[1] Titta Rosa's invitation was one of many launched by the literary establishment as part of a campaign to enlist the support of writers in the creation of a distinctly Italian and fascist model of modernity. As writers were organized into syndicates that would "discipline" their professional lives, they were also encouraged to generate works that, by disseminating the moral and spiritual values of Mussolini's revolution, would contribute to the cause of collective transformation. Titta Rosa's allusive language hardly conceals his attempt to conflate the representation of Italian modernity with the representation of the fascist era: in the years of the dictatorship, in fact, earlier calls for the modernization and nationalization of Italian literature became intertwined with the campaign to create a corpus of fascist works. Certainly, not all Italian writers and critics accepted the regime's claim to represent the nation, and few advocated an overtly political literature. Yet most did share the dictatorship's desire to foster the production of modern, identifiably national novels and stories that could be exported abroad. Aided by a literary etiquette that favored the use of inferential language in cultural debates, the vast majority of writers and critics participated in fascism's public literary culture, allowing officials to vaunt a formal consensus for their efforts to conscript the institution of literature for the battle of national regeneration.

For several reasons, the effort to inspire a literature reflective of a distinctly fascist modernity proved less than successful. The strength of Crocean injunctions against the politicization of art, and the desire to maintain the collective illusion of creative liberty under fascism, tempered impulses to realize an openly fascist literature. Many literary figures, even those of convinced fascist faith, considered it bad form to write overtly political works. This viewpoint was summed up in 1936 by the writer Arrigo Benedetti, who told the contributors to his new review, *Letteratura*, that "no one is talking about making political declarations. We may rarely write the word Fascism, even if I believe we cannot be uncertain in front of this term."[2] The influence of foreign literary models also worked against the production of a cohesive body of blackshirt works, as did market conditions that favored foreign translations and escapist tales of the type the regime had vowed to eschew.[3]

All the same, Mussolini's regime had far-reaching effects on the conceptualization, production, and critical reception of literary works in Italy. Although many authors managed to publish without joining the PNF, the state made full use of its powers to silence unacceptable voices and control the content and circulation of literary texts. Books and stories were routinely confiscated, altered by the censors, or condemned to oblivion through press directives that commanded critics to ignore them. In some cases, the censor's changes were extensive, complicating the issue of authorship. Other books were abandoned at the idea stage by their authors, who followed their instincts on what subjects to avoid. "I had a censor in myself," declared Alvaro a year after Mussolini's removal from office.[4]

The Italian dictatorship's policies toward writers and critics consisted of a mix of disciplinary measures and patronage. With subsidies and prizes came the controls exercised by the syndical system that, however, disciplined the individual rather than his or her work. Until 1935, book censorship fell to the prefectures, whose employees often had limited literary expertise. To save costs and protect themselves from capricious decisions, authors and publishers made recourse to informal procedures of preventive censorship, such as showing authorities synopses of book projects or asking advice on ideas. As in the post–World War II state socialist regimes of Hungary and East Germany, censorship functioned less through heavy-handed repression than through collaboration with authors who negotiated with authorities over a questionable tone or turn of phrase.[5] A separate system of censorship existed for the daily and periodical press, which hosted literary debates, criticism, and installments of some of the best-known novels of this period.[6] Every publication had to designate a prefect-approved individual who assumed legal responsibility, and directors of periodicals had to join the journalists' syndicate. Mussolini's Press Office distributed press directives and photographs, scrutinized publications, notified journalists of transgressions, and granted subsidies to newspapers, periodicals, and individuals.[7]

Critics constituted the final class of authorities who shaped the institution of literature under the dictatorship. In many political contexts, critics can position themselves as agents of canon formation for high culture and as tastemakers who seek to mediate the public's contact with Art. The first link in the chain of reception, they participate actively in the postproduction of a text by helping to determine its public destiny and readership.[8] Under a dictatorship, where the acts of interpretation and contextualization take on heightened importance, the critic's role is magnified. By editing out ambiguities, or by playing on the polyvalence of language, Italian critics could make texts perform as documents of an emerging fascist literature. Naturally, they could also exploit this same polyvalence to bring out the oppositional message of a work for their readers. Press policies ensured that many newspaper critics were staunch fascists, however, who often worked directly with the government.[9] In different ways, the texts that make up the literary history of these years bear the marks of a regime that arrogated the right to decide who could speak, what they could say, when and where they could say it, and to whom.

TOWARD A NEW ITALIAN LITERATURE

In the late twenties, though, before the regime had consolidated its disciplinary and patronage mechanisms, Italians writers and critics were not shy about denouncing the sorry state of their national literature. They charged that the continuing influence of liberal-era genres such as the lyrical prose fragment had left Italians incapable of producing what the young author Alberto Moravia called "a true and above all convincing representation of life."[10] For various reasons, many of them championed the novel as a means of reviving Italian letters. For some, the passage from the literary fragment to the novel would mirror Italy's own transition from a regional to a national consciousness during World War I. As the literary historian Salvatore Rosati and others envisioned it, the focus on personal experience would be replaced with an emphasis on what was "universally national" in the Italian consciousness, allowing the novel to communicate the new identities that accompanied the advent of Italy's "first truly national life."[11] Others argued that the novel's sweeping scope made it the literary form best suited to depict the complexities of mass society. The twenty-two-year-old critic and journalist Mario Pannunzio argued that only the novel could express the drama of the individual's destiny at a time of moral crisis and radical social transformations. He urged Italian writers to correct decades of reductivist Positivist depictions by narrating modern man "as a complete and whole figure who struggles with his fellow creatures, with nature, hunger, and death. The necessity of the novel today is a necessity for a return to the epic, in the etymological sense of the word; for a return to telling the stories of a perennially suffering humanity that is endlessly changing. It is a story that is all the more evocative and poetic for being real, true, and topical."[12] Other partisans of the novel had political as well as literary interests in mind. While not every intellectual who championed the novel in these years can be termed a convinced supporter of fascism, many considered it the best literary vehicle for the dissemination of the regime's ideals in and outside of Italy. Specifically, the novel's potential to offer a more integrated portrait of the individual appealed to those who wished to utilize literature to inculcate fascist values. The novelist, in this view, would disseminate a "new ethical attitude" by choosing to focus on contemporary moral dilemmas. In this way, Granata wrote in *Critica fascista*, writers would fulfill a social function by "giving life to works that can provide clarification for each person."[13]

This "ethical" novel would also show its transparency through the use of realist codes of representation, which found favor among a broad spectrum of literary intellectuals. Several factors account for this preference for realist aesthetics. The experience of World War I was a catalyst for some older intellectuals: as in other countries, it produced a predilection for prose styles that would reflect the harsh and essential quality of combat experience. Another factor was the influence of fascism. The merger between art and life that Mussolini had always advocated would find its clearest expression, some claimed, in aesthetics that "go directly to the essentials, destroying the literary means that were so dear to the decadent period that preceded ours."[14] Others, mindful of the didactic function the regime envisioned for culture, considered its communicative potential. After all, as the writer Massimo Bontempelli contended in 1933, the task of the new avant-garde was not to perfect "a rare language destined for the ears of a few initiates," but to learn how to deliver a message to twenty thousand people in an orig-

inal and entertaining way.[15] Finally, realism appealed to critics for its potential to perform as political speech while keeping up the appearance of artistic autonomy. Arnaldo Bocelli could thus couch his calls for a "new realism" in language that alluded to political as well as aesthetic necessities.
Realism would satisfy "a fundamental need of our time and spirit: to leave
behind old forms and formulas, to broaden our horizons, to look around us
with eyes that are free from preconceived ideas, to observe the life being
lived around us, to understand it, keep pace with it, and interpret it *from
within.*"[16] The formal consensus for realism among literary intellectuals
did not denote the existence of a unified school of realist thought or practice. Whereas in Soviet Russia several years of literary debates ended in
1934 with the establishment of socialist realism as state policy, in Italy a variety of realist tendencies received official support and patronage throughout the fascist period. In literature, as in art and film, the government's
main goal was to muzzle realism's critical bite, since officials knew that
asking Italians to record reality in their works could easily prove counterproductive. Bontempelli's "magic realism" provided one possible model,
but its stress on mythmaking and evasion gave it little appeal for younger
intellectuals who adhered to the thirties ethos of *engagement.* For the same
reason, many writers rejected Bottai's vision of the artist who "presents
and embraces all the particulars of reality in order to reconcile its contradictions," although this consolatory aesthetic inspired Italians in various fields
who embraced an illustrative and propagandistic model of fascist art.[17]

What held the most promise as a uniquely Italian and fascist literary
aesthetic was the notion of a "spiritual" realism that would "transfigure"
reality rather than merely register it. As presented by Bocelli, Titta Rosa,
and other critics, "spiritual realism" would avoid the pitfalls of materialistic aesthetics—such as Naturalism and the *Neue Sachlichkeit*—that "lost
sight of the individual." Ideals of impersonality and absolute objectivity,
they charged, made the writer into a "mere reporter of events" and
stripped him or her of the chance to use literature to actively shape new
values.[18] At the level of the text, this spiritual ethos would be expressed
through the inclusion of psychologically complex characters whose actions
were motivated by ethical concerns. This formula satisfied a variety of literary constituencies, as it preserved, at least in theory, Crocean notions of
the autonomy of art. Yet by assigning the writer a transformative role and
urging him or her to manipulate reality in the service of a moral vision, it
also conformed to the fascist requests for works that would foster changes
in collective behavior.

CRITICS AND THE CONSTRUCTION OF LITERARY IDENTITY

As in other realms of fascist culture, the definition of national literary aesthetics proceeded through a series of encounters with foreign texts. While the Italian market had always proved receptive to foreign works at both the popular and elite level, fascist goals of developing a modern and exportable literature increased support for an "open door" policy. Isolationist attitudes would further harm an already provincial literary culture, critics argued; to find audiences throughout Europe, modern trends should be "assimilated, rather than refuted; surpassed, rather than ignored." [19] As in other fields of cultural endeavor, younger intellectuals proved particularly open to influences from abroad. In a 1929 article, the twenty-one-year-old writer Elio Vittorini complained that neither Futurism, D'Annunzianism, Naturalism, nor *prosa d'arte* inspired his age-group. He concluded that Italy's new literary spirit would have to develop through a process of "exchanges and correspondences" with Europe.[20] For this generation, translating foreign authors proved to be a mechanism of cultural influence as well as a source of income. In the thirties and early forties, writers like Vittorini, Umberto Barbaro, Cesare Pavese, Moravia, and Enrico Emanuelli translated new Soviet, American, French, and German authors for the Italian market as they were writing their own works.[21]

In the early thirties, both commercial and political goals thus produced a climate of support for publications with a cosmopolitan character. Dailies like the *Corriere padano* and periodicals such as *Espero* and *Italia letteraria* purveyed prose by, and discussions of, a wide range of American and European writers.[22] In Rome, the journal *Occidente*, which billed itself as a "synthesis of the literary activity of the world," offered the works of authors such as Katherine Mansfield, Hans Fallada, Ramon Perez de Ayala, and Ernest Hemingway and advised Italians on new work coming out of Europe and North and South America. Book publishers' lists proved no less eclectic. Editorial houses such as Mondadori, Bompiani, and Corbaccio peddled translations of a wide range of American and European novels. Corbaccio's series "Writers from All over the World," which featured Leon Feuchtwanger, Alfred Neumann, Thornton Wilder, and John Dos Passos, mushroomed from twenty-six to sixty titles between 1933 and 1934.[23]

Soviet literature, like the rest of Soviet society, commanded much attention among intellectual circles and the educated public in the years of the depression. The market supported a specialized publishing house, Slavia, while periodicals such as *L'Italiano* and *Il Convegno* dedicated issues to Soviet literature.[24] Reviews of Russian literature often served Italian intellectuals to send messages to their peers on subjects—such as realism and the relationship between politics and art—that were hotly debated under Mussolini as well as under Stalin. Thus the critic Giuseppe Raimondi lauded Konstantin Fedin, Lydia Seyfullina, and other writers "who in the midst of a war and a Revolution kept their eyes open to be able to record all that they observed," and Barbaro suggested Seyfullina's lyrical prose as a model for Italian writers who wished to overcome the constraints of Naturalism.[25] Yet Italians also called attention to the loss of intellectual autonomy under communism. Lo Gatto, a University of Padua professor who headed the Institute for Eastern Europe, ended his chronicle of the first years of Stalinist rule with an account of the "artistic castrations" faced by Soviet writers. Stalin's literary policies were certainly more draconian than Mussolini's: they mandated manual labor for writers and the use of state-approved themes and styles. Such comparisons might also have placated Italian consciences, though, by furthering the notion that fascism was a regime that protected art and the liberty of thought. Thus Lo Gatto and others noted that Russian critics such as Vyacheslav Polonski had lost their jobs for opposing state literary policies, "forgetting" that the press had been purged, if in minor measure, at home as well.[26]

American literature drew even more interest from writers and critics under the dictatorship. As Pavese would later recall, Italians saw similarities between their own literary goals and the attempts of authors like Sinclair Lewis to create "a modern taste, a modern style, a modern world" in the years following World War I.[27] But the "documentary" realisms supposedly favored by Americans met with little favor from more traditional critics, who charged that they evinced a mechanistic mindset that was out of step with the Italian national character.[28] In an "open letter" from Ojetti to Dos Passos that appeared in *Pègaso,* Ojetti expressed admiration for *Manhattan Transfer* and *1919,* but criticized the American writer's "ruthlessly" objective narrative voice, which floated "like a perfect movie camera" from scene to scene. Ojetti concluded that Dos Passos's prose was "the opposite of what we Italians have written in the past, what we are writing now, and, I dare say, what we will write in the future."[29] Other reviewers, especially younger ones, did not agree. Dos Passos's continuous shifts in style and setting, they argued, allowed him to capture modernity's tempos and mentalities. *Orpheus* editors Luciano Anceschi and Remo Cantoni, who were studying phenomenology with Antonio Banfi in Milan, cited the American's writings as an example of how the abandonment of literary formulas and theories resulted in more authentic representations of reality.

Commenting on *Manhattan Transfer,* Anceschi noted that "social life itself becomes the protagonist of the novel. . . . He [Dos Passos] judges nothing, but merely accepts life and lets things speak for themselves: any judgment must necessarily come from the reflections of the reader."[30]

This praise for American literature did not, in most cases, imply sympathy for American democracy. For Pavese, who was ostracized for his antifascism from the start of his career, the study of American literature represented an opening to a world of greater civil and creative liberties. But the majority of Italian intellectuals did not associate freedom with American democracy in the early thirties. Even Moravia, who confessed to feeling "isolated and sad" in fascist Italy, returned from a two-month trip to America convinced that freedom "costs too much" there, given the unemployment and public poverty. As he informed Giuseppe Prezzolini, who had hosted him at Columbia's Casa Italiana, "liberty is culture" and America had very little of that (fig. 2).[31]

Weimar German literature provided a final reference point for Italians who sought to develop a national literary aesthetic. As an experiment in realist poetics, the *Neue Sachlichkeit* held much interest for writers and critics, and all of the major authors of the movement were translated and reviewed in the fascist press. Italians admired the Germans' readiness to break with past artistic canons and acknowledged the different kind of beauty produced by this aesthetic of concreteness. The novelist and German scholar Bonaventura Tecchi conceded that, in the hands of Alexander Döblin or Hermann Kesten, "the most brutal reality, the bare fact of chronicle[,] . . . can generate the most wondrous and modern poetic evocations."[32] The critic Enrico Rocca also praised works such as Ernst Glaeser's *Jahrgang 1902* for their "actuality," and hoped aloud that Italians would be inspired by them to write novels about "the dramatic and inviting events" that culminated in the March on Rome.[33]

These same commentators, though, also lost no occasion to emphasize the deficiencies of the *Neue Sachlichkeit,* which Titta Rosa characterized as a "pseudo-literature" of "crude content."[34] Discussing Döblin's novel *Berlin Alexanderplatz,* for example, Rocca lauded the German's inclusion of newspaper cuttings and other artifacts of "real life" but warned that the book's "coldly brutal" realism could only find success among a people who, like the Germans, were "antisentimental and frigid."[35] Still others objected to the cultural assumptions that undergirded many currents of the *Neue Sachlichkeit.* Alvaro noted during his stay in Berlin that the movement reflected a mentality that privileged the material, the quotidian, and the contingent. However remarkable its "poetic possibilities," he asserted, the

Figure 2. Alberto Moravia in New York City, 1935. Reproduced with kind permission of Carlo Cecchi and the Fondo Associazione Alberto Moravia, Rome.

Neue Sachlichkeit was ill-suited for "Latins" who valued the spiritual and the universal.[36]

At a time when facism wished to firm up its identity with respect to other models of modern civilization, reviews of foreign novels mapped the confines between the "national" and the "foreign" by signaling literary elements that were considered "anti-Italian." Following agendas of artistic normalization and national purification, they attempted to guide Italians away from trends and aesthetics that, they claimed, had no place under Mussolini's dictatorship.

THE REALIST NOVEL AND THE SEARCH FOR MORAL CHANGE

Not all Italian authors accepted these critical messages, at least not at the outset of their careers. In the midst of these discussions over foreign realisms, a group of novels appeared that pointed up the contradictions that beset the regime's projects for a national literature and a fascist style of modernity. Written by intellectuals in their twenties, these novels sparked much debate for their frank depictions of bourgeois moral corruption. While some critics saluted them as revolutionary contributions to the creation of new collective values, others decried their focus on illicit sex and financial scandal. In fact, the young protagonists of these works hardly fit the description of the regime's "new men," and the cosmopolitan demimondes they frequent had been targeted by fascist zealots for rehabilitation. I will discuss three of these novels, Moravia's *Gli indifferenti* (*The Indifferent Ones*, 1929), Barbaro's *Luce fredda* (*Cold Light*, 1931), and Emanuelli's *Radiografia di una notte* (*X-Ray of a Night*, 1932). While the first of these works remains one of the most famous twentieth-century Italian novels, the latter two have remained in the dustbin of literary history since World War II. Despite the different political stances of their authors — only Emanuelli was a convinced fascist — they are similar in tone and theme. Taken together, they raise questions about the role of biography, ideology, and language in the production and reception of fascist texts and shed light on a literary movement of the dictatorship that has yet to receive much critical attention.[37]

The denunciation of middle-class morality that pervades *Gli indifferenti* has led critics to classify it as an antifascist work and, more recently, as an expression of existentialist tendencies. Both these interpretations overlook the book's affinities with the causes of the fascist avant-garde, with which Moravia was associated in his earliest days as a writer.[38] In many ways, Moravia was an anomaly within the fascist literary world. First, an allowance provided by his wealthy architect father meant that, unlike most Italian intellectuals, he was under no duress to publish his work or accept the subsidies proffered by state patronage institutions. Second, family ties placed him in direct contact with both fascist and antifascist circles, although, by his own admission, he embraced neither creed with much conviction. His maternal uncle Augusto De Marsanich was a senator and a prominent fascist official, while his cousins Carlo and Nello Rosselli belonged to the *Giustizia e Libertà* opposition group. Thus even when he became a regular guest of Sarfatti, Ciano, and other dignitaries, he was intermittently tailed by the fascist political police.[39]

In light of these affiliations, it is interesting that Moravia chose to become involved in 1928 with the militant youth journals *I Lupi* and *Interplanetario*, the latter of which he helped to edit. Viewing fascism as a profound break with the past, these two reviews embraced experimental theater and other manifestations of the avant-garde as the foundations of a corresponding "cultural revolution" in Italy. To mark their distance from the literary styles of the war generation, they called for an "antiliterature" that would reflect fascism's concrete, fact-oriented mentality.[40] *Gli indifferenti* took shape in *I Lupi* and *Interplanetario* as a series of stories that display Moravia's sympathy for such views and provide clues as to the ideological climate within which the novel was developed and received.[41] A parable he contributed to the former journal constitutes the thematic nucleus of *Gli indifferenti,* as it mocks those who cannot decide whether or not to act in life. In his story "Villa Mercedes," which appeared in *Interplanetario,* a courtesan is killed and left in the attic of her belle epoque house as a not-so-subtle message about the obsolescence of liberal moral and aesthetic codes.[42]

A similar concern for ethical change pervades *Gli indifferenti.* Set in Rome in the mid-1920s, the narrative focuses on the society woman Mariagrazia and her children, Carla and Michele, who are both in their early twenties. Presented as an unsympathetic if pathetic figure, Mariagrazia passes her time with her best friend, Lisa, a lascivious divorcée, and her lover, Leo, a lecherous and violent man who plans to swindle the family out of their home. Carla communicates her disgust with the "oppressive, miserable and petty" climate in which she lives, while Michele distances himself by becoming an "indifferent" voyeur for whom "gestures, words, feelings, all were just a vain game of pretense."[43]

Making sexual conquest a metaphor for predatory behavior of other kinds, Moravia structures his novel around the parallel seductions of Carla and Michele by Leo and Lisa. Carla's sad future at Leo's side is presented as a foregone conclusion. With the first touch of Leo's hands on her skirt, she thinks, "There was just no way out of it, everything was fixed and governed by a wretched inevitability." For Michele, however, Lisa's unwanted attentions bring on a crisis. He ponders the ethical consequences of his indifference to the corruption around him, and nurtures a dream of living in a "paradise of concreteness and truth" where "every gesture, feeling, and word would have an immediate and direct connection [*aderenza*] with the reality that inspired them."[44] When Michele's halfhearted attempt to shoot Leo fails, he puts himself through a mock trial for his "sin of indifference" and concludes that he is guilty. "I have done nothing[,] . . . nothing but think. . . . that is my error," he reflects as the book ends.[45] Michele's condemnation of his own apathy sent a message that was not out of keeping with the current intellectual and political climate, as it raised the possibility of his transformation from amoral spectator to active agent of ethical change.

Published by Alpes, an editorial house owned by Mussolini's brother, Arnaldo, *Gli indifferenti* was an immediate succès de scandale. Catholics and conservatives objected to its frank language and depiction of youthful apathy, and a reviewer in the *Corriere padano* denounced it for spreading a "syphilitic Freudianism" that had no place in fascist Italy.[46] Many critics lauded the book for its penetrating exposé of the bankruptcy of existing values, however, arguing that it condemned indifference rather than encouraged it. As Tecchi commented, while many works of the *Neue Sachlichkeit* betrayed "a certain cynicism and moral apathy[,] . . . the merit of *Gli indifferenti*, in my opinion, is that Moravia has presented moral indifference as a problem, described it, and in a certain sense, judged it." While Moravia later claimed that his book had vanished into oblivion after being labeled a subversive work, *Gli indifferenti* quickly achieved canonical status as an example of the new Italian novel.[47] The work also enjoyed commercial acclaim. By April 1930 it had gone through four printings, and a deluxe edition had been prepared for collectors. Bompiani bought the rights and issued a second edition in 1934.

Motivated by similar moral concerns and, perhaps, a wish to share some of Moravia's success, other young writers published their own critiques of indifference in the early thirties. Euralio De Michelis and Elio Talarico, both convinced fascists, authored similar tales of the costs of apathy that ended with their protagonists' renunciation of decadent tastes and behaviors.[48] The twenty-nine-year-old Barbaro brought out *Luce fredda*, which was immediately placed alongside Moravia's as an example of the new realist school of writing. An autodidact of great talent about whom little has been written, the Sicilian-born Barbaro was a critic, editor, translator, novelist, filmmaker, screenwriter, and playwright. A specialist in Russian culture, he translated a variety of Russian and Soviet authors, as well as the works of Vsevolod Pudovkin and Sergei Eisenstein.[49] After 1935, he taught film theory and practice at the state-run Centro Sperimentale di Cinematografia (CSC), and emerged as a leading communist film critic after World War II.

His vast knowledge and diverse activities rank him as one of the most important mediators of European modernism in interwar Italy.

Both during and after fascism, Barbaro remained an uncomfortable figure for many, however, since his ideas and works play on the lability of the boundaries between rightist and leftist revolutionary discourse.[50] Barbaro's political and aesthetic roots lay in that segment of the Italian avant-garde that, in the early twenties, brought Futurists into an aesthetic alliance with leftist artists who could not find a place in the culturally conservative Italian Communist Party.[51] This heterodox formation honed Barbaro's skills at exploiting the polyvalent qualities of revolutionary rhetoric. This mastery of language, together with the protection he enjoyed from his friend Chiarini, allowed him to carve out a variegated career within the institutions of the regime.

Luce fredda is the product of an intricate web of cultural and political influences. Alternating between a satirical tone reminiscent of Mikhail Bulgakov (whose novel *Fatal Eggs* he was translating at that time) and *Neue Sachlichkeit* reportage, Barbaro employs an arsenal of experimental narrative techniques to tell a story that converges in many points with that of Moravia. His polyphonic narrative begins in May 1922 and continues into the late twenties. It darts in and out of the lives of characters who are introduced through interior monologues that jump, sometimes in midsentence, from the thoughts of one protagonist to those of another. This multiperspectivist approach, which recalls that of Döblin and Dos Passos, allows Barbaro to present a damning collective portrait of the Roman bourgeoisie. Sergio, the novel's apathetic young protagonist, hates the hypocrisy he sees everywhere in society, but lacks the resolve to change anything. As he reflects, "Is it possible to create a moral code for oneself that would be independent of and superior to the recognized and consecrated one? . . . Perhaps not, but certainly anyone who doesn't try is a contemptible person, no?"[52]

Such open-ended discourse conveys more than Sergio's perpetual state of indecision. It lends Barbaro's text an ironic, almost mocking tone that separates it from other contemporary realist works. Unlike Moravia's Michele, Sergio experiences no moment of moral clarity that might allow him to act as a guide for others in the future. Instead, he comes to see the wisdom of indifference, understood as a refusal to enter into a society governed by an authoritarian logic of binary oppositions. As he states, "There is no such thing as good and evil, beauty and ugliness, white and black as mutually exclusive things; all opposing things are absurdly intertwined and interlinked, all lying on the same plane of indifference, and life is all of a color[,]

. . . a fading white that is not yet black."[53] Toward the end of the novel, Sergio resolves to discard his pernicious "intellectualism" and "regain a sense of reality and the concrete." He then promptly falls asleep, allowing Barbaro to end his narrative in a dreamworld that vindicates those "evasions from the real" that Sergio had originally condemned.[54] At the close of the narrative, Barbaro's protagonist remains in his seedy Roman boarding-house, in a liminal and unredeemed mental and physical space. The disjunction between Sergio's thoughts and his behavior at the novel's end stands as a rebuke of fascist projects to mobilize youth and create a "new man" in whom, as one militant put it, "the virtues of thought and action would be harmonized."[55]

Despite Barbaro's apparent refusal to support the regime's projects of collective reclamation, fascist critics interpreted *Luce fredda* much as they had *Gli indifferenti:* as a protest against bourgeois corruption and the self-absorbed attitudes of the Italian intellectual class.[56] Bocelli depicted Barbaro as a messenger of moral activism and devoted a long article to him and the emerging school of "spiritual realism." Although Barbaro and other new writers had captured modernity's "fragmented and discontinuous" mind-set, they had steered clear of the Positivist tendencies that marred the *Neue Sachlichkeit.* Bocelli saw "behind all the pitiless analysis, an aspiration to harmony and synthesis; behind the ostentatious coldness and cynicism, a sincere need for faith and authentic human warmth; behind the orgy of the particular, a search for the universal. . . . man is being reborn in the writer today."[57] For other critics, though, the appearance of Barbaro's work on the heels of *Gli indifferenti* raised fears that the new Italian novel was taking a terribly wrong turn. The "magic realist" Bontempelli objected to these authors' materialistic focus on "corporeal necessities," while Giovanni Battista Angioletti decreed that the analytical tone and "abulic" protagonists of works like *Luce fredda* were elements that "we cannot embrace."[58]

Trepidation over the style and content of these new novels only increased with the publication of Emanuelli's openly experimental *Radiografia di una notte,* which chronicled six hours in the lives of a wealthy Milanese family. Like his friend Soldati, the twenty-three-year-old Emanuelli moved easily between reportage and literature. In the early thirties he journeyed to Spain, Libya, and Russia on assignment for newspapers such as *La Stampa* and *La Gazzetta del Popolo.* Emanuelli viewed the advent of mass society in Italy with ambivalence. His novel showcases modernity's social and psychological costs as much as its material enticements. Indeed, unlike Moravia and Barbaro, Emanuelli blames commercial culture as much as bourgeois convention for the erosion of meaning in contemporary life.

Don't these go hand in hand?

Like the Americans and Weimar Germans depicted by travelers such as Soldati, Emanuelli's modern subjects lack all sense of personal taste and volition; they are caught in the flow of commodities that characterizes contemporary Milan. Their stream-of-consciousness monologues contain recitations of advertising slogans, and they blindly consume the products offered them—women's magazines, radio programs, and other products whose ads Emanuelli inserts into the narrative.[59] Subjecting every character in the book to a pitiless "X-ray" light, the author develops images of a superficial nouveau riche society in which spirituality is considered a sign of weakness rather than a source of strength. Reflecting on her life of "horrible, degrading half-truths," Stefano's mother, Lucia, notes that "it would be too humiliating to ask for comfort and help from prayer, from faith."[60]

As in many *Neue Sachlichkeit* novels, generational conflict takes center stage. Stefano's father, who neglects his family for evening "business meetings" with his mistress, takes the brunt of the work's critical blow. The book's dénouement comes when Stefano confronts his father, who symbolizes the pervasive moral corruption that obstructs all ethical and social change. In the course of their quarrel, his father pulls out a gun, and accidentally ends up dead. "Someone must die here," Stefano's friend Giacomo muses at the end of the book as he tries to justify the tragedy. "Only then will everything change."[61] At the close of Moravia's novel, Michele can only condemn himself for his inaction, while Barbaro's phlegmatic Sergio cannot bring himself to do even that. By the end of Emanuelli's story, at least in one family, the stage is set for a purifying moral "revolution" that might underpin social change.

Like other realist works, this one met with mixed reviews. Younger critics like Vittorini praised the book's spirit of "moral resentment" and termed it "one of the most remarkable works of our time"[62] The book also gained Emanuelli an "encouragement prize" from the Italian Academy, although an internal Academy report that year noted that reservations had been expressed over the practice of rewarding youth such as Emanuelli who were "too acerbic."[63] Other critics accused him of imitating Moravia's and Barbaro's skeptical determinism and of borrowing the worst of contemporary modernism. As one charged, the novel was nothing but a "chaotic photomontage" of Dos Passos, Freud, Joyce, the Surrealists, and the "crude photographic verism" of the *Neue Sachlichkeit*.[64]

The issue of foreign influence proved to be the most sensitive for Italian commentators who had awaited this generation's contributions to the new national novel. Indeed, reviews of realist novels often became occasions for impromptu referendums on the applicability of modernist styles and techniques to the Italian fascist context. Even before Emanuelli's work appeared, fascist functionaries had joined critics in accusing realist writers of propagating foreign "decadence." In 1931, claiming that the new novelists had "confused modernity and novelty," Arnaldo Mussolini had warned students at the School of Fascist Mysticism away from books that propagated "sad foreign literary movements that aim at the degeneration of the dignity of man." The next year, Chiarini blasted young Italians who imitated "precious, deformed, and cerebral" foreign movements that obliterated "not only our national character, but the personality of the artist himself." By 1933, after several more realist texts had appeared, the journalist Carlo Villani proclaimed it a "national duty" to "save our youth from the tedious analytic examination of foreign fetishes. It is not just a question of literature[;] . . . the continued physical and moral integrity of our people depends on it." [65]

Moravia proved the most vocal in refuting charges of foreign influence. He justified his generation's recourse to "foreign experiences" as a means of representing an Italy "that is changed, ambitious, Europeanized, bourgeois, and pulsing with new needs whose commonality with those of other nations does not make them any less Italian." Other critics of Moravia's generation seconded his opinion. In *Saggiatore,* Pannunzio reminded the detractors of the new novel that his generation's goal remained that of creating a literary culture which, "while reaching out to Europe, remains Italian, giving us works that reflect *our* turmoils, *our,* hopes, in a word, *our* way of understanding and adapting to modern life." [66] Minister Bottai backed up Moravia and his peers. Asserting in *Critica fascista* that Italianness was a matter of spirit as well as of style, he proclaimed *Gli indifferenti* to be entirely consonant with "the ethical climate of fascism." Restating the arguments of the young Rationalist architect Rava, he concluded that the "transfiguration" and adaptation of foreign trends had long been recognized as a national trait.[67]

FASCIST LITERATURE AND THE FICTION OF THE UNPOLITICAL

Political as well as cultural designs lay behind Bottai's support for realist novelists. The early thirties witnessed the development of patronage strategies designed to control and neutralize young intellectuals. Academy awards, invitations to write for publications such as *Il Bargello* and *Critica fascista,* and public encouragement of "nonconformist" creative endeavors drew writers into cliental relationships with fascist authorities. Like Emanuelli, Moravia commenced a parallel career as a journalist for *La*

Stampa and *La Gazzetta del Popolo,* which allowed him the luxury of frequent foreign travel. At the same time, he became a fixture at the salons of
fascism's social and political elite and served on the jury of the San Remo
literary prize. With the help of his patron, Chiarini, Barbaro began to write
for the wider audiences of *Educazione fascista* and *Roma,* was hired by the
Cines movie studio as a documentarist and screenwriter, and in 1935 became coeditor of *Italia letteraria* and a teacher at the Centro Sperimentale
di Cinematografia.[68] Over the long term, the price of this access to power
would be the slow erosion of experimental impulses. As we will see, Barbaro and Emanuelli left behind their avant-garde ethos as they became
more immersed in the structures of the regime.   AND MORAVIA?

The utility that these new networks had for both patrons and clients
came through clearly in a 1932 debate about the relationship of literature
and politics under fascism. Functionaries who wished to speed up the development of a fascist literature supported the realists and their supporters
in their campaign for novels of actuality, offering them space in *Critica
fascista, Il Lavoro fascista,* and other publications. They also delivered their
own seemingly allied messages about the writer's duty to "immerse himself in life" and produce works that, as Chiarini wrote, reflected "the grand
problems of our time."[69] While this generic request may have seemed
innocent, its meaning in the context of fascist cultural politics proved easy
to decipher. Thus the writer and critic Angioletti, speaking for the anti-
realists, boldly decided to call the functionaries' bluff:

> Immerse ourselves in life. Very good. But we are already in life up to
> our necks, and one must not demand that we immerse our heads as
> well. . . . Does participating in the political life of a Country mean plac-
> ing art at the service of politics? Inviting the writer to illustrate certain
> principles? . . . If art must respond to certain presuppositions[,] . . .
> then writers have the right to be told openly. And then what will be
> discussed is the essence of art, its moral function and its limits in front
> of the collective interest; such a discussion could create a deep and un-
> breachable division among artists.

Angioletti's blunt statement infringed Italian literary etiquette but proved
effective. Chiarini immediately retreated, replying that "no one wishes to
make artists the executors of [Soviet-style] 'social commands' or propagandists: no one wants to impose limits to art or establish controls or censorship: I was simply speaking of the relationship between art and life."[70]
Casini, who would soon become fascism's chief literary censor, also denied
any censorial intentions. The call for a "literature of the present," he
claimed, was less a request for "an art that calls itself fascist[,] . . . a State

art enslaved to political ends," than a reminder that all writers had the responsibility to participate actively in the making of a modern society, which in Italy meant furthering the fascist revolution.[71] A few months later, speaking to the Italian Society for Authors and Editors, Mussolini delivered his own carefully worded message on the matter. While he disavowed any intention to establish a state literature, he chided his audience for not drawing more inspiration from two "capital events" such as the war and the revolution. Henceforth, writers must redouble their efforts to "immerse themselves in life" and become "interpreters of their own time," which, he specified, "is that of the fascist revolution."[72]

The discussions about the relationship of literature and politics also provided writers like Barbaro and Moravia with opportunities to publicly reinterpret their works to make them better conform to the current political climate. For intellectuals who were regarded with some suspicion, such "self-criticisms" had a precise performative value: they constituted political acts that could better one's position or at least keep persecutors at bay. "My aesthetic, in essence, concerns the relationship of art and life," Barbaro wrote in one of several articles that explained his literary philosophy in terms that conformed semantically both to contemporary communist and fascist cultural policy. "All of my work . . . denounces individualism and the inexorable destruction to which it leads; this is certainly a topical problem." *Luce fredda*, he intimated, should be seen as a demonstration of his "ethical commitment" as an artist, since its goal was to "cause the reader to acknowledge the problems of daily life . . . in order to give him an overwhelming urge to put an end to them, to transform himself and the world." Such was Barbaro's skill at the art of double entendre that, after his death in 1955, his friend and patron Chiarini could contend that "his writings contain not a line or a word that could be cause for shame or repentance."[73]

The same, perhaps, could not be said for Moravia, who had come in for the most criticism and proved an easy target for charges of anti-Italianness and antifascism due to his ties to the Rossellis and his Jewish heritage. Of course, Moravia had connections that worked for him as well: in 1931, Bottai had pointed out *Gli indifferenti*'s convergence with fascist concerns for moral renewal, and had reminded Italians that "the true fascist intellectual is known by his works and not by his party card or position."[74] In 1933, though, at the height of the polemics regarding literature's role in the fascist state, Moravia chose to repudiate his successful novel on the third page of the extremist (and anti-Semitic) paper *Il Tevere*. Comparing himself to "Saturn [who] eats his own children," the Roman writer claimed

OR PERHAPS NOT: B-G DOESN'T PROVIDE
THE EVIDENCE TO SUPPORT THIS

that "one fine day, taking *Gli indifferenti* in hand, I realized that it not only bored me but I really could not understand it. . . . I realized then that I was finally free of it and drew a sigh of relief."[75] His association with the militant literary review *Oggi* afforded him other occasions to make statements that might pacify conservative elements of the regime.[76] Although Moravia's private pronouncements of this period suggest that it is unlikely that he underwent a profascist political conversion, these changes in his public discourse allowed his work to be more easily appropriated by fascist critics. Thus Corrado Sofia could write a few months later in *Critica fascista* that *Gli indifferenti* and other realist novels had been the fruit of a phase of "cerebralism" that had since been left behind by the Italian intellectual class. "Not only has politics entered into every corner of the country, but ideas about art have become truer and more profound," Sofia observed with satisfaction.[77]

The more repressive climate that took hold after 1933 galvanized those who had long protested against political interference in art. The critic Franceso Bruno reminded his colleagues that foreign audiences would never accept novels "whose political and propagandistic function is too obvious."[78] The review *Italia vivente* chose the moment to publish a survey on "the art of our time" that contained refutations of state-inspired art. The poet Angelo Silvio Novaro took a pragmatic tack in his response, observing that "art cannot be created by invitation, much less intimidation. What would Fascism want with a lying art, anyway?"[79] Alvaro, who had long opposed the realists' agenda, played an antimodernist card, maintaining that "vulgar documentaries" further disseminated the foreign maladies of "hedonism, experimentalism, agnosticism, and objectivism." Today, he argued, living one's own reality "with the most complete adhesion" entailed the duty to produce works that were based on Italian, rather than foreign, ideals and experiences. The writer's task today was to create narratives that would convey Italy's "special way of living the problems of modernity" at home and abroad.[80]

THE ETHNIC AS NATIONAL: ALVARO'S ALTERNATIVE

Alvaro's literary production of these years suggests that he had been working overtime to fulfill this mandate. In 1930 alone, he published three volumes of stories and a novel. Few writers of the fascist era worked harder to understand the shifts in attitudes and social structures that accompanied the advent of mass society in Italy; few were more ambivalent about them. And few writers offer more insight into how political concerns could influence the production and reception of literary works in fascist Italy. A native of Calabria, Alvaro spent much of his life dealing with authoritarian personalities: first, his father, a small landowner who served as the village schoolmaster, then the Jesuit educators who expelled him for reading D'Annunzio, and later the officials of the fascist state, which he first opposed and then came to outwardly support. But Alvaro, too, had a deep need for order, which was continually frustrated by the interwar period's changing social and sexual mores. From his vantage point in Milan, where he worked as a journalist after fighting in World War I, Alvaro came to regard modernity as a manifestation of a historical crisis, and associated it with the end of comforting scenarios of gender and class stability. "Europe has become like an uncomfortable hotel. . . . all we can do now is wait for the flood," he observed uneasily in 1923.[81]

Unlike many intellectuals of the older war generation, though, Alvaro's concerns over the erosion of social and sexual hierarchies did not lead him to immediately support Mussolini's movement. Instead, a few months before the March on Rome, Alvaro joined the staff of Giovanni Amendola's liberal paper, *Il Mondo*, and wrote many antifascist columns before the paper was suppressed. After the political crackdown of 1926, this affiliation, along with his signature on Croce's opposition manifesto, targeted him for personal and professional marginalization. While his friend Bontempelli helped him out with a position at the journal '*900*, pressure mounted from authorities such as the PNF propaganda chief Franco Ciarlantini for him to intervene in ongoing debates over fascist art as a way of beginning the process of political rehabilitation. Alvaro could "liberate himself from the taint of antifascism and enjoy our free atmosphere," Ciarlantini advised Bontempelli, by authoring articles that would "clarify his political position . . . in a decisive and definitive manner."[82]

Unwilling to renounce his beliefs, Alvaro opted for exile, embarking on what he referred to as an "enforced vacation" to Berlin in 1928, when he was thirty-five. There, he wrote for the *Berliner Tageblatt* and *Weltbühne* and contributed articles on Weimar society and culture to several Italian publications. Judging from these essays, though, and from the story "Solitudine," discussed in chapter 1, Berlin made Alvaro as unhappy as Rome had. He disliked the politicization and pace of the German capital and felt physically ill at ease there. He confided to his diary that he was continually reminded of being "small and Southern" by the "gigantic women, with boots up to their knees," who accosted him on the streets.[83] As a writer, finally, he could not accept the "impersonal and collective tone, unheard of among us," that marked *Neue Sachlichkeit* literature and many other manifestations of Weimar culture. As he informed his compatriots back home, "For those of us who follow more lyrical impulses in our work, such an environment is almost incomprehensible and causes feelings of imbalance and panic."[84]

It was in this state of mind that Alvaro formulated a "plan of defense" that would allow him to live in Italy and practice his craft. As expressed in his diary and other private notations, this involved "defining a distinct personality as a writer" and "becoming successful" (*far carriera*) to minimize the power his enemies could have over him.[85] Whatever his motivation, by 1930 Alvaro had published one collection of stories, *L'amata alla finestra* (*The Loved One at the Window*, 1929), and had completed three more, including *Gente in Aspromonte* (*The People of Aspromonte*, 1930), a bittersweet paean to Calabria as a site of youthful struggles and dreams. As he prepared to return to Italy that year, he wrote an article for the peer journal *Italia letteraria* that began his rapprochement with fascism. He lauded "the war and the revolution" for creating the possibility of a "national world and a total civilization," and characterized his forthcoming work, *Gente in Aspromonte*, as a "last look behind" before he immersed himself in "a passionate present from which it is by now difficult to extract oneself."[86]

Gente in Aspromonte mixes individual and collective memory, history and myth, in narrating the demise of a rural civilization that Alvaro associated with his own childhood and with Italy's regional past. On the surface, it would seem that nostalgia had little place in Alvaro's book. Written in spartan prose, the novella-length title story records the injustices and misery of Calabrian life and the humiliations that those who wield power inflict on the poor.[87] Yet Alvaro's Calabria also embodies the sense of community that the writer found lacking in both Milan and Berlin. This longing for wholeness found expression in a vision of a society in which nature, humans, animals, and the built environment form one organic entity. While he builds on to Giovanni Verga's Naturalist narratives of regional life, Alvaro adds a mythic dimension to the people and places he describes, making them into emblems of a "universal" ethnic community. The slippage between realism and symbolism can be seen in the opening lines of the title story: "Life is not easy for the shepherds of Aspromonte, in the dead of winter when the streams rush down to the sea and the earth seems to float on water. The shepherds stay in huts of mud and sticks and sleep beside the animals. They go about in long capes such as those seen in depictions of ancient Greek gods on winter pilgrimages."[88] In this book, history gives way to legend, in the fashion of Novecentist prescriptions for a "magic realist" literature. At the same time, Alvaro's narratives further *Il*

Selvaggio's proposal to make provincial values the basis for national regeneration. Revisiting his region in order to bury regionalism, Alvaro made Calabria into a symbol of a generalized ethnic community that, he felt, represented Italy's truest national identity, one that could represent the country to the world.[89] Unlike the realist novels of younger intellectuals that depicted an urban Italy cast adrift from the national past, Alvaro's narratives pay homage to the specificity of Italian tradition.   *complimentary, no?*

In the months preceding the publication of *Gente in Aspromonte*, critics who accepted Alvaro's signs of repentance helped to prepare the ground for his return and political rehabilitation. The conservative critic Ojetti, who saw Alvaro's work as an antidote to foreign-influenced realist novels, published the title story in *Pègaso* and ran a full-page ad that presented Alvaro as "among the leading Italian writers of today." [90] Once the book appeared in the spring of 1930, reviewers seemed to agree with this judgment. Noting Alvaro's ability to blend lyricism with a "spare and naked" prose, Rocca and Tecchi praised his "humane" style that had none of the defects of the *Neue Sachlichkeit*: "Everything is precise, clean, simple, essential, and significant," wrote Rocca.[91] Later that year, Alvaro published *Vent'anni*, a novel that answered the calls of critics and cultural functionaries for a work that detailed Italy's regeneration from the ashes of World War I. Critics found it lacking, but read the writer's choice of theme as another sign of his willingness to reconcile himself with the fascist state. "It appears that this is Corrado Alvaro's moment," noted one skeptic. "Volume upon volume appears, and critics greet them all with abundant praise and with an enthusiasm that in truth I cannot understand." [92]

Alvaro's changing fortunes also reflected the power of personal connections in fascist Italy. Soon after his return, he met Sarfatti and, along with Moravia, became a regular at her salon and a judge for the San Remo literary prize. As he confided with relief to his diary, his appearances there "served to allay much rancor and suspicion," since Sarfatti and Mussolini were then lovers.[93] After Mussolini praised *Gente in Aspromonte* at a diplomatic gathering, Alvaro's literary and political position changed definitively. In 1931, with Sarfatti's help, he won the first *La Stampa* literary prize. Interviewed about the lucrative award, he emphasized his contribution to the revival of Italian letters and celebrated Mussolini for "creating an atmosphere that is very conducive to the development of a national literature. . . . I say these things with pleasure, knowing that, coming from me today they cannot be seen as either false or opportunistic." [94]

Displaying the zeal of a recent convert, Alvaro now lauded Mussolini as a "genius" who had invented "traditional solutions to the modern problems of Italian life," and claimed that liberal Italy had been a "dictatorship in disguise" for its neglect of spiritual liberty.[95] His literary production also changed direction. Following his own injunction to "adhere to the present," Alvaro produced volumes of literary reportage on Turkey, Russia, and the "new Italy," including a didactic book for the INCF that interpreted the government's extensive land reclamation (*bonifica*) projects as a symbol of national regeneration.[96] He also intervened more strenuously in the polemics against realist novels, issuing a challenge to younger Italian writers who "have let themselves be dominated by so-called European documentarism": "Will we have the courage to find nonimported roots, to derive our aesthetic directly from our own texts, remembering that we have our own classics[,] . . . which record how the processes of civilization and modernity have been lived in our own way?"[97]

Despite Alvaro's animosity toward recent realist novels, as the thirties progressed *Gli indifferenti* and other works like it were often listed next to his own writings in publications that charted the progress of the new Italian literature. For Titta Rosa and other critics, Alvaro and Moravia reflected a collective desire among Italian writers to achieve "a new culture, a new taste, a spiritual renewal" in Italy in their use of a modern language that "refuted all ornament."[98] Bocelli expressed similar sentiments. Although younger novelists like Moravia were still not "completely clear about their methods and goals," realism had emerged as "*the* tendency of today's literature" and shared a "secret and profound consonance with the fervid political and historical climate in which we live."[99]

Other critics dissented from these rosy views, complaining that the new national literature was anything but national. Arrigo Cajumi noted that Italian writing remained divided into two camps: the provincial and the European. The former, represented by Alvaro, idealized rural life, while the latter, best embodied by Moravia, looked at Italian society through the lenses of the latest foreign literary trends. The critic Alfredo Galletti pointed out that, Moravia apart, the new "national novels" were "unbearably boring" and had left both domestic and foreign audiences cold. Fortunately, Italian writers could offset these market failures by accepting the generous assistance that was now being offered them by the fascist state.[100]

Galletti's comment referred to the results of a 1934 reorganization of the fascist cultural bureaucracy that changed the conditions under which writers worked in Italy. A visit from the Nazi propaganda minister Joseph Goebbels the year before had convinced Italian officials to create a centralized office for propaganda and cultural policy.[101] Under the guidance of

Mussolini's son-in-law, Galeazzo Ciano, the Press Office evolved into an Undersecretariat for Press and Propaganda before becoming a ministry in 1935. Censorship now passed from the prefectures to a special office within this entity that oversaw book revision and confiscation. Literary criticism could also be controlled more closely, through daily directives (*veline*) that told reviewers which works to discuss and how they were to discuss them. An order of March 1935 noted that Moravia's new novel, *Le ambizioni sbagliate*, should receive only limited praise and attention.[102] At the same time, with help from Bottai, the thirty-year-old Ciano increased the patronage functions of his office. He helped young writers obtain jobs, arranged audiences for them with the Duce, and offered "fraternal" aid to authors like Vittorini when their work incurred the wrath of the government.[103]

Ciano also made censorship a more familial experience for the literary community. He hired the poet Adriano Grande to work in the Undersecretariat of Press and Propaganda, allowing Grande to continue on as director of the literary journal *Circoli*. For the duration of the dictatorship, the presence of such men in fascism's cultural bureaucracy would encourage writers of all ages to work with the state rather than struggle against it. Yet the generational fractures that had come to light over realism and the issue of foreign influence would not be sutured in the coming years. Rather, as we will see in chapters 5 and 6, as the 1930s progressed younger writers such as Moravia, Vittorini, and Paola Masino turned literature into an effective tool of internal critique. By then, the government was concentrating its attentions and resources on the cinema, which promised to be a more propitious medium for the dissemination of fascist models of modernity.

3   Envisioning Modernity

"Today films have replaced novels as the source of new models for youth," the journalist Leo Longanesi observed in 1933. "The situations, gestures, physiognomies and environments they see, like the words they hear, enter into their memories as real, lived experience; they stir up fantasies, stimulate dreams, and can even form characters. Many youth today possess a temperament that might be defined as cinematographic."[1] Since World War I, intellectuals throughout Europe had pondered cinema's capacity to represent the landscapes and rhythms of a rapidly changing world. Under Italian fascism, though, films came in for special attention from those who wished to bring about a lasting shift in collective values. Hailed as a new means of "writing and remembering," the cinema attracted many intellectuals from the journalistic and literary worlds who searched for other means to articulate the tastes and behaviors that might mark national models of modernity. By the end of the decade, Longanesi, like Moravia, Alvaro, and Alba De Céspedes, was writing scripts; Soldati directed movies as well, and Barbaro's multifaceted career in film had caused him to set aside his literary activities altogether.[2] Emanuelli, Pannunzio, and Vittorini worked as film reviewers; other writers and critics became film censors. A point of confluence for creative energies under the dictatorship, the movie industry became a laboratory for the formulation of new professional identities that, in many cases, carried over to the postwar era.[3]

Fascist officials also recognized cinema's extraordinary communicative potential and granted films a central role in their attempts to transform ideologies and lifestyles. After the establishment of a documentary production center (the Istituto LUCE) in the early 1920s, newsreels and instructional movies became frontline weapons in the *bonifica* campaigns that Mussolini's government unleashed on Italians. By the end of the de-

Figure 3. Cinema serving the regime. Projection car shown at the *Mostra del dopolavoro*, 1937. Partito Nazionale Fascista, *Prima mostra del dopolavoro* (Rome, 1938). Reprinted with permission from the Biblioteca Nazionale, Rome.

cade, a small fleet of trucks—modeled on those used by the Soviets—projected newsreels in piazzas and on large, freestanding screens in open fields throughout Italy (fig. 3). Feature films proved no less important to fascist plans for a collective transformation, since they were seen as an ideal way to transmit political messages unobtrusively. As one critic commented, they could impart "a particular vision of life and the world . . . to a multitude of persons who believe they are merely giving themselves an hour of innocent amusement."[4] Yet, as this chapter recounts, films also presented intellectuals and policy makers with a dilemma. Like German filmmakers under Hitler, Italians faced the challenge of making movies that would compete with immensely popular Hollywood productions on the domestic and foreign market. The need to strike a balance between ideological and commercial concerns guided the development of film culture under the dictatorship, influencing aesthetics, policies, and production preferences.

While Mussolini declared that cinema constituted "the regime's most powerful weapon," many Italians realized early on that it could prove to be a double-edged sword. Indeed, fascist films showcased the very sort of cosmopolitan glamour that the regime's populist arm had pledged to defeat, and they projected models of social and sexual behavior that were often at odds with those propagated in the official press. Moreover, as authorities well knew, the cinema offered opportunities for potentially emancipating social interactions. Nowhere more than under a dictatorship could movie theaters become "dream spaces," to use Walter Benjamin's term, public places where private desires might find free expression. "The darkness of the movie theater restores to us a sense of limitless liberty and the comfort of being able to strip off our morality," marveled the critic Giacomo Debenedetti in 1927. "As the faces of those near us descend into the shadows, all conventions can disappear." [5]

The cinema had long been associated with transgressive thoughts and practices, given that it grew out of a culture of mass spectacle that had worried intellectual, social, and political elites since the fin de siècle years. In Italy, as in France, Germany, and America, films were often shown in hippodromes or music halls as part of traveling programs that might include vaudeville acts, freak shows, and acrobats. While the liberal government passed measures in 1907 and 1913 to allow censorship of films on moral and political grounds, less could be done about the drunken rowdies, urinating children, and erotic adventurers, who, critics charged, made film going an unhealthy and corrosive experience. [6] The predominance of women in the audience also made cinemas an emblem of the dangerous social spaces created by mass society. Coded as female by intellectuals who found it both threatening and titillating, the cinema lay at the center of the gendered discourses about mass culture that emerged in the years before World War I. [7]

This mistrust of cinema as a form of spectacle and a site of social intercourse carried over to the fascist period, as did the use of a sexualized rhetoric in discussions of film's nature and its effects on the public. Adapting censorship mechanisms used by the liberal state, regime officials established commissions (composed of representatives of various fascist ministries, a judge, and a mother) to monitor the making of films from the script phase through the finished product. [8] Catholics took their cues from Pope Pius XI, who denounced movies as an occasion for "moral and religious shipwreck" and encouraged the development of a circuit of parish-linked theaters in order to control the conditions under which films were seen. [9] Other commentators claimed that films lacked the moral and aesthetic unity that distinguished all true Art. In *La Fiera letteraria*, Piero Solari decried the cinema as "a bastard, an unnatural child of many mothers and fathers, who have coupled by chance, in hurried unions of convenience: theater and photography, narrative art and melodrama, painting and mime, dance and sculpture, acrobatics and propaganda, finance and the aphrodisiac arts." [10]

For an increasing number of critics, though, such concerns appeared to be shortsighted. Bontempelli declared cinema to be "the most powerful expression of a race" and argued that its freedom from established aesthetic traditions was its greatest asset as an agent for cultural renewal. In similar terms, Corrado Pavolini complained that those who dismissed movies as "vehicles of moral infection" had not grasped their potential to wean domestic audiences from foreign models of taste and behavior. Unless Italy developed a "national cinematographic consciousness" that would permeate future productions, he warned, Germany and America would continue to conquer the country "through the seductive action of the screen." [11]

Like many other projects for national cinemas that circulated before and after World War II, this one proved difficult to realize. The concept of a national cinema has often implied the application of a coherent set of aesthetic and technical codes, the development of a coordinated production sector, and the diffusion of distribution and exhibition strategies that favor domestic films.[12] While a combination of protection and promotion starting in the late 1920s allowed the Italians, like the British and the Germans, to make strides in all of these areas, for several reasons the fascist goal of a "national cinema, immune from all dangerous foreign infiltrations," remained difficult to realize.[13] In Italy, as in other countries, national film aesthetics and policies were formulated with international considerations in mind; namely, the need to respond to a Hollywood studio system that produced consistently polished and engaging films "to be exported by the crate." [14] Although American movies were regularly denounced by Italian intellectuals and policy makers as symbols of mass society's leveling effects, their audience appeal and technical sophistication led even militant fascist filmmakers, along with their Nazi neighbors, to emulate and adapt their conventions, story lines, and star culture.[15]

Yet as purists pointed out, America was only part of the problem. As it evolved after World War I, filmmaking was an incredibly international enterprise. Actors, directors, producers, and technicians traveled among the production centers of Europe—Berlin, Budapest, Paris, Joinville, Rome—and to and from America, following the flows of capital that supported the industry. Migrations occasioned by coproductions, fluctuations in the fortunes of single national industries, political changes, the need to master new equipment, and the practice of making several versions of one film simultaneously created a cosmopolitan industry culture whose habits ran counter to the protectionist impulses of the 1930s. Max Ophüls and Walter Ruttmann were among the directors who made movies in fascist Italy; Sergei Eisenstein was also invited but crossed the Atlantic to make *Qué viva Mexico!* instead. Moreover, while both Nazi Germany and fascist Italy passed legislation requiring the use of all-national casts, crews, studios, and stories, filmmakers often made use of foreign stars and production spaces.[16] Story material also circulated beyond national boundaries. Remakes of foreign films were common in both democracies and dictatorships, as was the use of foreign theatrical and literary works as bases for screenplays.[17] More than literature, the cinema points up the limitations and paradoxes that characterized interwar initiatives aimed at the achievement of aesthetic autarchy.

STYLE AND IDENTITY: CREATING THE NATIONAL FILM

In the late 1920s, Italians who wished to utilize the cinema as a vehicle of national regeneration and international prestige faced frustrating circumstances. Before World War I, Italy had been a leading film power with a flourishing export trade. In Germany, for example, Italian films—which ranged from elaborate costume epics to realist street films—brought in profits close to those earned by American and French movies.[18] But the war spelled the end of this boom period. A consortium established in 1919 with money from banks, producers, distributors, and exhibitors (the *Unione Cinematografica Italiana*, or UCI) failed after only four years. In 1909, Italy had produced approximately five hundred feature films; by 1920, when German and America production was expanding considerably, this number had dropped to a few dozen, and, by 1928, to around twenty. The resulting exodus of Italian actors, technicians, and directors abroad led the playwright Anton Giulio Bragaglia to joke that the Italian cinema was being revived not in Rome but in Berlin.[19] As the Ministry of National Economy established a commission to study the situation, Stefano Pittaluga arrived on the scene. A Turin entrepreneur who enjoyed good relations with both the fascist government and American movie companies, he took over the UCI's holdings in 1926. While Pittaluga also purchased the silent-era powerhouse Cines studio in 1927, the first priority of his new company was not moviemaking but bringing profitable American sound films to the peninsula.[20] Nor was help for feature films forthcoming from the state. Despite entreaties from many in the industry, the fascists continued to concentrate their attention on documentary films, which Mussolini considered to be "the best and most suggestive means of education and persuasion."[21] When the regime passed a law in 1927 requiring theaters to reserve one-tenth of their programming for Italian productions, industry voices grumbled that such protectionist measures only underscored the dearth of national films to be protected.

Among the most trenchant critics of this situation was Alessandro Blasetti, whose day job as a lawyer for the Banca Popolare Triestina did not prevent him from becoming a protagonist in the campaign to revive the Italian film. From the mid-1920s on, he played a central role in the birth of a professional film culture in Italy. One of the country's first film critics (for the daily *L'Impero*), he founded specialized reviews such as *Cinematografo* (1927–31), which discussed film aesthetics, economics, and politics and helped Italians to clarify the roles that feature films—and their makers— might play within the fascist state.[22] In 1926, after viewing some of the first LUCE documentaries, Blasetti realized that "films in which the propaganda is not only not evident, but actually hidden" would be more effective emissaries of fascist ideals.[23] Non-Italian audiences would be especially alienated by political films, which would be "boycotted, rejected by the market, and forbidden by foreign censors." The solution, Blasetti concluded, lay in creating "entertainment films" that would "attract and convince" audiences at home and abroad by burying their prescriptive messages within a compelling dramatic or comedic narrative.[24]

To translate this program into reality, in 1927 the twenty-seven-year-old Blasetti founded a production house, Augustus, whose initial shareholders included members of the Italian nobility (such as the Marquis Roberto Lucifero), the fascist hierarchy (Bottai and Augusto Turati), and the less august intellectual class.[25] Its first and only film, *Sole* (*Sun,* Blasetti 1929), which glorified the fascist reclamation of the Pontine marshes, gained glowing reviews at its premiere on Rome's Via del Corso but failed to find a distributor.[26] One year earlier, the equally short-lived ADIA consortium had presented Mario Camerini's colonial movie *Kif tebbi,* which commemorated Italy's 1912 conquest of Libya. Released just as the government had begun its "pacification" campaign in the colony, it won a ministerial prize for the best film of 1928.[27] Although they were privately financed, these two films anticipated several features of future collaborations between filmmakers and the fascist state. Both treated political subjects of considerable importance to the government—colonialism and the *bonifiche*—and both appeared in conjunction with propaganda campaigns that exalted those subjects in the press. A similar "coordination" of art and politics would mark Italian film for the duration of the dictatorship.

As these and other movies were released, a culture of film appreciation also began to take shape. Cine clubs appeared that showed films whose experimentalism or political content kept them off commercial screens, and columns in the daily and periodical press hosted debates over which styles and subject matter would be most appropriate for the new national film.[28] As in the realm of literature, support emerged early on for realist aesthetics. Here too, realism had many different ideological connotations, and no unified school of realist theory and filmmaking emerged under the dictatorship. For those motivated by economic gain, realism represented the promise of a unique film style that could carve out a niche for the country on the international market. With its emphasis on outdoor shooting and nonprofessional actors, realism would constitute a nationally specific alternative both to diva-driven American movies and to European art films with avant-garde pretensions. Pavolini recommended that Italians look for actors "on the tram, in the public gardens, in offices and in the fields," and the editor and documentarist Mario Serandrei urged Italian directors to renounce "a cosmopolitan world of falsity, rhetoric, jewels, and femmes fatales" and feature "our own land . . . so rich in marvelous and beautiful things."[29] The idea of an aesthetic that would privilege the local and the distinctive also pleased intellectuals who viewed modernity as a standardizing force that threatened Italian traditions. As Alvaro observed, cinema, like the novel, had particular potential as an instrument for the documentation and articulation of "authentic national idioms."[30]

Realist codes of representation also interested politically minded intellectuals who wished to use feature films to communicate fascist values. Providing a "real-life" frame for fictional stories through the use of amateur actors, documentary footage, and location shots of recognizable places would encourage audience identification, endowing the people and places depicted with a collective, national resonance. Finally, the use of a realist aesthetic would also increase the power of feature films to act as agents for the expansion of influence abroad. Movies that included footage of the successes of fascist modernization schemes—new roads, sports stadiums, cities, and disciplined inhabitants—would begin the process of changing foreign opinion about fascism.[31] The support for realism created a climate conducive to stylistic experimentation. Integrating documentarist conventions into feature films, and manipulating the documentary form to incorporate elements from fictional films, fascist-era moviemakers created a hybrid aesthetic whose influences can be seen in the Neorealist films that flourished after World War II.[32]

Just as the debates over the Italian novel occasioned an exchange of views on the essential traits of the national character, so too the discussions of cinematic style and content in these years prompted reflections on the qualities that separated Italian audiences from foreign ones. Few intellectuals lacked firsthand familiarity with American films, since the major American studios had branch offices in Italy and showed their latest releases with little delay. For information on American audiences and their preferences and tastes, though, Italians relied on the reports of writers and journalists who had spent time overseas, since film professionals who had actually worked in Hollywood did not often put their thoughts onto paper.[33]

For these observers, the Americans' greatest gift was their ability to create spectacles that, like candy, pleased and absorbed the consumer despite their lack of substance. "They are silly films," declared Soldati after his two years in New York. "But they are astutely written and edited with a sure musical sense. . . . When you leave the theater, you might think: how stupid. But in the meantime you've stayed for the whole thing." These same commentators, though, observed that a steady diet of such escapist fare would prove indigestible to Italians, who preferred realism, common sense, and sobriety.[34] Soldati and Chiarini highlighted the different psychological impact cinema had on Americans and Italians as a way of dissuading their peers from imitating foreign films. Building on stereotypes of Americans as prone to infantile obsessions, they presented movie-going across the Atlantic as a "collective frenzy, a mass psychosis" that "fascinated, excited, and prepared the way for acts of madness."[35] Italians, in contrast, held "a critical attitude, a diffidence toward the easy incantations of the screen." The rags-to-riches narratives of American films would not appeal to them, Soldati claimed, since they were more skeptical about the possibility of social and economic elevation. "When things don't go well, one can always find one or two hundred people who are just as badly off but [who] instead of getting angry just go on with their lives," he wrote admiringly of the country he had chosen to return to.[36] This attitude of resilience and resignation, which proved perfectly suited to the needs of the dictatorship, permeated the plotlines of many films made under Mussolini, including those Soldati scripted and directed.

Discussions of the Soviet cinema provided another occasion to delineate the boundaries between foreign and fascist film cultures. In the early thirties, the specter of communism haunted Italians who postulated realism as the aesthetic of choice for the national film, since the Soviet industry had distinguished itself with internationally admired films that married technical sophistication to stories of a poetic simplicity. Compared to American productions, Soviet films remained relatively unknown in Italy. Although Russian movies could be seen in the cine clubs and at public expositions like the Milan Trade Fair and the Venice Biennale, the government remained wary of their potential as carriers of communist propaganda. A proposal by the Soviet embassy to mount its own film show in 1933, for example, was vetoed by Mussolini himself.[37]

What the Russian cinema lacked in mass circulation, though, it gained in the enthusiasm it generated in elites as an alternative to Hollywood. Intellectuals in their twenties, such as Raffaello Matarazzo, Serandrei, and the Moscow-born Vinicio Paladini, hoped that Italians would draw on the works of Dziga Vertov and other Russian realists as they forged their own "cinematography of real life." They praised the Soviets' ability to blend entertainment and political education, and admired their depictions of the new collectivist ethos of mass society.[38] Yet many of their peers still resisted communist films as models for the fascist cinema. Corrado Sofia, writing in *Critica fascista*, reminded readers that Soviet films aimed to make their spectators more critical, whereas American films merely drew the public into a "comforting world of illusions." Other intellectuals, using language that echoed current literary debates, maintained that Russian films failed to "transfigure" reality in ways that would satisfy the "spiritual needs" of the Italian people.[39]

The ambivalence with which American and Russian movies were greeted under fascism did not stop some intellectuals in the film world from observing that Italians needed more, not less, exposure to foreign cinema cultures. Like their colleagues in architecture and literature, they advocated a strategy of *aggiornamento* that would give Italians the knowledge needed to create national works with an international appeal. The critic and theoretician Eugenio Giovannetti recommended Soviet films for their superior insights on "beauty and form," American films for their mastery of "influence, genre, and stars," and Weimar German films as examples of overall filmic intelligence.[40] But, as a number of his peers observed, beyond the cine clubs, Italy did not have arenas where foreign films could be viewed in their original form, and amateurish dubbing practices distorted films shown in commercial theaters. "As a way of remaining in contact with the best of world production and possibly learning something from it," the critic Guglielmo Alberti asked, "why not follow the example of other countries and allow us to see some of the best films in their original form?"[41]

Government policies of the early thirties suggest that Alberti's request did not fall on deaf ears. At the same time that the regime subsidized internationally oriented literary publications, it set up special screenings of uncensored, undubbed foreign films for officials, journalists, and members of the Young University Fascist (GUF) groups. Starting in 1932, the Venice

Biennale included a Film Show that showed full-length, original-language versions of documentary and feature works from Italy and a dozen foreign nations.[42] The first edition proved to be a great success, attracting more than ten thousand spectators. Matarazzo wrote of the initiative that "one could imagine Lumière in a corner, crying with joy," and Mario Gromo, the critic for *La Stampa*, announced that the Biennale had done more for the knowledge of the film arts in Italy than "a half dozen treatises on the aesthetics of the screen."[43] But when other film festivals clamored for similar projection privileges, Biennale administrator Antonio Maraini reminded the government of the potential political fallout of such freedoms and recommended that such "very exceptional liberties" be restricted to the Biennale show alone.[44]

Even as the fascists established venues for the consideration for foreign films, they also took steps to promote the production of Italian ones. In 1931, with the national output totaling twelve films for the previous year, Bottai sponsored a law that subsidized domestic films on a competitive basis.[45] As was often the case with fascist patronage schemes, the prizes came at a price. Since they were awarded after an accounting of box-office receipts, rather than before shooting began, they guided filmmakers toward commercial films that would "demonstrate that they have known how to best interpret the tastes of the public."[46] As Bottai envisioned it, the law was an "act of resistance" against the hegemony of foreign entertainment films, as well as a message to Italian militants who continued to call for an overtly political cinema. "The public wants to be amused, and it is precisely on this point that we wish to help the Italian industry today," he explained soon after the law took effect.[47]

The regime's new enthusiasm for the feature film industry received impetus from the reopening of the Cines production complex, which was inaugurated in 1930 and boasted American equipment for sound recording. With a half dozen movies on the market and a host of others in progress, Cines was already a professional home for many actors and technicians who had decided to return to Italy despite the presence of the dictatorship. Under the guide of the writer and critic Emilio Cecchi, who was appointed artistic director when Pittaluga died suddenly in 1931, the studio emerged as a center of creative ferment as well. Cecchi sought the collaboration of the best new talent from other fields to maximize film's tastemaking potential. He encouraged Soldati, Barbaro, and other young authors to write treatments and screenplays and invited cutting-edge artists and architects to work as scenographers.[48] Cecchi also set the tone for Cines's political culture. A self-declared "apolitical" intellectual, Cecchi suited regime functionaries such as Chiarini and Bottai who continued to affirm fascism's commitment to creative liberties. While Cecchi, like Alvaro, had signed Croce's antifascist manifesto in 1925, his reputation and (a)political savvy allowed him to escape the kind of censure that Alvaro had faced. Seven years later, his avowed adherence to Crocean credos of artistic autonomy and his refusal to discuss politics made him a perfect boss for a host of intellectuals who, like their counterparts in Nazi Germany, wished to convince themselves that even a studio partially under state control could constitute an uncontaminated space.[49]

If the Cines studio symbolized fascism's intention to use cinema as a tool of collective transformation and cultural diplomacy, the movies made there attest to the difficulties that beset the project of creating truly "national" films. In the next section, I examine two Cines works, *Terra madre* (*Mother Earth*, Blasetti, 1931) and *Gli uomini, che mascalzoni!* (*Men, What Rascals They Are!* Mario Camerini, 1932), and a film by the SAFIR studio, *Treno popolare* (*Popular Train*, Matarazzo, 1933). The three movies convey the range of attitudes filmmakers and screenwriters of different generations and temperaments brought to bear on their explorations of modernity's impact on Italian social roles and national traditions. They showcase behaviors and attitudes that, according to their creators, were to characterize a distinctively Italian and fascist modernity. While only Camerini's film proved a hit at the box office, all of the above works display the tensions between commercial concerns and political ideology that characterized Italian cinema under the dictatorship. As we will see, in their quest to entertain as well as persuade, Italian filmmakers often showcased the very behaviors and values that the regime sought strenuously to contain and correct.

BLASETTI, CAMERINI, MATARAZZO: THREE VISIONS OF A DIFFERENT MODERNITY

At the center of many discourses of fascist modernity, I have suggested, lay the will to bring about a shift in national habits and tastes in both the public and private spheres. At the heart of these strategies of national transformation lay the idea of *bonifica*, or reclamation, which aimed to "conquer souls as well as the soil," changing Italians' behaviors, prejudices, and predilections.[50] The theme of reclamation pervades many films made under fascism and has a prominent place in early works by Blasetti. *Sole*, which was filmed partly on location in the Pontine marshes, presented the *bonifica* enterprise as a metaphor for the fascist plan to purify and rejuvenate Italy. Blasetti's next work, the Expressionist-influenced *Resurrectio* (*Res-*

urrection, 1931), concerned the redemption of an Italian composer from a degrading relationship with a Slavic femme fatale. The motifs of *Sole* and *Resurrectio* come together in *Terra madre,* which is structured around parallel narratives of redemption. Marco, a young nobleman, frees himself from an irresponsible urban existence and a controlling woman by returning to the country to rule over his family's estate. In doing so, he saves the land from speculators, restores its fecundity, and regains his sense of masculinity.[51]

By conflating sexual and social power dynamics in *Terra madre,* Blasetti sends viewers a message about the public consequences of private behaviors. He presents Marco's hesitation to become a padrone as stemming from his enslavement to his fiancée, Daisy, a debauched urbanite who derides country life as boring and primitive.[52] Only when Marco arrives at the estate does he begin to acquire stature and confidence. With typical fascist logic, Blasetti suggests that freedom will come when Marco accepts the dominance required of him by his gender and social station. Marco's "liberation" process is accelerated when he meets Emilia, a young peasant woman who comes into view as she helps a child to pray that the new boss will stay on the land. Associated with spirituality and maternity, Emilia is the perfect New Woman of fascist Italy. Soon after this encounter, in a scene reminiscent of American Westerns, Marco wrestles a bull to the ground, offering proof of his reawakening vitality.

To convince Marco to stay on as their padrone, the peasants organize a folk celebration, or *festa.* In this segment, which showcases folk songs and dances, *Terra madre* becomes an advertisement for the regime's "revival" of popular traditions, which glorified rural lifestyles at a time of low grain output and exodus from the countryside.[53] In effect, the movie accorded well with the fascist aim of encouraging the development of an alternative mass culture based on nationally specific aesthetic forms and styles (figs. 4, 5, and 6). Blasetti meant to underscore the differences between these "healthy" models of popular leisure and the decadence of urban nightlife by juxtaposing the *festa* with a party for Marco, which takes place inside the mansion at the same time. Yet his cinematography highlights the allure of the urbane indoor party. Continuity editing and long shots allow the audience full immersion in and enjoyment of the glamorous ambiance, which features swing music, flowing champagne, and women wandering about in beautiful gowns.[54] The end of the film, though, makes clear Marco's status as an emblem of the fascist style of modernity. Although he decides to move to the country, he makes the property a showpiece for new agricultural technology and techniques. A long, documentary sequence of tractors

Figure 4. Mass culture in the fascist manner. Traditional dress
and a *fascio* made of grapes at the Grape Festival, Tuscany, 1931.
Opera Nazionale Dopolavoro, *Cinque anni di organizzazione*
(Rome: Opera Nazionale Dopolavoro, 1931). Reprinted with permission from the Biblioteca Nazionale, Rome.

tilling the soil drives homes the point that modernity, when purged of its
associations with decadence and emancipation, can be a positive force for
national regeneration.[55]

While Blasetti always denied that foreign film cultures had any influence on his work, *Terra madre*'s editing and composition show a debt to Soviet and American cinema.[56] The director recodes these foreign-influenced
images as "Italian," though, by combining them with folk music and Catholic symbolism. These maneuvers were not lost on reviewers of the film,
who praised Blasetti's use of the latest foreign conventions in the service of
a "truly national" film.[57] Government officials liked the film enough to

Figure 5. Alessandro Blasetti in 1930. Courtesy of
Mara Blasetti, Rome.

Figure 6. The face of bourgeois decadence in Blasetti's *Terra madre*, 1931. Courtesy of
Mara Blasetti, Rome.

show it to the U.S. Bureau of Commercial Economics in Washington, D.C., as part of an information session on fascist reclamation policies. There, it also performed as a testament to Mussolini's success in reclaiming the "bohemian" world of spectacle, which had placed its creative energies at the service of fascism.[58]

Set in Milan, Camerini's *Gli uomini, che mascalzoni!* advocates no such "return to the soil" but makes an equally strong case against unchecked modernization. Like Emanuelli's novel *Radiografia di una notte,* which appeared the same year, it warns against mass society's pernicious effects on individual identities and family structures. Yet Camerini's critique is couched in screen images of bustling streets, streamlined art deco stores, vibrant trade fairs, and emancipated female shop workers that give Italy's burgeoning consumer society a glamorous sheen. Although the qualities that made the film a box-office success probably undercut its utility as a vehicle of fascist resocialization, it is not surprising that when the film premiered at the 1932 Biennale the press embraced it as a "profoundly" Italian film both for its subject and its style.[59]

The movie's aesthetic did reflect Camerini's formation at the crossroads of European and America film cultures. During the lean 1920s, the director had worked for the Paramount studios in Paris and Joinville, and his early movie *Rotaie (Rails,* 1929), showed the influence of Weimar German street films.[60] The sleek look of Camerini's films, and his predilection for romantic comedy, led him to be labeled by critics after World War II as a merchant of escapist fantasies. Yet Camerini's fascist-era production covers many of the themes and causes of the regime—such as colonialism (*Kif tebbi* and *Il grande appello,* 1936), labor (*Rotaie*), and the regime's natalist campaign (*T'amerò sempre,* 1933 and 1943)—and is bound by a social conservatism that preaches family values and the necessity of accepting one's assigned social station. In its focus on the human costs of mass consumer society, *Gli uomini, che mascalzoni!* also reflects the views of Soldati, who cowrote the story and the script with Camerini soon after his return to America.[61] Indeed, if the film's visuals celebrate the machines that power Italian modernity, its plot makes clear the price those machines exact from those who labor to keep them running.

The movie is nominally a romantic comedy about two young working-class protagonists (played by Lia Franca and Vittorio De Sica) who are united in their aspirations to social and economic elevation. Since Bruno works as a car mechanic and chauffeur, and Mariuccia is a salesgirl in an expensive perfumery, both are continually exposed to luxury products they could never afford themselves. As in many of Camerini's films, frustrations find an outlet in role playing, which creates temporary transgressions of normally rigid class boundaries. In this case, Bruno pretends to own a luxury convertible that he is repairing. He convinces Mariuccia to go on an outing to Lake Como, where the two fall in love. After many comic misunderstandings, he proposes in the back of a taxi which, coincidentally, is driven by Mariuccia's father. The film ends with Bruno moving from the back to the front of the cab so that his future father-in-law can transport a wealthy couple to their destination. Taking the message of *Terra madre* into the urban realm, *Gli uomini, che mascalzoni!* intimates that happiness comes from accepting one's inherited social station. By giving up false illusions of autonomy, both automotive and social, Bruno gains a family and a chance at finding inner peace.

While *Gli uomini, che mascalzoni!* made De Sica a star, its real protagonist is modernity. Mass society has created the film's locations and the psyches of its characters, who live an exciting but unstable existence. Bruno's temporary jobs—mechanic, chauffeur—and Mariuccia's father's position as driver of an all-night taxi are made possible by Milan's expanding consumerism and nontraditional leisure habits. Camerini's film captures a Milan whose networks of commerce, mass transit, and mass information bring people together and, just as easily, drive them apart. The director brilliantly underscores the provisional quality of modern relationships when Bruno attempts to follow Mariuccia after their initial encounter at a news kiosk. Filming from the windows of her tram, Camerini depicts Bruno pedaling furiously on his bike to keep up with her, as advertisements for Coca-Cola and other consumer products flash by. Throughout the movie, the two protagonists repeatedly lose each other in the flux of urban existence, and when they are together the city's voice (tram bells, taxi horns, and crowds) frequently drowns out their own.

The filmmakers' ambivalence in the face of consumer culture comes through most clearly in the scenes that take place inside the Milan Trade Fair. A minicity for the promotion of new European products, the fair attracted foreign and Italian vendors and visitors and played an important role in fascism's politics of image improvement.[62] In Camerini's hands, it serves to showcase both the perils and the pleasures that accompany modern urban existence. Blaring radio announcements and advertisements accompany people of different classes, genders, and nationalities as they try on new roles as consumer-citizens of an international marketplace. The chaotic environment of the "sample" fair *(fiera campioniera)* emphasizes the randomness and venality of modern social interactions. Bruno's job demonstrating machinery requires him to wear a primitive megaphone strapped to his head, which renders him almost unrecognizable. At the close of the film, his fate is decidedly mixed: he gains happiness and authenticity in his personal life, but loses his identity in the public sphere.[63] *Gli uomini, che mascalzoni!* does not reject modern existence, but, like much contemporary fascist propaganda, argues that it can be managed and humanized through investment in domestic and family identities.

If *Terra madre* projected a fantasy of orderly power relations in the reclaimed Italian countryside, and *Gli uomini, che mascalzoni!* suggested ways of negotiating the temptations and pitfalls of modern urban life, *Treno popolare* showcased the new forms of social interaction that might accompany the mass leisure activities of the fascist state. One of the most vocal advocates of the new Italian cinema, Matarazzo viewed films as agents of indoctrination at home and as ambassadors of the fascist revolution abroad. To advertise the uniqueness of the fascist model of modernity, he focused on the OND's program of popular trains that offered salaried employees cheap day fares to the countryside. By 1933, millions of men and women were participating in these outings, which aimed to nationalize Italians by exposing them to their "collective" cultural and historic patrimony.[64] Shot entirely on location in Orvieto and in the carriages of popular trains, *Treno popolare* furthers the message conveyed in *Terra madre* and a host of other fascist texts: pruned of all decadent offshoots, modernity can become a productive force, helping Italians to reclaim their past as they refashion themselves for the future.

Although *Treno popolare* was lauded by one critic as "the film of our new collective life," it also highlights the potential for social disorder that came with that life.[65] While the OND's outings were designed to give Italians a break from the strictures of lower-class urban life, regulations that prohibited "improvised activities" and individualized itineraries communicated the limits of the government's escapist invitations.[66] Matarazzo's film indulges official fantasies about the regimented nature of fascist mass leisure and reminds future OND travelers that increased mobility brings new disciplinary demands as well. Yet the director also looks with humor upon Italians' attempts to use these trips as occasions for infidelities and other evasions of daily life, leaving the door open for male and female spectators to conclude that participation in the public activities of the regime could facilitate the realization of private fantasies.

Matarazzo was just twenty-three years old when he made *Treno popolare*, and his film reflects his generation's claim that they alone would carry out fascism's moral, social, and aesthetic revolutions. The cast and crew— which included the young composer Nino Rota—were all in their twenties, and the script, which Matarazzo cowrote, reflects his cohort's disdain for those who, whatever their chronological age, continued to embrace liberal-era values and tastes. An attitudinal contrast divides the protagonists as soon as they board the train. Carlo's sporty dress, athletic physique, and confident manner mark him as a symbol of fascism's new modern man. Giovanni's anachronistic attire (straw hat and bow tie) and inept manner reference contemporary American comedy idols such as Harold Lloyd and Stan Laurel but also deride the "little Italy" of the liberal period. Indeed, Giovanni's attractive coworker Lina jokes about Giovanni's masculinity and abandons him for Carlo during the trip.

The group's visit to Orvieto's famous medieval cathedral offers the young filmmakers an opportunity to argue that, for Italians, becoming modern meant repositioning themselves with respect to their formidable cultural patrimony. The director fulfills his self-imposed educational mandate by integrating LUCE footage that shows the cathedral's facade. Yet his young protagonists wear the burden of their national history lightly. Carlo is not ashamed that he cannot tell Lina when the cathedral was built; his strength, he tells her, is "living things. . . . I can show you the environs [of Orvieto,] which are magnificent." While Carlo respects the accomplishments of national history, he remains firmly grounded in the present. He avoids the violent repudiations of the past that characterized the Futurist avant-garde, as well as the fetishistic attitudes of conservatives, represented here by Giovanni, who drones out details about Orvieto's monuments gleaned from his touring guide. Matarazzo's film suggests a model for Italians' relationship to their past that found an echo in the contemporary youth press. As a writer for *I Lupi* asserted, the modern Italian did not fall prostrate in front of national tradition, but "leaves the great things of the past in their niches and tips his hat to them when he walks by." [67]

United by their contemporary tastes and their mutual attraction, Lina and Carlo lose Giovanni and depart on an outing that tests their worthiness as modern subjects who know how to discipline their libidinal energies. Until this point, Lina has been presented as an confident New Woman whose platinum hair and assertive demeanor signal her disruptive potential. Thus, when Carlo takes her out in a rowboat and she asserts her autonomy by attempting to guide the boat herself, the script calls for her to fall in the water so that she can be rescued by Carlo. The two, in their underwear, then take shelter until their clothes dry and Carlo has a chance to demonstrate his self-control. The chastened Lina, too, fulfills her didactic function by exchanging Giovanni for Carlo, the new man who is capable of both conquest and continence. The film's gender politics echo those of most of

the fascist youth press, showing the limitations sex bias placed on generational camaraderie. Still, female spectators might have taken away a more
emancipatory message, seeing Lina as a woman who makes the most of opportunities for personal pleasure, even on a work-related outing sponsored
by the fascist regime.

Ultimately, *Treno popolare* testifies to the difficulties fascist filmmakers
of all ages faced in making films that were profitable as well as politically
minded. Although Matarazzo had begun his career as a documentarist for
Cines, he shared Blasetti's belief that entertainment films formed the best
means of calling attention to the values and achievements of the dictatorship.[68] The result is a rather awkward blend of romantic comedy and didactic documentary. The contrast between the glamorous actors and the peasant extras merely emphasizes the constructed nature of the fiction film,
creating tears in its diegetic fabric. Most reviewers, however, greeted *Treno
popolare* as a step toward the development of a uniquely "national" cinema
in Italy. The director's integration of documentary footage and romantic
comedy conventions distinguished his film from most American productions and from Soviet realist works.[69] Other reviewers, impressed by the
film's "freshness and simplicity," labeled the film a "small jewel" that held
hope for a still-fossilized industry. Since the late 1920s, Matarazzo had
claimed that the younger generation was best equipped to carry out a revival of the national film industry. In their articles on *Treno popolare*, critics conceded that, if this film were any indication, Matarazzo might just be
right.[70]

THE DEVELOPMENT OF FASCIST FILM POLICY, 1933–35

By 1933, the revival of the national film industry seemed to be well under
way. Although imports still far outnumbered domestic production, twenty-
seven Italian films appeared that year (about half of them from Cines),
as did ten new production houses. Exhibition networks also continued to
develop, and most movie theaters in big and medium-sized urban areas
boasted sound equipment.[71] Judging from the opinions expressed outside
the mainstream press, though, the situation remained catastrophic. Longanesi observed in *L'Italiano* that the national film, as it had developed so
far, stood out only for its silliness and monotony. "We have learned nothing from America, Russia, and Germany," he charged. "Next to them, we
resemble those black kings who think they're dressing in the European
style just because they wear top hats and pajamas."[72] Independent youth
reviews echoed this feeling of collective failure. In *Saggiatore*, Pannunzio

blamed uneducated critics and commercial pressures for the prevailing climate of "idiocy and bad taste," while *Orpheus* placed the burden on directors who made "false" films that imitated foreign works. The young journalist Giulio Santangelo charged that the "new" national cinema was merely recycling old people and ideas. "As in literature, architecture, and sculpture," he concluded, "we need a revolution."[73]

Fascist officials like Luigi Freddi listened attentively to these complaints in the cultural press, since, in fact, Italian audiences continued to prefer foreign films to domestic ones. Freddi held a similarly low opinion of the national industry, and the former PNF propaganda chief was determined to improve the situation. A two-month fact-finding mission to Hollywood in 1932 had made him an admirer of the American studio system, and a May 1933 visit from Goebbels, who spoke about the new Nazi state film office (the Reichsfilmkammer) had left him convinced of the merits of government intervention.[74] The first fruit of these encounters was an October 1933 law that rewarded quality as well as commercial success. A fund directed by the Ministry of Corporations offered subsidies to Italian movies that "show particular artistic dignity and technical expertise." The films made would also benefit from added screen time, since the law also required Italian movie theaters to show one domestic film for every three foreign ones.[75]

While industry observers applauded these measures, for Freddi they merely formed part of a larger plan. Taking advantage of the momentum created by the decision to establish the Undersecretariat of Press and Propaganda, in February 1934 he drafted the first of a series of reports to persuade Mussolini to establish a separate film bureau as well. Echoing the dire judgments in the youth press, Freddi declared the industry a disaster zone. Instead of defining "an original, Italian 'type' of cinematography," Italian filmmakers had persisted in "imitating—badly—what others have already done well," which had led to their movies being scorned at home and ostracized abroad.[76] In this report and a second one he sent to Ciano some months later, Freddi introduced the idea of a centralized state office, or Direzione Generale di Cinematografia, that would oversee film planning, patronage, and censorship.[77]

In September 1934, under Freddi's lead, the Direzione Generale began operation with a small staff that included Chiarini and young intellectuals like Santangelo and Attilio Riccio of *Saggiatore*.[78] Inspired by Goebbels's Reich Film Chamber, it would serve as the model for the Direccíon General de Teatro y Cine in Franco's Spain. Indeed, Freddi's inaugural speech emphasized the authoritarian nature of the new entity. It would not only offer financial assistance to finished films, as in the past, but would intervene in the moviemaking process from the treatment phase through postproduction, giving officials a say in a film's subject matter and dialogue and in the selection of actors and technical personnel. Film patronage and policing were now the domain of a single office, and policies of preventive censorship made the cooperation of film professionals with the regime a foregone conclusion. As in the realm of literature, the small size of the Italian creative community meant that "revision" meetings often took the form of amiable, if forced, conversations between officials who were anxious to keep up the appearances of artistic freedom and intellectuals who became adept at censoring their own work.[79] Although post-1945 auteur theories have led film historians to focus attention on directors, screenwriters were also accorded considerable creative and political responsibility under fascism. They bore the burden of getting potentially profitable projects approved, since advance production funds depended on officials' judgments of a script's "moral and professional qualities."[80] Political and commercial concerns thus combined to create a feature film culture that tended to neutralize avant-garde and experimental tendencies. By the late 1930s, some younger Italians, Roberto Rossellini among them, looked instead to documentary filmmaking as a means of developing an individual voice.[81]

In the early thirties, this younger generation became the target of a host of government policies designed to train the "future technical and managerial elements of the national [film] industry."[82] From 1933 on, the GUF organizations included cinema sections that gave youth experience in screenwriting and 16 mm film production. The semiprivate National Film School had also opened its doors one year earlier, under Blasetti's direction. Modeled loosely on foreign institutions such as the Soviet School for the Art of the Screen, the school's instructors included Barbaro, Camerini, Blasetti, and the architect Virgilio Marchi, who had worked with Le Corbusier.[83] In 1935, though, Freddi shut the school down and transferred its equipment and instructors to the new government-controlled Centro Sperimentale di Cinematografia (CSC), which, after 1935, offered classes to Clara Calamai, Dino De Laurentiis, Michelangelo Antonioni, and other protagonists of the post-1945 film industry.

Although the CSC has attained semimythical status in Italian film history for its role in training those who would achieve fame in the postwar period, it also holds interest as an institution whose policies sum up the contradictory impulses that characterized Italian fascist film culture. First, while it was created "to make film production one hundred percent Italian," as its new director Chiarini declared in his inaugural speech, the CSC soon became a prominent site of international cultural interchange.[84] Rudolph Arnheim taught aesthetics there after he emigrated from Nazi Germany, and foreign directors making movies at the nearby Cinecittà studios (which opened in 1937, after Cines burned down) often gave talks. Barbaro and other teachers routinely showed original-language foreign films to students, and the Center's publications, which were utilized in the classroom, featured the writings of Raymond Spottiswoode, Paul Rotha, and other prominent foreign intellectuals.[85]

Second, while the Center certainly fulfilled Freddi's wishes for a school that would produce commercially viable films on the American model, it also propagated more militant approaches to filmmaking that would survive into the postwar years. Chiarini may have professed discomfort with overtly political movies, but the medium's potential for mass persuasion prevented him from maintaining, as he had in earlier literary debates, that the fascist government did not wish to create political art. In his inaugural speech, Chiarini specified that the creation of an "Italian" cinema meant the production of works that "express our fascist world, our sensibility. I have said 'our fascist world' for a reason: the State has the right and duty to ask that a powerful instrument like the cinema respond to its political needs." Although he added that the word *political* was to be understood in a "universal" sense, he had sent a message about the new school and the kind of cinema he wished to come out of it.[86]

Third, although the CSC aimed to socialize younger Italians and instill in them a "political conscience," the climate of relative cultural openness that reigned there encouraged a degree of individual initiative and critical thinking. Young women, in particular, gained a sense of personal fulfillment at the Center that countered the antifeminist messages they received from their surrounding society. To protect gender hierarchies in the film profession, women could, in theory, enroll only in courses on acting, makeup, and costume and set design. Yet a number of women took courses in directing and production and went on to have successful careers. Luisa Alessandrini, who completed the production course in 1936, served as assistant director on several films in subsequent years, while Marisa Romano, who took directing with Blasetti in 1935, became an accomplished documentarist before she died five years later at the age of thirty-six.[87]

The CSC's "liberatory" role should not be overstated, however. The school aimed to normalize and politicize young people who might have considered the cinema an entrée to a glamorous or bohemian lifestyle. Students were required to wear uniforms, could not move about the premises unaccompanied, and followed a schedule of military precision that kept them occupied from nine in the morning until eight at night.[88] Soon after the inauguration of the Center, both Chiarini and Freddi delivered speeches that emphasized cinema's contribution to the regime's goals of social engineering. Freddi placed the CSC within the context of fascism's "organic reordering" of Italian society, and Chiarini reminded younger Italians that their films were to contribute to the "great work of human reclamation" *(bonifica umana)* that the regime had undertaken. Speaking in August 1935, as Italian troops mobilized for the Ethiopian invasion, Chiarini appealed to "those youth who have felt the new climate of this warlike Italy" to "enter the ranks" of Italian film.[89] Chiarini's remarks preview the martial concerns that would permeate Italian society in the coming years, placing new demands on filmmakers to serve the state.

From the early thirties on, the cinema had attracted many young Italians as an art form whose canons and traditions were still in flux. A primary signifier of modernity, the cinema seemed to offer an escape from the burden of Italy's cultural patrimony and a chance to develop a language that could capture the spirit of a new collectivist age. Yet the regime valued films too much as potential vehicles of propaganda and profit to permit them to convey critical or autonomist tendencies, as Soldati, Matarazzo, and others in their twenties discovered as they built careers under the dictatorship. To explore the alternative models of fascist modernity that this generation proposed in these years, we must turn to the independent cultural press. The following chapter brings into focus the generational conflicts over the meaning of fascism and Italian modernity that structured debates over the new national novel and film. I examine the endeavors of young intellectuals who were being groomed to serve as the regime's next cultural elite. To the dismay of their official patrons, their writings on subjects such as corporativism and feminism exposed the disjunctures between fascism's emancipatory rhetoric and its disciplinary imperatives. As we will see, once Italy began to mobilize for the Ethiopian war, the government quickly moved to silence them, ending a phase of cultural policy that had won the support of intellectuals of all ages for Mussolini's dictatorship.

4 Class Dismissed
Fascism's Politics of Youth

Like many dictators, Mussolini showed little interest in grooming a successor. Ego, pride, and the need to project an aura of uniqueness and infallibility prevented him from ever anointing a political heir, and the timorous and sycophantic officials who surrounded him for twenty years were not about to press the issue. Yet the Duce and his functionaries had been preoccupied with problems of succession and continuity from the inception of the regime, since they viewed fascism less as a traditional political party than as a "way of life" that would give rise to a new civilization. Accordingly, even as the question of a future leader remained suspended, the government spared no resources to create a new leadership class (*classe dirigente*) and millions of "new men" and "new women" who would perpetuate fascist behaviors and values. From the early 1920s on, alongside the Soviets in Russia, the Italian fascists pioneered techniques of mass socialization and political identity formation that would subsequently mark the youth policies of other European dictatorships.[1]

The cult of youth that proved so central to fascist ideology had its origins in the broader trend toward generational thinking that began in the fin de siècle period. The increased mobility that came with modernization weakened family and communal ties, and age-group identification joined the list of collective allegiances that would structure political and social life in the mass societies of the future.[2] In Italy, a rhetoric of rejuvenation had characterized Italian Nationalist schemes of political and demographic renewal, as well as the cultural programs of the Futurists and the Florentine avant-garde.[3] There, as elsewhere in Europe, World War I consolidated the spread of a generational consciousness. A sense of camaraderie and shared trauma united veterans and separated them from their children, who developed group identities around the issue of nonparticipation. The social and cultural changes that followed the war caused further generational division. The influence of American mass culture led many Italian young people, like their counterparts in France and Weimar Germany, to adopt styles and attitudes that bore little resemblance to those of their parents. By the late 1920s, the breach between age-groups had become a popular theme in the press and in novels and films across the continent. "Tradition no longer has any value, and the thoughts of my elders can no longer determine my path," wrote one French university student in 1930, expressing feelings that spanned national boundaries. "By my own choices, I will decide my life."[4]

Generational thinking was an important defining element of Italian fascist ideology, and the separatist sentiments held by many young Italian intellectuals stemmed in part from the regime's own propaganda and policies. Even before the March on Rome, Mussolini had shrewdly cast youth as protagonists of the fascist political drama: by 1921, secondary school and university students made up 13 percent of fascist supporters. Participants in squadrist actions included many former members of the Italian *arditi*, or World War I shock troops, who were in their twenties at the close of the conflict.[5] Once in power, the fascists took steps to strengthen their image as a youthful and forward-looking political force. Official publications such as *Critica fascista* repeatedly declared fascism's intent to "replace an entire class of men . . . with a new class, a new ruling elite," and the new government cabinet announced in 1929 included the thirty-four-year-old Bottai (minister of corporations) and his contemporaries Dino Grandi (minister of foreign affairs) and Italo Balbo (minister of aviation).[6] During the depression years, when the fascists advertised themselves as the antidote to European decline, fascism's "youthfulness" became a central component of the propaganda directed at foreign nations. Youth not only served as an unparalleled emblem of fascism's regeneration of the Italian nation but provided the blackshirts with a mobilizing myth that differentiated them from the communists, who emphasized class struggle, and, before 1938, from the racially obsessed National Socialists. Inside Italy, the dictatorship's youth policies, like its other measures, functioned to reinforce class boundaries and further restrict opportunities for social mobility. From the early thirties on, postsecondary school males were channeled into distinct groups—the *fasci giovanili di combattimento*, for lower-class Italians, and the GUFs—that separated the rank and file from the future managerial class.

Young intellectuals occupied a special place in the formation of this new elite. Those born roughly between 1905 and 1915 enjoyed privileges (patrons, professional training programs, relaxed censorship) meant to create a group of specialists who would manage fascism's new civilization in the future. As the regime well knew, they were also the group who, along with urban workers, had demonstrated the most open disaffection. In 1931, as the depression hit Italy with full force and unemployment mounted, police informers' reports from Turin, Rome, and other cities related that "antagonism, diffidence, and demoralization" reigned among university students, who viewed the dictatorship's youth-promoting rhetoric with skeptical eyes. "This Regime, which claims it wants to valorize youth, is actually trying to clip their wings and protect the old guard," reported one Neapolitan spy in summing up their feelings. Faced with these findings, the youth group official Carlo Scorza confided to Mussolini that "young intellectuals feel spiritually uncertain because they are confronted with two great events, war and revolution, which they did not take part in and to which they made no contribution. [They] are searching for something they feel instinctively, but are not yet able to define."[7]

The regime responded to this situation with a new set of policies and propaganda themes meant to convince young intellectuals that the regime was going to "make way for youth" (*far largo ai giovani*). These measures favored Italians under thirty in competitions for civil service posts, spawned new postgraduate professional schools such as the Fascist School of Journalism, and established patronage programs for young intellectuals within the Italian Academy and other institutions. Bottai was the architect of many of these policies that complemented his promotion of young writers and filmmakers such as Moravia and Matarazzo. In a 1933 article that sparked much commentary in the youth press, he reassured his followers that the regime intended to "give youth their own voice within fascism, from the party to the syndicates, from the center to the periphery, a voice that is listened to, that will count in the elaboration of doctrine, in the formation and transformation of institutions, and in the renewal of myths."[8]

As young women soon found out, the fascists considered such self-expression primarily a male prerogative. Far from opening up new opportunities for women of this generation, the new policy became one more vehicle for the reinforcement of gender hierarchies. Transmitting authority and privilege as well as political ideology, "making way for youth" served as a conduit into a system of patronage relationships and power networks from which women were largely excluded. Although a few young female intellectuals—such as the writers Anna Maria Ortese and Margherita Guidacci—received encouragement prizes from the Italian Academy, juries and prize committees routinely discriminated against women. GUF programs such as the Littoriali competitions, which provided male university students national exposure for their debating skills and creative work, came into being for women only at the end of the regime. As we saw in the case of the cinema, some young women did flourish within the GUFs and other male structures. Others formed their own networks through organizations such as the *Alleanza muliebre culturale italiana*, which championed women's rights within the "intellectual professions." But the sex biases of fascist youth policies and patronage structures, coupled with the prejudice young women often faced from their male peers, meant that gender identity often overrode Italian women's sense of generational affiliation and conditioned their experiences as revolutionaries who, like men, saw fascism as a vehicle for the transformation of Italy and the world.[9]

Although the policy of "making way for youth" favored men over women in matters of public recognition and professional advancement, it formed part of a totalitarian program of political socialization that was essentially nondiscriminatory in its aim of co-optation and control. Discussing his agency's new "encouragement prizes" in 1930 with his fellow Italian Academy officials, Alfredo Panzini reasoned that subsidizing youth who reveal "singular attitudes in any field of human activity" would ensure that "when they start to act in their lives, the State can benefit from it."[10] In fact, as the regime expanded its programs of mass mobilization throughout the thirties, fascist youth policies were harnessed to state social engineering schemes, producing initiatives like children's holiday camps (*colonie*) that offered mountain and sea cures while inculcating obedience to authority. As Bottai maintained in a 1932 article, fascism's youth policies would provide a critical test of its innovative "therapeutic approach" (*politica terapeutica*) to governance, since the formation of new generations of fascists depended on the reform of character and spirit as well as custom and behavior. Mirroring the regime's "coordination" of national energies and interests under the aegis of a central managerial power, the state would actively intervene to "cure" youth of both sexes of any deviant impulses, channeling young energies "into a circulatory system that will conquer and dissolve any objects that would hinder its vital flow."[11]

Ultimately, the Italian dictatorship's youth politics and policies ended up exposing the disjuncture between the regime's revolutionary rhetoric and its normalizing imperatives. They mirrored larger contradictions within fascist ideology that were exacerbated by political directives that worked at cross-purposes. A labyrinth of depression-era laws and measures aimed to simultaneously quell popular discontent, neutralize the PNF as a vehicle of domestic revolution, present fascism abroad as a revolutionary rival of communism, and mobilize Italians in the regime's new collective organizations. Even as Mussolini launched a purge of the PNF that expelled many former squadrists for excessive political ardor, he put the language of his socialist past to work in incendiary speeches that promised to bring Italians sweeping social change and economic parity.[12] By 1932, the year the Exhibition of the Fascist Revolution was inaugurated in Rome with great fanfare, intellectuals of the war generation such as Bontempelli and Camillo Pellizzi were warning that the gap between rhetoric and reality would eventually alienate the brightest members of the new generation. The government was playing a dangerous game by preaching change and demanding continuity, these men intoned, since "one cannot serve the cause of revolution and reaction at the same time."[13]

The consequences of these contradictory policies can be most clearly tracked in the writings and experiences of those who had been targeted as fascism's future political and cultural elite. As we have seen in previous chapters, the debates over the realist novel and the lineaments of the national film revealed a generational gap that stemmed from divergent visions of the meaning of Italian modernity. To Alvaro and others of the war generation who asserted that fascist culture would be founded on a harmonious melding of tradition and modernity, Italians in their twenties replied that the advent of modernity made most traditions irrelevant.[14] Against a backdrop of official exhortations to "keep alive the national personality" as future cultural managers and producers, they announced their intention to elaborate a new culture that dispensed with "all the ideologies that were the patrimony of the old generations."[15] As a united front began to coalesce among youth who wished to modernize Italian culture, the young art critic Mario Tinti warned that his peers harbored an "antiofficial mentality that would be a true and proper oppositionism if transferred to the political sphere."[16]

Here I take a broader view of the issues that structured the debates over literature and film in the early thirties, exploring the social and political causes that underwrote younger Italians' campaigns for cultural and ethical change. The corporativist state, a social revolution, a new moral order— these interlinking causes engaged philosophers, architects, filmmakers, and writers in their twenties who saw them as the cornerstones of the edifice of fascist modernity. For them, the development of new aesthetics and modes of cultural practice that addressed the problems of mass society formed but one part of a thorough reconsideration of the relations among the cultural, social, economic, and political realms. An article by Mario Zagari published in the youth journal *Camminare* conveys a sense of the urgency many in their twenties felt to actuate a new postliberal, postleftist civilization. Zagari observed, "Young people are affirming the need to take an inventory of their world, to understand every aspect of it and resolve its problems at a chaotic time when everything seems to be in gestation, there are no stable and definite values, the future is uncertain, and material limitations are the order of the day."[17]

The attempts of young men and women to fulfill this mandate under the dictatorship compose a chapter of Italian history that, until fairly recently, was often seen through the lens of post–World War II political positions. Its reigning interpretative paradigms were developed soon after the fall of fascism by memoirists and historians, many of whom belonged to this cohort. They set a course for the public memory of the dictatorship's extensive youth culture that glossed over the extent and duration of their generation's support for the regime. One influential scheme depicted young intellectuals' critiques of fascist institutions as a *fronde* that led ineluctably to dissidence and on to the Resistance. Another interpretation tended to abdicate agency completely: it portrayed younger Italians as "seduced and abandoned" by older generations who had socialized them to believe in ideologies and practices that had then been hastily repudiated.[18] Both of these models minimize the complexity of relations between young intellectuals and the regime, and obscure a set of power dynamics that characterized other twentieth-century dictatorships as well.

Foremost among these dynamics was leader worship, which translated into a tendency to blame the limits of the fascist "revolution" on inept bureaucrats, conservative interest groups, saboteurs—anyone but Mussolini.[19] The elaborate patronage system set up for young intellectuals also structured power relations under fascism and contributed to the genesis and development of its youth culture. *L'Universale* and journals like it that voiced "frondist" visions of fascist modernity did not enter the public sphere through a backdoor: each issue was approved by the censors for publication, and each review had official patrons (most often Bottai or Ciano) who arranged subsidies, gave editorial suggestions, and smoothed out any political difficulties that might arise. The dictatorship's policies toward young intellectuals lend truth to Michel Foucault's observation that power often works not by repressing dissent but by organizing and channeling it, creating an opposition that in some way serves the interests of the hegemonic power.[20]

At the same time, it is clear that the youth reviews under discussion here exposed the contradictions of fascist ideology in ways that garnered them attention from antifascists abroad and government censure at home.

I track their increasing radicalization to analyze how it affected their creators' status as clients within fascist patronage networks and as test subjects of policies designed to produce a new elite. As we will see, discussions of corporativism and the social mandate of the revolution, no less than the debates over the national film and novel, revealed that differences of opinion about the meaning of Italian modernity often derived from divergent interpretations of the nature and mission of fascism. As the young art critic Nino Bertocchi observed in 1932, the polemics between his cohort and older intellectuals not only concerned "the style of contemporary Italian life" but also "the way we should proceed down the path that Mussolini has forged."[21] Examining the blueprints for change produced by this generation clarifies the meanings fascism held for them: rebellion against authority, the promise of collective justice and personal realization, and the chance to realize a unique model of mass society that could be imposed on the world.

TOWARD A FASCIST MODERNITY:
THREE VOICES FOR CHANGE

"Isn't it wonderful that there are all these young people who live hundreds of kilometers apart and are working in the same direction without ever having met?" the twenty-five-year-old writer and critic Dino Garrone marveled to his friend Berto Ricci in 1929. Garrone referred to his literary peers, but the appearance of independent youth journals in Rome, Florence, and other cities over the next few years allowed like-minded youth from many fields to come together to "fashion a new realm of endeavor and understanding."[22] These intellectuals had adopted the cause of cultural change as their unique contribution to fascism but viewed culture as an expression of larger moral, political, and social imperatives. As the editors of Pannunzio's review *Oggi* noted in 1933, their generation was reacting "less against a specific poetics or aesthetics than against a spiritual attitude that influences not only art but all of life. The old attitude holds that only the individual exists in the world (in politics, liberalism). . . . the new attitude is that the individual exists only insofar as he has relations with the world around him (in politics, fascism)."[23]

While local patronage networks and institutional contexts gave each journal its own allies and adversaries, they shared several beliefs and concerns. First was the perception that fascism constituted the political manifestation of the condition of modernity. Like Stefan Zweig, Karl Mannheim, and other European intellectuals, these young Italians believed that modernity necessitated a "multidirectional and active" outlook that took immediate contingencies rather than rigid theories as guides for action. They claimed that fascism shared that same outlook; anti-ideological and eclectic, it was the only political movement in existence that could cope with the "infinitely diverse and mutable" conditions of the modern world.[24] Mussolini encouraged such perceptions, boasting that fascism's independence from fixed formulas allowed it to flourish in the condition of protracted transition and crisis that characterized modernity. As he asserted, "Fascism did not come to power with a tidy prepared program to implement. Had it had such a program, it would have been a failure by now. Nothing is more ruinous than parties that have their doctrinal baggage all tidy and packed and still delude themselves that they can keep up with the grand and mutable reality of life."[25]

The second shared belief was a belief in corporativism as a key component of fascist models of modernity. At its most basic, corporativism organized the economy by category rather than by class. Capital and labor were to be grouped into hierarchical units, or corporations, which would oversee issues relating to their sector of economic life. The corporation would also represent its group politically in a corporative parliament, which was to replace the Chamber of Deputies. Private enterprise and initiative would not be suppressed, as in communist Russia, but merely "coordinated" by the government, which would discipline and control production and consumption. Paralleling the rhetoric used by Rocco, Bottai, and other officials to justify the advent of the managerial state, the original corporativist charter of 1922 asserted that "the nation—considered a superior synthesis of all material and spiritual values of the race—is above individuals, groups, and classes, [who are] made use of by the nation to gain a better position."[26] Emphasizing collective sacrifice rather than individual gain, corporativism would allow Italians to "industrialize ourselves following our own traditions," forestalling the development of American-style atomization. Putting aside both personal and class interests for the good of the entire social body, Italians would pioneer a system "in which oppression, aggression, immorality, fraud, and the lack of social solidarity are strictly forbidden," as one particularly idealistic supporter put it. Like other programs of the fascist *bonifica*, corporativism thus mandated changes in Italians' collective behavior. As Mussolini asserted in a speech that would be widely quoted in the youth press, it represented Italy's solution to a crisis "of the system" that called not only for new economic arrangements but for new values as well.[27]

The prospect of a system that would regulate capitalism and enhance labor's powers convinced syndicalists like Sergio Panunzio and Edmondo Rossoni, who came from the ranks of the pre–World War I left, to cast their lot with fascism.[28] Yet corporativism also reflected the coercive strategies adopted by conservative coalitions in the face of widespread demands for democratization. In Italy, as in Germany and France, the state took on new roles during World War I in regulating production and mediating social conflict. Under fascism, industrial and business elites countenanced corporativism to retain their privileges, not lose them altogether.[29] They engineered the breakup of the fascist syndical structure in 1928, and made sure that state-interventionist enterprises such as the Institute for Industrial Reconstruction operated outside of the corporativist system. They also lobbied successfully to have Bottai removed as minister of corporations in 1932. Bottai was no syndicalist but viewed the corporations as checks on the development of monopoly capitalism in Italy.[30] When the corporations did appear in 1934, their repressive potential led some young intellectuals to worry openly that corporativism without syndicalism resembled a "state capitalism, the last defensive bulwark of the capitalistic bourgeoisie."[31]

Ultimately, corporativism served the regime best by functioning as a symbol of fascism's revolutionary will to forge an antileftist, antiliberal "third way" to modernity. It was the subject of extensive interest from foreign economists and policy makers and earned the regime good press in America, Britain, and other countries.[32] This public relations success owed much to Bottai, who served as the patron saint of a burgeoning corporativist subculture that encompassed institutes, academic programs, and publications that exposed a new generation of Italians to the ideas of leftist thinkers such as Marx, Stalin, Arturo Labriola, and Sidney Webb.[33] Corporativist propaganda, with its promises to "eliminate the economic ruling class," convinced many younger intellectuals of the regime's political good faith and its commitment to anticapitalist agendas.[34] For this generation, corporativism meant more than the attainment of specific economic goals such as the regulation of production and the redistribution of wealth. It promised a new relationship between the individual and the state and the triumph of a new code of values that would underwrite fascism's programs of collective transformation. As the editors of the youth review *Cantiere* wrote, "The corporative revolution knows no compromises. . . . it touches everything in our lives, transforming our way of thinking, our moral and social relationships as well as economic ones. . . . No reformism, no reaction, just revolution. This is fascism."[35]

Thus defined, corporativism provided Italians of this generation with an official reference point for ideas about the function of culture and the intellectual's political role that, in other countries, often fueled political opposition. In France, the notion of *engagement* sustained Raymond Aron, Alexandre Marc, and other young rightists who wished to carry out a "total revolution" against the Third Republic. In journals such as *Réaction, Esprit,* and *L'Ordre nouveau,* they called for a "revision of all values" as a first step to collective change. As Marc stated succinctly in 1933, in the art of revolution, *"Tout se tient:* no new order without a new man, no new man without a new thought [*sagesse*]." [36] In Italy, in contrast, where the cult of commitment (*impegno*) took shape within the context of the regime, it served young people to denounce their compatriots who were hindering the fulfillment of fascism's full transformative potential. Writing in the independent journal *Saggiatore* two years before he became a government censor, the journalist Attilio Riccio demanded that novels and other creative works express a "constructive" mentality and attacked those who shied away from involvement in the fascist syndicate system. The ideology of *engagement,* mediated by fascist power structures, here aids the realization of a totalitarian agenda: "Fear of contact with reality, retreat from action[:] . . . these are sins that can no longer be pardoned. Intellectuals must not see the artistic world as a golden exile or an aristocratic refuge, because art has no worth if it does not contribute to a superior goal." [37]

A brief look at three youth journals that appeared in these years in Rome, Milan, and Florence—*Saggiatore* (1930–33), *Orpheus* (1932–34), and *L'Universale* (1931–35)—clarifies the cultural, moral, and social agendas that characterized this generation's visions of a fascist modernity. *Saggiatore's* central mission was one of cultural modernization. Edited by two students in the University of Rome philosophy department, of which Gentile served as chair, the journal attacked Idealist philosophy for its attachment to abstractions and "metaphysical concerns." Domenico Carella and Giorgio Granata proposed that Italians use the insights of pragmatist philosophy and psychoanalysis to fashion new values that would reflect the "decisive and anti-ideological" nature of modernity and fascism. [38] For *Saggiatore,* cultural change also mandated a transfer of cultural authority. The Roman context in which these intellectuals operated made them acutely aware of the hegemony that cultural bureaucrats such as Gentile exerted through a web of governmental institutes and university chairs. [39] In 1932, demonstrating the enterprising spirit that would mark their postwar careers as journalists and cultural organizers, they asked Bottai and other prominent figures to comment on the attitudes and behaviors that differ-

entiated the war and "postwar" generations, and then summed up the responses in ways that showcased their own ideas.[40] Rejecting the idea that
Italian culture must be updated within the framework of tradition, they argued that the "dynamic multiplicity" of modern life had rendered obsolete
all absolute values and past legacies. Cultural ideals, like ethical and political ones, should arise "directly from practical circumstances, adhering to
the different situations in which man finds himself. . . . Emphasis is placed
on action rather than principles." They thus supported the work of realist
novelists and Rationalist architects as expressions of a "sincere" and "responsible" cultural practice that found its rationale in the realities of contemporary life.[41]

Saggiatore's presumption to speak for a generation of Italian intellectuals did not offend *Orpheus* editor Enzo Paci, who wrote from Milan that his
group shared many attitudes with their Roman peers. Rejecting Idealist
philosophies that "presented everything as closed and systemized," Paci
and his coeditor, Anceschi, gravitated toward doctrines such as phenomenology, which "instead invite us to start from scratch in our studies of the
diverse phenomena of life and consciousness."[42] Students of the philosopher Antonio Banfi, who had worked in turn with Georg Simmel and was
close to Edmund Husserl, Paci and Anceschi became important thinkers in
their own right after World War II. Banfi's view of the crisis as a productive
moment of transition between two opposing systems of values inspired
them to work for a new worldview adapted to mass society. They did not
accept their teacher's antifascist politics, however: for them, as for the editors of *Saggiatore*, Mussolini's anti-ideological stance was proof of fascism's
modern and "phenomenological" nature. "Fascism means coming into contact with the life of one's people," the editors asserted in 1933. "[It] means
feeling and living the problems of the moment."[43] Here, as in other realms
of culture, fascism provided a political context for impulses and interests
that were common to this generation throughout Europe. A few young
French thinkers also felt the pull toward "the concrete" and looked beyond
Idealism to phenomenology and psychology. In 1933, the twenty-eight-
year-old Jean-Paul Sartre took off for Germany to study with Husserl and
Martin Heidegger, motivated, as he would later recall, by a desire to "find
something solid."[44]

Compared to *Saggiatore*, *Orpheus* reflected the greater space given to
experimentalist and modernist tendencies in the Lombard city. Affiliated
with the Superior School of Culture and Art in Milan, whose instructors
included several Rationalist architects, its directive was to "diffuse the principles of modernity" and create a culture adapted to mass society.[45] With a

director (the musician Pietro Tronchi) who urged the journal's editors to "always remain in the avant-garde," *Orpheus* soon became a leading voice of a new collectivist-minded culture among youth that took its cues as much from the *Neue Sachlichkeit* as from the speeches of Mussolini. The editors had a Berlin correspondent (Grete Aberle), devoted much attention to Weimar German films and novels, and helped to arrange a local exhibition of the work of Otto Dix. In the spring of 1933, while *Saggiatore* expressed concern over preserving the personhood within the collectivity, *Orpheus* spoke approvingly of recent German literary trends that "have killed off the ego of the artist and substituted the ego of the mass."[46] As Paci stated in a programmatic article later that year, the crisis had impelled his generation to "take a new look at everything [and] understand culture from a completely different viewpoint . . . that finds its rationale in the changed conditions of life as they find expression in social relations."[47]

This "different viewpoint" mandated a redefinition of the intellectual's role. Like other youth journals, *Orpheus* applauded corporativism for providing a new context and discipline for the practice of culture. As the corporativist syndical structure weeded out anarchy and egotism in the social and economic realms, so would it banish the residues of liberal-era individualism in culture. For the editors of *Orpheus*, no less than those of *Saggiatore*, corporativism's disciplinary mandate resocialized intellectuals who had remained attached to bourgeois notions of high culture. In the corporativist state, they asserted, "the new intellectual will have his work to do, and he must have the modesty to consider himself a man who works like others. . . . What counts, it seems to us, is the function and not the individual, the work and not the personality who produces it."[48]

Orpheus's project for a fascist mass society also entailed the recasting of gender roles in Italy. Paci and Anceschi advocated the development of a new "sexual ethics" founded on the assumption of male-female parity, and their many female collaborators denounced job discrimination schemes that would keep women out of public life.[49]

Orpheus's progressive positions and its editors' willingness to let women speak for themselves were rare in a world where male solidarity tended to prevail over generational kinship. As Victoria de Grazia has shown in her study of women under the dictatorship, young women with professional ambitions bore the brunt of the generational strife of the interwar years. Bombarded with misogynistic messages from the regime's press, they also risked parental censure if they experimented with styles and attitudes that departed from traditional models of Italian femininity. The Bolognese writer Daria Banfi Malaguzzi, who championed careers for women, did not hesitate to lambaste her younger sisters for their cropped hair and "cheeks yellowed by the fox-trot [*sic*]."[50] Moreover, many young male intellectuals did not wish to work with women and excluded them from their publications; no women wrote for *Saggiatore* or *L'Universale*. As one twenty-seven-year-old specified, "We want women to be real companions[,] . . . but they should not imitate our lives and our mentalities. . . . they should respect our work."[51]

Throughout its brief existence, *Orpheus* served as a forum for young female intellectuals who sought to reconcile feminism and fascism by emphasizing the modernity of both. An article about the condition of women under fascism by the University of Pavia student Clara Valente gives some sense of the contradictory agendas that shaped the thinking of these women. For Valente, "The fascist family is not irregular, divorced, Americanized" but rather "the first nucleus of the fascist state" in that "the liberty of every member is subordinated to the entire familial community." She also argued that professional women had the right to contribute in their own way to the collective good, however, and criticized the press for its obsession with the themes of "maternity, infancy, family, and the return to the home."[52] Giovanna Libani and Clara Albini also defended the choice to combine marriage and professional life. They reminded men that the days when women served them as "domestics, cooks, and lovers" had ended. Economic necessity and the social conditions of modernity had made the working woman "a social fact that must be accepted."[53]

One suspects that fascist feminists would have had little place in the modern civilization envisioned by the Florentine journal *L'Universale*. Its director Ricci and editors such as Romano Bilenchi came from the ranks of the Strapaese movement, and this review shared something of the boisterous homosociality that characterized *Il Selvaggio, Il Bargello*, and other populist publications of Tuscan origin.[54] More than other youth journals, *L'Universale* conveys the feeling of being "born too late" that haunted many would-be revolutionaries of this generation. The grandiose air of the review's initial editorial—"We start this paper with the will to act upon Italian history"—masked a fear of having no impact at all in a society that made military conquest a measure of political faith and masculinity.[55]

L'Universale did constitute an important voice in the youth campaign to develop a uniquely Italian and fascist model of modernity. Unlike *Il Selvaggio*, the journal supported Rationalist architecture, seeing it as an important symbol of "an Italian modernity . . . that would permeate our customs, thought, and the very physiognomy of our cities."[56] Along with *Saggiatore* and *Orpheus*, the editors of *L'Universale* also championed corporativist reforms. Corporativism would eliminate class tensions and close the gap between city and country lifestyles, they argued, creating one unified national collective in Italy. These Catholics also polemicized with the post-Concordat Catholic Church for its seeming neglect of its social mission. No less than capitalism, Christianity had entered into a phase of decadence and decline, L'Universale concluded in its January 1933 manifesto.[57] The journal was even more hostile to Judaism, showing marked anti-Semitic tendencies. The editors assured their readers that they received no funding from "rich Jews," and—practically alone among youth reviews—greeted the Nazi takeover with enthusiasm. Warning that Italy's reborn "civil tradition" must be free of any Jewish influence, Ricci aired views that would become widespread a few years later during the state-sponsored anti-Semitic campaign.[58] Finally, L'Universale's vision of modernity also offered Italians a plan for containing globalization's threat to white European racial hegemony. As Ricci wrote in a 1931 book that dictated the journal's ideas on the subject, advances in travel and communications between peoples rendered inevitable the erosion of national cultures. Barriers would fall first within Europe and then on a global scale, creating civilizations "with which every race and Country will probably collaborate." Rather than resist this process, Italy could guide its development by creating an imperial "union of peoples" under its control. Here the idea that Italy should absorb the best of other peoples took on an overtly colonialist cast. Fascism would act as a "catalyst to cosmopolitanism of the Italian type," supervising the mixing of races and peoples to ensure that its own genes dominated in the multiethnic empires of the future.[59] Combining corporativist designs for national unity with calls for the end of the nation-state, L'Universale embodies the tensions between protectionism and internationalism that characterized the cultural life of the dictatorship. The journal can also be located within the universal fascist movement of interwar Europe that refuted leftist internationalism but conceived of fascism as a transnational phenomenon. While neither Saggiatore nor Orpheus supported universal fascism, Ricci's anticapitalist position resonated with many of his generation who believed that the solution to the crisis lay "not in the system, but beyond it."[60]

By 1933 the editors of L'Universale, Saggiatore, and Orpheus had forged informal alliances based on their shared goal of modernizing Italian culture and making it conform to corporativism's egalitarian imperatives. They made mutual advertising agreements and toyed with ideas for a "united youth front" with headquarters in Milan and Rome.[61] In the summer of 1933, Granata asked Anceschi to assess the emerging "new culture" for a special triple issue of *Saggiatore* that would "review all the youthful forces that are currently at work in Italy." [62] The majority of the fifty-seven mini-essays that appeared in the fall lambaste the war generation for failing to address the "urgent and serious problems" of modernity, and call for new models of mass civilization. Their contributions confirm that this generation of fascist intellectuals wished less to recast bourgeois Europe than to send it to its grave.[63]

THE DISCIPLINE OF REVOLUTION

For regime officials, the *Saggiatore* survey was not a welcome event. It confirmed suspicions that had been brewing for several years: that fascist culture, as conceived by youth, owed more to modernism than to Mussolini. In 1932, during the debates over realist novels, Chiarini and other functionaries had warned youth against thinking that "a revolution is real only if it makes a tabula rasa of all that preceded it." [64] By January 1933, after the publication of provocative manifestos by *L'Universale* and *Saggiatore*, the government began to rethink its policies that had allowed this youth culture to develop. Like National Socialist officials, the fascists had strived for "generational mobilization without generational conflict"; now they found that they had encouraged autonomist sentiments that worked against the formation of a new elite. A press order that month told journalists that emphasizing the issue of generational conflict constituted

> a gross error that only fuels the anti-Fascist press abroad in its claim of a breach between the new generations and Fascism—they even write, as has [the antifascist historian Gaetano] Salvemini, that it will be the youth who will carry out the revolution against Fascism. The truth is the opposite: if there is faith and fervor for Fascism it comes above all from youth. So these silly attacks must be stopped.[65]

The effort to reign in heterodox tendencies also led officials to downplay fascism's ideological indeterminacy. Chiarini attacked youth reviews' "mania for innovative and revolutionary programs, grand syntheses and original interpretations" and reminded young intellectuals that the regime "already has a perfectly defined history and doctrine." [66] In a series of critiques of *L'Universale* and *Saggiatore*, Casini struck a similar chord. He stated the regime's intention to "exert control over emerging tendencies" and warned youth away from "negating" existing values and institutions. "Woe to those who do not understand that . . . the new reality must follow the path laid out by fascism," he concluded ominously.[67]

As the government grew more worried about the separatist tendencies of young intellectuals, it employed patronage strategies tried out earlier on older intellectuals to bring them under control. First, officials subsidized youth reviews and their contributors, who, as they knew, were perennially starved for cash. *Saggiatore, L'Universale,* and those who wrote for them were given funds by Mussolini's Press Office and the undersecretary of press and propaganda (after 1933), by individual officials acting as private contributors, and by the Italian Academy.[68] Second, the regime used job offers to neutralize those with overly independent tastes and temperaments. This tactic was used with Rationalist architects whose work had long been suspect for its affinities with European modernism. Since the inception of the movement, authorities such as Bottai and the architect's syndicate head, Alberto Calza-Bini, had sought to place it under syndical control "in order to guide its development and ensure that the new tendency would have an openly Italian character." Now, at the time when the young designers had made news outside Italy with high-profile state commissions such as the Florentine train station (1931) and the facade of the Exhibition of the Fascist Revolution (1932), officials took further steps to curb their autonomy. They created "special positions" (*incarichi speciali*) for them within the architect's syndicate that drew them into the regime's disciplinary system, and invited them to write for the syndical journal *L'Architettura.*[69]

Officials proffered collaborations to youth in other fields as well. By 1933, Bilenchi, Brancati, Carella, Granata, and Ricci wrote for Bottai's *Critica fascista,* Vittorini, Ricci, Brancati, and De Michelis contributed to Casini's syndicalist newspaper *Lavoro fascista,* and Mussolini's own *Il Popolo d'Italia* featured bylines by Bilenchi and other editors of *L'Universale.* Bilenchi turned down Bottai's offer of a job with the Ministry of Corporations but accepted the cookery column Ciano got him at the Florentine paper *La Nazione.* For Vittorini and other individuals of modest means, these collaborations signified much-needed extra cash and a wider audience. Their purpose, though, was to normalize young intellectuals by drawing them into closer relations with the government. The double edge of the dictatorship's largesse is evoked in Bilenchi's postwar recollection that "they told us to write whatever we wanted, with full freedom, but to send our articles to the Press Office of the Head of the Government [the censor's office] rather than directly to the newspaper."[70]

The political reasoning behind fascist youth patronage comes through most clearly in the case of Gastone Silvano Spinetti, who became a press censor in 1933 at the age of twenty-five. Spinetti had come to the attention of fascist officials early that year when he began to publish *La Sapienza,* a confused but enthusiastic review that combined anti-Idealist, universal fascist, and Catholic orientations with calls for a return to the revolutionary spirit of 1919.[71] Gaetano Polverelli, the head of Mussolini's Press Office, decided to offer Spinetti a job as a censor, and wrote to the Duce in March that Spinetti seemed "particularly prepared for propaganda work."[72] Spinetti agreed to write for *Il Popolo d'Italia*, but turned down the job; he was busy organizing an Anti-Idealist Congress, which was to be held at the University of Rome in June. According to police informers' reports, hundreds of youth turned out to hear Spinetti call for a "cultural revolution" that would curtail the influence of Gentile and other authorities with ties to the liberal era.[73] After the congress, the job offer was renewed, with the stipulation that Spinetti cease all activities as a journalist and cultural organizer. In October, Spinetti suspended publication of *La Sapienza* and began work in the Press Office, where he "revised" the writings of his former comrades until the fall of the regime.[74]

The push to curtail young intellectuals' autonomy also led to a series of initiatives designed to bring their leisure-time activities under state authority. The GUF sections, which had been viewed with diffidence by students, were now expanded to include cinema, radio, and theater sections that allowed youth to make 16 mm films and produce experimental plays and radio programs. By 1936, with over seventy-five thousand members, the GUFs had become an important part of cultural life under the dictatorship.[75] The Littoriali competitions, which began in 1934, were another success, as they gave GUF members a relatively free environment in which to debate topical issues such as corporativism, cinema, and mass culture. Anceschi and other students who most impressed the judges—1934 juries included Giuseppe Ungaretti, Enrico Fermi, and Ottorino Respighi— received cash, a medal, and a handshake from Mussolini. As with Hitler Youth activities in Germany and the programs of the Youth Front of Franco's Spain, personal and career concerns as well as political zeal motivated Italians' participation in GUF programs. The GUFs offered opportunities for national and international travel, socializing, exposure to new ideas, and the chance to acquire professional skills. In later years, the Littoriali also became a place where youth came into contact with antifascist recruiters, giving new meaning to Bottai's comment that the competitions served young Italians who would "discover our 'truths' for themselves."[76]

This climate of camaraderie did not normally extend to female students. As Clara Valente charged in *Orpheus*, the generational solidarity of the GUF broke down when it came to collaborating with women "who read Mussolini's speeches and play sports." GUF statutes made no provision for separate female sections and severely restricted female participation in

GUF activities.[77] Littoriali competitions for female students did not appear until 1939. Thus female students whose interests diverged from child care, family hygiene, and social welfare often had to depend on the goodwill of their male peers to gain entry to officially sponsored cultural activities. Yet many enterprising women utilized the GUFs to their advantage. Eva Weinberger of the Milan GUF worked as a camera operator on the award-winning 16 mm film *Fonderie d'acciaio* (*Steel Foundries,* Ubaldo Magnaghi, 1933), and a number of women authors who achieved prominence in the post-1945 period, such as Milena Mileni, got their start writing articles for GUF reviews.

Self-realization and personal emancipation for young Italians of either sex did not figure in official calculations about the long-term effects of GUF initiatives, however. As the reviews *Gioventù fascista* and *Critica fascista* reminded their readers, the GUFs had been assigned a "totalitarian task" by the government: that of instilling in younger Italians "the spirit of collaboration and discipline for work."[78] *Acciaio* (*Steel,* 1933), a film made by the Cines studio under Cecchi's supervision, showcased the type of the redemptive transformations the regime envisioned for younger Italians. Directed by the German filmmaker Walter Ruttmann, the movie's ideology and cinematography also owe a debt to Soldati, who served as assistant director and cowrote the script.[79] Based loosely on a story by Pirandello, *Acciaio* tracks the rehabilitation of the young worker Mario from a disruptive element to a productive member of the national collective. While its protagonists are members of the working class, the lessons they learn about the need to curb their desires for emancipation were applicable to intellectuals of this generation as well.

Acciaio's plotline plays on the tensions between individual initiative and collective duty that were of prime concern to the fascist regime. Mario's success in cycling championships during his military service has left him with dangerous dreams of heroic individualism. He is unable to make the transition back to his mundane job as a steelworker, and he cannot control his anger at his fellow laborer Pietro, who has become engaged to his former girlfriend, Gina, while he was away. Working amid huge tongues of fire and scorching slabs of metal, he smokes and ignores other rules of collective safety. Finally, he provokes a conflict that ends in Pietro's death. Ostracized by the entire village, Mario flees on his bicycle and bursts illegally into the Tour of Italy racing championship, which is passing through Terni, but rapidly falls behind in the race. He becomes a lone figure who peddles desperately away from his village against the tide of workers who, on their own bicycles, flood toward the factory for the next shift. In the film's climactic moment, at least according to Cecchi, who worked on the script, "the discipline of work and his love for Gina and his birthplace stop Mario on the threshold of liberty."[80] Mario turns around and follows his peers to the factory, slipping in just as the heavy doors slam behind him. Ruttmann conveys the inevitable and "natural" quality of this decision to rejoin the collective in his favorite formalist manner. An overhead shot of the workers joining up on the main road to the factory cuts to an image of many small streams merging into Terni's majestic waterfall. Once in the factory, Mario is given an assignment that requires him to sit inside a sort of cage, away from the other men. His egotistical behavior will never really be forgiven, and has barred him from the fellowship of the laboring life.

Ruttmann came from the ranks of the German avant-garde, and *Acciaio* draws on the documentarist strain within modernist cinema. Shot on location in the Terni steelworks, it features local steelworkers and other non-actors in leading roles. The framing and composition of some shots recall images from Vertov's film on the steel industry (*Enthusiasm*, 1931), as well as those of Soviet photographers such as Arkady Shaikhet and Anatoly Skurikhin. Ruttmann's primary interest, though, was to exalt the power and beauty of machines, as he had in his 1927 documentary, *Berlin*. The film features lengthy sequences of white-hot forms emerging like ghosts in the blackness of the steel mill. This sense of labor as spectacle is reinforced when the film cuts to a group of middle-class visitors who watch the steelworking process with the aid of binoculars, as if they were attending a sporting event. The aestheticized view of labor and laborers bothered the procorporativist editors of *Oggi*, who complained that industrial workshops were not "a sort of grandiose studio in which one can produce interesting photographic and acoustic effects. They are places where an infinite number of men labor, sweat, earn their living, and feel anger, sadness, and cheer."[81]

Oggi's dissatisfaction was echoed by Italian spectators, who stayed away from *Acciaio* in record numbers. But critics gave the film mostly glowing reviews. Luigi Chiarelli felt that the *Acciaio* would "open a window on Italy for foreigners," and the critic Alberti called it "a European as well as Italian film."[82] In fact, *Acciaio* communicated the disciplinary demands of fascism as seen by both Italian and German governments. It anticipated Ruttmann's films on the steel industry for the Nazi Bureau of Labor, and was well received in Hitler's Germany, where it was shown with the title *Arbeit macht glücklich* (*Work Makes for Happiness*).[83] The film also illustrated the kind of therapeutic transformations that the Italian regime wished to bring about. Like the waterfall in *Acciaio*, which reminded Terni's workers of the one-way trajectory they were to follow, fascist youth activities were intended to instill a disciplinary ethos that would become naturalized, stilling any currents of internal opposition. Noting the nonconformist views of many participants at the 1934 Littoriali competitions, one commentator observed that the government's task in the coming years was to "guide the energies of youth like the bed of a great river in which the powerful and disorderly rushing waters of spring will soon be dammed."[84]

The normalizing messages delivered in *Acciaio* and other films were undercut, though, by the government's decision to intensify its revolutionary rhetoric in view of the upcoming inauguration of the corporations. In a series of speeches in late 1933 and 1934 that were extensively cited in the youth press, Mussolini declared the death of capitalism. The solution to the European crisis lay "beyond the system," he asserted, in the new socioeconomic order of the fascist corporativist state. Declaring "bourgeois" and "fascist" to be mutually exclusive spiritual conditions, Mussolini announced his intention to entrust "production to the producers." These included workers as well as employers, he told his working-class audience, since fascism recognized "the equality of all individuals with respect to labor and the Nation."[85]

Although such speeches restated themes and ideas that had been circulating in *Critica fascista* and the syndicalist and youth press, they fueled the fervor of those intellectuals whom the regime had been trying to regiment. Taking to heart the Duce's invitation to "act and think as revolutionaries," the editors of *Saggiatore* and *Orpheus* now adopted more radical positions on corporativist and cultural affairs. Inspired in part by the imminent creation of the corporations, in March 1934 they dissolved their reviews and created one unified journal, *Cantiere*, reaffirming their status as militants "ready to do anything in order to realize that reality which Mussolini wishes to give to Italy." As Granata specified in an internal memo to Anceschi, the journal's focus on labor was not to stop at the title. Rather, its entire program should reflect the "new spirituality that interprets cultural events in a 'political' and 'social' light."[86] *Cantiere* considered the improvement of worker's rights to be the central task of corporativism, and corporativism to be a central contribution of the fascist model of modernity. The journal argued against salary reductions for workers and conducted investigations of labor conditions in fields and factories. One reporter wrote a two-part study on Sicilian sulphur workers and concluded that their circumstances had worsened considerably after twelve years of fascist rule.[87]

Other youth journals also manifested more intransigent positions on labor issues in 1934–35. Bilenchi and other contributors to *L'Universale* denounced employers' associations as the "adversaries" of worker's rights and pointed out loopholes in corporativist legislation that allowed capitalism to continue to flourish.[88] Anticapitalist sentiments also permeated *Camminare*, a Milanese journal run by the publishing heir Arnaldo Mondadori. *Camminare* championed corporativism as a means of "definitively eliminating liberal concepts of private property and individual initiative."[89] The proworker, procollectivist arguments advanced by these journals led the exiled socialist Pietro Nenni to remark from Brussels that young fascist intellectuals had "become socialists without wanting to or even knowing how."[90]

While corporativism brought some youth together in 1934–35, collectivism pulled others apart. As elaborated in both *Cantiere* and *Camminare*, fascist mass society demanded that the individual put aside all partisan interests and identify with the sentiments of the group. Only through this process of "depersonalization" could men and women produce works that reflected the realities of contemporary life. As Anceschi explained it in *Cantiere*, "The sense of the 'mass' replaces that of the 'individual' as a center of life; an anonymous 'production' replaces the ambitious 'personality.'" For intellectuals, this entailed abdicating all eccentric and individualist tendencies and accepting "programs fixed by the collective."[91] In the realm of letters, *Cantiere* called for a "social literature" that would demonstrate that collectivism had entered *"in interiorem hominem."* When the publisher Valentino Bompiani launched a provocative proposal in March 1934 for a "collective novel" that would recount only "collective facts," Anceschi and Mondadori applauded the idea as an example of "depersonalization" applied to art.[92]

For Anceschi and other former contributors to *Orpheus*, the leap to *Cantiere* had not been a very large one, since they had long supported collectivism and the spread of an "objective" mentality along the lines of the *Neue Sachlichkeit*. No such linear development marked the youth of *Saggiatore*, whose views underwent an about-face when they created *Cantiere*. "Pernicious egalitarian collectivism is a utopia, an absurdity," Carella had written in *Saggiatore* nine months earlier. "The task of the new generations is to define the personality of man within the collective organs of society."[93] The radicalizing effect that Mussolini's deployment of leftist rhetoric had on some of his more militant supporters can be seen in the changing views on collectivism that accompanied the transformation of *Saggiatore* into *Cantiere* (fig. 7).

Relatively few youth, though, followed the editors of *Cantiere* and *Camminare* down the path of "depersonalization." Regardless of their age,

COLLETTIVISTA D'IERI E COLLETTIVISTA D'OGGI
— Giovanotto, per aver avuto le vostre idee, io, quindici anni or sono...

Figure 7. "Collectivists of Yesterday and Collectivists of Today." "Young man, for having held your ideas, fifteen or so years ago, I . . ." Lampooning the antibourgeois radical-ism of young bourgeois fascist intellectuals. *Il Selvaggio*, May 15, 1934. Reprinted with permission of the Biblioteca Nazionale, Rome.

most educated Italians—who were formed by humanistic educational and cultural traditions—could not accept the negation of individual agency and creativity implied by this concept. Since the inception of the regime, most discourses of fascist modernity had hinged on the notion that Mussolini's state would protect the individual against the leveling tendencies of capi-talism and communism. Even when the regime's totalitarian politics made clear its intent to annihilate individual will and action, many intellectuals continued to assert that fascism was a defense of personhood against the standardizing imperatives of "Soviet-American barbarism."[94] As we have seen in preceding chapters, this comforting fiction had structured Italians' perceptions of foreign models of modernity when they traveled abroad and their reception of the foreign films and novels they consumed at home. Corporativism, the ethical state, universal fascism—what tied these doctrines together, however loosely, was the idea that fascist collectivism would strengthen and complete the individual, not negate his or her existence altogether. Indeed, *L'Universale* maintained in its manifesto that "respect for the human personality" was the only principle of Western civilization worth saving. Thus Ricci protested privately at *Cantiere's* "materialistic and stupid collectivism" and argued publicly that doing away with economic privilege did not mean the destruction of individuality. What made fascism unique, according to Ricci, was that all its initiatives had an educative and spiritual dimension.[95]

Cantiere's brand of collectivism also produced a breach in the youth front that had developed around the cause of realist literature. Pannunzio had founded the literary review *Oggi* in 1933 to support realism and other modernist tendencies in Italian letters. Fearing that the collective novel would lead to "a State art, to the suffocation of all high aspirations, to the heaviest and darkest kind of Bolshevism," he and his friend Moravia began a public campaign against their peers in the press. Moravia lambasted the collective novel as the triumph of a "mechanical mentality" over poetic inspiration, and Pannunzio published an anticollectivist article in *Oggi* that revealed his deep ambivalence towards mass society. In it, he charged that the "multiple, confused, and artificial" reality of modernity had compromised the individual's ability to order his or her world. "Firm ideas" had given way to a "swirl of chaotic cognitions" that reflected the latest trends propagated by movies and the press. Stripped of the ability to think critically and act autonomously, he argued, modernity's sorry subjects were powerless to resist "the absorption of man by the collectivity, the advent of the mass-man, an individual who is undifferentiated and anonymous; the affirmation of a mechanical world of men without souls, enslaved to a purely material goal that will bring humanity to decadence, decrepitude, and death."[96]

Pannunzio's polemic created a schism within the ranks of *Oggi* that led to the journal's demise later that year. Accusing him of being "individualist and bourgeois," a group of *Oggi's* procollectivist collaborators migrated to *Cantiere*. Moravia remained with Pannunzio to found a new literary journal, *Caratteri*, which promised its collaborators "maximum liberty of expression" to voice "personal discoveries and convictions . . . each according to their own temperament and preferences."[97] While *Caratteri* lasted but four issues due to financial difficulties, it holds interest as a reaction within the youth ranks against the turn to collectivism that some intellectuals were taking. It also rehearses the debates Pannunzio would engage in with Italian communists after World War II as an editor of liberal publications such as *Risorgimento liberale* and the influential *Il Mondo.* Granata would contribute to both of these journals (as would Moravia), having turned away from collectivist positions after the experience of *Cantiere.*

The radicalization of youth culture also changed the course of this generation's cultural production. Labor now became a preferred subject for younger Italians, who saw the regime's attacks on the "parasitical" middle class as a guarantee of its progressive politics. The twenty-five-year-old Bilenchi published a novel entitled *Il capofabbrica* (*The Foreman,* 1935), in which a young fascist revolutionary and a communist worker find common ground in their fight against bourgeois corruption. Barbaro now shifted his focus from the bored bourgeois youth of his 1931 novel *Luce fredda* to the laboring class. He urged Italian writers to depict the world of work with its "ink-stained fingers and broken nails" and made a short film for Cines on the activities of a naval shipyard.[98] Significantly, Barbaro had sat in on the editing process of *Acciaio,* and his documentary *Cantieri dell'Adriatico* (*Shipyards of the Adriatic,* 1933) seems to comment on the aestheticization of labor that marked the former film. Barbaro focuses not on the machines themselves but on the impact they have on those who operate them. Neither does he heroicize the workers in the manner of many Soviet films of the time. Through real-time pacing and a matter-of-fact point of view, he places the accent on the relation of the laborers with their tools and their surrounding environment.

Other works communicate the frustration provoked in many young intellectuals by Mussolini's calls to revolution, which reminded them that their own rebellious urges could find expression only in the discursive and cultural realm. Even if they believed that corporativism was "the most radical reform in the history of modern times," as Mussolini maintained, it could hardly compete with the clubs and castor oil that had propelled the revolution in its earlier phase. "Ah, the attraction of the word anti-bourgeois!" exclaims a character in Vittorini's 1933–34 novel *Il garofano rosso* (*The Red Carnation*) who has missed all the action. "And what a longing for rifle shots!"[99] Vittorini, Bilenchi, and their cohort wrote about squadrism in these years to claim a place for themselves in fascism's collective history and remind Italians of the radical elements in fascism's family tree. The interest in squadrism also expressed this generation's desire to experience the "unlimited liberties" they believed had marked the years of Mussolini's rise to power.[100] The desire for such freedoms is most clearly conveyed in *Il garofano rosso*, which Vittorini wrote at the age of twenty-five. Set in the months following Matteotti's 1924 assassination, the novel captures fascism as it evolved from a revolutionary movement to a bureaucratic regime bent on collective normalization. During the course of the narrative, the rowdy young squadrist Tarquinio, who believes in a "revolutionary and antibourgeois" fascism, becomes a conformist who thinks only about getting a job.[101] Sixteen-year-old Alessio lives vicariously through his hero Tarquinio at first, and he eventually leads a student action to occupy a school. Yet, he ultimately finds more satisfaction hiding out in a brothel with the prostitute Zobeida, who stands for an illicit and unrepressed realm of life that, in Vittorini's eyes, had fallen victim to the dictatorship's moralizing imperatives. In fact, Alessio and Tarquinio discover a group of younger boys, representative of a newer generation raised entirely under fascism, who are drafting a mock code of law to regulate sexual affairs in Italy. Giving voice to official desires to alter Italians' sexual and social behavior, the boys ban prostitution as well as "occasional physical relationships that are the fruit of frivolous impulses . . . and passing sexual desires." Here Vittorini seems to lampoon the "social hygiene" campaigns that resulted in more stringent regulations on prostitutes and other supposed "delinquents." The book's ending raises the possibility that Alessio may have also internalized fascism's new disciplinary codes: he reflects that, although he has not stolen or killed, he feels the need to be "convicted."[102] Not surprisingly, the novel angered the censors when it appeared in installments in *Solaria*. One segment caused the review's April 1934 issue to be confiscated on charges of immorality, and the government subsequently denied Vittorini permission to publish *Il garofano rosso* in book form.[103]

The antibourgeois sentiments expressed in *Cantiere* and *Il garofano rosso* unsettled intellectuals of the war generation such as Pellizzi, who had been warning government officials for some years that encouraging the radical tendencies of youth would impede the formation of a new ruling elite. In a spring 1934 issue of *Critica fascista*, Pellizzi urged Bottai to punish those who were trying to revive the atmosphere of the early 1920s by "excluding them from every delicate activity and social endeavor, as befits an unassimilable and disorderly element in national life." Bottai's reply was designed to acknowledge Pellizzi's concerns without jeopardizing his own status as patron and protector of all things modern and revolutionary. He admitted that young intellectuals had "given a different meaning" to fascism's cardinal ideas, particularly in the area of labor relations, and reminded them that "this time of fascism is not, as some say, one of transition from one phase of the Revolution to another (to clarify: from a political to a social or economic phase)." At the same time, he refused to condemn their interpretations of Mussolini's movement: "Where we have seen an end, they see a beginning. They have taken us seriously. We have spoken, they want to act[;] . . . and even where we have acted they glimpse new roads to take that they don't intend to renounce. . . . [But] it is precisely from the youthful penchant to make surveys, ask questions, and mine old themes for new solutions that the dialectic intrinsic to the revolutionary movement has received its vital impulse."[104] Bottai did heed Pellizzi's admonition to "be afraid of words." A June 1934 note in *Critica fascista* entitled "Revolution" exhorted youth to be more prudent in their use of this term "and others that are just as beautiful and just as dangerous." With Pellizzi's help, Bottai also organized a forum on "the relationship between language and revolution" in the youth review *L'Orto*. The forum aimed to establish a consensus on the meanings that socialist-linked terms such as "labor" and "revolution" should take on within the fascist state.[105]

That the regime had become more wary of its critics is evidenced by the intensified action of patronage and policing directed at the editors of *Cantiere* and other youth journals in the summer of 1934. Anceschi and Mondadori were followed by fascist informers and visited at home by agents who urged them to drop their publishing activities. At the same time, *Cantiere* received government funding through the intervention of Ciano, who then began to suggest themes that the journal might emphasize or avoid. A request by Ciano in April 1934 to launch a campaign against National Socialism was promptly obeyed, as was a tip—coinciding with the censorship of Vittorini's *Il garofano rosso*—advising them to minimize attacks on the bourgeois conception of the family. By March 1935, *Cantiere* counted Augusto De Marsanich, Bottai, Casini, and other functionaries among its contributors, and its articles on Ethiopia resembled the propaganda put forth in the mainstream press.[106]

L'Universale came in for similar double-edged attention. Ricci was called in for additional "consultations" with Spinetti and other censors, and the police began to survey printing operations of the journal in order to sequester any offending issues before they went on sale. At the same time, the review's editors came into closer contact with the government. Ciano arranged an audience for them with Mussolini in July 1934 and placed many of them on the pay lists of the undersecretary of press and propaganda.[107] The creeping conformism that resulted from such cliental relationships was not lost on the readers of youth publications, at least according to one police informer. Reporting from Ancona in the summer of 1934, he related students' dismay at the "loss of spontaneity" in the "independent" youth press. "The feeling is that [the editors] have become slaves to political figures who fund their reviews but ask for the most complete servitude in return," the spy stated.[108]

At the beginning of the decade, informers' accounts of young Italians' apathy toward fascism had given rise to the set of policies and privileges that went under the rubric of "making way for youth." By 1935, a new round of reports told officials that this strategy had backfired by raising expectations of mobility that could never be fulfilled. Students had begun to see fascism as a "repressive and authoritarian system," spies reported from Milan. "Discontent and opposition are notably spreading . . . even among those students who had always been disinterested in politics."[109] The bad faith of fascist officials must certainly have been apparent to the students who attended the "Italian-French Conference on Corporativist Studies" held in Rome in May. Bottai and other blackshirts danced around the questions put to them by Emmanuel Mounier and other Gallic intellectuals on the rights of the individual in the fascist state. "We defend the dictatorship because it is the revolution, and consider the problem of liberty to be a secondary, if not altogether irrelevant, question," contended the head of the agricultural worker's federation early on in the proceedings, setting the tone for the responses to come. Once back in Paris, Mounier directed his praise to the younger Italians with whom he had talked before and after the official presentations. The new generation of fascists is "radically anticapitalist and audaciously constructive," he concluded, "with profound roots in the proletariat." That same month, *L'Universale* editor Indro Montanelli, who had attended the conference, expressed irritation and amazement that some French youth thought of fascism as a "nationalistic movement of the extreme Right."[110]

Within a few months of the conference, the nonconformist attitudes Mounier had admired became untenable in Italy. Ricci had already been expelled from the PNF in March for one year for an overly critical article in his journal. Now preparations for the upcoming invasion of Ethiopia resulted in demands for internal unity and precluded attacks on the capitalists who were to arm Italy for war. The government suppressed both *Cantiere* and *L'Universale* in the summer of 1935, leading Nenni to proclaim from Brussels that Mussolini had "decapitated the left wing of fascism."[111] *Cantiere* had no time to make final statements, but *L'Universale's* editors put a patriotic face on things, announcing that the time had finally come for their generation to act, rather than merely write about the actions of others. Ricci's expulsion from the PNF did not affect his faith in fascism, and he volunteered for the Ethiopian War, along with Paci, Montanelli, and a number of other intellectuals their age. Although he intended to resume *L'Universale* and its campaign for social justice when he returned, the new Ministry of Popular Culture denied his request.[112]

As Italian intellectuals of all ages soon realized, the start of the Ethiopian War ended a phase of cultural policy that had taken shape as fascism evolved into a mass regime. Two intertwined exigencies had determined the directives of this period: the need to clarify the contours of fascist ideology and culture for domestic and foreign consumption, and the desire to develop a model of modernity that would supplant liberal and leftist conceptions of contemporary life. In the early thirties, these goals produced a consensus in government circles for an "open door" stance that encouraged Italians to explore and assimilate the latest foreign trends. This position earned the regime some good press abroad and allowed policy makers to sidestep the long-debated problem of how to build a national culture in a country that lacked a shared legacy of national traditions. As Bottai wrote in 1932, Italy's greatest asset was its ability to "reelaborate and unify all the observations, critiques, and systems of knowledge produced in other countries," whether in cultural or corporativist matters.[113] This wish to take the best from other nations never dissipated, but the autarchic climate that was imposed in Italy after 1936 made most officials more wary about encouraging the investigation of foreign trends. New networks of cultural exchange developed based on the Rome-Berlin Axis, and military imperatives, rather than modernist trends, proved a prime inspiration for many future visions of fascist modernity.

The Ethiopian War also ended an era of cultural debate that many intellectuals would remember as the most intense and engaging period of the dictatorship. As we have seen, fascist officials facilitated this generation's aesthetic experimentations by allowing them ample exposure to foreign modernist movements and subsidizing their works. Yet the attempts of younger Italians to translate their visions of modernity into cultural production met with a decidedly ambivalent reaction. After 1935, many in their twenties would discover that the interests Bottai and others had encouraged them to develop had less and less place within the regime. Even Bottai began to search for another cause around which to organize his campaigns for a fascist model of modernity, once he perceived that corporativism had little future as a means of collective transformation. "If we realize tomorrow that the end will be achieved by different means than those we had envisioned until now," he reflected late in 1935, "we will not hesitate for a moment to change direction."[114] For Bottai, that means proved to be anti-Semitism. After 1938, under his lead, racism became a new vehicle for the expression of antibourgeois and anticapitalist elements of fascist ideology, and the latest curative instrument of a "therapeutic politics" that aimed at the abolition of moral and cultural decadence in Italy.

Temperament, talent, personal finances, and patronage connections determined how each individual navigated the shifting sea of fascist culture in these years. With few exceptions, the climate of conformism and intimidation had a normalizing effect on the comportment, career choices, and creative work of intellectuals of all ages. Alvaro saw the start of the imperial enterprise as an opportune time to renew his public commitment to fascism. Interviewed in November 1935, he emphasized that he had left a lucrative screenwriting job in Vienna "to be in Italy at such an important moment for our Country." Such pronouncements earned him a prominent place within fascist culture and a series of subsidies that culminated in a 1940 Academic Prize from the Italian Academy.[115] Barbaro's itinerary ended up resembling those of the Soviet intellectuals he so often wrote about. As he became immersed in the fascist film industry, his exaltations of the independent artists' transformative powers gave way to praise for the taste-making potential of state institutions.[116] Emanuelli, too, steered away from the avant-garde impulses that had informed his novel *Radiografia di una notte*. As was the case with many of his peers, his antibourgeois and experimentalist tendencies peaked in 1934, when he published a volume of stories (*Storie crudeli*) that show the clear influence of the *Neue Sachlichkeit*. Scathing reviews and his increasing militancy led Emanuelli to favor journalism over literature for several years, and his later literary works are much more traditional. He volunteered for the Ethiopian War and combined his combat duties with those of war correspondent for the Genoese daily *Il Lavoro*.

Some intellectuals of Emanuelli's generation retreated temporarily into more private worlds. Granata turned his attentions to teaching, Anceschi concentrated on his academic writing, and Pannunzio took up his profession as a lawyer. "Heavy old furniture, portraits of the King, of the little Prince, of the Duce. A telephone. Electric lights. A map of Rome on the wall. . . . what a terrible sadness," Pannunzio wrote of his new surroundings at the end of 1934.[117] Moravia dealt with his own "sadness and solitude" in a predictably patrician manner. Having repudiated *Gli indifferenti* and published a second book that critics had been ordered to ignore, he sailed for New York and, following in Soldati's footsteps, spent five months at Columbia's Casa Italiana before going on to vacation in Mexico. In the coming years, journalistic assignments would allow him frequent trips abroad, but he never seriously considered emigration. Moravia's belief that leaving Italy would constitute an evasion of moral responsibility, together with the privileges afforded him by his relationships with many of fascism's social and political elite, kept the half-Jewish writer in his native land even after the promulgation of the racial laws.[118] Soldati, who had been fired from Cines in 1934 after *Acciaio*'s box-office failure, ended a hard-luck year with a gesture of public self-criticism of the type most dictatorships demand as a prelude to rehabilitation. In the preface to *America primo amore*, which appeared in 1935, he characterized his attempted emigration from Italy as a "sin" and a "youthful error." Reassuring his readers that he had abandoned his cosmopolitan leanings, Soldati announced his intention to "stay here, ringing the bells, singing in churches and taverns, burying the dead."[119] A year later, he was in Ethiopia with Camerini, working on a film sponsored by the Ministry of War, which narrated a wayward expatriate's transformation into a martyr for the fascist cause.

From the southern village of Brancaleone Calabro, where he had been confined for antifascism, the twenty-seven-year-old Pavese recorded his own responses to the paroxysms of patriotic rhetoric that surrounded him. In the early thirties, when Soldati decided to return to fascist Italy, Pavese had tried to emigrate to America but had been stymied by lack of funds and contacts. By 1935, he had resigned himself to remaining in his native land, but his diary testifies to the restrictions and isolation he faced. Observing his cohort's enthusiasm for Italy's new imperial enterprise, Pavese asked himself if he too could become inspired by the "moral atmosphere of the revolution." He concluded that he lacked the interest in "blood and triumphs" that animated many of his generation. "I can only hope that I will encounter historic moments other than violent revolutions, and be able to depict them in my own way," he wrote in October 1935, as Italian soldiers, his literary peers among them, poured into Ethiopia.[120]

5 Conquest and Collaboration

The invasion of Ethiopia constituted a watershed in the history of the Italian regime. Spurred by fascist dreams of creating a Mediterranean and Red Sea empire, it set in motion a chain of events that destroyed millions of lives in and outside of Italy. By the end of 1937, Italy had left the League of Nations and formed an alliance with Nazi Germany that had lasting repercussions on fascist foreign and domestic policies. War now provided a new context for fascist social engineering schemes: combat and the colonial experience were envisioned as crucibles of a "new type of humanity" suited for conquest and rule. Departing from the premise that effective persecutors do not allow themselves to feel for their victims, official discourses of fascist modernity centered increasingly on the production of a subject capable of disciplining affects as well as thoughts and behaviors. As Bottai boasted in December 1935, emotional and physical composure would mark the new Italian, who "no longer becomes a soldier[,] . . . [he] 'is' a soldier, naturally."[1]

The takeover of Ethiopia also marked the apex of the fascist myth of national regeneration. Celebrated as a triumph of collective action that would free Italy from the "prison" of the Versailles treaty, the colonial enterprise provided putative proof that Mussolini had transformed Italians from spectators to agents of historical change. As men braved bullets for the blackshirt cause, women demonstrated their patriotism by donating their wedding rings in a national "Day of Faith" in December 1935. This symbolic reconciliation between state and society was heralded by propaganda that posited the new empire as a solution to problems that had plagued Italy throughout the liberal period. Southern cities such as Palermo and Catania would enjoy a renaissance as the cultural, industrial, and commercial centers of a new Mediterranean-based civilization, and peasants would be allotted land in Ethiopia, alleviating some of the misery that had led to past waves of emigration.[2]

Ironically, the invasion of Ethiopia, saluted as "the Nation's first autonomous act," also intensified anxieties about Italian subalternity. Even as fascists celebrated the modernity of their imperial enterprise, they worried about the degenerative effects of miscegenation and the civilizing abilities of "backward" Italian colonists. These heightened fears about "blood contamination" gave rise to colonial racial legislation that prepared the terrain for the fascist anti-Jewish laws.[3] The alliance with Nazi Germany that came out of the Ethiopian War prompted further insecurities about Italian authority. The Nazi's aggressive bid to become the undisputed rulers of the "new Europe" alarmed fascists who had seen the Rome-Berlin Axis as an alliance of two powers of equal rank. All too quickly for Italian tastes, the National Socialists became the standard-bearers of rightist totalitarianism, and the Nazi Aryan the emblem of the purified and disciplined fascist subject. These two developments led the Italians to accelerate their efforts to engineer a race of hard-edged conquerors. In 1938, as new racial laws defined Italians as "Aryans," the Duce ordered a "reform of custom" that mandated the goose step and other practices designed to inculcate a command mentality. "[Italians] must learn to be less *simpatici* and become tougher, implacable, odious: that is, masters," he told Ciano that year.[4]

This chapter examines how the Ethiopian War and the events that followed it influenced ongoing discourses and debates about Italian and fascist modernity. I emphasize the links between foreign and cultural policies but also underscore the national concerns that motivated some intellectuals to support measures that are sometimes viewed as anomalous to Italian society and Italian fascism. In this scheme, the regime's cultural autarchy directives not only constituted pragmatic responses to contingent international developments but also answered long-standing anxieties about cultural colonization. The campaign of cultural reclamation (*bonifica della cultura*) that began in 1938 aimed not only to ban Jewish influences from Italy but American and French ones as well. With its arts and letters purged of all elements "that do not fit the particular characteristics of our race," Italy would at last bring a distinctive product to the international cultural marketplace.[5] Similarly, the anti-Semitic laws that targeted Jews for discrimination were modeled on recent German legislation but also built on existing Italian concerns about national unity. Anti-Jewish measures soon became a central component of Mussolini's plans to carry out a totalizing transformation of Italian society, and "Aryanization" the final step to overcoming what Mussolini referred to as a national "inferiority complex."[6]

This chapter also examines the impact of the Axis alliance on cultural policy and cultural production. Mussolini's project to forge a new international order modified official notions about the role of culture and changed the landscape of fascist cultural institutions. New cultural exchange networks took shape between Germany, Italy, Japan, and Spain that rivaled the League of Nations' "cultural internationalism."[7] I look at policies designed to reorient public tastes away from the culture of France and other "plutocratic" powers, and explore how intellectuals responded to the changing political climate. Both documentary and feature directors—among them Soldati, Camerini, and Barbaro—answered the government's call for films that would celebrate its new imperial profile, and cinema soon lay at the center of fascist strategies of continental cultural domination. The government hoped for a similar response from literary figures, and established so many prizes to spur the production of exportable fascist prose and poetry that a government "Commission to Discipline Literary Prizes" was established in 1938.[8] In the end, though, Italians waited in vain for the epic novel of Mussolini's revolution. As we shall see, the works produced by Alvaro and by younger novelists such as Moravia and Paola Masino in the late 1930s cast a skeptical eye on totalitarian projects for collective change. At the same time, it would be wrong to conclude that writers were antifascist or apolitical, since many of them, Alvaro included, worked on colonial and military films that they would strike from their résumés after 1945.[9]

FASCIST MODERNITY AND COLONIAL CONQUEST

In planning their conquest of East Africa, the fascists could draw to some extent on their experiences in Libya, which had been held by Italy since 1912. After Mussolini visited Libya in 1926, the country was targeted to become an overseas outpost of fascist modernity. Land reclamation schemes, tourist developments, and comprehensive urban planning schemes would realize the regime's claim that Libya constituted "Italy's fourth shore." In the early thirties, when resistance was at its fiercest in the inland Cyrenaica region, the fascists subjected the civilian population to gassings and confined eighty thousand Libyans in concentration camps, where vast numbers perished from the rampant disease and starvation rations. Future "improvement" campaigns created more victims. Altogether, about one-tenth of the Libyan population died during two decades of fascist colonial rule.[10]

The fascists employed similar totalitarian tactics during their rule of East Africa. Like other imperialist powers, the Italians billed their colonial war as a modernizing mission that would deliver the Africans from backwardness, slavery, and chaos. Fascist propaganda depicted the Italians as an army of tireless altruists who built roads and bridges, transformed deserts into gardens, and brought peace and prosperity to the indigenous peoples.[11] Traveling through Ethiopia on assignment for the newspaper *Il Lavoro* in the spring of 1936, the writer Emanuelli highlighted the humanity of the Italian troops and the "discipline and civility" that governed their behavior toward the Ethiopians. "Indignant and vindicatory, yes; uncivil and barbarians—we Italians—never," Emanuelli asserted.[12] Foreign journalists and relief workers were free to tell a different story about Italian colonialism—one that archival documents corroborate. As in Libya, gassings formed a prominent part of the fascists' conquest strategy. Between 1935 and 1939, in defiance of the 1925 Geneva Protocol bans on the use of chemical weapons, 617 tons of gas were shipped to Ethiopia. Together with slaughter from conventional weapons, gassings caused a quarter million Ethiopian deaths by 1938. As Ethiopian resistance continued after the proclamation of empire, the Italians combined old-fashioned savageries (decapitations, castrations, and burning and razing of civilian quarters) with industrial killing methods (aerial gas bombings and efficient open-grave executions) that are more commonly associated with Hitler and Stalin's soldiers than with Mussolini's rank and file. Indeed, the slaughter in Ethiopia was so out of keeping with Italians' self-perception as the more "humane" dictatorship that it has been edited out of popular and official memory. Until 1995, the Italian government, and former combatants such as Indro Montanelli, denied the use of gas in East Africa.[13]

If the Ethiopian War hardly lived up to the Duce's boast that it constituted "the most gigantic spectacle in the history of mankind," it did bring the dictatorship a new level of popular acceptance and acclaim within Italy. The victory of May 1936 not only seemed to settle an old score with the Africans (Italian troops had been defeated at Adua forty years earlier) but also avenged Italy's mistreatment by European powers at the Paris Peace Conference in 1919. With League of Nations sanctions in force against Italy after November 1935, Mussolini depicted his country as a "virtuous victim" of the dominant powers. Even as he ordered gas attacks on the Ethiopians, he lashed out at the League's unjust punishment of Italians who, he claimed, were merely trying to "bring civilization to backward lands, build roads and schools[, and] diffuse the hygiene and progress of our time."[14] Such statements united many Italian intellectuals in patriotic outrage during the war and brought forth a show of support for fascism once empire was declared. "After the victory, almost everyone became a fascist," Soldati recalled in a postwar interview in which he identified the conquest of Ethiopia as the peak of his own enthusiasm for the Italian regime.[15]

For intellectuals of Soldati's generation, the Ethiopian War offered a chance to finally translate their political faith into concrete action. A special Universitarian's Battalion allowed young writers, journalists, and others to serve as volunteers. With their journals shut down by the government, Paci of *Cantiere* and Ricci and others from *L'Universale* left for Africa in the fall of 1935; Vittorini's attempt to enlist failed due to bureaucratic complications. In Milan, the nineteen-year-old aristocrat Luchino Visconti had an impulse to volunteer "to make the Patria greater and stronger" but went to Paris to begin a career in film instead.[16] For these men, the Ethiopian war confirmed, rather than contradicted, the regime's intention to carry out its long-promised social revolution. Provided that capitalist speculation and individual greed did not gain the upper hand, they asserted, Italian Africa could become the site of a great social experiment. Corporativist principles of collaboration would now find application in the colonies, so that Africans would be enriched rather than exploited. Exporting Mussolini's revolutionary movement to Africa, youth like Vittorini and Ruggiero Zangrandi believed, would convince the world of fascism's "modern and progressive" nature.[17]

Fascist officials envisioned Ethiopia as a laboratory of another sort. For this generation of men, whose lives had been irremediably marked by their participation in World War I, the battlefield remained the supreme arena for the refashioning of Italians. Calling the Ethiopian invasion the start of a "gigantic work . . . of human reclamation [*bonifica umana*]," Mussolini posited the war as a practicum for the disciplinary education received in schools and fascist mass organizations. Combat and the collective nature of military life, his followers asserted, would eliminate tendencies toward "moodiness," "impulsiveness," and "romanticism" in the national character, producing a new breed of hard-edged Italians. To set an appropriately tough and virile tone, the press was forbidden to depict "sentimental and tearful" family scenes that accompanied Italian troops' departure for Ethiopia, as well as any emotionalism shown by soldiers in Africa.[18]

Although the conquest of Ethiopia was to accelerate the creation of a fascist model of modern existence, it led to heightened fears of social disintegration and degeneration. Concerns over white population numbers had informed fascist social policy since the late 1920s but took on new urgency with the diffusion of crisis ideologies during the depression. By 1934, the

Duce worried aloud that the "numeric and geographic expansion of the yellow and black races" meant that "the civilization of the white man is destined to perish."[19] The Ethiopian invasion was seen as an opportunity to correct this situation. Fascist policies of "demographic colonization" that foresaw the creation of permanent Italian settlements would not only solve Italy's land hunger problem but begin the repopulation of East Africa as a white European space.[20] More broadly, the conquest of Ethiopia created a new forum for the expression of existing fears about mass society and modernity. Building on worries about the loss of hierarchies that marked fascist discourses on modern life in the metropole, intellectuals and functionaries had argued that Ethiopia's "unimaginable ethnic confusion" was responsible for its social chaos and political disintegration.[21] Likewise, when colonial experts such as Raffaele Di Lauro (professor of colonial history and policy at the University of Rome) insisted on the need for gradual modernization in East Africa to prevent "disorder, chaos, and corruption" among the indigenous population, they drew upon some of the same anxieties over the social consequences of rapid change that had informed films and writings about mass society earlier in the decade.[22]

The agenda of maintaining racial boundaries, which lay at the heart of fascist colonial culture, motivated many intellectuals to place their skills at the service of the regime. Architects and urban planners utilized race as the overriding criteria of spatial organization in Ethiopia, following mandates to keep Italian and African cultures separate and unequal. Laws passed in 1939 "for the protection of racial prestige" regulated interracial social contacts, and a new city plan for Addis Ababa enforced racial segregation.[23] Sponsored by the Italian Academy and the National Council of Research, ethnographers and scientists who had earlier mapped Italian ethnicity as part of the regime's "revival of tradition" now began to investigate the inhabitants of East Africa. Demographers designed a vast census of the tribes that would allow for the compilation of a massive "ethnographic atlas" of Italian East Africa, and colonial experts displayed their classification of East Africa's "racial types" in periodicals such as *Etiopia* and *Africa italiana*. The development and exhibition of these taxonomies of colonial knowledge drew on technologies of social control and population management that had informed official blueprints for a fascist modernity since the inception of the regime.[24]

In reality, racial boundaries proved difficult to police and administer, especially in the sphere of sexual relations. As we saw in the 1933 film *Treno popolare*, the regime demanded that its unmarried "new men" learn the virtues both of continence and conquest and worked to reroute female sexuality into procreation. Once Italian troops invaded Ethiopia, the specter of miscegenation imparted a new urgency to ongoing state efforts to modify comportment, affects, and primal drives. Now, the true fascist was less a fearless conqueror than a man "with the attributes of his virility firmly in place."[25] Miscegenation thus received much media attention as a practice that caused physical and psychological decrepitude. Journalists warned Italians that many Ethiopians were of "beautiful appearance and noble bearing," and speakers at colonial preparation courses for women reminded their audiences that heat caused the female sex to "put up less resistance to men." The filmmaker Giulio Brignone delivered a similar warning to Italian men with his 1937 film *Sotto la croce del sud (Under the Southern Cross)*, which was filmed on location in the colony. The movie narrates the temptations faced by Paolo, a normally disciplined young engineer who stands for fascism's ideal modern subject, when he meets Mailù, a mixed-race former prostitute, who embodies the threat of degeneration.[26]

Such messages did little to alter the realities of colonial life. The motivating power of individual fantasies and emotions rendered official exhortations against miscegenation rather ineffectual, as did a tradition of fetishizing the female black body that had permeated Italian high culture and commercial culture by the 1930s.[27] More concretely, very few women accompanied their husbands to Ethiopia, ensuring that sexual relationships between Italian men and African women were frequent and enduring. Although the government continued to urge colonists to bring their wives with them, they also established state-run brothels and traveling "Venus cars" (*carri di Venere*) filled with women recruited from the ranks of Italian prostitutes and domestic servants. The journalist Luigi Barzini Jr. profiled the most popular Italian-staffed brothel for *Esquire*, noting that it was as packed "as a movie house on rainy days." In 1937 miscegenation became a criminal offense for all Italians, punishable by five years in prison; women who were discovered having relations with African men were publicly whipped and sent to concentration camps.[28]

Official desires for the new colony to perform as a laboratory of the fascist social engineering projects produced codes of collective comportment for other spheres as well. Many Italian colonial authorities and experts felt that assimilationism on the French model led to the loss of white prestige by encouraging the colonized to mimic their European rulers. They advocated the propagation of a politics of difference that would continually remind the Africans of their inferior status. Put another way, it was no longer enough for Italians to know how to "believe, obey, and fight"; now, they also had to learn the art of command. Image control, as articulated in the notion of prestige, had been a central part of daily life in all European colonies, where power was maintained not only by repressing the ruled but by rituals that reaffirmed the superiority of the ruler. For French, British, and Dutch imperialists, the notion of the "civilizing mission" entailed the diffusion of upper- and middle-class norms of culture and comportment, even though the colonies often attracted the poor and those who wished to escape rigid social norms.[29]

Class tensions marked Italian colonialism as well, but were often couched in a rhetoric that built on preexisting anxieties—usually heard in statements about the South, long seen as Italy's own "Africa"—about national "backwardness" and servility. Indeed, Mussolini and his officials believed that Italian colonists' ragged appearance and crude manners had cost them Africans' respect, and routinely blamed them for the ongoing Ethiopian rebellions. "The Italians present the indigenous with a quite unimperial spectacle," Farinacci complained to Mussolini after a trip to Ethiopia in 1938.[30] Colonial manuals and laws for the protection of "racial prestige" thus ordered Italians to abandon behaviors that "diminished the Italian in native eyes." Asking Africans for loans, carrying their bags, having sexual or social relations with them, and exhibiting public drunkenness and excessive emotion were prohibited as practices that undermined Italian authority. In his book *Il governo delle genti di colore (Governing Peoples of Color)*, Di Lauro appealed to the Italian tradition of *fare bella figura* (cutting a fine figure) in highlighting the links between comportment and prestige. He instructed colonists to "take care with your clothing, err on the side of vanity. . . . If you have to receive dirty or rag-clad natives, dress elegantly, as though you were going to receive a beautiful woman."[31]

The notion of prestige occupies a central place in all colonial discourse but may have held a special meaning for Italians, who viewed empire as an escape route from a subordinate international position. Worried about foreign perceptions of the insufficiently imperial demeanor of many soldiers and colonists, the Minister of Colonies Alessandro Lessona complained that it was a waste of time to "bring the colonial problem onto the international stage" if Italians were not up to the task of rule. Remaking Italians in the image of imperious commanders became an important theme of the dictatorship's colonial culture; "civilizing" Africa presented an opportunity for the fascists to refashion and modernize Italians in ways that would improve their image and prepare them for the demands of total war.[32]

BETWEEN EXPANSION AND AUTARCHY:
ITALIAN CULTURE IN THE AXIS YEARS

The Ethiopian War began a new era of policy making in cultural as well as foreign affairs. The continuing revolts in the new colonies, as well as the German alliance and Italy's entry into the Spanish Civil War, mandated the maintenance of the new level of propaganda control that had begun during the conflict. To handle the increased attention to censorship and image management, the Ministry of Press and Propaganda was transformed into the larger Ministry of Popular Culture (MCP) by the end of 1937. The architect of this expansion was Dino Alfieri, a former journalist and an admirer of Goebbels, who took over as Italy's cultural minister in June 1936. While Alfieri never carried out a *Gleichschaltung* of culture on the Nazi model, his three-year tenure did result in greater state control over Italian cultural life. The ministry took over direct management of bodies such as the Istituto LUCE and the Society for Italian Authors and Editors and encompassed five General Directorates (press, propaganda, cinema, tourism, and theater). Alfieri's innovations were welcome news to hundreds of underemployed and unemployed intellectuals. The Propaganda Services Directorate hired many photographers, filmmakers, artists, and architects, and the expanded Press Directorate, headed by Casini, engaged writers, critics, and journalists to censor their colleagues. Its new Book Division alone boasted forty employees who reviewed about seven hundred titles a month.[33]

The more efficient policing of cultural production afforded by this centralization process affected every area of creative life. Recalls and sequestrations increased dramatically for newspapers and periodicals; in April 1937 alone, the press office recalled forty-four daily editions and issued 120 telephonic warnings. That same month, Casini's Book Division ordered publishers to inform the government of all forthcoming books in order to streamline the process of sequestration. As a result, fiction and nonfiction texts not only disappeared from shops and libraries but an increasing number of books never made it to public venues at all.[34] Movie censorship also became more comprehensive. To eliminate unacceptable ideas as early as possible, the regime now required filmmakers to get official approval of their projects before writing the script.[35] The new conditions required intellectuals to become vigilant self-censors if they wished to remain productive members of the fascist cultural community. Alvaro revealed to his diary the toll this practice took on his creative process as a writer and screenwriter: "One sits before a stack of paper and stops oneself, dismayed, at each new vain desire, before giving up entirely."[36]

The strict controls on movies reflected their status as the regime's instrument of choice to fashion a colonial culture and shape public opinion of the Ethiopian War. Propagandists identified three distinct audiences and agendas for colonial films. First, they were to instill in Italians an "imperial and racial consciousness," persuading them to emigrate to East Africa and furnishing guidelines for their behavior once they were there. Second, they would indoctrinate the peoples of East Africa. In the cities, Africans viewed censored versions of Italian feature films, and mobile LUCE projection units screened documentary films and newsreels for rural dwellers.[37] Finally, at a time when Italy faced sanctions from the League of Nations, films that showed the beneficial effects of Italian colonization in Africa might improve the regime's international standing. For all these reasons, after 1936 the regime accorded film an even more prominent role in its strategies of international influence and domestic control. As one journalist reminded his peers, the establishment of empire did not mean that fascists could rest on their laurels; rather, "it has never been more vital or necessary to increase the scope and power of our actions of *observation;* it has never been more important to have a systematic plan designed to *diffuse knowledge* of our truths, ideas, conquests, and achievements. *Getting to know others better; making others know us better;* this is the objective and program of our imperialist cultural politics."[38]

Two films made under government auspices in 1936 shed light on how Italian filmmakers responded to this multiple mandate. Composed of documentary footage shot by LUCE's Africa Unit (fig. 8) and edited by Corrado D'Errico, *Il cammino degli eroi (The Path of the Heroes)* offers a vision of a bloodless war engineered by a highly efficient army of soldier-workers. Interestingly, only two of the film's twelve sections cover the military conflict, which appears as a brief disruption of the fascists' civilizing mission. Instead, we see endless footage of smoothly running machines that produce food, airplane parts, and other necessities of war. The movie celebrates less the conquest of Ethiopians than the conquest of Italians—who, along with the machines they operate, now serve the ends of the regime. D'Errico's heroes are not brave pioneers, as one might expect from the film's title, but faceless laborers who have subjugated their individual desires and identities to suit the needs of the collectivity. D'Errico's vision of war is close to that of Walter Ruttmann and other National Socialist intellectuals who drew on the productivist and rationalizing imperatives of the *Neue Sachlichkeit.*[39]

Figure 8. Istituto LUCE filmmakers shooting a documentary during the Ethiopian War. Reproduced with permission of the Istituto LUCE, Rome.

D'Errico came to colonial filmmaking from the ranks of the theatrical and cinematic avant-garde, and his career offers an example of a journey into totalitarianism completed by some modernists in the interwar period. His first film, a documentary short (*Stramilano,* or *Supermilan,* 1929), resembles the formalist city-films made by Ruttmann and other avant-garde directors. In it, D'Errico utilized split screens and other creative montage techniques to render the multiperspectivist mindset and frenetic rhythms of modern life. Within the director's itinerary as a fascist intellectual, then, *Il cammino degli eroi* may be considered an act of self-discipline. Disavowing an avant-garde vision of modernity as chaos and fragmentation, he presents a vision of reality that is visually and ideologically overdetermined.[40] D'Errico appropriates the Russian Constructivist technique of "baring the device" to illustrate how cinema may further the disciplinary aims of the regime. Devoting an entire sequence to the activities of LUCE cameramen, he shows them shooting the aerial and ground footage that will compose his film. This is not done to expose the fabricated nature of the movie, as would be the case in Constructivism, but rather to emphasize cinema's total integration into the ranks of the regime. Even as the cameramen observe the troops in battle, D'Errico tells audiences, they are themselves being observed by a higher authority. This chain of surveillance and domination ended, of course, with Mussolini, who lost no chance to remind Italian directors of his own uncontested vantage point. In this movie made for an international audience, with intertitles in French and German, D'Errico advertises the domestication of modernism and modernity by the fascist regime.

The moral and political rehabilitation obtained by those who submit to the discipline of a higher cause is also a primary theme of the commercial film *Il grande appello* (*A Call to Arms*, Camerini, 1936). Here, the colonial war becomes a catalyst for the consolidation of the national community and for the redemption of those Italians who had remained outside the fold. Written by Camerini, Piero Solari, and Soldati, the film tracks the transformation of its protagonist, Giovanni, from cynical expatriate to martyr for the national cause. The proprietor of a seedy hotel in the French colonial city of Djibouti, Giovanni symbolizes the ruin that resulted from a rootless cosmopolitan lifestyle. Married to a Spaniard, with a résumé that includes stints in Brooklyn, Brazil, and Shanghai, Giovanni is fluent in English, Spanish, French, German, and Amharic—everything, seemingly, but Italian, a language he has not spoken in twenty years. His hotel, a meeting place for individuals of many peoples and races, is a colonial version of that metropolitan consumerist crossroads—the Milan Trade Fair—which Camerini and Soldati had critiqued in *Gli uomini, che mascalzoni!* four years earlier. Here, Giovanni tends bar as African women and European men flirt in French and Amharic against a backdrop of advertisements for Schweppes beverages and Texaco Motor Oil. Most significantly, Giovanni is a traitor who is arming the Ethiopians even though his son, Enrico, is fighting for the Italian cause. A journey Giovanni makes to Ethiopia occasions a reunion with the culture of his youth. While the hard-nosed Enrico mistrusts him, he is accepted by Italian workers, for whom his heritage is proof enough of his patriotic potential. In their company he drinks Chianti for the first time in decades and sings a long-forgotten Italian song. Touched and tantalized by the prospect of belonging to a genuine community, Giovanni realizes the error of his ways. As the film ends, he blows up a shipment of arms meant for the Ethiopians, fatally injuring himself. A note to his son and his dying words—"Italia!"—let audiences know that his moral transformation is complete.

The brainchild of film official Freddi, *Il grande appello* enjoyed the financial and political support of the Ministry of Press and Propaganda and the Ministries of Colonies, Aeronautics, and War, and it paints a comforting picture of the colonial conflict. As in *Il cammino degli eroi* and *Lo squadrone bianco* (*The White Squadron*, Augusto Genina, 1936), the Ethiopians seem well armed in the battle scenes, and fascist commanders and troops exude humanity and bonhomie. While heavy regional accents underscore their diverse origins, they are linked by common language, customs, and enemies. The movie also supported the government's agendas of national reconciliation by indicting emigration as immoral and unpatriotic. Here the filmmakers clearly drew on Soldati's personal experience. The language Soldati uses to describe Giovanni's odyssey in a prerelease interview strongly recalls his account of his own attempt to emigrate from Italy in *America primo amore*. Like Soldati, Giovanni had given in to his "youthful instincts of evasion"; unlike Soldati, Giovanni had remained abroad until he had lost all national and familial allegiances. Seen in this light, *Il grande appello* is not only a work of colonial propaganda but also a reenactment of Soldati's self-imposed exile and voluntary return. It represents his response to increased official pressures on intellectuals to give up their dreams of cosmopolitanism and serve the fascist state. While Camerini would also express remorse about making this film, there is a double meaning in Soldati's postwar confession. "Although I was never a fascist, *Il grande appello* constitutes my contribution to the regime," the screenwriter would state in 1974. "I too committed an error."[41]

Il grand appello's call for Italians to renounce foreign tastes found a complement in the cultural autarchy policies that followed the conquest of Ethiopia. The advent of League of Nations sanctions in 1935 and Italy's adherence to the Anti-Cominterm Pact two years later ended the policy of purposeful "openness" that had exposed Italians to cultural trends from Los Angeles to Leningrad. In cultural as in economic affairs, autarchy involved the reduction of exports and the substitution of national products and tastes for foreign ones. Although Italian literary and film markets continued to depend heavily on translations and importations, an openly xenophobic atmosphere took hold in the late thirties that further reduced support for cultural tendencies with a foreign flavor. Now, fascist cultural policies aimed to "bring the Italian race back to its authentic origins, freeing it from all pollution."[42]

Government-linked publications communicated the shift in official humors starting in 1936. In a volume written for the INCF, Chiarini warned writers and critics that "supernational European" art no longer had any place under fascism. Using Moravia's *Gli indifferenti* as an example, Chiarini asserted that such "immoral" and "pessimistic" works would no longer receive the indulgent treatment of earlier years. "Fascism refutes and rejects all literary movements of an international character," he intoned. "[It is] a return to the purest Italian tradition." A PNF handbook on fascist culture Bocelli authored that same year underscored how military culture had now become the referent for manifestations of fascist modernity. Eliding years of debates over the influence of the *Neue Sachlichkeit* and other foreign movements on the new Italian novel, Bocelli cited Mussolini's *Diario di guerra* and other works of combat literature as the inspiration for realist works that celebrate "a sense of the concreteness of life." [43]

In other areas of culture as well, intellectuals generated new genealogies for contemporary Italian movements that minimized their connections with European modernism. In a 1938 essay on the history of avant-garde cinema, the critic and film functionary Jacopo Comin minimized the influence of surrealism, expressionism, and other movements on the development of Italian cinema. Similar agendas inspired the writings of Giuseppe Pagano and other architectural authorities, who satisfied autarchic axioms of self-sufficiency by creating a national lineage for rationalism that distanced it from the International Style. Pagano proposed vernacular constructions as emblems of an uninterrupted functionalist tradition in Italy and organized an exhibition of rural architecture for the 1936 Triennale to demonstrate the inherent Italianness of flat roofs, simple white boxes, and other signifiers of architectural modernism (fig. 9).[44]

The proclamation of autarchy also galvanized intellectuals who had long sought to valorize the nationally specific against the internationalizing tendencies of mass culture. Official institutions such as the Italian Academy, the Biennale, and the Triennale supported revivals of those decorative arts that had earned the country acclaim in past centuries. The former Futurist Gino Severini was among those artists and artisans who collaborated with architects to produce mosaics, frescos, and sculptures that would give contemporary buildings an undeniably Italian stamp. Inaugurating a conference on the relationship of architecture and the decorative arts that was attended by Le Corbusier, the Academy official Carlo Formichi asserted that "every people can and must have different desires in art that depend not only on their race but also on their climate and general life conditions. The result is an artistic nationalism that often goes hand in hand with political nationalism and is certainly no less consequential." [45]

Italians did not stand alone in their heightened concerns to protect the local and the particular. In the thirties, democracies as well as dictatorships demonstrated an increased interest in their national heritage, prompting state support for folkloric revivals, mass tourist initiatives, and realist painting styles that displayed local landscapes and physiognomies. French modernists like Le Corbusier and Fernand Léger integrated vernacular, ornamental, and nostalgic elements into their works, repudiating the machine aesthetic's universalizing imperatives. In Nazi Germany, *volkisch*

Figure 9. Rural architecture as Italian modernism. Photograph featured in the 1936 Triennale Exhibition of Rural Architecture and in Giuseppe Pagano, *Architettura rurale italiana* (Milan, 1936). Reprinted with permission of the Biblioteca Nazionale, Rome.

elements now combined with the aesthetics of technology inherited from the *Neue Sachlichkeit*. The Arbeitsstil favored by Paul Bonatz, who designed bridges for the new Autobahns, melded modern building principles with the use of stone and other traditional materials.[46] This desire for differentiation reflected trepidations over cultural standardization as well as the protectionist ethos that overtook depression-era Europe. The shift in mood was captured by Albert Laprade, a cultural official of the French Popular Front. Writing after the 1937 Paris Exposition, he noted that the international and European spirit of earlier years had given way to a focus on the national and the provincial.[47]

In Italy, such sentiments also found support as part of a larger effort to contain the influence of "enemy" ideologies and cultures. Thus the folklore-oriented *cultura popolare* diffused by the regime would protect the Italian heritage, weaning people away from foreign consumer and cultural products. Reviving mosaic making and mural painting would renew Italian traditions, but would also bring artists into the public realm to work "in intimate contact with the people." [48] In his capacity as minister of education, Bottai played an important role in these efforts to nurture the national patrimony. After 1938, his efforts resulted in the establishment of a Central Institute for Restoration and increased funding for artistic, ethnographic, and historic preservation. This culture of conservation developed in tandem with initiatives that would defend Italy from foreign "contamination," most notably anti-Semitic measures by which Bottai intended to curtail Jewish influences on the nation. [49]

As the fate of the fascist campaigns for linguistic and cinematic autarchy demonstrate, the trend toward internationalization in interwar Europe complicated attempts to purge Italian culture of foreign influences. Linguistic reform had long been seen by many officials as a primary means of reshaping collective mentalities, but with over 20 percent of Italians communicating exclusively in dialect as of 1931, the diffusion of Italian remained the main priority of fascist language policies. [50] Purist initiatives also had their place from the start, though, as a means of removing all emblems of foreign influence and ethnic diversity. Starting in the mid-1920s, families of German and Slavic origin had been forced to change their surnames and even modify family tombstones, and foreign words had been banned from public signage. [51] After 1938, purist measures accelerated: the government ordered Italians to use the *Voi* form of address (for the formal *you*) rather than the supposedly Spanish-derived *Lei*, it banned the use of foreign words in advertisements and business titles, and the Italian Academy set up a Commission for the Italianness of the Language in 1941 to provide substitutes for foreign words of common usage in Italian. The absurdity of the commission's recommendations destined this project to failure. Few Italians relished asking for an *arlecchino* or a *coda di gallo* instead of a *cocktail,* and fewer still wished to drink those cocktails in a *bottigliera* rather than a *bar*. Most significantly, the rhetoric of American mass culture had become so entrenched in Italy by World War II that the Academy resigned itself to the permanence of terms like *sport, vaudeville, fox-trot* and *film* in Italian. [52]

Cinema provides another example of the difficulties the regime faced in its efforts to legislate changes in collective tastes. At a time when the fascists faced widespread international reprobation for their seizure of Ethiopia, films were at the forefront of government plans to retain influence through "two peaceful but very powerful weapons: culture and commerce." Officials thus added new emphasis to old requests for movies "of a national character and an international appeal" that would publicize Italian values and ways of life.[53] Arguing that autarchy entailed the valorization of national resources, Freddi and other militants recommended that directors feature the country's photogenic mountains, coastlines, and monuments, as well as the latest products of Italian fashion and design. "Being a nationalist in the cinema is not only an act of faith, but good business as well," one pragmatist concluded.[54] Film authorities also attacked the industry practice of basing Italian movies on foreign texts and asked writers to create original stories for the screen. As the lighting expert and CSC teacher Ernesto Cauda told his peers, an "autarchic cinema" would be possible only if intellectuals committed to a state of "spiritual and artistic hygiene."[55]

A 1938 law that severely reduced the importation of foreign films into Italy offered the most concrete manifestation of the desire for internal purification. This measure, known as the Alfieri law, gave the state a monopoly on the purchase and distribution of foreign films. The resulting taxes on non-Italian movies caused large American houses such as MGM and Paramount to desert the national market. In the words of Mussolini's son, Vittorio, and Chiarini, the law would combat Hollywood's "Jewish-communist center" and "detoxify the public from the subtle poisons of films made in the USA."[56] The law soon cut American profits by a third in a market where, in 1938, forty-odd Italian releases had competed (badly) with over two hundred American films. New government subsidies for domestic films also caused Italian production to double.[57] The appeal of Hollywood, though, resisted policy changes. Italians flocked to see the small-label Westerns and B movies that continued to circulate; high- and low-brow cinema periodicals lavished attention on American studios and stars; and some critics even advised Italian studios to imitate American publicity tactics if they wished to launch their stars with national audiences.[58] To the consternation of officials and militants, French social realist films—associated with leftist sympathies and the Popular Front—also enjoyed a new popularity in Italy after the Alfieri law took effect. Whereas box-office receipts for National Socialist films remained relatively stagnant, they tripled for works such as Marcel Carné's *Le jour se lève (Daybreak)*, which one critic found to be "filmically excellent" but "sick and morbid" in its ideology.[59]

Finally, the internationalism of the film industry also mitigated autarchic tendencies. The opening of the Cinecittà production complex allowed the Italians to lure foreign directors such as Jean Renoir to Italy by offering them favorable working conditions. Rome also became home to refugees from Nazism, such as the Austrian director Max Neufeld, who made fifteen films in Italy between 1938 and 1943, and the German Jewish director Hans Hinrich, who worked despite the presence of fascist anti-Semitic laws. Foreign texts also continued to form the basis for Italian films, despite the contributions of many writers to the national industry. The colonial film *Lo squadrone bianco*, which won the Mussolini Cup of the Biennale Film Show for "best Italian film," was based on the novel *L'Escadron blanc* by the French author Joseph Peyré, who also helped to write the script. Even during World War II, a chain of intertextuality linked many national films to a transnational narrative community. Over one hundred Italian films released between 1940 and 1943 were based on central European theatrical and literary texts, one-quarter of the total production. At the height of fascist protectionism, then, Italy's film industry remained among the most cosmopolitan in Europe.[60]

A different set of cultural exchange networks were occasioned by the Axis alliance, which affected both the structures and content of Italian intellectual life. As we have seen, the fascists had long used cultural activities such as exhibitions and festivals to improve their image and keep open channels of influence to the democratic world. Yet the League of Nations sanctions that followed the Italian invasion of Ethiopia delivered a blow to the "Europeanist" policies of the early thirties. The Italians were shut out of organizations such as the International Committees on Popular Arts and Traditions and lost their leadership role in the International Institute for Educational Cinematography, a League of Nations–linked body, with headquarters on the grounds of Mussolini's Villa Torlonia. Collaborations with the Germans compensated for these exclusions and appealed to more militant fascists as a chance to build a new international order based on antidemocratic principles. Indeed, Mussolini's December 1935 propaganda accord with Hitler came just one month after the declaration of League sanctions. In the coming years, the strengthening of personal ties between the two dictators created many occasions for contact between Italians and German journalists, documentary filmmakers, and writers. A formal cultural agreement was reached in November 1938, and a Italian-German Cultural Commission began work in 1939, when other cultural accords brought Italians together with Japanese and Spanish intellectuals.[61]

The cultural accord offered each regime new markets and audiences for its intellectual and artistic production and created innumerable occasions for travel, work, and recreation between for the two peoples. It provided for mutual language instruction and additional Italian language chairs in German universities, and it established Italian as an approved subject for state examinations in Germany. Exchange programs for university students also multiplied, giving younger Italians a chance to study in Germany; Carlo Azeglio Ciampi (future president and prime minister of Italy) was among those who spent the dramatic year 1938–39 in Berlin. German exhibitions of Italian art also multiplied, and the German presence increased at the Biennale art and film shows. The cinema became a primary site of cross-cultural collaborations. Camerini and other filmmakers traveled to Nazi Germany and Franco's Spain for coproductions or new versions of Italian films, and Germans and Spaniards shot dozens of movies in Italy. In 1942, the film show was rebaptized as the Italian-German Cinema Exhibition.[62] The Dante Alighieri Society, like the National Institute for Fascist Culture, sent Italian classicists, folklorists, and other scholars to speak in Germany, and the Istituto di Europa Giovane, like the Istituto di Studi Germanici, invited Nazi intellectuals to Rome. Although Nazi literature never aroused the same interest in Italy as the novels of the *Neue Sachlichkeit*, Italian and German writers also interacted at readings and lunches. Animating many of these collective endeavors was the sense of weaving a cultural fabric that would support the spread of a new civilization on the continent. Thus Casini referred to Axis exchanges as events "destined to decide the future of Europe . . . and the course of history.[63]

Within this whirl of comradely activity, the multimedia frenzy occasioned by Hitler's May 1938 visit to Italy stands out. One hundred and twenty filmmakers, artists, and photographers worked overtime for the Istituto LUCE, producing fifty thousand postcards, thirty thousand photographs, and dozens of newsreels that celebrated the Führer's visits to Rome, Naples, and Florence. These cities were adorned with displays of flags, banners, and lights artfully crafted by architects and set designers, and Hitler was showered with more than twenty important gifts from royal and political authorities. Intellectuals who wished to secure a foothold in the cultural life of the new Europe vied for invitations to banquets, concerts, and art openings; 150 of them attended a reception in Hitler's honor in Florence. Along with the other ceremonials of the culture of Italian-German collaboration, this special occasion was conveniently forgotten after World War II.[64]

Two works of 1937–38 testify to the range of reactions provoked among intellectuals by the regime's new cultural and foreign-policy directives. Barbaro's film *L'ultima nemica (The Last Enemy)* and Alvaro's novel *L'uomo è forte (Man Is Strong)* are both highly topical texts that performed in the service of, respectively, the regime's imperialist and anticommunist agendas. Yet they may also be read as public meditations on the destiny of the Italian intellectual class under fascism and the place of the individual under a dictatorship. Although the authors' conclusions reflect their diverse political provenances (communism for Barbaro, liberalism for Alvaro) both of these works play on the ideological lability of the notion that the state should have a primary role in the remaking of collective morality and behavior.

Through the experiences of Franco, an Italian tropical disease specialist, *L'ultima nemica* points out the national advantages to be gained by a culture of state intervention that manages and funds intellectual endeavors. As in Matarazzo's 1933 movie *Treno popolare*, discussed in chapter 3, the state appears as a paternal force that places the resources of modernity at Italians' disposal in return for increased obedience and discipline. In Matarazzo's movie, made during the consolidation of mass mobilization programs, progress allows the regime to nationalize Italians; in Barbaro's film, made soon after the proclamation of an Italian empire, it also instills an international consciousness that will extend Italian influence throughout the world.

As in so many fascist texts, the trope of *bonifica*—remaking the individual and his or her environment—drives the narrative forward and structures its plot. Positing a parallel between the *bonifica agricola* and the *bonifica umana*, Barbaro and his cowriter, Francesco Pasinetti, set their characters' interior journeys against a landscape that changes from malarial marshes in the liberal period (the film begins in 1920) to a modern New Town in the present. The chain-smoking bourgeois and diseased prostitutes who populate the film's early scenes convey a sense of an unhealthy society that neglects its human resources. The state provides no support for scientific research, so that Franco's experiments share space with bread crusts in his living room. When his kitchen-counter methods of practicing science lead to the death of a former prostitute, who infects herself with Tasmanian fever in his home, Franco's mentor denounces his lack of discipline but can do nothing to better his working conditions.

The film then jumps to the fascist period and a new era of state support for scientific activities. Franco's mentor is able to invite him to an International Congress of Tropical Diseases held in the Italian capital and give him a state job in the sleek, modernist quarters of the University of Rome's new Institute for Tropical Diseases. Barbaro highlights Italy's newly global reach and heightened prestige in a scene where visiting Japanese functionaries express their esteem for Franco's work.[65] When his old love, Anna, a rich and spoiled young widow, contracts Tasmanian fever while cruising the Indian Ocean, Franco tests his vaccine and also demonstrates "recent Italian inventions" in communications and medical technology. By the end of the film, Anna regains her health and has a moral reawakening, intimating that modern science, helped by the fascist state, can cure diseases of both body and soul. The film advertises the achievements of fascist modernity in other ways as well. As it moves from the liberal to the fascist period, dizzyingly eclectic sets are replaced with a rigorous Rationalist aesthetic that communicates hygiene and efficiency. Exterior shots show only the revamped University of Rome and the clean lines of Littoria, a New Town reclaimed from the Pontine marshes, while indoor scenes advertise functional Italian designs (such as convertible sofa beds, which we see in action) that had been introduced at the 1936 Triennale.[66]

One of the foremost authorities on Soviet culture in fascist Italy, Barbaro had always sympathized with the revolutionary aims of communism. It is not surprising, then, that the totalitarian transformations envisioned in this film converge at many points with communist schemes of collective renewal. The movie's many references to the achievements of Mussolini's era, though, made it easy for Chiarini and others to present it as a profascist text. *L'ultima nemica* certainly sent an unambiguous message about the benefits of state intervention in the modernization process. In Barbaro's 1931 novel *Luce fredda*, examined in chapter 2, Sergio wished for a Rationalist-style house that would help him become a more disciplined individual. Instead, he ended up asleep and unredeemed in his grungy boardinghouse room. By 1937, in line with Barbaro's own progressive immersion in government film structures, Sergio has metamorphosed into Franco, a limpid and infection-free modern subject who works in streamlined surroundings provided by the fascist patron-state. Barbaro often told his students at the CSC that films were "the most powerful taste-shaping instruments that humanity possesses." With this movie, he advertised a model of modernity founded on totalitarian transparency. The "last enemy" referred to in the film's title is not only tropical disease but the residues of a bourgeois individualism—nemesis of both fascism and communism—that might obstruct the internalization of state disciplinary norms (fig. 10).[67]

Alvaro's novel *L'uomo è forte* offers a quite different view of the individual-state relationship and of interwar experiments in social engineering and state taste formation. Set in Stalinist Russia, it evokes a nightmarish world of paranoia and betrayal similar to that of Arthur Koestler's contemporaneously written work *Darkness at Noon*. Possessing none of Barbaro's spirit of revolutionary optimism, Alvaro suggests that the desire to produce a "new humanity" can lead instead to humanity's destruction.

Figure 10. Umberto Barbaro during the filming of *L'ultima ne-mica*. *Cinema*, June 10, 1937. Reprinted with permission of the Biblioteca Nazionale, Rome.

The narrative revolves around the actions of Dale, an engineer who returns to his native country after fifteen years abroad. There, he resumes a relationship with Barbara, a radio technician, only to become a target of state inquisitors who wish to destroy "all that is private, personal, and intimate." When the couple's fear and guilt cause them to view "every act, every touch, every word" as a possible crime, they are ripe to become puppets in the hands of the state.[68] Barbara denounces Dale to the authorities, and Dale becomes an informer who is then himself driven to commit crimes in the name of the new collective morality. He kills his boss—a first-hour revolutionary, like Koestler's Rubashov—giving the state an excuse to "impose order" through a purge. Too late, Dale realizes that he has become part of a system that aims to make all men and women criminals to justify its own criminality. At the novel's end, he is planning his escape.

Alvaro's indictment of Stalinism in *L'uomo è forte* is also an attack on the evils of mass society. As in his 1935 book of Russian reportage, Soviet society stands for a collectivist modernity that suffocates individuality and demands a total rupture with past traditions and ideals. Long-standing anxieties about modernity's destructive potential that inform all of Alvaro's writing are given a new political context and form. The rootless crowd of prior works becomes a howling mob whose murderous humors are literally infectious. Describing a group of Russian agitators, Alvaro writes that "their cries seemed like groans of pain; the women yelled as though taken by a ferocious pleasure; as if on a gigantic body belonging to everyone, the crowd's movements left repugnant growths and tumors that nourished its screams." [69] Bringing decades of pessimism about mass society into focus, Alvaro produces an apocalyptic vision of a pathological society that admits of no bond outside that which links the individual to the state.

Alvaro's denunciation of Soviet tyranny came at an opportune moment. Anticommunist diatribes had increased in the fascist press due to the Spanish Civil War, Italy's upcoming adherence to the Anti-Cominterm Pact, and the work of a new anticommunist propaganda section within the Ministry of Popular Culture. Following suit, Italian critics received *L'uomo è forte* well on ideological and artistic grounds and saluted it as a searing portrait of the contemporary Russian soul.[70] Still, Alvaro's contemporaries could hardly ignore the signals his tale sent about the nature of their own political enterprise. The inquisitioner's dreams of constructing a "new world" and a "new race" closely resemble the utopian aspirations of the Italian fascists and the Nazis, while a scene in which young intellectuals are branded as counterrevolutionaries for translating foreign literary works clearly comments on fascism's own autarchic atmosphere. That Alvaro felt almost as oppressed as the characters in his novel is clear from a 1936 diary entry in which he confesses that "day by day, relationships and friendships come to an end. You hear that someone has spread a rumor about you. . . . So now you could be a police informer or someone who associates with shady elements. In any case you too are now someone to be avoided. So you avoid others as well. Even family ties suffer if they are not strong. And in despising others, one comes to despise oneself."[71]

To head off possible "misreadings" of *L'uomo è forte*, censors ordered Alvaro to include a prefatory note that let readers know the book was about Russia. Yet the novelist's statement there of his reasons for writing the

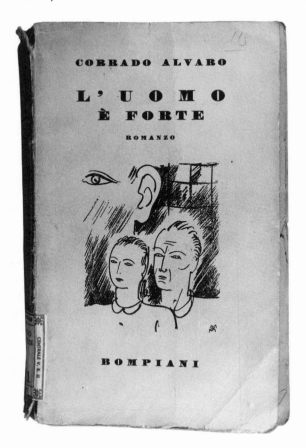

Figure 11. The eyes and ears of the totalitarian state. Cover of Corrado Alvaro's *L'uomo è forte*, 1938. Reprinted with permission of the Biblioteca Nazionale, Rome.

work—"I wished to describe the condition of man in a state of terror"— only underscored his narrative's universalizing implications. Interestingly, some publicity for the book, as well as an early cover, played on the ambiguity of Alvaro's antitotalitarian message. A November 1938 ad in the review *Omnibus* consisted only of the book's title and the phrase "there's someone listening," and the cover drawing of a 1938 edition showed a large ear hovering over the heads of Dale and Barbara (figs. 11 and 12). The book also catered to the culture of self-deception that existed among Italians,

Figure 12. Advertisement for Corrado Alvaro's *L'uomo è forte* in *Omnibus*, October 8, 1938. Reprinted with permission of the Biblioteca Nazionale, Rome.

however, by depicting the infringement of personal liberties as characteristic of "foreign" regimes. As we have seen, Alvaro and other intellectuals had long maintained that fascism protected the individual against the leveling effects of Russian communism and American consumer capitalism.[72] In the coming years, as anti-Jewish measures gave a new and terrible twist to campaigns for national purification, the specter of Stalinist brutality would help to quiet restless consciences by reassuring Italians that things were not that bad at home.

ARYANS AND OTHERS: THE FASCIST WAR AGAINST THE JEWS

As we have seen, racial thinking had informed Italian fascist doctrines since the first decade of the regime. Building on fears sparked by declines in European fertility, it had a place in the crisis ideologies that proved so persuasive to many Italian intellectuals. The conquest of Ethiopia gave a new focus to these diffused anxieties and produced a slew of official efforts meant to inculcate a "racial consciousness" that would combat miscegenation and ensure the smooth workings of colonial domination. Anti-Semitism, in contrast, had little or no place in fascist doctrine before 1938, reflecting the Italian Jewish community's relatively pacific existence on the peninsula. The tiny size of the country's Jewish population (about 44,000 out of 44 million), the frequency of intermarriage, the physiognomic and cultural similarities that linked Italians of Catholic and Jewish faiths, and the absence of popular anti-Semitic violence had allowed the Jews to enjoy a relatively harmonious existence in Italy throughout the liberal period.[73]

Before and after Hitler's rise to power, Mussolini had publicly rejected credos of biological racism as utopian and ahistorical and had authorized a public attack against Nazi racial doctrines in 1933–34. We should be cautious in interpreting this as a denunciation of anti-Jewish sentiments, however, since anti-Semites like Longanesi, Maccari, and Ricci participated in the campaign.[74] More than any support for Jews, fascist antiracism of the early thirties reflected the Duce's desire to portray Italian fascism as different and superior to the ideas being propagated by the parvenu Hitler. During twenty years of rule, Mussolini's attitudes toward the Jews were guided by a similar pragmatism. When he felt that the Jews would help him attain his domestic and foreign policy goals, he was for them; when the Axis alliance led him to perceive the Jews as an obstacle to reaching those goals, he did not hesitate to turn against them.[75]

Just two months after the formation of the Rome-Berlin Axis, in fact, Mussolini published the first a series of anonymous interventions that set the tone for the dictatorship's new attitude toward Italian Jews. Dismissing centuries of historical and theological debate, the Duce explained that "anti-Semitism is inevitable wherever there is exaggerated Semitic visibility, interference, and arrogance. The excessive Jew gives rise to the anti-Jew [*Il troppo ebreo fa nascere l'antiebreo*]."[76] Mussolini's remarks unveiled the new rhetoric of Axis Italy to the international community but also anticipated the different attitudes and aims that separated the Italian and the German racial campaigns. For Mussolini and most of his officials, unlike the Nazis, national prerogatives almost always took precedence over racial ones, and fascist anti-Jewish measures were envisioned as an addition to existing social engineering programs that aimed to solve nagging questions about Italian unity and strength. The removal of *il troppo ebreo* (literally, the overly Jewish) from Italian society mandated qualitative as well as quantitative changes in the national collective. The Italians sought less to eradicate Jews entirely from society, as did the Nazis, than to coerce changes in those Jewish behaviors and customs that had long frustrated Italian and Catholic fantasies about a total Jewish assimilation.[77]

Departing from this premise, I argue in this section that, although anti-Jewish policies were modeled on the Nazi Nuremberg laws, they also built on and responded to national issues and traditions. First, as Carl Ipsen has contended, anti-Semitic policies must be seen in the context of a series of official demographic measures that aimed to create a race of hardy conquerors and childbearers.[78] Second, they were an important, if not inevitable, outcome of fascist projects for a model of modern existence that would protect Italy's autochthonous traditions. Third, they provide another example of the fascist intent to mobilize state resources to cure the national collective of tendencies and traits that had supposedly contributed in the past to Italian "backwardness" and national fragmentation. The Jew emerged after 1938 as a primary symbol of the forces that had consigned Italy to a position on the margins of modernity. The fascist anti-Semitic campaign shared images and legal provisions with other countries and reflected Mussolini's desire to remain at the forefront of Axis Europe's "new order," but it also offered an occasion for the articulation of specifically Italian grievances and goals.

The "Manifesto of Racial Scientists," which appeared in the fascist press on Bastille Day 1938, signaled the start of the official anti-Semitic campaign. Written by the Duce in collaboration with a group of scholars, the manifesto established an irremediable divide between Jews and Italians. The former were now defined as an "unassimilable population composed of non-European racial elements," and the latter as a "pure" people of Aryan origin and civilization. While the document warned that Italian racism recognized only racial differences, as against German ideals of racial superiority, it legitimized anti-Semitic prejudice by inviting Italians to "proclaim themselves openly racist."[79] In subsequent communications, the Duce proclaimed his intention to "adjust" Jewish participation in the state to reflect Jews' minority status, even as he admonished his audience that "discrimination does not mean persecution."[80]

A September decree marked the start of this discrimination process. It forbade Jews to teach or attend schools and universities (those currently enrolled in postsecondary schools were allowed to finish their degrees) and expelled them from academies and cultural institutions. This decree brought the Minister of Education Bottai out of the closet as an anti-Semite whose intransigence surprised even Ciano (who had himself confessed that he cared little for Jews). Publicizing the names of Jewish professors who had been terminated, Bottai's ministerial bulletin, *Vita universitaria*, expressed its "unconditional admiration" for a measure that would "liberate us from a treacherous people, rejuvenate the University, and purify the race." [81] Over the next year, further provisions modeled on the Nuremberg laws restricted Jews' earning potential and policed their public and private activities.[82] A bureaucratic apparatus dedicated to the implementation of racial policy also emerged, centered on the Interior Ministry's new General Directorate for Demography and Race. Demorazza, as it became known, provided employment to journalists and to scholars who had failed to find a foothold in the university system, and hired other intellectuals for consulting jobs and publishing ventures.[83] To underscore the primacy of nation over race in Italian doctrine, exceptions were granted for proven patriots and others Jews of "exceptional merit," and the juridical category of "Aryanized Jew" exempted politically meritorious and appropriately "non-Jewish" Jews.[84]

This was small consolation to Italian Jewish intellectuals, for whom the racial laws meant the sudden loss of jobs, friendships, and community ties. They especially shocked prominent fascist intellectuals such as Margherita Sarfatti, the corporativist expert Gino Arias, and the composer Renzo Massarani, all of whom emigrated to South America.[85] While these elites, and internationally known scholars such as Arnaldo Momigliano and Enrico Fermi, managed to leave the country, most intellectuals were not so fortunate. The literary community was particularly hard hit, due to Casini's concurrent campaign to "take Jewish writers out of circulation" by prohibiting them from publishing their works (the *bonifica del libro*). Although exemptions were eventually made for "classic interpreters of the human spirit," critics would rarely touch books by Jewish authors. In the face of these restrictions, writers depended on help from their "Aryan" colleagues, who arranged ghostwriting jobs and pseudonymous collaborations in the cinema and the press. Giorgio Bassani, whose novel *Il giardino dei Finzi-Contini (The Garden of the Finzi-Continis,* 1962) describes the awful effects of the Italian racial laws, adopted a semiunderground existence as he embraced antifascist politics and the pen name Giorgio Marchi. Moravia had Aryan status (his mother was Catholic, and he had been baptized), but he became a target of virulent anti-Semitic diatribes anyway. In 1941, the government banned any reviews of his new novel, *La mascherata (The Masked Ball)*, which will be discussed below, and forbade the printing of a second edition. He began to write under the name of Pseudo, and worked uncredited on several films. Jewish-owned publishing firms had to take on new names and remove Jewish writers from their lists. Treves thumbed its nose at officials by calling itself T.R.E.V.E.S., but the house of Formiggini came to a tragic end: Angelo Formiggini jumped off the Ghirlandina Tower in Modena, prompting the PNF secretary Starace to remark that Formiggini "died like a Jew—he threw himself off a tower to save the cost of a bullet."[86]

As in Nazi Germany, state anti-Jewish provisions also created numerous occasions for displays of opportunism and conformism among the intellectual class. While many members of Italy's cultural community greeted the news of the racial laws with horror, none resigned from the institutes and academies that their Jewish colleagues were forced to abandon, and very few refused collaborations with or awards from papers and agencies engaged in anti-Semitic propaganda. Alvaro noted his protector Sarfatti's fall from grace in his diary with evident unease, but turned his back on her in the wake of his success with *L'uomo è forte*. A year later, he accepted a lucrative Mussolini Prize from the virulently anti-Jewish Italian Academy.[87] Other intellectuals, including the supposedly philo-Semitic Marinetti, aided racist initiatives such as Casini's Commission for the Reclamation of the Book Industry (*Commissione per la Bonifica Libraria*), which aimed at purging Jewish influences from Italian literary culture. Finally, Italians also besieged the Ministry of National Education with requests for the secondary school and university posts that Jews had been forced to vacate. Such jobs became valuable capital in the hands of education minister Bottai, who used them to consolidate his patronage relations. When the writer Bontempelli refused Bottai's offer of Attilio Momigliano's chair in Italian literature at the University of Florence, his show of conscience angered officials. After giving a public speech that augured the rebirth of "ideals of good, friendship, concord, abnegation, intelligence, chivalry, piety, in sum humanity as liberty and poetry," Bontempelli found himself expelled temporarily from the PNF.[88]

If anti-Semitism became an ordinary component of many visions of a fascist modernity after 1938, then a great deal of the responsibility lies with the intellectual class. Like other directives of the dictatorship, the racial laws were interpreted, debated, and disseminated to millions of Italians by journalists, writers, archeologists, musicologists, folklorists, historians, and other cultural authorities. Joined by new "racial experts," established intellectuals pontificated in print, on the radio, and in public lectures

Figure 13. Racial education. Lecture by a university professor, "How We Defend the Race," January 14, 1939, Rome. Reproduced with permission of the Istituto LUCE, Rome.

funded by the OND, the Dante Alighieri Society, the INCF, and other institutions (fig. 13). The culture of racism also produced its own university chairs, as well as periodicals such as *Difesa della razza, Razza e civiltà,* and *Il diritto razzista.* Anti-Semitism was also front-page news in the *Corriere della sera* and other established dailies.[89] Even *Difesa della razza,* which embraced biological racism on the German model, was sponsored by Bottai's Ministry of National Education, and its editors (also the authors of the "Manifesto of Racial Scientists") all held full-time positions within the Italian university system.[90] Long excused as the product of German pressure, or marginalized as the work of an extremist fringe, anti-Jewish propaganda was a normal component of Italian fascist culture and a routine category in the résumé of Italian fascist intellectuals in the last five years of the regime.

Nor was Catholic culture extraneous to the diffusion of anti-Jewish doctrines and policies. Catholic intellectuals could take their cues from the pronouncements of Church officials, who delivered decidedly mixed messages that accorded well on several central points with the position of the fascist government. A month before the promulgation of the racial laws, Pius XI asked why "Italy has made the disgraceful decision to imitate Germany," and he subsequently lodged repeated private protests with the fascist government. Yet, as would Pius XII, he showed caution in directly criticizing the regime's racial policies in public and saved his strongest pronouncements for the foreign press and for condemnations of Nazi-style biological racism of the sort that many Italian fascists rejected as well.[91] More damaging at the grassroots level were the ambivalent positions of the Catholic press and Italian clergy, many of whom had long wished for a greater rate of Jewish assimilation. They condemned German racism for its materialism and determinism but gave the basic goal of Italian racial policies—limiting Jewish influence and encouraging conversion—their public support. The Vatican daily, *L'Osservatorio romano*, reasoned that restrictions on Jewish liberty had been routine for centuries and reassured its readers that Jewish treatment by the fascist state would not be worse than that meted out by popes in the past.[92]

Still, there were many ways to be a racist in fascist Italy, and not all of them implied the embrace of anti-Semitic sentiments. The word race (*razza*) had long been used in Italian as a synonym for people (*popolo*), nation (*nazione*), and stock (*stirpe*). Before and after 1938, folklorists, demographers, and social welfare experts used it in reference to campaigns to increase the population and protect popular traditions. Slippage between the terms *race* and *stock* was particularly common, since most Italian fascists viewed race as an spiritual identity based on common history, language, and traditions rather than on a community of blood as in the Nordic racist school. The lability of the word *race* allowed intellectuals who may not have been anti-Semites to take part in the regime's racist subculture and gain credit for toeing the line.[93]

This stated, it is important to consider what needs the racial ideologies did fulfill under fascism. For if Italian racism borrowed much from Nazi Germany, it also reflected national concerns. Indeed, the delineation of a peculiarly "Italian" brand of racial thought, which conceived of race as a mostly cultural and spiritual construct, became a point of pride for fascists who wished to assert their autonomy within the Axis alliance. For many fascist intellectuals, race proved most compelling as a rubric under which ongoing discussions about Italian national identity and modernity found new expression. A site where diachronic and synchronic issues coalesced, racial discourse answered long-term worries about Italian "backwardness" and lack of national integration, as well as interwar anxieties about the erosion of national and racial boundaries. It represented the culmination of a strain of fascist thinking that aimed to forge an Italian mass society purged of all degenerate influences.

First, the characterization of Italians as a homogeneous Aryan people responded to historic concerns about Italy's supposedly "weak" national identity. Before World War I, with his usual bluntness the writer Giovanni Papini had reminded his peers that the country's eclectic ethnic profile made it difficult to define an essential Italian identity. Reflecting on the many conquerors who had sojourned on Italian soil, Papini asked, "in all this flow of names and glories, how do we distinguish between . . . the autochthonous and the imported[;] . . . what merits inclusion and what must be extirpated; the eternal and the transitory; the Italian and the non-Italian?"[94] Prior to 1938, fascist ideologues had responded to this challenge by arguing that the Italian people constituted a superior distillation of the genetic and cultural offerings of the Romans, Etruscans, Greeks, Normans, and other past colonizers. "Italians can boast of being the result of all the races, perfectly fused into a national unity of clear, precise, and easily recognizable traits," asserted Luca Dei Sabelli in a 1929 INCF-sponsored study on nations and ethnic minorities. Although Dei Sabelli observed that European Jewish communities often stood apart from this fusion process, remaining "closed groups, inviolable islands within society," he complimented Italian Jews for their "full solidarity" with the nation and for their willingness to "make the passage to Catholicism."[95]

The onset of the anti-Semitic laws and the campaign for Italian "Aryanization" both built on and modified such views. Italians reacted sharply to occasional assertions by Nazi ideologues that "Negro blood" was common in southern and central Italy, and argued that any "foreign" influences had long since been absorbed into an Italic culture of "purely European physical and psychological characteristics." Moreover, Italian Jews were now grouped with others of their race who refused to assimilate into their "host societies." This racist rewriting of the national past not only placed a comforting gloss of genetic continuity on Italian history but justified the exclusion of the one remaining "extra-European" group within state boundaries on ethnic and cultural as well as biological grounds.[96]

Second, the racial laws represented the culmination of a tradition of blaming internal Others for Italy's supposed backwardness and subordinate position in the hierarchy of European nations. These concerns had traditionally received expression in discussions of the Italian South, which had been marked as a realm of primitivity and deviancy since the Risorgimento period.[97] By heightening fears about degeneration, the Ethiopian War created new occasions for the airing of such sentiments, which found expression, however, only in diaries, government memos, and other private notations. Indeed, fascism's nationalizing imperatives mandated the suppression of antisouthern rhetoric from public discourse, leaving the door open for other groups to assume the discursive burdens of the internal enemy. After 1938, the Jew took on this function, becoming a repository for all the negative qualities and tendencies—individualism, criminality, lack of martial feeling—that had long been used to characterize southern Italians, and that had long formed part of foreigners' stereotypes of Italians as a whole. Reconfigured as "Aryans," the racial theorist Giulio Cogni reasoned, the Italians would no longer be seen as "short and dark singing simpletons[,] . . . blasphemous bandits with brown faces and assassins' eyes": Jews now had a monopoly on that image instead. Depictions of Jews as atavistic and criminal forces inside the nation were the stock-in-trade of anti-Semitic propaganda everywhere in Europe. Among Italians who were haunted by the specter of backwardness, the racial laws may have had a vindicatory as well as a unifying function.[98]

Third, fascist anti-Semitism addressed issues of the erosion of racial barriers that had grown more urgent with the invasion of Ethiopia. The antimiscegenationist rhetoric that accompanied the Italian colonial enterprise was extended to Jews once they too were defined as a non-European race. Indeed, official pronouncements on racial issues considered the anti-Semitic measures and colonial legislation together as measures designed to ensure that Italians' Aryan and European characteristics would "not be altered in any way." Both the Grand Council's "Declaration on Race," and Mussolini's Trieste speech in the fall of 1938 spoke of the anti-Jewish laws as part of a larger effort to create a "racial consciousness" that would allow Italians to avoid "bastardization" as their empire expanded throughout the world.[99]

Fourth, the anti-Jewish legislation expressed anxieties proper to the interwar period about the erosion of national identities. Annexed onto existing autarchic impulses, racist rhetoric that inveighed against the Jew as the "incarnation of the international" fueled the fires of those who had long wished to cleanse Italian society of foreign and modernist influences. In the early thirties, as we have seen, functionaries such as Casini and Chiarini had been wary about younger intellectuals' attempts to create a fascist culture in line with modernist trends. By 1938, the review *Cinema* saluted the racial campaign as a reaction against "a cosmopolitanism that only neutralized our ethnic and racial resources," and Casini had begun a crusade (the *bonifica della cultura*) to purge Italy of a culture "led by Jews or by

Jewish sympathizers . . . without countries, ideals, or traditions." In this context, the concept of race performed as a safe house for putatively "national" customs, behaviors, and psychological traits. It expressed fantasies of wholeness in an era of increasing pluralism, and dreams of permanence when everything seemed in a state of continual crisis and change.[100]

The attribution of "Jewish" qualities to modernism spurred the Futurist Marinetti and other champions of modern culture to begin a debate in the fall of 1938 that revealed the extent of anti-Semitic sentiments among certain members of the intellectual class. Marinetti, Ricci, Bottai, and others who defended the cause of modern art made use of stock anti-Semitic stereotypes and prejudices to claim that Jews had had no influence on the development of Italian modernism. Marinetti emphasized that Jews' talents lay in the commercial rather than the creative sphere, while both he and Ricci asserted that Jews lacked the audacity of spirit that marked true aesthetic innovators. "The Jew does not make his own revolutions: he merely climbs onto those made by others," Ricci intoned. Claiming that Jews "have never managed to corrode our traditions," Bottai constructed a Christian genealogy for Italian art and culture and called for a "revision of the principles and intuitions of modern art through the lens of racism." After World War II, amid a general amnesia about the racist element within fascist culture, the positions taken by these men and their allies in favor of modern art would be taken as evidence of their philo-Semitism. In reality, their attempt to sever any association between modern art and the Jews played into the culture of Italian racism. It formed part of an ongoing fascist strategy to develop a model of Italian modernity free from all degenerative or foreign elements. It is no accident that Bottai chose that moment to publish an editorial that justified the exclusion of Jews from fascist culture as a means of "cleaning up" a national body that had been soiled by an "invisible atmosphere [and] fluid mass."[101]

Indeed, racism represented the most radical initiative of the fascist project of remaking Italians as a way of regenerating the Italian nation. Coinciding with the 1938 "reform of custom" and antibourgeois polemics, the racial crusade may be considered the cruelest means by which the state intended to "revolutionize" Italian society by transforming collective morals and behaviors. As the former syndicalist Luigi Fontanelli argued in 1938, fascist racial policies would not only discipline the Jews but strike at all those "gray zones" that sheltered the remnants of bourgeois corruption and liberal life.[102] Certainly, not all Italian intellectuals who championed the regime's social revolution supported the regime's racial policies; for some, such as Bilenchi, the racial laws occasioned a definitive break with the regime.[103] Yet it is not surprising that many other members of the *L'Universale* group reemerged in the late 1930s as exponents of a totalitarian program of renewal that conflated Jews and bourgeois as carriers of corruption. For the former *L'Universale* collaborator Alberto Luchini, now head of the MCP's Race Office, the Jew, like the bourgeois, constituted a "moral cancer" that undermined fascism's work of "renewing the nation . . . and reconstructing the world" on the basis of a purified and improved Italian race. Since fascism was a "way of being" rather than a mere political party, only the Jew who had been Aryanized could, along with the reformed bourgeois and the rehabilitated deviant, claim a place under Mussolini's dictatorship.[104]

That racism became one more means of advancing the fascist revolution's therapeutic and disciplinary imperatives is evident from an important speech Mussolini gave to the PNF's National Council in October 1938. In it, he cited the reform of custom, the antibourgeois campaign, and the racial legislation directed at Jews and Africans as individual elements of a comprehensive strategy of eradicating attitudes and behaviors that in the past had relegated Italy to the rank of secondary power. The goose step would build physical endurance, while the abolition of the *Lei* form of address would be a sign of the end of servility to foreign ways. The racial laws would end a shameful "inferiority complex" caused by the lack of national unity and a racial identity. In a dazzling display of deductive logic, Mussolini told his officials that "we are not Camites, Semites, or Mongols. And if we are none of these races, we are evidently Aryans, and we came from the Alps, from the North. We are therefore Aryans of the pure Mediterranean type." Armed with this knowledge, he argued, Italians could manifest their "racial dignity" and fulfill their function as colonizers. On the home front, too, the Italians must act as conquerors; any sympathy shown toward Jews was out of place.[105] From the mid-1930s on, then, official visions of fascist modernity hinged not only on the creation of obedient soldiers and willing child bearers but also on the relentless cultivation of a culture of command that would allow Italians to assume a dominant position in the world.

POLITICS AND IDENTITY IN FASCIST YOUTH CULTURE, 1936–39

The transformation of Italian society in the wake of the German alliance and the racial laws met with mixed reactions among those who were to serve as fascism's next ruling elite. Many young intellectuals who had lived under

Mussolini's rule for most of their lives greeted most new developments after 1936 with enthusiasm, including the laws against Italian Jews. A smaller group found their fervor diminishing, replaced with anxiety about their futures in an increasingly uncertain economic and international climate. As military life became the referent for official visions of fascist mass society, and Nazi Germany replaced Weimar Germany as the official touchstone for cultural trends, some young intellectuals began to wonder about fascism's ideological orientation and their role within the regime. A few worried that the government's policy of "making way for youth" now meant that they would be used as frontline cannon fodder, while others lost their martial zeal at the prospect of fighting the Nazis' battles. The indefinite goals of the Italian-German alliance and Italy's Spanish involvement also deepened a generational identity crisis that had been brewing since the start of the decade. "Who are we anyway?" asked one young Italian in August 1937. "Against whom do we struggle? If we stay in the ranks they condemn us, but where do they want to send us next?" That same summer, an informer confirmed the "discontentment" that prevailed among many Italians in their twenties. "We are talking about youth who have lived under fascism since birth, and have grown up in an atmosphere of nationalism and patriotism," the spy wrote with an perplexed air.[106]

This slow burn of resentment spread further among the ranks of some young intellectuals throughout 1938. A year marked by Hitler's takeover of Austria, the Munich crisis, the Kristallnacht pogrom, and the onset of the Italian anti-Jewish laws, 1938 proved to be a turning point in some younger Italians' relations with the regime as well. The "notable dampening of fascist faith" that informers observed among Milanese high school and university students in January became a nationwide "hostility to the Rome-Berlin Axis" following the Anschluss in March 1938. After students booed newsreels and lectures on Nazism, GUF organizations were banned from public rallies when Hitler visited Italy two months later.[107] For young Jewish fascists and some of their Catholic comrades, the racial laws provided further proof that fascism had abandoned its attempts to install a new social and moral order. Bottai's sudden conversion from corporativism to racism, along with the government's new campaign against modern art, left some of his former clients feeling bitter and betrayed. In September 1938, as the laws against the Jews were announced in the press, the young critic Giulia Veronesi commented on the moral dilemmas now faced by her and her peers: "Each one of us lives timid and uncertain in the midst of this deepening discomfort: we hardly recognize each other. We'd like to justify the compromise in which we live to ourselves, but at root there is also the question of our cowardice, and how can we justify that? . . . It seems that we must begin everything again, in solitude, without indulgences or concessions." [108]

In the majority of these cases, disillusionment did not translate into antifascism but led to a process of detachment or depoliticization that was neither linear nor steady in its psychological and political trajectory. Many youth repudiated certain developments within fascism, such as the alliance with Hitler, but continued to identify strongly with Mussolini. Most followed complex and sometimes tortured itineraries as they grappled with a rapidly changing political climate and the contrasting messages they received from family, peers, the mass media, and their own consciences. The twenty-five-year-old writer Vasco Pratolini, editor of the Florentine youth review *Campo di Marte,* had since adolescence embraced fascism as a populist and modernizing force. As late as 1937, writing in the PNF review *Il Bargello,* he had celebrated the conquest of Ethiopia and fascism's forging of a "social and revolutionary conscience." By October 1938, though, in an atmosphere of anti-Semitism and cultural autarchy, Pratolini announced that his age-group harbored "a troubled desire to discern, to take another look, to 'document ourselves' on the *reality* of doctrines, ideologies, actions as a means of clarifying the basis of a joint truth." [109]

Two novels by members of Pratolini's cohort, Moravia's *La mascherata* (*The Masked Ball,* written 1939; published 1941) and Paola Masino's *Nascita e morte della massaia (Birth and Death of the Housewife),* written 1938–39; published 1945), convey the increased sense of oppression some young intellectuals felt in the late thirties. Both works comment on fascism from a generational point of view, denouncing the deleterious psychological and moral effects produced by its aggressive campaigns of collective socialization. Moravia and Masino also use satire to puncture the aura of power that protected Italian authorities, depicting the rituals and hierarchies of fascist society in a grotesque and mocking light.

The political consequences of the fascists' raw abuses of power are made most explicit in *La mascherata,* in which a masked ball to be given by an aging aristocrat occasions a web of political intrigue at the highest level. The story is set in the reign of the dictator Tereso Arango, whose "regular and hermetic" rhythms are disturbed only by his desperate pursuits of women. In the tradition of many twentieth-century despots, Tereso wishes to replace the "old and ferocious companions" who helped him come to power years ago with a "new man, an ordinary bureaucrat, faithful and regular, with clean hands and a clean past." [110] His seasoned police chief, Cinco, who knows he is next in line to be purged, invents an assassination attempt on Tereso for the evening of the ball that, when foiled, will reaffirm his own power and indispensability. Cinco calls on his master operative, Perro, a younger man who embodies the values of high totalitarianism. Perro is a functionary rather than a revolutionary, who prefers "the usual blind faith" over "embarrassing enthusiasms"; his political vision hinges on the disappearance of all politics and the triumph of fear. It is far more effective and powerful to "make men speak of their most secret and dangerous passions," Perro reflects, than to "make them march in formation with their rifles on their shoulder[s]." Tereso comes off as a ridiculous and farcical figure, caught between childish rages and the abjections of his middle-aged passions, but there is nothing humorous about Perro. His precise and unfailingly logical mind, his cold brutality, and his desire to "transform the entire country . . . into an orgy of betrayals" make him the fascist equivalent of the functionary-executioner Gletkin, who stands for the new face of Stalinist communism in Koestler's *Darkness at Noon*.[111]

A master of deception, Perro is playing his own double game. He has created a secret opposition party "of the most violent sort," which serves as a steam valve for the energies of dissidents and guarantees his own political survival in an eventual post-Tereso age. Instructed by Cinco to find a "deluded, crazy, ingenuous" individual to carry out the assassination attempt, Perro turns to Saverio, a young party militant with a large library of forbidden left-wing propaganda. Saverio lives to "serve with closed eyes and absolute faith," and revolutionary doctrine provides him with a ready-made set of principles by which to judge all of history and humanity. He sees his assignment as a chance to help destroy a society that is "rotten to the core" and create "a new world, a new way of feeling, a new civilization." In some ways, Saverio is the book's only "pure" individual: he believes in the power of politics, rather than in the politics of power, and stands out among the book's many schemers and informers for betraying no one. Yet Saverio does not hesitate to assassinate an innocent person who threatens to derail the unfolding of "revolutionary logic." Although Saverio ends up dead, killed by Perro himself, Moravia does not paint him as a particularly sympathetic figure. Rather, Saverio's dogmatism serves the author by raising questions about the consequences of utopian thinking, which Moravia viewed as applicable to fascism as well.[112]

Although Moravia's biting exposition of the workings of totalitarian mentalities links his book to Alvaro's *L'uomo è forte*, *La mascherata* is a story told from the perspective of a generation of intellectuals who had come of age under fascism. Sebastiano, Saverio's stepbrother, communicates Moravia's own views on politics: his "deathly hatred" for mass politics and his "complete skepticism about the fate of humanity" echo sentiments expressed in Moravia's reportages and fiction of earlier years.[113] Alvaro's ill-fated engineer, Dale, who belonged to Alvaro's own generation, had believed he could "create something around himself, and find something real in the void of the life"; Sebastiano, a decade younger, has no such illusions. His participation in the assassination plot is motivated by a private intrigue of seduction (he and Tereso are rivals for the same woman) rather than by ideology or a desire for justice. As Moravia tells us, Sebastiano "belonged to a generation that believed in nothing, as though it had been rendered indifferent before birth by the recent ultraviolent events. It believed neither in the state, nor in the revolution, neither in liberty, nor in authority."[114]

Although *La mascherata* conveys the feelings of disorientation and detachment that had then begun to overtake some young intellectuals of Moravia's generation, its plot and tone also reflect the toll of two events of a more personal resonance. First was the promulgation of the Italian racial laws. Catholic on his mother's side, Moravia fared better than most Italian Jews in 1938; he and his siblings were granted "Aryan" legal status after his mother changed the family name to Piccinini. In 1941, Moravia was able to wed the novelist Elsa Morante in the ultra-Jesuit *Chiesa del Gesù* in Rome. His uncle Augusto De Marsanich, then undersecretary of communications, attended with other fascist officials, and the officiating priest was Father Tacchi-Venturi, who had supervised the concordat between Mussolini and the Vatican. However, as the critic Renzo Paris argues, the new political climate that took hold with the passage of anti-Semitic legislation caught Moravia by surprise. He found that his "Aryan" status mattered little to ideologues who publicly decried his work as a symbol of Jewish immorality, and he saw his primary high-society patron—the Countess Pecci-Blunt, a woman of Jewish origins—summarily dismissed from the social elite.[115]

Second, the book may constitute a response to and reenactment of the 1937 murder of Moravia's exiled antifascist cousins, Carlo and Nello Rosselli, by French Cagoulards. The supremely pragmatic Moravia had always considered the Rossellis' crusades against the dictatorship to be ill-advised, and held misgivings about Carlo's revolutionaries' view of the value of the individual in history. The foolishness and dogmatism he attributed to the idealistic Saverio may stem from his anger at the Rossellis, who, like Saverio, ended up assassinated on official orders. Certainly *La mascherata* conveys the feelings of insecurity and victimization that may have been raised in Moravia by the convergence of the assassination of the Jewish Rossellis and the racial laws. His physical description of Saverio-Carlo is as telling as it is striking, given the context in which it appeared. With thick glasses and a thicker body, covered in blood from a beating he's received from neighborhood boys, Saverio is the antithesis of the now-Aryanized fascist "new man": "[He] had an huge head, with hair as curly as sheep's wool, oversized glasses for his nearsighted eyes, a crooked nose, and a wide pale face covered with pimples. His large unformed mouth was so inexpressive as to make one think he was a deaf-mute. . . . The final monstrosity, the voice that came out of that foaming mouth was shrill, feminine, and stammering." The conflation of the Jewish, the feminine, and the grotesque in Saverio builds on Moravia's long-standing ambivalence to his Jewish heritage but also points to his internalization of the anti-Semitic stereotypes and caricatures that circulated in the fascist press. The conduct of the character Sebastiano, who is indifferent to everything but his own interests, offers an additional clue as to Moravia's tortured mentality. Sebastiano is the only person who might save Saverio, but he is repulsed by his "ugly, deformed, [and] badly dressed" stepbrother and collaborates with both Perro and Saverio without taking either side.[116] As the novel reaches its dénouement, Sebastiano slips out of the narrative, neither victim or perpetrator, while his relative is killed at the hands of the state. Moravia later recalled that he remained "traumatized" by the Rosselli murders, which were not discussed at home for fear of informers. *La mascherata* might thus be seen as an early working-through of grief and anger about his cousins' death that, twelve years later, would find a fuller narrative expression in the novel *Il conformista (The Conformist,* 1951).[117]

A different kind of victimization at the hands of fascist society is related in Masino's *Nascita e morte della massaia.* Born in Pisa one year after Moravia, Masino shared the Roman writer's precocity: her first novel, *Monte Ignoso (Mount Ignoso,* 1931), appeared when she was twenty-three years old and won a gold medal at the Viareggio literary competition; and her second one, *Periferia (Periphery,* 1933), took Viareggio's second prize. While she lacked Moravia's opportunistic nature and his predilection for salon life, she was equally cosmopolitan. From 1929 to 1933, Masino lived in Paris with her lifelong companion, Bontempelli, and worked at the League of Nations–sponsored Bureau International de Coopération Intellectuel. Although her highly original and sophisticated works drew praise in the 1930s from some Italian critics and from foreign observers such as Benjamin Crémieux, her name is rarely listed with Moravia's in post-1945 discussions of interwar Italian literature. Still less has she been accorded a place next to Vittorini or Ignazio Silone in the pantheon of dissenting or antifascist writers (fig. 14).[118] Yet *Nascita e morte della massaia* constitutes one of the most incisive critiques of fascist attempts to (re)socialize, mili-

Figure 14. Paola Masino with the artist Mirko Basaldella, Venice, 1938–39. Reproduced by permission of Alvise Memmo and the Getty Research Institute, Research Library.

tarize, and discipline Italians. Along with De Céspedes's *Nessuno torna indietro* (*There's No Turning Back,* 1938), which I will discuss in chapter 6, it
complements better-known narratives by younger male authors that illuminate the workings of tyranny and the struggle to preserve a sphere of
privacy. Masino's critique of fascist remaking schemes is refracted through
the lens of gender, and her microhistory of a "birth and death" brings into
relief the extent to which the fascists intended biology to be destiny for
millions of Italian girls raised under Mussolini's rule.

Set in a society mobilized for permanent war, it tells the story of a woman
who is driven to her death by her decision to become an exemplary housewife and perfect autarchic subject. At the start of the book, Masino describes
the refuge created by her protagonist, an upper-class adolescent who has
chosen to rebuke both fascist and consumerist ideals of womanhood:

> Reclining in a trunk that served her as a closet, bed, sideboard, table,
> and room, full of shreds of blankets, pieces of bread, books, and relics
> of funerals[,] . . . the girl engaged in daily meditations about death. . . .
> Dust from the ceiling fell on her and settled like dandruff on her head,
> crumbs and bits of paper were imbedded under her nails, musk grew
> among the cracks of the trunk; and the blankets . . . were encrusted
> with mold and spiders' webs.[119]

Her existential ponderings about birth and death alarm her mother, who
mounts a campaign to save her daughter by finding her a husband. Spurred
by a desire to win her mother's approval, she agrees to remake herself into
an attractive and marriageable young woman. Her "coming out" is a literal
one: she leaves her trunk and begins an existence as the wife of an rich, el-
derly uncle (identified only as "the Husband") who believes that home and
family are "sacred institutions that must be respected and defended." She
tries to become a socialite but muses at night about the conditions that
define her sex's existence: "food, forced labor, an eternal conversation with
ignorance, petty complication, and quotidian necessity. Mother."[120]

The Housewife's struggles to come to terms with her duties as wife and
padrona of a vast staff allow Masino the opportunity to expose the rituals
and conventions that undergird power differentials in fascist society. As she
tours her new possessions, human and material, she is introduced into a hierarchical world of "social and domestic bureaucracy" that, as Lucia Re has
observed, mirrors that of Mussolini's state. The *padrona* soon finds herself
a prisoner of this small authoritarian world of privilege and of the conformism and brutality of her surrounding society. To escape, she travels
and takes up residence apart from her husband, only to discover that, outside of her long-discarded trunk, there is no escape from the insidious pro-

cesses of moral compromise and corruption.[121] The Housewife thus decides to embrace her sacrificial role, making every autarchic mandate into a guiding principle. After she wears a coarse sack at an aristocratic soirée, she is toasted as a "National Example" of wartime renunciation. She becomes a perfect self-sufficient subject, dismissing her staff and turning her home into a social welfare center and command post in the home war against defeatism. As she "distributes prizes and punishments" to the populace, she also tries to eradicate her own idiosyncrasies; by the end of the novel, her mind is free of all "arbitrary digressions," and "she has even succeeded in disciplining her dreams, something heretofore unheard of," as Masino notes with irony.[122]

Although she has fulfilled her narrative mandate, the Housewife does not have the luxury of slipping out of the story, as Moravia's character Sebastiano does. As a woman, her duties are as unending as the war. She comes to believe that death holds the only possibility of escape, and orchestrates her own funeral before she expires at the close of the book. Like Alvaro and Moravia, Masino comments on the disappearance of civic values under fascism, and the triumph of a culture of betrayal and terror. Yet she also reminds her readers of the additional masks women must wear to appear "normal" under the regime, and argues that, for women, becoming a good fascist subject ultimately leads to self-immolation. Despite her personal *bonifica* and political orthodoxy, then, Masino's Housewife ends up no less a victim than Moravia's Saverio, the revolutionary outsider who is used and killed by the state. Not surprisingly, both of these works met with hostility from fascist censors. Masino's novel was judged "defeatist and cynical," and she was ordered to remove all terms and descriptions that would identify its setting as Italian. An Allied bombing of the Milan warehouse that held copies of the revised volume then intervened to prevent its release, and the book appeared only in 1945. Moravia's novel did not have a much better fate. Mussolini had initially approved the publication of *La mascherata*, but more stringent wartime censorship led to orders to limit reviews and prohibit further printings.[123]

The censorship of Moravia and Masino communicated the government's intention to intensify its policing of young intellectuals. To avoid the reappearance of polemical journals such as *L'Universale* and *Cantiere*, the government restricted the number of independent periodicals. Ricci appealed in vain for the right to revive *L'Universale* in 1938, and Bilenchi's attempt to start a review that year proved futile as well.[124] At the same time, the regime expanded its patronage programs to counter disaffection and bring more young people into contact with official institutions. Mussolini allocated more resources for the GUFs: by 1939, fifty-four GUF groups boasted cinema sections, and those of Naples, Milan, Turin, Bari, Genoa, and Rome developed into busy centers of 16 mm film production. The Milanese cinema section became a training ground for future directors such as Alberto Lattuada, Renato Castellani, and Luigi Comencini, while the Bologna section showed eclectic programs of uncensored, undubbed films by Eisenstein and Carné to young intellectuals like Pier Paolo Pasolini. The activities of the cinema sections produced a new generation of film professionals and critics and created an informed interest in film among the educated public that would sustain Italy's lively cine-club culture after 1945.[125]

The Littoriali competitions for GUF members also expanded after 1936. New themes on radio, photography, and race brought entry categories up from twenty-one in 1934 to thirty-one to 1939. Despite the imposition of fixed themes on the contestants, the Littoriali still attracted the most promising youth from diverse areas of endeavor. Aldo Moro, Mario Alicata, Ettore Sotsass, Paolo Emilio Taviani, Lattuada, Paci, and Renato Guttuso all won prizes there between 1937 and 1940.[126] From 1939 to 1941, female students had their own Littoriali. Women often had to overcome parental opposition to their participation in order to debate their peers on topics such as "The Role of Women in Racial Policy" and "Women and Sports," and they received little support afterward from the male-controlled youth press. All the same, the Littoriali became a place where independent-minded university women were recognized for their intellectual abilities. Here, too, victors included individuals—such as the writers Margherita Guidacci, Anna Maria Ortese, and Milena Milani—who enjoyed successful careers after 1945.[127] GUF programs like the Littoriali offered younger Italians of both sexes a space of moderate nonconformism and the chance to gain professional experiences and contacts. "I took advantage of the GUF to change my status in life, to pass from a simple office worker to the creative and independent work of the intellectual," recalled the journalist Antonio Ghirelli, who joined a GUF in the Neapolitan hinterland and wrote for the GUF review *IX Maggio* during the war.[128]

A few young Italians found that the knowledge and contacts they gained through GUF programs caused them to move away from fascist militancy. Exploiting the more tolerant censorship guidelines the regime granted them, young cultural organizers tried to keep alive alternative political ideologies and visions of cultural modernity by exposing their peers to works that the regime had banned from public circulation. In 1940, Lattuada showed Renoir's pacifist work *La grande illusion* in Milan by giving the event a GUF affiliation. "In authoritarian regimes there are spaces that one can exploit," Lattuada reflected years later. "There were odd ways to utilize the margins to one's advantage." The Littoriali, too, functioned as points of encounter and education for those who had begun to question fascist dogma. Giuseppe Melis Bassu came away empty-handed after traveling from Sassari to Bologna for the 1940 competitions, but recalled the Littoriali as an experience that "opened my eyes" to the range of opinions that his age-group held about fascism.[129] PCI officials also utilized the Littoriali as recruitment and intelligence-gathering sites, sending young operatives such as Eugenio Curiel who knew how to manipulate fascism's revolutionary rhetoric. Curiel attended the Littoriali competitions in 1938 as a correspondent for the PCI exile paper *Lo Stato operaio* and the GUF paper *Il Bò*. In the former publication he stressed the growing disaffection with Italy's autarchic policies and military involvements; in *Il Bò* he augured the emergence of young people who "do not accept political solutions passively, but think them through thoroughly for themselves."[130]

The broadening fissures within fascist youth culture may be tracked most clearly in the review *Corrente di vita giovanile*. Founded in January 1938 with the intention of "stimulating the preparation of tomorrow's leadership class," by 1940 the sympathies of its contributors ranged from Nazism to communism.[131] Directed by an eighteen-year-old student, Ernesto Treccani, *Corrente* displayed the influences of its two very powerful patrons: Ernesto's father, Senator Giovanni Treccani, a Lombard textile baron and backer of the *Enciclopedia Italiana*, and the senator's close friend Alfieri, then minister of popular culture. Alfieri's input accounts for the journal's orthodox stances on foreign policy. *Corrente* exalted Franco and the fascist takeover of Albania, published paranoid philippics against the threat of world communism, and claimed that Nazism had given Germany "intellectual and national dignity." The journal also enthusiastically supported the anti-Semitic laws. "We frankly proclaim ourselves to be racists," wrote Claudio Belingardi for the journal in December 1938. Like many in the mainstream press, *Corrente*'s collaborators justified Italian anti-Semitism as a "moral racism" because it converged with Catholic exhortations for Jews to assimilate and convert.[132]

On cultural issues, though, *Corrente* forged an independent path. In the face of autarchic provisions, the journal defended Italians' right to have access to the latest trends of foreign culture in the name of "a true and legitimate development of the tradition of modernity." Its long list of collaborators included many rising stars of the newer generations: philosophers (Anceschi, Paci), literary figures (Vittorini, Vittorio Sereni), cineastes (Lattuada, Luigi Comencini), and a large group of artists (Renato Guttuso,

Figure 15. From *Vita giovanile* to *Corrente*, 1938–39. Reprinted with the kind permission of Ernesto Treccani and the Fondazione Corrente, Milan.

Renato Birolli) whose works were often featured in the review. By 1940, the journal had added an art gallery on Via Spiga and an imprint that published poetry and photography, and had introduced Italians to Walker Evans, Sartre, Federico García Lorca, and other contemporary cultural figures. In the space of a few years, *Corrente* became a movement that united youth who wished to find an alternative to fascist culture by immersing themselves "in the living heart of modernity, in the vital problematic of our time." [133] The group's transformation can also be traced in the evolution of the journal's masthead. In the course of one year, the editors took off the fasces and distinctive Mussolinian signature that framed the original title (*Vita giovanile*, chosen by Alfieri), removed the Duce's dictum ("We want youth to pick up our torch"), and demoted *Vita giovanile* to tiny letters beneath the word *Corrente* (fig. 15). Their actions testify to the abandonment of their original mission—the creation of a new fascist political elite—and to the growing importance culture took on for this age-group as a means of connecting with a world outside the dictatorship.

Indeed, *Corrente's* cultural pages signal the start of a phenomenon that would grow more prevalent during World War II: the subversion of the realist rhetorics and aesthetics that had underwritten projects for a fascist culture since the early 1930s. The journal's few Marxist contributors, such as the critic Raffaele De Grada and the painters Guttuso and Birolli, augured the birth of a new "social conscience" among intellectuals who would be inspired to illuminate "the profound connections between art and the social and economic spheres." For De Grada, who became a leading proponent of social realism after 1945, artists' constructive role in society lay in their function as "witnesses" who testified to humanity's current travails. He and other dissidents embraced realism in the years surrounding World War II as a movement that would imbue art with moral force, allowing it to become an instrument of liberation. In *Corrente*, Realism denoted less a specific style of art than a desire to break out of the anaesthetized creative climate produced by two decades of censorship and self-censorship and achieve a "dramatic rediscovery of life." [134]

Other contributors to *Corrente* still believed in the feasibility of a distinctly fascist modernity and continued to work for a culture that would express fascism's revolutionary and dynamic nature. As a philosophy student in the early 1930s, Paci had argued in *Orpheus* that fascism's "antisystematic" politics and thought were perfectly adapted to the mutable character of contemporary life. By 1940, now a professor at the University of Padua and an ardent Axis supporter, he was in the forefront of Italian thinkers who wished to integrate fascist and existentialist thought. Including Nazism in his argument, Paci asserted in *Corrente* that fascism's essential modernity lay in its definition of history and reality as an unfolding problematic. At a time of endemic crisis in Europe, the Hitler and Mussolini regimes answered a need for "the concrete, the positive, for a clear look at the limits and possibilities of the real." [135]

Paci was among those youth who envisioned the Axis's New Order as an antidote to a bankrupt bourgeois civilization. Like their counterparts in Nazi Germany, these individuals accepted racism as an unproblematic element of fascist ideology. Many university students who demonstrated against Hitler in the aftermath of the Anschluss, for example, took issue with Hitler's disrespect of Italy's own territorial ambitions, not with Germany's state anti-Semitism. Indeed, the youth press and institutions such as the GUFs and the Scuola di Mistica Fascista stand out on the map of fascist racism for the quantity and vitriol of the anti-Jewish propaganda they produced. Their lecture series, books and articles, slide lectures, and radio programs formed the building blocks of an edifice of racist culture that was hastily forgotten after the war.

Aided by its links to the anti-Bolshevik and antibourgeois campaigns, anti-Semitism became the cause of the moment in many youth circles, just as corporativism had been in the early thirties. "Two new words light up the Italian sky: autarchy and race," crowed the young journalist Giorgio Vecchietti in December 1938 with the same enthusiasm he had earlier shown for corporativism. Ambitious professionals took care to integrate racial themes in their work: In 1939, the thirty-one-year-old economics professor Amintore Fanfani (prime minister of Italy in 1954 and 1958–59) argued in the *Rivista internazionale di scienza sociali* that the exclusion of Jews from economic life would guarantee "the power and the future of the Nation." The writer Giampaolo Callegari, one year Fanfani's senior, published the anti-Semitic novel *Il cuore a destra* (*The Heart on the Right*, 1939) the same year he won the Biella literary prize.[136] It is sobering to think that many Italian intellectuals spent some of their formative years steeped in the racist propaganda that permeated the schools and the fascist press. "I dedicated many hours of study to racism," recalled the journalist Ugoberto Alfassio Grimaldi, who won third place in the 1940 Littoriali competition for best "racial monograph," at the age of twenty-five. Alfassio Grimaldi joined the Resistance in the fall of 1943, but other GUF members who came from this climate were drawn to the Republic of Salò. In fact, to those who did not travel abroad and who received no conflicting messages from family, mentors, or peers, all of fascism's causes and campaigns might have appeared perfectly normal and natural. In the recollection of the filmmaker Renato Castellani, "We were like canaries born in a cage with no idea of what existed outside. . . . one lived in a world organized in a certain manner, and one went ahead agreeing more or less with what this world did."[137] This circumstance enabled younger Italian intellectuals to sustain their support of fascism through the alliance with Hitler, the racial laws, and the restrictions of cultural autarchy. World War II would test the political faith of these youth and that of intellectuals of all ages, as early military defeats cast a shadow over fascist projects for a model of mass society that could be exported throughout the continent.

6 The Wars of Fascism

In June 1940, as German Panzer Corps swept into the heart of France, Mussolini announced Italy's entry into the war. Low monetary reserves and an antiquated arsenal had prevented the fascists' mobilization in 1939, and many top government advisors had recommended continued neutrality. Yet the Duce did not want to miss a prime opportunity to secure Italy's leadership role in the New Europe. Nonintervention, he announced to the Italian public, would "downgrade Italy for a century as a great power and for an eternity as a Fascist regime." Building on two decades of crisis thinking, Mussolini billed the war as the climactic moment of years of revolutionary developments meant to reinvent European civilization. This face-off between "two centuries and two ideas," he declared, pitted "young and prolific nations" against "sterile and declining" ones. World War II would definitively defeat the forces of decadence that had necessitated fascism's arrival onto the scene of history some twenty years before.[1]

The Duce's calculations proved badly mistaken. Rather than bringing fascism renewed prestige and popularity, World War II turned many Italians against the regime. The failure of fascist Italy's bid for international prestige disillusioned even the armed forces and political militants. Early setbacks in Greece, Albania, and North Africa ended the Italian dream of a "parallel war" fought independently of the Germans. By the end of 1941, Mussolini had admitted to Ciano that the Italians were destined to be very junior partners in the Nazi-dominated "new order." German behavior toward the Italians during the disastrous Russian campaign of 1942 further injured morale and increased fears that for Italians the New Europe might mean renewed subordination within a different international system. Yet disappointment with Mussolini's regime did not necessarily imply the end of fascist sympathies: many die-hard fighters and ideologues, along with younger Italians who had been educated to hate both socialism and democracy, continued to support the idea of a New European order.[2] These groups formed the core of Italian supporters who cast their destinies with the Republic of Salò after September 1943.

This chapter explores the function of culture in articulating shifting concepts of Italian and fascist modernity and nationhood during World War II. I will argue two points. First, as the Italian military effort stalled, culture took on increased importance as a means of asserting the fascists' independence within the Axis and their influence throughout Europe. Second, culture became important terrain on which Italians would contest their own government and reveal the bankruptcy of official conceptions of fascist modernity. As in the early 1930s, a round of debates over the lineaments of the national novel and film offered occasions for the expression of frustration and discontent. Yet the polemics of the early forties saw the debut of a new generation of intellectuals who matured in a climate of state-sanctioned racism, food lines, and growing political crisis. Along with Vittorini and others in their thirties who had become disillusioned with the dictatorship, a few in their twenties reappropriated official rhetorics of social revolution and collective refashioning for antifascist purposes. In the final years of fascism, as popular discontent increased and military morale crumbled, fissures widened within the dictatorship's youth culture that would find political expression after September 1943.

Looking back on the catalogue of disasters that marked Italy's military experience in World War II, it is easy to forget that many Italian intellectuals initially supported the conflict as a final strike against the state system established by the Versailles treaty.[3] Like the Nazis, many fascists rejected Wilsonian concepts of national self-determination as encouraging ethnic anarchy, and conceived of the New Europe as a "hierarchy of peoples." Whereas the Germans planned to occupy the apex of this hierarchy, though, the Italians posited the Axis as an alliance of powers who would become separate and equal managers of a new world civilization.[4] For the fascists, World War II was above all a means of realizing autonomy and prestige. Coming on the heels of the Ethiopian success, it would prove that they were no longer spectators of events that took place "without their participation and against their will and rights," but "protagonists" who would "decisively and definitively transform the face of Europe and the world."[5]

The fascist government also viewed World War II as the supreme test-ing ground for its experiments in social engineering. In 1940, as in 1914 and 1935, Mussolini saw war as a formative and constructive mass experi-ence. He argued that combat would serve as the final "kick in the ass" (*cal-cio nel culo*) Italians needed to become a great and modern people.[6] Erasing the lines between civilian and military endeavor, the war would transform the country into a single productive unit. The experience of war would also eradicate residual pernicious traits in the national character. Laziness, whining, flightiness, disorganization, and other "famous defects" would disappear in the face of the grave task of "defending one's own country and civilization . . . against a grim coalition of demoplutocrats, Masons, and Jews." Three months into the war, one linguist who studied "war neolo-gisms" claimed that Italians had at least assimilated the language of fascist modernity: terms such as *efficiente* and *efficienza* (*efficient* and *efficiency*) had become a normal part of the Italian lexicon.[7] Finally, combat would continue to reshape Italians' affective propensities. Sentimental and pietist attitudes would be replaced with hatred, which was defined as "the will to render the maximum harm to the enemy until he is annihilated." Some intellectuals justified the normalization of the killer instinct by depicting the war as a continuation of the "surgical violence" that had characterized squadrism and other defining moments of the fascist revolution. Others claimed that this "warrior conscience" was a sign that Italians had inter-nalized the purificatory and expansionist agendas of fascist modernity. By the early 1940s, "modern" Italians were those who were able to discipline their emotions and execute the violent acts the state demanded of them.[8]

The expansion and radicalization of the culture of racism after 1940 sug-gests that the dictatorship did not entirely fail in its goal of producing a piti-less people. The anti-Semitic propaganda disseminated by the press and GUF organizations grew more vitriolic, labeling Jews as warmongers, trai-tors, and saboteurs. In Turin and other cities, manifestos appeared that in-cited Italians to kill and imprison local Jews, sometimes listing their names and addresses. A new compulsory labor program forced Jews to work out-doors as street sweepers, where they were subject to insults and physical attacks. The program had been instituted to still complaints that Jews—who had been ejected from their jobs by the racial laws—had become work-shy parasites who lived off the state. As the war continued to go badly, Jews became a convenient scapegoat for anger that could not be expressed against the regime, and incidents of spontaneous anti-Semitic violence accompanied requests for more radical action by the state. In a 1941 article in *Critica fascista*, Domenico Vanelli demanded a more "totalitarian" and "revolutionary" treatment of the Jewish question: "Isn't it time to take ruthless and inexorable action against a race that bears the enormous responsibility of having poisoned the world and started the war?" Vanelli and other Italian proponents of eliminationist anti-Semitism would take heart in the genocidal policies followed during the Republic of Salò.[9]

Before the fall of 1943, though, such a German-identified course of action found little support in a country with no tradition of pogrom-style violence. Most intellectuals and policy makers continued to favor policies such as ghettoization and expulsion, which they saw as consistent with those followed in past centuries by Church and secular authorities. After 1940, a network of concentration camps appeared from Calabria to Ferrara to intern foreign Jews who had no money to emigrate. Approximately fourteen thousand Jews had come into the country in the 1930s on temporary visas and had stayed on as exiles from Germany, Poland, and other central European nations. Among these was the German Jewish philosopher Karl Löwith, who had emigrated to Rome in 1934 after his expulsion from the German university system. In the mid-1930s, cheered by the absence of state anti-Semitism, Löwith had imagined that "the Italian is humane even in a black shirt." He changed his mind once he, like other foreign Jews, was forced to choose between expulsion or imprisonment. Löwith was one of the fortunate ones: he got a job in Japan in 1940 and soon settled in the United States. The majority of his peers lived in difficult conditions in Italian concentration camps until July 1943, and many who were interned in the North were later handed over to the Germans, along with Italian Jews who had by then been targeted for deportation.[10]

A CULTURE OF WAR, 1940 – 43

As millions of Italian soldiers set off for the battlegrounds of Europe and North Africa, new cultural policies appeared that sought to extend state controls over high culture and assert Italy's agenda of cultural imperialism. The most immediate task was managing the war's presentation and reception in order to manipulate public opinion of Italy's allies and enemies. To ensure a "coordinated" media coverage of the conflict, the MCP ordered directors of major dailies to attend weekly briefings in Rome, and created a new Press Entity to regulate provincial papers. The Press Office of the Armed Forces eventually gained first right of censorship on dispatches from the front, but the MCP retained the authority to shape everything else that Italians heard, saw, or read in those years.[11] Book censorship guidelines also became more stringent after 1940. As the MCP official Fernando Mezzasoma argued, the war made it necessary to ban or sequester hundreds of volumes that were "absolutely incompatible with the new foreign policy directives and the current military situation." By 1943, only one-third of the volumes inspected received the censors' green light; one-third were marked for major revisions, and another third were banned altogether.[12]

World War II also occasioned a final round of initiatives to prevent the circulation of foreign books and films in Italy. Autarchic measures such as Alfieri's 1938 import taxes on American films found new legitimation once England, France, and the United States became official enemies. As one commentator averred in 1940, the war would at last allow the triumph of "traditional Italian genius" by purging cultural materials that were "extraneous to our character, our life, and the social and political humanity of our people." Keeping up with the latest party line, Bottai and others further disavowed their previous internationalist policies. Bottai claimed that a "strange mix of errors, blindness and modishness" had led Italians to believe that cosmopolitanism was the best route to a national culture. Now, freed from "the slavery of foreign ties," they would act as innovators rather than imitators in the cultural sphere.[13]

This new round of protectionist measures occurred too late to have much effect. Policies that drastically reduced the number of translations from foreign literature were not implemented until 1942–43, and 1941 quotas on the importation of foreign-language books failed due to the popularity of such books with educated readers.[14] The government did better in the realm of the cinema. There, the sharp reduction in American imports, coupled with the increase in national production, caused Italian films to make more money than foreign ones by 1942, leading Vittorio Mussolini to boast that only a few "excellent" American movies would be allowed into the postwar Italian empire.[15] By the early forties, though, America had become such a potent symbol of liberation for many Italian youth that the absence of its films did little to dampen its appeal. In 1943, five years into the ban on American films, the young critic Giame Pintor observed that American cinema constituted "the greatest message our generation has received. . . . this serenely revolutionary arm has abolished political frontiers and made us conscious of the most urgent issue of our time, that of the unity of all races."[16]

Of course, the psychological power of the cinema had never been lost on fascist officials, who assigned films a key role in the manipulation of public opinion regarding the war. In 1923, Mussolini had proclaimed the cinema to be fascism's strongest weapon; now, when early military failures ended fascism's bid for prestige through armed combat, the regime poured resources into its filmic front. The Istituto LUCE sent seven squads to shoot footage of battles and all other aspects of combat life. LUCE newsreels followed the progress of Italian troops—or masked the lack of any progress when necessary—fashioning a repertory of images of the nation's allies and enemies.[17] To exert close control over the development of war-themed feature films, the government created a Committee for War and Political Cinema in 1941. Staffed with representatives from the PNF, LUCE, Cinecittà, and other official bodies, the committee approved a production plan for the next few years that included two movies on the navy, two on the air force, three on the army, and a "grand anti-Jewish historical film." The government also increased the staff and budget of military filmmaking centers such as the navy ministry's Cinematographic Center.[18]

Through the efforts of such entities, the military documentary attained a particular prominence within fascist film culture as a site for experimentation in the art of filmmaking as well as the science of propaganda. State-sponsored military cinematography had its genesis in Italy during World War I and gave rise to such agencies as the Royal Navy's Special Office of Cinematographic Reportage.[19] During the Ethiopian War, films such as D'Errico's *Il cammino degli eroi* signaled the beginning of a period of formal innovation with the documentary genre that bore fruit during World War II and influenced the development of the postwar Neorealist movement. Critics labeled the works made by directors such as Francesco De Robertis and Rossellini for the navy's Cinematographic Center as "novelized documentaries" (*documentari romanzati*) for their blend of documentary and feature film conventions, realism and melodrama. These full-length movies, which enjoyed commercial releases, made reviewers enthusiastic for the "unheard-of possibilities" they raised for the future of political filmmaking and the affirmation of a uniquely "Italian" realist aesthetic.[20]

The role such military movies had in disseminating the norms of fascist modernity can be seen in De Robertis's *Uomini sul fondo* (*Men on the Bottom*, 1941), which recounts the drama of sailors whose damaged submarine has sunk to the seafloor. Made by a director who was himself a navy officer, employing a cast composed mostly of full-time military operatives, the documentary promised viewers an "authentic" view of the new Italian soldier. The film's opening titles, which announce the work's intention to "make known the great renunciations, mute heroisms, and silent joys" of combat life, flag the merits of the modern subject who has learned to discipline his affects and his behaviors. Calm professionalism and a collective spirit reign supreme even in the midst of a life-threatening situation. Answering years of griping among fascist ideologues about the persistence of national "defects" that damaged prestige and efficiency, De Robertis offers a vision of a people who have eliminated all indices of excess and sentimentalism. His sailors do not gesticulate or emote, and their rarely used voices are always low and controlled; the news of their rescue elicits only a laconic "finally." The film thus showcases both the modernized navy and the "new man" produced by twenty years of fascist remaking schemes. It is not surprising that critics saluted *Uomini sul fondo* as a truly "national" film that vividly conveyed "our pure and sincere character; a precious and fragrant *italianità* pervades its settings and its protagonists." [21]

Uomini sul fondo also puts a wartime twist on ongoing discourses about the function of technology within the fascist model of modernity. In films such as Matarazzo's *Treno popolare*, D'Errico's *Il cammino degli eroi*, and Barbaro's *L'ultima nemica*, technological advance (trains, hygienic and scientific advances, communications equipment) is turned to the task of reconfiguring the boundaries between public and private, colony and metropole. Like other military movies, De Robertis's film showcases new communications technology (radio towers, telephonic buoys) and depicts technology's potential to obliterate the divide between home and front, creating a new kind of national collective marked by a totalitarian transparency. Here the radio serves as the conduit of public power into the private domain. As in Nazi Germany, war bulletins and other radio programs became a mediating force between home and front, and the radio became a main mouthpiece of state authority. In a scene so artificial as to seem comical, the submarine's drama is broadcast to the populace and Italians freeze at the sound of their master's voice: a mother's hand stops in midair as she serves dinner, a family swivels wordlessly in unison toward its dining-room radio. At home as on the submarine, silence and obedience mark the new breed of permanently mobilized Italians, who, the film tells us, "have the ultimate privilege of being unable to distinguish between their 'peacetime life' and their 'wartime life.'" In *Uomini sul fondo*, form and content conjoin to create an homage to aesthetic and psychological discipline that stood in sharp contrast with Italy's messy performances on the battlefield. By 1942, in the wake of additional combat debacles, De Robertis's film was cited as a model for future documentaries that could be "taken abroad to make known Italy and the Italians." [22]

In fact, as mounting military defeats created new tensions within the Axis alliance, the cinema became a primary site of competition between Italy and Germany for economic and cultural control of the New Europe. Although the war consolidated rightist cultural exchange networks, ongoing fascist misgivings about the Nazi's hegemonic intentions put a damper on initiatives meant to bring about an Italian-German "cultural fusion." The fascists felt that Italy's glorious artistic heritage made it a natural leader in the cultural realm, while Goebbels and other Nazi officials saw Italian ambitions as "interfering" with their own plans for domination.[23] Nowhere was this tension more evident than in the struggle for continental film markets. In 1935, the Nazis had founded an International Film Chamber whose stated purpose was to unite the global movie industry against American productions. Forty nations signed on to this organization, which folded with the onset of World War II. In 1941 it was resurrected to facilitate Germany's filmic expansion throughout Europe. Goebbels assured representatives from Denmark and other member nations that his country's goals in this area were "altruistic," but his policies left no doubt that the Germans planned to pillage the industries they professed to protect. Polish cinema was all but destroyed when the Germans commandeered equipment and personnel for its own production centers in Berlin, Munich, and Vienna. In France, a branch of the German film company Ufa produced 30 of the 220 French films made during the Occupation. With the help of many local allies of the Nazi cause, movie theater chains, distribution networks, and studios passed into German hands at a blitzkrieg pace all over Europe after 1940.[24]

To Goebbels's consternation, the Italians also saw the benefits of cultural imperialism and pursued their own expansionist strategies in the film markets of wartime Europe. Mussolini's movie moguls were well positioned to undertake their own "parallel war": the influential industrialist Count Giuseppe Volpe di Misurata then served as president of the International Film Chamber, and the Italians hosted the prestigious Biennale film festival. The fascist film industry also boomed during World War II: production increased from 83 films in 1940 to 119 in 1942. Exploiting shifts in trade networks occasioned by wartime political upheavals, the fascists made inroads into eastern European markets that formerly had generated little revenue. In Bulgaria and Hungary, military movies such as *Il grande appello* and *Uomini sul fondo* garnered more attention and profits than German films. Paralleling their trajectories of economic expansion, the Italians invested heavily in Romania, where they bought interests in studios and established joint-venture production companies. Italian imports rose sharply there; 90 Italian films came into Romania in 1942, as opposed to 30 the year before. Overall, export sales for Italian films rose from L19,000,000 in 1940 to almost L31,000,000 in 1941, and Pavolini, the minister of popular culture, estimated that this figure would double by 1943. These developments irritated Goebbels, who ordered German functionaries on missions to Italy to do everything possible to undermine the Italians' programs for cinematic expansionism. "The Italians are creating every sort of difficulty for us," he observed in his diary in June 1941. "They want a piece of the pie at all costs and on this subject there is no reasoning with them." [25]

A blend of cooperation and competition characterized Italian-German wartime relations in other realms of culture as well. Italian intellectuals were present in numbers at the numerous German-sponsored cultural events held in both countries, even in the face of the Nazis' obvious intentions to establish "a European cultural front that gravitates around German culture," as the German ambassador Alfieri warned from Berlin in 1942.[26] Alfieri's comment was prompted by the unveiling of the European Union of Writers, one of Goebbels's most ambitious projects for Nazi cultural hegemony. Presumably a means of gathering authors from Germany, Italy, and the occupied countries to plan the literary life of the new Europe, the union soon emerged as a vehicle of German cultural imperialism. The Italian writer Papini addressed the problematic nature of Nazi patronage that month at a preparatory meeting in Weimar in March 1942. With his usual bluntness, Papini told Goebbels that the "spiritual unity" vaunted by the union "can and must not mean the overwhelming of one culture by another, but must express the same understanding and collaboration that is at work in political and economic life." [27] Bottai's influential wartime journal *Primato* aired the critiques of the young Giame Pintor, who warned Italians of the political and cultural consequences of the Nazis' "adoption of war as a way of life." In October 1942, though, he, Cecchi, Falqui, Vittorini, and six other Italians donned black shirts to spend a week in Weimar at the Germans' expense. The double edge of Nazi patronage was everywhere evident; the Nazis treated their guests to "innumerable toasts, speeches, outings, and concerts," but Hitler Youth guards and swastikas filled the ballroom where Cecchi and other non-Germans delivered their speeches. At the concluding ceremonies, the Gauleiter of Thuringia spoke of the ongoing crusade against Bolsheviks, democrats, and Jews, while Goebbels informed the audience of the Reich's latest literary directives. When the French purge trials began a few years later, attendance at this conference was used as evidence of pro-Nazi sentiments. In the Italian context, the Weimar junket formed one page in a history of cultural collaboration that was buried along with Mussolini in 1945.[28]

GENERATIONS AT WAR

Although some younger intellectuals also saw World War II as a prime opportunity to achieve an Italian cultural primacy in Europe, many supported the conflict as a means of sweeping away the detritus of a bourgeois society that had hindered fascism's radical restructuring of relations among economics, politics, and the social realm. Buoyed by official predictions of a short war with long-term gains in international influence, intellectuals like the philosopher Paci greeted intervention with great enthusiasm. Paci, now twenty-nine years old, had fought in Ethiopia and supported the Nazi-fascist alliance. He asked his peers to join him in volunteering for a war "through which we will authentically determine ourselves in history[,] . . . so that each of us can truly contribute to the new community and social organization we want to actuate through our revolution." A year later, the nineteen-year-old poet Milani urged her own age-group to support the war, envisioning an "armed femininity" that would be realized in 1943–44 with the appearance of female Resistance fighters and Salò's women's auxiliary corps. For many in their twenties and thirties, World War II represented a chance to defeat the "plutocrats" who had long obstructed the expansion of fascism's social revolution. As presented in some GUF reviews, the war would bring about a revival of the spirit of 1919—the original fascist radicalism—that had been diluted by years of corruption, compromise, and creeping embourgeoisement. Bottai encouraged this train of thought by depicting the fascists as underdogs in a struggle against the "barbaric and bloodthirsty" bosses of international finance. "The peace that will come will be the first real world peace; we will be able to say Patria, without meaning national hatred; Man, without meaning slave or master; Labor, without meaning capitalism," he told a gathering of young Italians in 1942 (fig. 16).[29]

The zealous support for the war that these Italians showed in 1940 contradicts the notion some historians have advanced of a mass disaffection with the regime among youth after 1938. As we saw in chapter 5, a small group of young intellectuals had begun to distance themselves from fascism by 1940. Yet MacGregor Knox's observation that defeat, not war, turned Italians against fascism is especially valid for fascism's younger generations.[30] What soured many youth against Mussolini and his regime was

Figure 16. Wartime priorities of the youth review *Book and Musket. Libro e moschetto*, February 15, 1941. Reprinted with permission of the Biblioteca Nazionale, Rome.

not the racial laws or the end of nonbelligerency, but their experiences on the battlefields of North Africa, Greece, and Russia. Even then, some intellectuals died in combat with their fascist faith still intact. One of these was Berto Ricci, for whom World War II represented the last occasion to realize the fascist civilization he had advocated since the days of *L'Universale*. Although Mussolini's alliance with Hitler worried him, as did the campaigns for autarchy and against modern art, he embraced the war as a revolutionary strike at the international forces of wealth and privilege. He volunteered for the front in 1940, at the age of thirty-five, but was assigned instead to a naval unit stationed near Pisa. After pleading with officials to be transferred to the African front, he arrived in Libya in January 1941, only to be killed a month later after a surprise attack by English bombers. Although Ricci was commemorated as a martyr for the fascist cause, his life and death demonstrate the powerful hold that fascism exerted on a generation of Italians who searched for an antiliberal, antileftist model of modernity in the interwar years. "Fascism has made us suffer in the past and it will make us suffer in the future," Ricci had written presciently to a friend in 1937. "But fascism is our life and our destiny."[31]

By the end of 1941, with military defeats piling up, such fanaticism must have been particularly valued by the dictatorship. Even as the GUF press declared that a new generation of university students was ready to serve Mussolini and fascism, officials' diaries, informer's reports, and other private documents convey a collective recognition that the regime was rapidly losing its battle to form a new elite. While active antifascism was confined to a very few individuals, a growing number of young intellectuals had become pessimistic about fascism's transformative intentions. "As the Duce once said, every revolution has three moments: it begins with mysticism, continues with politics, and ends up as administration," wrote one young journalist with more than a touch of sarcasm that year.[32] Several factors contributed to this disillusionment, which dampened martial and political zeal. First and most concretely, the antiquated arms and often incompetent direction young soldiers received on the battlefield made a mockery of fascism's claims to constitute a modern regime. On the frozen steppes of Russia, as mule-riding Italians watched Germans speed by on trucks, resentment commingled with admiration for the perceived superiority of the Nazi military machine. This experience of a "subaltern war," as the historian Giampiero Bernagozzi has called it, turned some fascists against the Germans and prepared others to support them during the Republic of Salò.[33]

Second, the increased political fragmentation within Mussolini's movement due to internecine rivalries left many youth unsure about fascism's ideological identity and impeded the formation of a united fighting front. The "absolute confusion about the most basic ideas of [fascism]" that Gastone Spinetti perceived among militants in February 1940 translated into uncertainty among conscripts over Italy's war role and aims. Without a cause that united Italians the way race did the Germans, the regime found it difficult to mobilize young intellectuals for a "national" struggle that would take them far from home.[34] Finally, the internationalist tendencies within fascist ideology, which found expression during World War II in visions of a rightist European federation, left some young intellectuals uncertain about the future of the nation-state they were supposed to be fighting for. *Critica fascista*, one of the papers followed by young intellectuals, argued that the war was revolutionary precisely because it would inaugurate "a manner of thinking and acting that is more consciously international." Several Italian observers commented on the psychological conflicts created in Italian combatants by the collision of the rhetorics of protectionist and universalist nationalisms. Was the war being waged to defend Italy, or to transform it beyond recognition? As one young journalist wondered in 1942, "Will we still speak of the nation, or will we consider it a completely obsolete concept?"[35]

For Bottai and other officials who believed that culture constituted fascism's surest road to influence in a German-dominated Europe, the apathy and disaffection that had overtaken Italy's most talented youth posed a grave problem. "Culture arrives at this war without any capacity to participate, dispirited, indifferent, even hostile, in a state of reaction against the revolutionary movement that spins ever faster around the Rome-Berlin Axis," Bottai told Mussolini in a confidential 1940 report on the problem. The only option, as he saw it, was to "reanimate culture by concentrating on its youthful elements, inciting and committing it to affront the problems of the new Europe's social, political, and economic order."[36] To this end, Bottai founded the cultural review *Primato*, which aimed to resolve two intertwined issues that took on new urgency during the war: winning the unconditional support of the intellectual class, and creating a modern culture that would represent Italian fascist interests abroad. While neither endeavor proved particularly successful, Bottai did make good use of consensus-building tactics that had been cemented over two decades of cultural debate. The review sponsored surveys on current topics such as existentialism and proffered promises of creative freedom to all contributors. Although neither Jewish nor female intellectuals were welcome in the journal, *Primato* attracted dozens of contributors of all ages, who included the most talented male and "Aryan" representatives of mid-twentieth-century Italian culture and thought.[37]

Bottai's aim was not merely to collect intellectuals, though, but to mobilize them to advance fascist agendas of Italian cultural hegemony. His initial editorial thus challenged intellectuals to put aside their differences and form a united cultural front that would be fascist Italy's most valuable wartime weapon. Introducing the figure of the soldier-scribe, an elite counterpart to the soldier-worker, *Primato* elaborated a program of "cultural interventionism" that gave intellectuals a frontline role in the defeat of liberal-democratic ideals as well as Nazi plans for cultural hegemony.[38] Intellectuals from a variety of fields answered the call. Emanuelli contributed a short story set in Italian-occupied Dalmatia, and articles by linguists on Italian speakers in Dalmatia, Malta, and Corsica advanced claims of a historic "Italian Mediterranean." Historians profiled the protagonists and debates of the Risorgimento—the review's title made reference to nineteenth-century visions of an Italian-led Europe—and noted that World War II offered a similar opportunity for Italians to reshape their collective destiny. As the Italian war effort stalled, however, the fear that Italy might become a glorified Nazi satellite imparted a more anxious tone to *Primato*'s discussions of nationalism and federalism. By 1942, historians cautioned against plans for European unity that foresaw the primacy of a single power, and one reminded his readers that Italy and Germany had historically acted "with absolute autonomy" even when they shared similar sentiments and goals. The "imposition of one race on another . . . would create a state of chronic crisis and foment new disorders and the most violent reactions," concluded one *Primato* editorial in August of that year.[39]

The sense of Italy's growing political impotence within the powerful Axis war machine made it more urgent for the Italians to position themselves as the exponents of fascist modernity in the cultural realm. To have any chance at cultural leadership in postwar Europe, Bottai reasoned, Italians must study the contemporary crisis in order to anticipate the lineaments of the new order that would emerge from the ashes of the war. Thus in the spring and summer of 1941, as fascist troops foundered in North Africa, *Primato* organized a discussion around the topic of "a new Romanticism." The term Romanticism here referred to a historical moment when, as in the early 1800s, war and revolution stimulated artistic innovation and an ethos of intellectual *engagement*. Summarizing the concerns of the debate, the philosopher Galvano Della Volpe asked, "How can we get our bearings now that Anglo-French culture is collapsing? What will take its place?" Clearly, only a "truly renewed culture, one that has the modernity of our time" would make inroads in the new Europe. But how should modernity be understood in light of the war, and what role should intellectuals play at a time of crisis and transition?[40]

Although the delineation of new cultural paradigms and political roles occupied intellectuals throughout the continent, they had a particular resonance for Italians who struggled to make sense of fascism's future in a German-dominated New Europe. Many intellectuals had invested years in working to bring about a movement that would supplant a moribund liberal-democratic civilization. Yet the rapid collapse of the old order in the face of Nazi firepower left some unexpectedly ambivalent. France's speedy capitulation to the Germans came as a particular shock to Italians who scorned the Gallic political system but still held its culture in high regard. Moreover, the war threw into relief the extremism of Nazi ideology, causing some Italians to take a second look at the disciplined Aryan conquerors whom Mussolini held up as paragons of fascist style. Pintor, whose job with the Italian Commission for the Armistice with France took him frequently to Germany, warned his compatriots repeatedly that the Nazis' mastery of the "modern" virtues of order and efficiency came at a deadly price. The growing fears of national decline and cultural colonization during World War II sparked a new round of debates over the issue of *engagement* and prompted some intellectuals to reconsider their allegiance to a fascism that had come to signify cold-blooded conquest and war.[41]

This did not mean that Italians wished to return to the prefascist past. Most still believed that the liberal-capitalist order had dug its own grave. Rather, the perception of a national crisis brought out tensions about the meaning of fascism and Italian modernity that had structured generational debates since the early 1930s. As we have seen in previous chapters, many of the World War I generation had been drawn to fascism as a defense of tradition against the interwar period's emancipatory and standardizing tendencies. This age-group had combated the efforts of younger intellectuals to advance models of fascist modernity based on collectivism and cultural modernism. Even those who had backed corporativism as a means of revolutionizing Italian society, such as Bottai and Casini, had censured *Cantiere*'s and *Camminare*'s visions of fascist mass society as unacceptably anti-individualist and materialistic. As they argued, Mussolini's "third way" was meant to protect personhood and spirituality, not do away with them altogether. This official commitment to "humanist" positions was, if anything, strengthened with the advent of the Axis alliance, when Bottai and other Italians countered the Nazi's genealogy of Nordic superiority by highlighting the legacies of Renaissance humanism in Europe.[42]

A similar spirit informed a March 1941 article in *Primato* by Manlio Lupinacci that began the "new Romanticism" debate. In it, Lupinacci blamed the current "social disorientation" in Italy on the erosion of the values of "moral courage and human sympathy." He urged intellectuals to act as forces for stability by "returning to the places they had left vacant" in the ranks of the bourgeoisie.[43] Lupinacci's essay provoked a storm of criticism from intellectuals who charged that such sentimental paternalism would have no place in postwar mass society. For Della Volpe, who foresaw a mass society defined by the values of technology and labor, Lupinacci's request smacked of "the old mentality of the Enlightened intellectual, of the *clerc*." Younger intellectuals took particular umbrage with Lupinacci's vision of intellectuals as agents of bourgeois and traditional interests. Indeed, antibourgeois sentiment was common among both fascist and antifascist respondents who had grown up with fascism's revolutionary rhetoric. Thus Paci averred that taking refuge in the ivory tower of "liberal optimism" would do nothing to ensure Italy's survival in the present crisis. Instead, Italians must abandon any residual bourgeois trust in the forces of history and shape their own destinies by assuming "the responsibility of an act of choice." Fascism intended to kill off the bourgeois order, he argued, not rehabilitate it.[44]

The twenty-three-year-old communist Mario Alicata also denounced liberal humanism and called on intellectuals to act as a clear-eyed vanguard of national renewal. Born just four years before the March on Rome, Alicata had supported universal fascism in the mid-1930s before making a permanent commitment to another kind of internationalist doctrine. Lupinacci's article expressed the viewpoint of a bygone age, Alicata asserted boldly, since bourgeois culture was in a state of "mortal crisis . . . that no old measures, instruments, or therapies will be able to cure." He asked his fellow intellectuals to "gather the courage to go down among the others [*scendere fra gli altri*] and search for the new conditions of our existence among other men." Alicata's proposal had nothing to do with fascism's mandate to "go toward the people." He envisioned a radical break with existing Italian society, which, given his involvement in PCI clandestine activities, also reads as a statement of psychological preparation for the rigors of underground life. To bring about a new society, Alicata concluded, Italian intellectuals must learn to "repress the humanitarian beliefs and impulses of placid well-being in the name of refusing all compromises and in the desire to search out suffering and pain. A new Romanticism? We believe it can only mean the ability to distance ourselves from things, habits and affections that might continue to sweeten our existence. . . . One must not be moved by loved ones or by one's own tradition."[45]

Lupinacci responded with a defense of blackshirt "humanism" that posited Mussolini's movement, squadrism included, as a defense of "bourgeois, Christian, and European" values. Piety and respect for the individual defined a Western tradition that fascism, as he understood it, had pledged to protect. If modernity entailed the abandonment of these qualities, then Lupinacci was having none of it: "Society is indeed in a grave crisis when the will to remain unmoved by loved ones and one's own tradition causes . . . qualities and virtues that make up man's essential dignity with respect to himself and his neighbor to be rejected as prerogatives peculiar to a given 'outdated' generation."[46] After the philosopher Ugo Spirito backed up Lupinacci two weeks later with an essay that invoked fascism's respect for the heroic individual, the twenty-two-year-old critic Pintor contributed an essay that concluded the debate on a sober note. Neither a communist like Alicata, nor a fascist like Paci, Pintor shared both men's belief that the current national crisis necessitated a concerted action by the intellectual class. As a Germanist and a Vichy-based attaché with the Italian-French armistice commission, Pintor had a privileged knowledge of the Nazi mentality. He thus warned that "decadent" attitudes such as Spirito's "Romantic pathos" and Lupinacci's "human sympathy" would only further weaken Italy's position. The new European era would favor those who were able to exercise "extreme coldness of judgment" as they confronted the central problem of the day: that of "choice and active polemic. [It is] the problem of the road to choose, in which individual solutions have a secondary importance."[47]

Pintor's article confirmed that the ideology of commitment and collective action had assumed an importance in the worldview of younger Italians that spanned political boundaries. For the fascist Paci, the "responsibility of choice" led to a decision to volunteer for "a war that will establish us in history"; for the antifascist Alicata, it led to the risky life of a communist operative.[48] Pintor would nurture his own plans for antifascist action from his base in Vichy. The positions these young intellectuals took during *Primato*'s 1941 debate foreshadowed the fracturing of the Italian nation in the coming years of political crisis and civil war. By the end of 1943, Paci would be doing time in a German prison camp, Alicata would be tasting freedom after nine months in a fascist jail, and Pintor would be dead, killed by a mine as he brought arms to Italian partisans.

The articles of Alicata and Pintor also testify to the failure of Bottai's consensus-building strategies. Designed to attract youth to serve a new fascist cultural front, *Primato* became a space for young antifascists to display their disaffection. *Primato* documents the political and moral dilemmas faced by Italian intellectuals of all ages during the dramatic years of World War II. The psychological costs of the regime's increasing fragmentation come across clearly in the pages of *Primato*, as do the war's effects on conceptions of Italian modernity and nationhood that had been developed over a decade of debate. In the final section of the chapter, I will discuss how the crisis of fascism found expression in literature and film in the last years of the regime.

OTHER ITALIES, OTHER MODERNITIES

Since the early thirties, the regime had assigned literature the task of elucidating the ethical values and codes of taste that might mark fascist modernities. The realist novels of the years 1930–35 had engaged with moral questions in ways that converged with blackshirt cultural policy, but their antibourgeois agendas and stylistic affinities with modernist movements had led some critics to exclude them from the pantheon of the new "national novel." In the long run, Alvaro's fiction and literary reportages proved most congenial to the fascist literary establishment, since they put forth a model of Italian modernity that preserved provincial and ethnic values within the national community. By 1940, Alvaro's "glorious country narratives" earned him an Academic Prize, and several of his books were reissued. Among these was *Itinerario italiano (Italian Itinerary)*, a 1933 collection of literary reportages that presented Italy as a land of folklore festivals, gleaming Dopolavoro centers, and industrious individuals. In the early thirties, reviewers had praised *Itinerario italiano* as a contribution to the individuation of a distinctly Italian and fascist style of mass society. Ten years later, though, Alfonso Gatto and other young reviewers of the new edition ignored the book's politics and highlighted Alvaro's affirmation that "exploring Italy is like exploring ourselves." Now, critics noted, writers were less concerned with "exterior aspects and problems of life" than with "moral documentation" and "a free artistic conscience." As the twenty-six-year-old critic Giancarlo Vigorelli observed, his peers had taken the old mandate to "return to the novel" as an invitation to engage in "a 'meditation on man': the *recherche* of the authentic novelist depends not on chronicle but on the notion of man." By the early 1940s, rather than map the sites of a fascist modernity, Gatto and others his age began to look outside of fascist social and political networks for "our forgotten parents, the types of an uncorrupted society."[49]

Themes of space and identity dominate the fiction by younger writers that appeared during the regime's final years. I will discuss two novels, De Céspedes's *Nessuno torna indietro* (*There's No Turning Back*, 1938), which became a best-seller in the war years, and Vittorini's *Conversazione in Sicilia* (*Conversation in Sicily*, 1941). Both works assert the need for new geographies and communities that would facilitate their generation's search for identities untouched by fascist social engineering schemes. De Céspedes's novel, though, also highlights how gender politics conditioned young women's experiences of modernity and mobility under the regime. Indeed, while Vittorini's protagonist's journey back to his native Sicily occasions his rediscovery of an antifascist history and identity, De Céspedes's characters find that there is "no turning back" for women who have rejected the roles and roads marked out for them by the dictatorship.

One of the greatest publishing successes of the fascist period, De Céspedes's novel reached a wide audience and can be read on a number of levels. I will focus here on the author's exploration of the relationship of gender and modernity and her skillful subversion of official discourses about both themes. First, De Céspedes highlights the constructed nature of "natural" discourses about female socialization and reclaims the sphere of

Figure 17. Alba De Céspedes and Paola Masino (second from left and far right), with friends in Cortina, 1941. Reproduced with permission of Alvise Memmo and the Getty Research Institute, Research Library.

choice for women by capturing her eight protagonists at the moment they make decisions about their destinies. The women, most of them college students, live in a nun-supervised boardinghouse (the Pensione Grimaldi) whose strict curfews and routines give it the feel of a prison; it is a static space that keeps them "cloistered," they complain, while "outside life flows by." As the women test out the lives they envision for themselves after graduation, De Céspedes reminds her readers that adopting the role of wife and mother is a choice rather than an automatic or ineluctable decision. There may be "no turning back," but there are many ways to go forward (fig. 17).[50]

The multivocal novel also exposes the gendered nature of fascist discourses about modernity. Rebuking prevailing ideas about the overdetermined nature of gender and social roles under fascism, it emphasizes women's role in the construction of their own personal histories and their right to "begin again, remake oneself from scratch," in the words of one protagonist. As we saw in chapter 2, themes of identity construction and the experience of spatiotemporal provisionality characterized the modernist novels of Emanuelli and Barbaro. De Céspedes views these themes through the lens of gender. She focuses on the tension between the rhetorics of expansion and possibility that form part of the modern ethos and the conditions that, in practice, conspired to curb female autonomy and exploration. Reflecting on the life she and her peers lead at the Grimaldi, the young intellectual Silvia characterizes their situation as "without traditions, without precedent or future. . . . not all of us will be here next year. It is as though we were on a bridge. We've left one shore, but have yet to reach the other. What we've left is behind us, and we don't even turn back to look at it. That which awaits us is still shrouded in fog, and not even we know what we will discover when that fog lifts."[51] Similar rhetoric marked the pronouncements of many male intellectuals of De Céspedes's generation (she was born in 1911, the same year as Paci and Anceschi) who proclaimed the liminality of their times and their intent to play a leading role in the shaping of a new society. Yet the writer shares none of her male cohort's utopian aspirations, and her characters lack female mentors and role models. Rather, her eight characters' stories confirm how difficult it was for young women to reconcile their ambitions with the constraints imposed by a highly traditional society. "We can't turn back again," observes the struggling writer Augusta. "If our parents knew this they would never send us to the city. Because afterward, even if we return home, we are bad daughters, bad wives. Who can forget how to be one's own mistress? . . . And those who remained [at home], who passed from the rule of the father to the rule of the husband, cannot forgive us for having had the keys to our own room, for having come and gone as we pleased."[52]

Through intertwined narratives of eight lives, De Céspedes offers a range of responses to the challenge of constructing a modern female subjectivity in fascist Italy. Space becomes a metaphor for identity in the book, as each character struggles to claim a place outside the Grimaldi in which to develop personally and professionally. Some find that "success" as women requires them to assume false identities. Xenia drops out of college and becomes a kept woman with a fake aristocratic pedigree to avoid returning to the provinces. Emanuela is forced to hide her illegitimate daughter away, censoring her identity as mother and constructing a "niche of lies" to conform to social expectations. To escape this system of repression and live openly with her daughter, she opts for the liminal space of an extended cruise around the Mediterranean at the novel's end. Anna is the exception here: her traditional temperament leads her to return home to marry and live as a rural landowner. "Everyone today wants to rise beyond their original status and live above their possibilities," she complains of her parents' modernist tastes and their ambitions to join urban high society.[53]

Female characters who harbor strong professional ambitions fare little better if they do not wish to compromise their independence. The feminist writer Augusta remains estranged from her surrounding society. With her "masculine attitudes and gestures" and disdain for prevailing gender codes, she can find no congenial public to inhabit and no audience for her antimale books. She remains alone at the Grimaldi but does avoid a domestic fate she regards as "slavery." Silvia is determined to succeed in her academic career and forges ahead with the help of a male mentor. "It is necessary to know how to be the person who walks in front of the others," Silvia muses. "I won't stay in the platoon, in the herd; women often let themselves be tamed by the senses or by the little faith they have in themselves." Yet De Céspedes offers a mixed message about the consequences of her success as a female professional in fascist Italy. Silvia hopes that her new teaching position, in the fascist New Town of Littoria, might offer more freedom from established gender roles, but she finds it difficult to gain social acceptance as a woman intellectual. Barbaro celebrated Littoria's totalitarian modernity in his film *L'ultima nemica,* but De Céspedes intimates that it obliterates all sense of community and self. Writing to her friends, Silvia reflects that she feels the need for a "refuge" in this town where "everything is clear, transparent, you see your reflection everywhere, your image comes at you in a thousand ways, you can never forget you exist. . . . No one has an intimate life of their own; you still feel the need for an organizing community that could help to overcome the coldness of the buildings and streets." [54] Like Vittorini in *Il garofano rosso,* De Céspedes also denounces the effects of fascist socialization schemes on an even younger generation of Italians. At the book's close, Emanuela perceives that younger girls who made up a new generation of Grimaldi residents had already lost their individuality and vitality: "In the new students the taste for debate had disappeared; their personalities seemed faced with stone and covered by the same varnish." *Nessuno torna indietro* revealed the constructed nature of fascist conceptions of social identity, offering women and men a message of resistance against the regime's assault on the self. [55]

The need to chart new geographies as a prelude to the construction of antifascist identities also forms a central theme of Vittorini's novel *Conversazione in Sicilia.* Mixing autobiography and fantasy, Vittorini recounts a journey home that becomes an occasion for the recovery of the self. Structured as a series of encounters and dialogues that generate progressive self-understanding, the novel takes readers into an Italy that has escaped transformation by fascist social engineering schemes. In "the pure heart of Sicily," the dictatorship's discourses have all been subverted. Alienation and sickness are signs of health, disobedience and skepticism indicate integrity, and language has taken on an allusive and coded quality that works against mass indoctrination. Language becomes an instrument of resistance against power in the novel in several ways. First, Vittorini uses ellipses to assert his right to a sphere of privacy and free thought. "That winter, I was taken by abstract furies. I won't say which, that's not what I set out to talk about," he writes teasingly in the book's opening lines. Second, Vittorini calls attention to the extent to which language can support or undermine existing political systems. At the start of the novel, the thirty-year-old protagonist, Silvio, withdraws from a world of conversation and debate that had previously excited and sustained him. Echoing the sentiments expressed by Vittorini's peers in the cultural press, he reflects that "it was as if I had nothing to say, nothing to affirm or negate, nothing of my own to stake a claim with." By the end of the book, though, he finds a place among Italians who communicate through evasive, jumbled stories and hermetic "sealed words" (*parole suggellate*, such as "Hmm" and "Ah!") that are incomprehensible to the authorities.[56]

As Silvio travels to Sicily for the first time in fifteen years, he recovers parts of himself that he had neglected or willfully repressed in order to conform to his surrounding society. His moral renewal begins on the train when he meets a man who expresses a desire for a "fresh conscience" that would inspire Italians to carry out "other duties" than those specified in the current ethical code. In his natal village, Silvio reunites with his mother, who symbolizes the ability to heal that has survived despite the welfare programs of the "therapeutic" state. He accompanies her as she visits the sick, and realizes that he, too, has harbored an illness that has blocked him from seeing the suffering around him. He then journeys further into Sicily, to a place "with no women" that is "not yet contaminated by the offensive things that are taking place on the earth."[57] In this all-male realm, he meets three artisans who prepare to resist, armed only with the tools of their trade and their desire to alleviate human misery. Silvio's final "conversation" is with the ghost of his brother, a casualty of the Ethiopian War. In a devastating indictment of the fascist cult of military martyrdom, his brother tells him that he is wounded anew by "every published and spoken word, every millimeter of bronze erected" in memory of wars undertaken in bad faith.[58] At the end of book, all those whom Silvio has encountered in his journey gather before a huge statue sent by the state to commemorate the local dead. Through a dialogue composed mostly of "sealed words" that the attending policemen cannot understand, Vittorini communicates his rejection of the rituals, symbols, and language of Mussolini's Italy. Like De Céspedes, Vittorini subverts official rhetorics about the collective remaking of their generation, but he also marks antifascist militancy as a male space, as would many participants in the upcoming Resistance.

Vittorini originally wrote the book in 1937–38 in reaction to the Spanish Civil War, and when it first appeared in the journal *Letteratura* his references to "massacres" and "suffering humanity" referred to the fate of Spanish Republicans. Indeed, Italy's alliance with Franco in the Spanish Civil War opened his eyes to the tyrannical nature of the regime he had supported for more than a decade. The book thus marks the beginning of Vittorini's own journey away from fascism. In his 1933 work, *Il garofano rosso*, he had celebrated squadrism as a liberatory force; he now took up the cause of all those who suffered from violence and abuses of authority. "Not every man is a man," the thirty-year-old protagonist Silvio muses midway through his trip: "One persecutes and the other is persecuted; so the human race is not all human, but only that part which is persecuted. Kill a man; he will be more of a man. The same is true of a sick man, a starving man; one who dies of hunger is more human than the rest of the human race." [59] By returning to Sicily, the land of his childhood, Silvio recreates a memory and history for himself outside of those instilled by the regime. Significantly, his escape from the official past liberates him from the influence of paternal authority: his trip to Sicily is initially prompted by his father's abandonment of his mother, who tells Silvio that his father had always been cowardly and weak. When the father finally returns home in the book's epilogue, Silvio leaves without speaking to him. At a time when Vittorini had been temporarily expelled from the PNF for his Republican sympathies, the novel's assertion of filial independence communicated a real-life rebellion against Bottai, Mussolini, and other father figures who had given him a false conscience and language.

The political implications of *Conversazione in Sicilia* resonated even more strongly with Italians by the time the story appeared in book form in the spring of 1941. By then, Vittorini was on his way to joining the communist underground, and many of his peers had begun to question fascism's claim to represent the Italian nation. For this audience, the "suffering humanity" of which the book speaks referred not only to fascism's victims but to their own struggles of conscience as they grew uncomfortable with their positions within fascist political and patronage networks. One of them, the military attaché Pintor, alluded to the book's multiple significance when he commented that "in no recent novel has the pain or anguish, the human element . . . appeared so plainly, so little obscured by the literary plot. For this reason *Conversazione in Sicilia* has the absolute value of an allegory." Other young antifascist critics also drew attention to the book's moral messages. Alicata praised Vittorini's "courageous sincerity of passions," while Giorgio Bassani, writing pseudonymously due to the racial laws, lauded the novelist's focus on the dilemmas faced by the individual in a society divided between "offenders and offended, the inert and the virile, the living and the dead." [60] Critics who opposed Vittorini's book attacked its "American" tone and rhythm as a way of labeling it as an outsider work. Certainly, they had plenty of ammunition: Vittorini had recently put his name to translations of Faulkner, Steinbeck, and Saroyan for the Bompiani publishing house and had begun work on a well-publicized anthology of American literature. Speaking for many, an anonymous critic lambasted the Sicilian writer in *Primato* for his "contamination" by American style. "When will Vittorini liberate himself from this extraneous weight that continues to impoverish his work?" [61]

The discussions over foreign influences on the work of Vittorini and others of his generation continued until the end of the dictatorship. In 1942, a decade after its first survey on the novel, the *Corriere padano* sponsored a discussion that revealed the continuing insecurities of the literary establishment about the existence of a new national novel. Reprising a provocative question Papini had raised in 1929, the newspaper asked Italian writers and critics if Italians were especially indisposed for novel-writing, and whether younger Italian novelists had been successful in assimilating foreign techniques, styles, and "civilizations." Many respondents objected to the insinuations about the Italian novel's failure to take off but gave only vague answers or cited writers who had flourished in the prefascist period. Most felt that it was too early to judge Vittorini, Emanuelli, and others of their age-group, but several expressed doubts that their works would ever qualify as art. While the antifascists Eugenio Montale and Francesca Flora were included in the survey, the respondents were all roughly fifty years old. The survey thus comes across as a collective disavowal of a generational literary project that dated back to Moravia's *Gli indifferenti* and had aimed to create works that "reach out to Europe, but still remain Italian," as Pannunzio had envisioned it in 1932. [62]

By the early 1940s, in any event, that literary project was undergoing an internal evolution. Not only were the politics of some of Vittorini's age-group beginning to shift, but an even younger generation—that of Alicata and Pintor—had emerged to advance its own visions of a modern Italian literature. As in the pages of the journal *Corrente*, the notion of realism took on new meanings in the hands of Alicata and other antifascist critics. In April 1940, Alicata became the editor of the literary review *La Ruota*, which was financed directly by the MCP. *La Ruota* counted other young communists, such as Antonello Trombadori and Carlo Muscetta, among its editorial committee, and it soon became a site for the articulation of critical methodologies that might underpin an antifascist culture. Unlike the intellectuals of Vittorini's generation, though, who had worked to forge an Italian culture that would be in step with the European modernism, the horizon of Alicata and his peers did not reach much outside the borders of Italy. In *La Ruota* and then in *Cinema,* they proposed a new realism that built not on Dos Passos or on the *Neue Sachlichkeit* but on the ideas of late-nineteenth-century Italian figures such as Francesco De Sanctis and Verga. De Sanctis's realism shed the Naturalist doctrine of impersonality for a belief in artistic transfiguration. The notion that reality must be interpreted, rather than reproduced, had been a cornerstone of fascist realist doctrines throughout the thirties, and calls for a "return to De Sanctis" had been issued intermittently in the fascist press. Alicata, Muscetta, and other antifascists, though, viewed De Sanctis's ideas as a means of restoring art's function as a force for social liberation. Thus Alicata's first editorial differentiated between writers who "remain completely 'written' or 'painted' by prevailing tastes," and those who "go beyond and transfigure them [these tastes] into their own definitive and immutable expression." In the post-1945 period, Alicata served as a PCI senator and headed the party's cultural committee, and Muscetta became an important communist critic who edited De Sanctis's works. The pages of *La Ruota* contain the outlines of a future communist model of cultural modernity that proved almost as ambivalent about European modernism as fascism had been.[63]

At the same time Alicata edited *La Ruota,* he and other leftists in their early twenties also authored articles in Vittorio Mussolini's *Cinema* that applied their ideas on realism to the realm of film. Indeed, cinema became the arena in which realism found its fullest development as an oppositional aesthetic and as an instrument for the discovery of an Italy that had been screened out of official visions of national community. As we have seen, realism had long been identified by fascist intellectuals as the basis for a uniquely "Italian" film product, and military filmmakers had been experimenting with an "Italian" documentarist aesthetic since the start of World War II. At the same time, the national film market remained dominated by foreign-derived romantic comedies and the stylized historical films made by Soldati and other directors of the emerging formalist school. Operating in this context, the *Cinema* group proposed a "transfigurative" realism that would combat "escapist" films without supporting the status quo. As in the case of literature, realism also offered an occasion to return to national tradition. Alicata and the twenty-four-year-old critic Giuseppe De Santis proposed the "essential and violent language" of Verga as the basis for "a revolutionary art inspired by a humanity that suffers and hopes." To these youth, Verga's narratives of struggling peasants and fishermen had a very contemporary appeal. They communicated a "faith in the truth and the poetry of the truth, faith in man and in the poetry of man" that could inspire other Italian stories about the "new and pure life" emerging from the country's streets, fields, ports, and factories. The *Cinema* group's recourse to a prefascist past reflected a search for an untainted national history that inspired Vittorini in these years as well.[64] At the heart of this discourse on realism lay a desire to achieve a more wholistic depiction of individuals as creatures intimately connected to their natural and social surroundings. For both De Santis and Alicata, the focus on environment and landscape (*ambiente* and *paesaggio*) signified more than a change in stylistic codes: it came to stand for the will to break through the prevailing alienation and dehumanization of fascist society. In a December 1941 article, De Santis made clear the political agenda that lay behind the crusade for a new national cinema: "Perhaps little by little we will be able to reanimate and warm the solitude of those characters. . . . perhaps we'll be able to restore a conscience to everyone, to find again the ancient ties between man and nature. . . . [We ask for] a 'choral' cinema that would keep pace with the problems and aspirations of our souls: be it a ruthless critique of a fat bourgeois world, or the depiction of a world in which man is sullied and corrupted by solitude and oppression."[65]

The 1942 film *Ossessione (Obsession)* represented the *Cinema* group's contribution to this collective moral and cultural renewal. Alicata and De Santis were among the screenwriters of this movie directed by Visconti, who had become an antifascist while working with Renoir in Paris on Popular Front films such as *La vie est à nous*.[66] Visconti had joined up with De Santis, Alicata, and other young dissidents to make a film from Verga's work *L'amante di Gramigna*, but that script was vetoed by the MCP for its allusions to brigandage. The group then produced a script from James Cain's novel *The Postman Always Rings Twice*, which had already inspired a 1939 film by Pierre Chénal. Although Cain's tale of domestic tragedy hardly counted as a national-popular work, its emphasis on the power of the passions to alter individual destinies pleased both the sensualist Visconti and the pragmatic Alicata. In their hands, this American story became the basis for a dramatic commentary on an Italy that had been impoverished rather than transformed by the fascist revolution.

With its desolate landscapes and its characters who act on their desires at whatever cost to prevailing laws and morals, *Ossessione* signaled the failure of official schemes to remake and discipline the Italian countryside and national character. With the exception of Bragagna, the innkeeper who falls victim to a murder plot by his wife, Giovanna, and her lover, Gino, all of the film's protagonists remain outside of fascist productive and reproductive networks. Giovanna avoided having children with the fat Bragagna, whom she married for survival rather than for love, and Gino became a vagabond after he completed his military service. Moreover, the film replaces secondary characters from Cain's book who represent state authority with nonconformist figures—such as the dancer Anita and the Italian showman known as "the Spaniard"—whose itinerant and bohemian existences contrast starkly with the structured lifestyles exalted in *Treno popolare* and other fascist films. "The Spaniard" is particularly important in this regard. His homosexuality (which is alluded to) and his scorn for money, fixed domiciles, and other bourgeois accoutrements ensure his outsider status in current Italian society. He offers Gino an entrée into a world of libidinal and spiritual freedom that stands in opposition to the capitalist and familialist orientations of fascism. It is not surprising that the film's original title was *Palude,* or *Marshes:* the filmmakers expose viewers to a world little touched by the *bonifica* enterprises that marked fascism's modernizing schemes.

Although the antifascist sympathies of *Ossessione's* authors were no secret to the government, the film received state financing and encountered few obstacles with the censors before it premiered. Visconti's movie also received advance billing in official organs such as *Lo Schermo* and *Bianco e nero,* both of which published laudatory articles while the film was being shot between June and November 1942.[67] Yet when the film opened in May 1943, Catholic critics denounced its erotic elements, and nationalists attacked it as a decadent imitation of French verist cinema. Foreshadowing practices of the cold war period, priests "purified" movie theaters after showings of *Ossessione,* and prefects made impromptu cuts to "improve" the film's moral tenor. Alicata and fellow screenwriter Gianni Puccini followed the fuss from their jail cells: they had been arrested for antifascism in December 1942 and remained in Rome's Regina Coeli prison until August 1943.

Released in the regime's final months, Visconti's film occasioned an exchange on national film style that became an implicit referendum on the results of fifteen years of fascist film policies. The critic Guido Aristarco praised *Ossessione* for providing an alternative poetics to the "decorativism" of the formalists and the escapism of the Camerini school. Bringing a documentarist sensibility to the world of the passions, the film had created "an intimate fusion of stylistics and human values" that was deeply moral and uniquely Italian. In his review, Aristarco cited a passage from an article by Barbaro, who now renewed his public support for realism after spending the war years at the Centro Sperimentale scripting the formalist films of his patron, Chiarini. "If we truly want to abandon the muddled historic epic . . . and the cute little comedy we must try the realist film," Barbaro wrote in a June 1943 essay that postwar critics would come to see as an early Neorealist manifesto.[68]

In December 1939, on the occasion of the first *Corrente* art exhibition, *Corrente*'s editors had observed that realism was "a problem that concerned young people above all, because a condition of our spiritual certainty was a free examination of that 'reality' which was being created around us, a 'reality' that we had to conquer with our own strength to feel it truly ours, beyond any doubts. Realism—without the Naturalistic connotations the word has had in various ages—was essentially our problem." Throughout World War II, in painting, literature, and film, realist discourses served intellectuals in their twenties and thirties to articulate new agendas of individual and national regeneration. As in the early thirties, when it had been at the center of plans for a new fascist aesthetic, realism implied less a specific set of principles than an attitude toward the practice of culture that placed an ethical value on intellectual *engagement*. A decade later, though, those disenchanted with fascism gravitated to realism as a means of conveying emotions and aspirations that could find no public outlet as yet in the political realm. As the antifascist painter Renato Guttuso argued in August 1941, art formed an important arena in which Italians could work to express their struggles, anger, and hope. "It is not necessary for a painter to be of one party or another, or for him to make a war or a revolution," Guttuso commented, "but it is necessary that when he paints, he acts in the same way as someone who does—like someone who dies for a cause."[69] Guttuso, Treccani, Mario Mafai, and other artists put this attitude into practice during the war with works that depict the killings and tortures perpetrated by the Axis powers.

In fact, fascist officials showed a new touchiness during World War II about realism's potential as an instrument of political protest. In 1940, the MCP head Pavolini released a report on the state of the Italian cinema that augured a greater attention to "present-day" Italian life. Using language that foreshadowed Christian Democratic attacks on postwar Neorealist films, Pavolini intoned that realism should not entail a focus on the "deleterious aspects of a society. . . . do we ask that everything be seen through rose-colored glasses? . . . Certainly not, but we require that films reflect not only the bad parts of Italian life but also and above all our collective and continuous well-being."[70] One year later, the government made it clear that these guidelines applied to other cultural activities as well. The Milan prefect temporarily blocked the release of a book of photographs by Lattuada on the grounds that it presented an unflattering picture of Italian life. One suspects, however, that it was the book's preface rather than its images that unsettled officials. In clear and courageous words, Lattuada denounced the collective moral and human failings that had driven Italians to collaborate with fascism for twenty years and had left them divided against each other: "The absence of love brought many tragedies that might have been averted. Instead of the golden rain of love, a black cloak of indifference fell upon the people. And thus people have lost *the eyes of love* and can no longer see clearly; they stagger in the obscurity of death. Here are the origins of the disintegration of all values and the destruction and sterilization of conscience: it is a long chain that is anchored at the devil's feet."[71]

A final exchange between the *Cinema* group and the government two weeks before the fall of the regime emphasized the extent to which Italian intellectuals had learned to exploit the polyvalence of realist rhetoric. In the early thirties, critics such as Bocelli had used allusive language to cushion their requests for a fascist literature. A decade later, such strategies had been mastered and appropriated by younger intellectuals, who used them to advance antifascist agendas. Thus, when the new MCP head Gaetano Polverelli asked filmmakers to "immerse ourselves in our times," *Cinema* responded with a cunning editorial that turned Polverelli's words back on him. With Alicata and Puccini in jail, and other editors facing constant police harassment, they wrote: "We are in accord with his Excellency Polverelli's directives: we believe that 'immersing ourselves in our times' is the healthiest and most constructive thing one can do today. . . . We have always argued for 'a cinema that would interpret Italian life, our civilization, our sensibility, and the character and genius of our race.' "[72]

By then, the Italian life these youth wished to depict depended on communist rather than fascist visions of society and nationhood. As for Vittorini, Treccani, and Guttuso, communism offered new identities and allegiances that saw them through the next few years of national strife. Most of their peers, though, had yet to find alternative models of national community. For many intellectuals, the disastrous war effort and the erosion of fascist authority set off a crisis of national identity that continued into the postwar period. By 1942–43, despite their fear at the consequences of national military defeat, it had become difficult for many youth to support Mussolini's government. The Jewish writer Primo Levi, who was targeted for compulsory labor and deportation during the war, summed up the dilemmas faced by many younger Italians. Describing a lieutenant in his twenties, Levi wrote,

> One could see that he wore his uniform with some disgust. . . . He spoke of fascism and of the war with reticence and with a sinister gaiety that was not hard to interpret. It was the ironic gaiety of an entire generation of Italians who were intelligent and honest enough to reject fascism, but too skeptical to actively oppose it and too young to passively accept the tragedy that was shaping up and despair about the future; I myself would have been part of this generation, had the racial laws not intervened to mature me precociously and guide me toward a choice.[73]

The crisis of national authority also invested the general population in the years 1942 to 1943. Material conditions worsened considerably as food supplies decreased, and Allied bombings drove millions of Italians to the countryside or to shacks on the urban peripheries.[74] Continued defeat on the battlefield also eroded confidence in the Italian army and revealed the emptiness of official boasts about fascism's modernity. Morale was lowest, and desertions highest, on the infamous Eastern Front, where the seeds of some future communist conversions were sown: a few Italians came away impressed with the results of the revolution made by their enemies and horrified by the brutality of their Nazi allies.[75] By 1943, the hunger and misery produced by the war had given rise to widespread discontent with fascism, and rumors flew throughout Italy that the Duce was ill or even dead. Some Italians took to the streets and squares with a fervor not seen since the Ethiopian War, this time to strike and protest the government. On July 11, 1943, two days after Allied troops landed in Sicily, Treccani predicted that their continued advance would "cut Italy in two, and we will have a civil war."[76]

The Allied invasion opened a window of opportunity for those who wished to end the fascist dictatorship or at least the rule of its leader. By then, Mussolini's cavalier and capricious actions had alienated many of his top officials, and even first-hour fascists had begun to make provisions for a postfascist future. On July 25, Ciano and Bottai, along with seventeen other officials, voted to remove Mussolini from power. The king oversaw Mussolini's arrest and the appointment of Marshal Pietro Badoglio as the new prime minister. A master of political survival, the seventy-two-year-old Badoglio had much blood on his hands. He had accepted the post of chief of staff for all the armed forces during the 1925 political crackdown, he bore responsibility for Italian military disasters in two world wars (most notably Caporetto and the Greek invasion), and he had overseen the extermination of hundreds of thousands of Libyans and Ethiopians in concentration camps and in gas attacks. Badoglio's stewardship may have sent a comforting message about the continuity of Italian institutions, but it also expressed a disregard for the moral implications of fascist violence at home and in the colonies that would be reinforced at the close of the war. After Badoglio surrendered to the Allies on September 3, some Italians would display their continued loyalty to fascist causes by serving the Republic of Salò, while others would commit to the antifascist Resistance. In the meantime, Germans flooded into the country from the North, and the Allies continued their sweep through southern Italy. "Half of Italy is German, half is English, and there is no longer an Italian Italy," remarked the young partisan Emmanuele Artom on September 9.[77] Since 1922, Italians had supported fascism as a means of bringing Italy international prestige, national unity, and a new style of modernity. Two decades of dictatorship left the nation bankrupt, occupied by three different foreign powers, and divided against itself.

Epilogue

As the forces of the Resistance and the Republic of Salò faced each other in January 1944, the philosopher Gentile posed a question to his fellow intellectuals that dramatized the fracturing of their country's national identity: "For which Italy should one now live think teach make poetry write?"[1] The choices Italian intellectuals made in response to this question not only determined their immediate future but also conditioned their views of their immediate past. Between September 1943 and April 1945, against the backdrop of the Holocaust and foreign occupation, a new moral universe took shape that ultimately facilitated the nation's self-absolution of responsibility for fascism. By the end of the war, the terms "collaborator" and "resister" referred to Italians' allegiances during the nineteen months of the Republic of Salò, rather than to their actions and attitudes over two decades of dictatorship. Collaborators were those who had aided the German occupiers, not those who had killed other Italians in the name of the Duce. Resisters included longtime opponents of the regime, but also formerly fervent fascists and anti-Semites who had chosen to fight Mussolini after September 1943.

Whether they wished to avenge the crimes of fascism or atone for their part in them, Italians embraced the Resistance in numbers that made it the largest such force in Western Europe. From an initial core of about 9,000, partisan numbers reached 90,000 in the spring of 1944 and swelled to 250,000 by the Liberation. At least 35,000 women fought in partisan formations, and another 70,000 were active in Women's Defense Groups. The communists' "Garibaldi Brigades" were the largest and best organized and financed, but the Action Party, the socialists, the Christian Democrats, and many other political groups also undertook courageous actions alongside Allied troops against the Nazis and fascists in northern and central Italy.[2]

Many reasons led Italians to risk their lives for the Resistance. Patriotism, family traditions, class biases, rebellion against authority, personal vendettas, hatred of the Nazi occupiers, antifascist political beliefs, and the desire to avoid conscription into military and labor units were among the most common motivations. The new networks of community and companionship created by the Resistance countered the climate of dehumanization created by the regime. For older antifascists such as Ada Gobetti, who had been condemned to years of isolation during the dictatorship, the Resistance meant the recovery of "friendship—a bond of solidarity, founded not on a community of blood, country, or intellectual tradition, but on a simple human relationship, the feeling of being at one with many."[3]

Billed as the "rebirth" of the nation, the Italian Resistance also attracted many youth. In August 1944, the now thirty-three-year-old Pannunzio noted the war's dramatic effects on a generation that had been "'educated' by the dictatorship to hate dictatorship itself." The withdrawal and lassitude that had marked his age-group's attitudes in the last years of fascism, he claimed, had given way to a desire for political activism. "For too many, the twenty years passed under the dictatorship have been like a long dream. Heavy, exhausting, full of fear and sweat. The war served as a wake-up call."[4] Others in their twenties and thirties who had believed in Mussolini's movement until the end felt particularly betrayed by the outcome of the war; they threw themselves into the cause of antifascism with what one called an "intense and insatiable hatred."[5] Among intellectuals who had benefited from the regime's patronage networks, the desire to expiate guilt feelings and escape the past proved a primary motivation. Although Italians of all ages conceived of the Resistance as a morally transformative event, images of purification, absolution, and rebirth recur with particular frequency in the writings of those who had been groomed as the regime's next ruling elite. In 1944, the partisan Teresio Olivelli, who had taken top prize for his racist essay at the 1940 Littoriali, interpreted the Resistance as a revolt

> against a system and an epoch, against a mode of thought and a mode of life, against a conception of the world. We never felt so free as when we found in the depths of our conscience the capacity to rebel against the passive acceptation of brutality. . . . we have burned all bridges: the extreme pain and suffering of the war have cleansed us of all impurities: we want to sweep away any residues. We are in a hurry to construct and reconstruct.[6]

The desire for purification also influenced youth who had a history of moral opposition to fascism. Franco Calamandrei, recipient of a bronze medal in the 1935 Littoriali competitions, wrote of "all the impurities that remained, incorrigible, inside of me" as he embarked on a series of dangerous Resistance operations. Although he feared he would be "a mediocre partisan," the twenty-three-year-old Pintor decided to joined the armed Resistance as well. From January to August 1943, Pintor had formed part of the Italian military delegation in Vichy, where he had lived among French and German officials in a state of moral unease about his "comfortable refuge." In November 1943, after concluding that "there can be no salvation through neutrality and isolationism," he set out on a mission that led to his death just four days later.[7]

Not everyone resisted on the battlefield. Many writers and critics who have been discussed in the course of this book used their creative talents to publicize antifascist causes. Treccani and other *Corrente* artists painted searing denunciations of fascist and Nazi atrocities. Alvaro directed the liberal paper *Il Popolo di Roma* between July and September 1943, and Soldati served as a war correspondent for the Socialist paper *Avanti!* before he oversaw, along with Camerini, Barbaro, and Visconti, the Allied-sponsored purges of the Italian film industry. After several months' imprisonment, Pannunzio started the journal *Risorgimento liberale*, while De Céspedes worked for Radio Free Bari and founded the periodical *Mercurio*.

For large numbers of Italians, however, the road to national renewal still led through Mussolini. The Fascist Republican Party numbered 487,000 members by March 1944, and almost 400,000 men and women served in Salò's various military and security forces. The state's army counted a quarter million members, and the Female Auxiliary Service troops, which were instituted in the spring of 1944, attracted almost 6,000 volunteers by April 1945. Salò's numerous police units engaged another 140,000–150,000 Italians, and another 20,000 joined the German-controlled Italian SS.[8] Certainly, duty rather than zeal motivated many who answered Salò's draft call. Yet for those habituated to dictatorship, Salò also represented legitimacy and continuity and closed a psychological void that had been created by the Duce's ouster on July 25. The need for order was particularly strong in younger Italians, for whom the German alliance, state anti-Semitism, and Mussolini's rule were normal rather than exceptional conditions of existence. Although most Italian intellectuals in their twenties and thirties sympathized with the Resistance, many of their age-group who had been trained to "believe, obey, and fight" were inclined to follow the Duce, even when he became a German puppet dictator.[9]

Some Italians, in fact, viewed the collaboration with the Nazis as a final chance to realize their dream of a fascist new order. For followers of first-hour revolutionary fascism, Salò represented an opportunity to enact the radical measures foreseen in the original San Sepolcro program of 1919 without obstructions from the monarchy, the Church, and other traditional institutions. For others, it meant a chance to complete a cleansing *bonifica* of the national collective that would bring Italy in line with its German ally. Defined as "enemy aliens" in November 1943, the Jews became the chief target of this campaign of "social hygiene." Although mass extermination of the Jews remained primarily a Nazi goal, the fascists were present and active in many Holocaust operations in Italy and were in charge of the "Jewish question" there until February 1944. Indeed, the Holocaust in Italy relied on measures and mechanisms that had been created by Mussolini's dictatorship. Censuses, concentration camps, and confiscation of Jewish assets now became essential links in a chain of persecution that culminated in the deportation of over seven thousand Italian Jews to German death camps by April 1945.[10]

Several factors worked against a collective reckoning with this state-sponsored racism after the close of the war. First, the courageous behavior of many non-Jews, who may have remained silent in 1938 but risked their lives during 1943 to 1945 to aid Italian Jews, contributing to their 83 percent survival rate, one of the highest in Europe.[11] Second, the Nazi's obsession with annihilating the Jews made it easy for the Italians to displace blame for their actions onto their German occupiers. As in Germany, functionaries involved in racial policy could shield themselves from guilt by claiming knowledge only of their own specialized bureaucratic domain. But the fact of German occupation meant that all Italians who lived under Salò could claim that they had been subsidiary agents who "just followed orders." After 1945, the use of the term "Nazifascist" to refer to supporters of Salò continued to link national racial violence to a foreign agenda, allowing for a continuing externalization of responsibility for state anti-Semitism.[12]

The events of 1943–45 complicated the process of coming to terms with fascism in other ways as well. The trauma of national division and defeat made it difficult for Italians to recriminate themselves for their past actions. Alvaro's 1944 characterization of Italy as a "poor lamb, offered up in holocaust, which fights to defend itself the best it can" contained an implicit disavowal of Italians' former identity as colonizers and conquerors that would be maintained in popular memory for years to come.[13] Badoglio's surrender to the Allies, which relieved many Italians, humiliated others who had supported fascism as a means of increasing Italy's international authority and who now found themselves invaded by their former German ally. Over six hundred thousand soldiers from the Italian fascist army were immediately deported to Germany as conscripted laborers; they joined one hundred thousand Italians who had emigrated to the Third Reich as "guest workers" in the industrial and farming sectors and who now became little more than slaves. Paci, who had admired the Nazis and volunteered for the war, found himself a German prisoner. By the time the philosopher left the *Lager,* he had changed his mind about fascism's modernity and its potential for human liberation.[14]

Many of the intellectuals whose careers have been followed here endured difficult conditions that seemed to mitigate memories of earlier compromises and collaborations. Those who came out as antifascists after July 25 were particularly at risk. In December 1943, Alvaro fled to the city of Chieti in the Abruzzo region, where he survived by tutoring local children. Vittorini spent a month in prison and went underground, working with the communist resistance in the mountains as he wrote his partisan novel *Uomini e no* (*Men and Not Men,* 1945). Moravia and his wife, Elsa Morante, spent a "sad and squalid" year in a peasant's pigsty in the Ciociara region after they were unable to find assistance at various Roman convents. Bottai, who was on the run from antifascists, experienced no such problems: the nuns of the Institute for the Children of Prisoners outside of Rome gave him shelter, as did a convent in the capital.[15] Emanuelli, who had remained a regime supporter until the end, cloistered himself in occupied Milan. In October 1943, he confessed to his diary that what he feared most was "my judgment of myself," but by 1944 had concluded that the sufferings of the war represented punishment enough. The experience of blood and pain, he confided to his diary, "has allowed the soul to free itself from all that moral laziness had made it taste in the past years. In this way wars cleanse many sins of the spirit."[16]

Those who did try to make sense of fascism after September 1943 often placed blame for the dictatorship with other Italians, drawing dichotomies within the national self based on class or age-group affiliation. Like many German youth after World War II, Italians who had grown up under the dictatorship pointed accusing fingers at their elders. In August 1944, as the first purge proceedings got under way, Pannunzio blasted older Italians who had "deceived" his generation by encouraging them to believe in fascism. The same year, Alvaro criticized elites who had supported fascism out of a desire to modernize Italy. Throughout the thirties, Alvaro had gained points with conservative elements of the fascist cultural establishment for his antimodernism. He preserved this point of view as an antifascist, charging that fascism had betrayed the Italian heartland through its bourgeois fetishization of the new and the foreign. Yet he also minimized collective responsibility for fascism by asserting that the "Italian of the people" had remained "civil and humane" under Mussolini. [17] Alvaro's characterization of fascism as a "flight from Italian reality" found confirmation at this time in the writings of the philosopher Croce, who depicted the dictatorship as a pathological "parenthesis" in the flow of national history. Although Croce denounced Italians for their embrace of fascism, his desire to improve Italy's standing with the Allied occupiers led him to depict fascism as something of foreign rather than Italian origin. [18]

Such ideas did not go uncontested. Before his death in December 1943, Pintor had responded that fascism "was not a parenthesis, but a grave malady that had corroded every fiber of the nation." Carlo Levi and other members of the Action Party would reiterate this message in the coming years, arguing that Italian fascism was an Italian phenomenon that had involved individuals from all regions and walks of life. [19] The communists also took issue with the idea of fascism as a parenthesis in Italian history. Togliatti's explanation of fascism as a bourgeois phenomenon with a mass basis made it difficult to perceive of the dictatorship as something extraneous to national life, and the communists proved more eager than most to see a widespread punishment for fascist wrongdoing. Yet the agenda of "progressive democracy" the PCI adopted in 1944, along with the party's need to establish a mass base of supporters, tended to work against impulses to implicate Italians at the grassroots level. [20]

Paradoxically, the impulse to forget fascism helped to guarantee a large degree of institutional continuity between the regime and the republic. With so many intellectuals entangled for so long with the fascist patron-state, a climate of collective complicity prevailed that worked against formal and judicial attempts to renew Italian cultural life. Although the purges of fascist culture have yet to be fully studied, evidence suggests that those who held power and influence during the dictatorship remained in place to shape the new republic's public discourses and institutions. Although Mussolini's regime lasted five times as long as that of Vichy France, far fewer Italian intellectuals stood trial for fascist sympathies, and no Italian writers met the fate of the French author Robert Brasillach, who was executed in February 1945. Rather, informal processes of censorship and exclusion determined the composition of the postwar Italian literary community. The squadrist writer Marcello Gallian, for example, was shunned by his peers, and died in poverty after selling cigarettes for several years in front of Rome's Termini rail station. Bontempelli had to give up a parliamentary seat he won in 1948 on a Popular Front ticket after a protest about his fascist past, but as late as 1953 he received payments for his service to the Fascist Confederation of Professionals and Artists. None of the writers and critics who have been discussed in this book met with sanctions, even those who, like Cecchi, had participated in the cultural life spawned by the Nazi-fascist alliance. On the contrary, all of those who had been involved in the campaign for the development of a "national novel" throughout the thirties and early forties were able to participate in the reshaping of a collective memory about literary life under the dictatorship.[21]

To some extent, this situation resulted from the same factors that limited defascistization activities in other realms—such as a lack of consensus on purge policies among Italians and their Allied occupiers, both of whom began to conduct purges in 1944. The socialists, communists, Actionists, and other elements in the government that took over from Badoglio in June 1944 had resolved to use the purges to do a thorough housecleaning. This brought them into disagreement with the Allies, whose goals of installing a liberal-conservative government and containing social disorder led them to favor continuities in the realms of finance, industry, and bureaucracy. By June 1945, when Action Party politician and partisan Federico Parri took office as Italy's first postwar prime minister, the sweeping purges and reforms he had envisioned had been constrained both by cold war and domestic exigencies.[22]

The cinema offers a good example of the factors that tempered tendencies toward collective punishment. First, preventive censorship and state sponsorship of the Italian industry had made it difficult to avoid working closely with the government, so that even those intellectuals chosen by the Allies to oversee purge proceedings for the cinema had produced films that exalted the causes of the regime. This collective entanglement in the patronage structures of fascism ensured that, as in the literary world, few Italians wished to push through purges. Carmine Gallone, Augusto Genina, and Goffredo Alessandrini were temporarily banished from Italian studios for their work on imperialist and war films, but all returned to work in the fall of 1945. Even those who had chosen to work for Salò did not see studio privileges suspended. Francesco De Robertis, who had been a major figure in Salò's cinema, continued to make military films in the postwar period, while the screenwriter Piero Tellini moved directly from the circles of Salò to those of leftist Neorealism.[23] Economic factors—namely the sorry state of the Italian film industry—also prevented peer censure. Cinecittà had been stripped of movie cameras by Luigi Freddi and others who had gone over to Salò, and its soundstages had been turned into wartime shelters. The American occupiers gave little aid, since Italy's disabled industry suited

America in its goal of expanding its own film markets, and some officials viewed the Italian industry as tainted by its connections to Mussolini's regime.[24] Under such conditions, many Italians were loathe to deprive their national cinema of experienced talent. The result was a substantial continuity of institutions and personnel between fascist and postwar cinema. Even Chiarini, who had served as director and vice-director of the CSC until the fall of the regime, managed to return to power as vice-president in 1948.

Chiarini's political savvy could not help him save the career of his friend Barbaro, whom he had protected during years of dictatorship. After the fall of Mussolini, Barbaro had emerged as a leading proponent of communist social realism and had been appointed Extraordinary Commissar of the CSC in 1946 when the Italian left's hopes for power in Italy were at their peak. In 1947, though, the left was expelled from the government, and the Christian Democrat official Giuliano Andreotti began a minipurge of communist intellectuals that cost Barbaro his job. That year, Barbaro emigrated to Poland, as his peers pursued the challenge of constructing a new Italy amid the constraints of the cold war.[25]

This book has explored the role of culture in the making and unmaking of projects for a fascist model of modernity. Against a backdrop of the spread of mass culture, the Italians, like their Nazi neighbors, lent their support to a utopian vision of a society that would defend national traditions and forestall further social emancipation. As I have argued, the goal of *bonifica*, or reclamation, provided a unifying framework for many fascist policies. Mussolini intended to create a new breed of conquerors and child bearers who would reverse European decline and put to rest nagging questions about Italian identity and prestige. Mussolini's vow to make Italy a leading international power proved to be a source of his personal popularity with intellectuals of all generations throughout two decades of dictatorship.

Culture had a central role in these projects of national reclamation and international expansion. Here, too, official agendas promised to resolve long-term questions about Italian unity and influence. The creation of distinctly national works that would advertise fascist values abroad inspired those who wished to build on the prestige of Italy's artistic patrimony, while autarchic measures appealed to those who felt that Italy had become a cultural colony of more dominant nations. More broadly, culture also became an important site for the articulation of fascist solutions to the contemporary crisis of modernity. Films, novels, and the cultural press reaffirmed the new behaviors, tastes, and values augured by *bonifica* schemes. Yet they also signaled the emergence of alternative visions of fascist modernity, and in the early forties, the rejection of fascist models of society and nationhood.

Ultimately, Mussolini's plans to transform Italy's domestic and international profile proved less than successful. After 1936, even as Italians consolidated their control of Ethiopia, the escalation of Nazi German aggression consigned the country to a subordinate role within the emerging Axis state system. Mussolini's decision to enter World War II brought Italy's great power ambitions to a crashing halt, leaving a legacy of bitterness and humiliation that was exacerbated by the loss of the Italian empire to the British in 1941. More complex is the issue of whether and in what ways fascism modernized Italy and Italians. The example of culture partially confirms the conclusions reached in studies of fascist economic and social policy: although Italy did modernize during the years of Mussolini's rule, it did so on terms somewhat different from those desired and planned by the fascists. As in other realms, state intervention was greatly expanded; the desire to manage and preserve the cultural patrimony provoked planning measures, as did the goal of attaining controls over the organization of high and popular culture. Intellectuals were organized and mobilized within state structures and were shaped by the regime's patronage and disciplinary measures. Like other Italians, though, many found ways to utilize these spaces and maneuver within them to facilitate the realization of personal and professional aspirations.[26] The cultural realm also illuminates how the tension within fascism between the autarchic and the international complicated the achievement of a distinct fascist model of mass society. Cinema, which became a primary emblem of fascist modernity, provides a crucial case in point. The internationalism of interwar film culture, as well as regime pressures on filmmakers to make movies that would sell abroad, led to works that showcased the very sorts of emancipated behaviors that the regime sought so strenuously to defeat.

Although fascist modernization schemes may have had unintended consequences, we should not assume that the dictatorship did not alter the landscape of Italian intellectual life. Theories of federalism and managed economies came out of the crucible of interwar Italy, as did the concern with a "return to man"—born from thirties' fears about the loss of identities—that informed postwar Italian movements such as existentialism, organic architecture, and Neorealism. Likewise, the collectivist concerns advanced by *Orpheus* and other avant-garde journals in the early thirties would find an echo in Italian neo-avant-garde movements three decades later.[27]

Among younger intellectuals in particular, the fascist dictatorship left a legacy of attitudes and practices that continued under different political rubrics. Consider the notion of intellectual *engagement,* which undergirded so many thirties projects of cultural revolution. In a 1933 article in *Saggiatore,* Paci had thus summarized fascism's greatest lesson to his generation: "There is no division between ideas and life, between systems and their application. One doesn't write history, one makes it."[28] The call for intellectual mobilization and the concept of culture as a privileged agent of social and collective change both found new life in the postwar period. They proved especially compelling among communist and socialist intellectuals as a means of compensating for restrictions on their parties' political influence. Certainly, intellectuals such as the future PCI cultural policy maker Mario Alicata, who began to work as an antifascist organizer while he edited a MCP-run journal, learned lessons about the power of cultural politics that served them well during the cold war.[29] For two decades, fascism provided the context for the reception of messages about Self and Other, Italy and the world, that would be transformed in the postwar period. The collective inquiry about the relationship of politics and culture and the meanings of modernity in Italy initiated during the dictatorship would continue to shape national intellectual life after 1945.

Notes

For list of abbreviations, see bibliography.

INTRODUCTION

1. Renato Poggioli, review of *L'Europa d'oggi*, by G. B. Angioletti, *Pan* (May 1934).

2. Aspects of the European crisis are discussed in Peter Stirk, "Introduction: Crisis and Continuity in Interwar Europe," in *European Unity in Context*, ed. Peter Stirk (London, 1989), 1–23; Michela Nacci, *Tecnica e cultura della crisi, 1914–39* (Turin, 1982); James Wilkinson, *The Intellectual Resistance in Europe* (Cambridge, Mass., 1981); Jay Winter, "War, Family, and Fertility in Twentieth Century Europe," in *The European Experience of Declining Fertility*, ed. John Gillis, Louise Tilly, and David Levine (Cambridge, 1982), 291–309; Dagmar Barnouw, *Weimar Intellectuals and the Threat of Modernity* (Bloomington, Ind., 1988).

3. Jeffrey Herf, *Reactionary Modernism* (Cambridge, 1984); Zeev Sternhell, *Neither Right nor Left* (Berkeley and Los Angeles, 1986); Michela Nacci, "I rivoluzionari dell'apocalisse: Società e politica nella cultura francese fra le due guerre," *Intersezioni* (April 1984): 85–123.

4. On the uses of racial thinking in agendas of social policing within Europe, see Anne McClintock, *Imperial Leather* (New York, 1995); Ann Laura Stoler, *Race and the Education of Desire* (Durham, N.C., 1995). The cultural implications of technological advance in this period are finely analyzed by Stephen Kern, *The Culture of Time and Space, 1880–1918* (London, 1983).

5. Gustave Le Bon, *The Crowd*, trans. and ed. Robert Nye (1895; reprint, New Brunswick, N.J., 1995); Scipio Sighele, *L'intelligenza della folla* (Turin, 1903). On this racialized discourse, see Daniel Pick, *Faces of Degeneration* (Cambridge, 1989); Susanna Barrows, *Distorting Mirrors* (New Haven, Conn., 1981); Patrick Brantlinger, *Bread and Circuses* (Ithaca, N.Y., 1983).

6. Jean Clair, ed., *The 1920s* (Montreal, 1991); John Willett, *Art and Politics in the Weimar Period* (New York, 1978); Richard Stites, *Revolutionary Dreams* (New York, 1989); Peter Wollen, "Cinema/Americanism/The Robot,"

in *Modernity and Mass Culture*, ed. James Naremore and Patrick Brantlinger (Bloomington, Ind., 1991).

7. Karl Jaspers, *Die Geistige Situation der Zeit* (Munich, 1931), 120; Alberto Pirelli, "Luci e ombre della moderna civiltà meccanica (Impressioni di un viaggio negli Stati Uniti d'America)," *Gerarchia* (July 1931); Henri Daniel-Rops, *Le Monde sans âme* (Paris, 1932). The ambivalence to modernity among European intellectuals in the 1930s is addressed by Nacci, *Tecnica e cultura della crisi.*

8. Luca Dei Sabelli, *Nazioni e minoranze etniche* (Bologna, 1929), 1:2; Antonio Gramsci, *Quaderni del carcere*, ed. Valentino Gerratana (Turin, 1974), 2:862–63. An interesting case study of the war's effects on the body and psyche is Joanna Burke, *Dismembering the Male* (Chicago, 1996).

9. José Ortega y Gasset, *The Revolt of the Masses* (1930; reprint, Madrid, 1964), 154. For fears about the reversal of racial hierarchies, see Oswald Spengler, *Der Mensch und die Technik* (Munich, 1931), 95; M. C. Catalano, "Giappone in marcia," *Politica* (July–August 1933). For worries about female emancipation, see Lucien Romier, *Qui sera le maître, Europe ou Amérique?* (Paris, 1927), 86–105; Karl Jaspers, *Die Geistige Situation der Zeit*; G. B. Angioletti, "Sogni e storture della Germania," *Italia letteraria* (January 24, 1932). On the nexus between changing gender relations and the ideology of the crisis, see Mary Louise Roberts, *Civilization without Sexes* (Chicago, 1994); Atina Grossmann, "*Girlkultur* or Thoroughly Rationalized Female: A New Woman in Weimar Germany?" in *Women in Culture and Politics*, ed. Judith Friedlander et al. (Bloomington, 1986), 62–80; Victoria de Grazia, *How Fascism Ruled Women, 1922–45* (Berkeley, 1992). Alice Jardine, *Gynesis* (Ithaca, 1985), looks at the philosophical legacy of this gendered interpretation of the Occidental crisis.

10. Umberto Bernasconi, "Vita di masse," *Gioventù fascista* (May 1, 1935).

11. Benito Mussolini, "Al gran rapporto del fascismo," in Mussolini, *Scritti e discorsi*, ed. Valentino Piccoli (Milan, 1934), 7:148.

12. This point is also made by MacGregor Knox in his works *Mussolini Unleashed, 1939–41* (Cambridge, 1982), and "Expansionist Zeal, Fighting Power, and Staying Power in the Italian and German Dictatorships," in *Fascist Italy and Nazi Germany*, ed. Richard Bessel (Cambridge, 1996), 113–33. Tim Mason, "Italy and Modernization: A Montage," *History Workshop* 25 (1988): 127–47, provides an overview of the debates over the relation of Italian fascism and socioeconomic modernization, as does Carl Ipsen, *Dictating Demography* (Cambridge, 1996), 5–12.

13. "Bonifica libraria," *Critica fascista* (January 1, 1939). The agricultural *bonifiche* and the creation of New Towns are discussed in Riccardo Mariani, *Fascismo e "città nuove"* (Milan, 1976); and Diane Ghirardo, *Building New Communities* (Princeton, 1989).

14. On the transformation of the Italian avant-garde, see Emilio Gentile, "The Conquest of Modernity: From Modernist Nationalism to Fascism," *Modernism/modernity* 1, no. 3 (1994): 55–87; Walter Adamson, *Avant-Garde*

Florence (Cambridge, Mass., 1993); Emily Braun, *Mario Sironi and Italian Modernism* (Cambridge, 2000). I also drew on the insights of Peter Fritzsche, "Nazi Modern," *Modernism/modernity* 3, no. 1 (January 1996): 1–21; Boris Groys, *The Total Art of Stalinism*, trans. Charles Rougle (Princeton, 1992); Modris Eksteins, *The Rites of Spring* (Boston, 1989).

15. See the memoir of the Italian artist-squadrist and World War I veteran Ottone Rosai, *Dentro la guerra* (Rome, 1934); and the testimonials by German veterans and Freikorps members in Klaus Theweleit, *Male Fantasies,* 2 vols. (Minneapolis, 1989). On postwar violence as a reaction to wartime traumas, see Omer Bartov, *Murder in Our Midst* (New York, 1996), 40; Mario Isnenghi, *Il mito della grande guerra da Marinetti a Malaparte* (Bari, 1971). On the war as a crusade of national regeneration, see Emilio Gentile, "Un'apocalisse nella modernità: La Grande Guerra e il Mito della Rigenerazione della politica," *Storia contemporanea* (October 1995): 733–87; Robert Wohl, *The Generation of 1914* (Cambridge, Mass., 1979); Adamson, *Avant-Garde Florence.*

16. Francesco Orestano, "Adunanza inaugurale," in *Convegno di scienze morali e storiche: L'Africa* (Rome, 1939), 1:49; Benito Mussolini, quoted in Luigi Preti, *Impero fascista, africani ed ebrei* (Milan, 1968), 68; Lelio Melani, "Battaglia del grano e psicologia rurale," *La Conquista della terra* (October 1930).

17. Bartov, *Murder in Our Midst,* 5; Fritzsche, "Nazi Modern," makes a similar point.

18. Benito Mussolini, "Discorso sull'Ascensione," May 26, 1927, in *Scritti e discorsi,* 6:59; "Senilità," *Critica fascista* (January 15, 1932); "Come coprire i vuoti," *Vita universitaria* (October 5, 1938).

19. See David Horn, *Social Bodies* (Princeton, 1994); Ipsen, *Dictating Demography;* Giorgio Israel and Piero Nastasi, *Scienza e razza nell'Italia fascista* (Bologna, 1997).

20. Francesco De Sanctis, *Storia della letteratura italiana (1870–71)* (Milan, 1960), 2:463. For concerns about prestige, modernity, and nationalization in the liberal era, see Silvio Lanaro, *Nazione e lavoro* (Venice, 1979); Gentile, "The Conquest of Modernity"; Richard Bosworth, *Italy: Least of the Great Powers* (Cambridge, 1980). Emilio Gentile has taken the goal of national regeneration as a unifying framework for fascist policies in his *La via italiana al totalitarianismo* (Rome, 1995); as has Roger Griffin, *The Nature of Fascism* (London, 1993).

21. Benito Mussolini, "Il discorso dell'Ascensione," *Scritti e discorsi,* 6:77; Mussolini, quoted in Giuseppe Bottai, *Diario, 1935–44* (Milan, 1982), 187.

22. Aspects of this aestheticized politics are analyzed in Simonetta Falasca-Zamponi, *Fascist Spectacle* (Berkeley and Los Angeles, 1997); Jeffrey Schnapp, *Staging Fascism* (Stanford, 1996); Mabel Berezin, *Making the Fascist Self* (Ithaca, 1996).

23. G. P. [Giuseppe Pagano], "Falsi e giusti concetti nella casa," *Domus* (March 1938); and Nino Bertocchi, "Tempo d'arresto," *Domus* (March 1938).

24. F. Zannon, "Per una maggiore diffusione della cultura coloniale," *Ger-*

archia (February 1923). On this point, see Roger Griffin, "The Sacred Synthesis: The Ideological Cohesion of Fascist Cultural Policy," *Modern Italy* (May 1998): 3–24.

25. Giuseppe Pagano, "Dell'uso di certi aggettivi," *Casabella* (July 1930); Mario Labroca, "Per la conoscenza dell'Italia nel mondo," *Critica fascista* (February 1, 1933). For similar sentiments in earlier decades, see Giovanni Papini, "La tradizione italiana," *Quaderni della Voce* (April 1915): 70–78; Giosuè Carducci, *Confessioni e battaglie*, 3 vols. (Rome: A. Sommaruga, 1883–84), 3:239.

26. Raffaele Calzini, ed., *Ventennio: Italia, 1914–34*, special issue of *Domus* (December 1933). Literacy rates were 38 percent in 1881, 74 percent in 1931; dialect speakers were 97.5 percent in 1871, 30 percent in 1931. David Forgacs, *Italian Culture in the Industrial Era, 1880–1980* (Manchester, 1990), 18.

27. Piero Bargellini, "Schiamazzo in salotto," *Frontespizio* (January 1936).

28. Some exceptions are Luisa Mangoni, *L'interventismo della cultura* (Bari, 1974); Giuseppe Carlo Marino, *L'autarchia della cultura* (Rome, 1983); Alexander De Grand, *Bottai e la cultura fascista* (Bari, 1978); Falasca-Zamponi, *Fascist Spectacle*.

29. In the past, Bottai, for example, has often been labeled as a moderate based on his support for modern art, freedoms for younger intellectuals, and corporativism. His zealotry for racist causes was consistently downplayed in Italian histories of fascism. See for example Giordano Bruno Guerri, *Giuseppe Bottai* (Milan, 1977; reprint, Milan, 1996). De Grand, *Bottai e la cultura fascista*, is much more balanced.

30. Rino Longhitano, "Il patto a quattro: Ricostruzione fascista dell'Europa," *Critica fascista* (July 1, 1933). On the regime's natalist measures, see de Grazia, *How Fascism Ruled Women*. On the *Opera Nazionale Dopolavoro's* mass programs, see de Grazia, *Culture of Consent* (Cambridge, 1981); Stefano Cavazza, *Piccole patrie* (Bologna, 1997).

31. Alberto Olivetti, "Il punto debole della economia capitalistica e il tallone d'Achille della dottrina marxista," *La Stirpe* (July 1930).

32. Benito Mussolini, "Quando il mito tramonta," *Il Popolo d'Italia* (December 23, 1921), in *Scritti e discorsi*, 2:230.

33. See Emilio Gentile, *Il culto del littorio* (Bari, 1993). Berezin, *Making the Fascist Self*, analyzes fascist cults of martyrdom.

34. The stress on spirituality also led foreign Catholic thinkers, such as Emmanuel Mounier and Daniel-Rops, to fellow-travel with fascism, drawn by certain similarities it seemed to have with their Personalist movement. For differing views on Personalism's ideological implications, see John Hellman, *Emmanuel Mounier and the New Catholic Left, 1930–50* (Toronto, 1981); Sternhell, *Neither Right nor Left*, chapter 4.

35. Camillo Pellizzi, "Per la difesa dell'uomo," *Critica fascista* (January 15, 1936).

36. Marla Stone and Roger Griffin use the terms "aesthetic pluralism" and "totalitarian pluralism," respectively, to refer to the regime's tolerance of di-

verse cultural tendencies. Stone, *The Patron State* (Princeton, 1998); Griffin, "The Sacred Synthesis."

37. Information on informers from "Elenco nominativo dei confidenti dell'OVRA pubblicato ai sensi e per gli effetti di cui all' art.1 del R.D. legislativo, May 25, 1946, n.424," in *Gazzetta ufficiale della Repubblica italiana*, supplemento ordinario n. 145, July 2, 1946, 1–18.

38. This strategy proved particularly useful with the issue of anti-Semitism. As Meir Michaelis and Michele Sarfatti have argued, Mussolini utilized militant journalists (most notably Telesio Interlandi) and scientists to broadcast his own racist views. See Michaelis, "Mussolini's Unofficial Spokesman: Telesio Interlandi," *Journal of Modern Italian Studies* (fall 1998): 217–40; and Michele Sarfatti, *Mussolini contro gli ebrei* (Turin, 1994), for this argument.

39. For the attitudes of university students, see the police reports in ACS, MI, DPP, Affari per materia, pacco 149, f.21, K112; see also Tracy H. Koon, *Believe, Obey, Fight* (Chapel Hill, 1985), 184–252. For workers' attitudes, see Tobias Abse, "Italian Workers and Italian Fascism," in *Fascist Italy and Nazi Germany*, ed. Richard Bessel (Cambridge, 1996), 40–60.

40. De Grazia, *How Fascism Ruled Women;* Cecilia Dau Novelli, *Famiglia e modernizzazione in Italia tra le due guerre* (Rome, 1994). For levels of participation in fascist mass organizations, see Philip Morgan, *Italian Fascism, 1919–45* (New York, 1995), 116–24.

41. For consumerism and American mass culture as agents of new identity formations, see Victoria de Grazia, "Mass Culture and Sovereignty: The American Challenge to European Cinemas, 1920–1960," *Journal of Modern History* (March 1989): 53–87, and her "Nationalizing Women: Competition between Fascist and Commercial Cultural Models in Mussolini's Italy," in *The Sex of Things*, ed. Victoria de Grazia (Berkeley and Los Angeles, 1996), 337–58.

42. Lucien Romier, *Qui sera le maître, Europe ou Amérique?* (Paris, 1927), 7. Aspects of the revival of traditions in interwar France, Germany, and Italy are discussed in Herman Lebovics, *True France* (Ithaca, N.Y., 1992); Christian Faure, *Le project culturel de Vichy* (Lyons, 1989); James R. Dow and Hannjost Lixfeld, *The Nazification of an Academic Discipline* (Bloomington, Ind., 1994); Cavazza, *Piccole patrie*. On interwar advertising cultures, see Victoria de Grazia, "The Arts of Purchase: How American Publicity Subverted the European Poster, 1920–40," in *Remaking History*, ed. Barbara Kruger and Phil Mariani (Seattle, 1989), 221–57; Karen Pinkus, *Bodily Regimes* (Minneapolis, 1995).

43. Knox, "Expansionist Zeal, Fighting Power, and Staying Power in the Italian and German Dictatorships"; Emilio Gentile, "La nazione del fascismo," in *Nazione e nazionalità in Italia*, ed. Giovanni Spadolini (Bari, 1994), 95–100.

44. F. M. Pacces, "La terza alternativa," *Critica fascista* (November 15, 1936).

45. See Guy Michaud, ed., *Identités collectives et relations inter-culturelles*

(Brussels, 1978); Gregory Jusdanis, *Belated Modernity and Aesthetic Culture* (Minneapolis, 1991); Harold James, *A German Identity, 1770–1990* (New York, 1990); Lydia H. Liu, *Translingual Practice* (Stanford, 1995); Winichakul Thongchai, *Siam Mapped* (Honolulu, 1994).

46. Just after Unification, the politician and critic Francesco de Sanctis had exhorted Italians to "convert the modern world into our world" by "studying, assimilating, and transforming" the achievements of others. De Sanctis, *Storia della letteratura italiana*, 2:463.

47. Giulio Santangelo, "Lo vogliamo fare?" *I Lupi* (January 20, 1928). For earlier (and more muted), similar statements, see Napoleone Colajanni, *Latini e anglosassoni* (Rome, 1906); Scipio Sighele, *Il nazionalismo e i partiti politici* (Milan, 1911), 26–30.

48. Mezzasoma to Pavolini, note of February 15, 1943, in ACS, MCP, b.28, f.413.

49. The phrase is from "Sulla nuova generazione," *Occidente* (January–March 1933).

50. Indro Montanelli, "Noi giovani," *L'Universale* (December 1933).

51. See Millicent Marcus, *Filmmaking by the Book* (Baltimore, 1993); and Lino Micciché, "Cinema italiano sotto il fascismo," in *Modelli culturali e Stato sociale negli anni trenta*, ed. Carlo Vallauri and Giuseppina Grassiccia (Florence, 1988), 173–98.

CHAPTER 1

1. Benito Mussolini, "Stato, anti-Stato, e fascismo," *Gerarchia* (February 25, 1922).

2. The best book on the rise of fascism is Adrian Lyttleton, *The Seizure of Power* (London, 1973). On the movement's early appeals to women and students, see Denise Detragiache, "Il fascismo femminile da San Sepolcro all'affare Matteotti, 1919–24," *Storia contemporanea* (April 1983): 211–51; and Paolo Nello, *L'avanguardismo giovanile alle origini del fascismo* (Bari, 1978). On the securing of conservative interests, see Charles Maier, *Recasting Bourgeois Europe* (Princeton, 1975); Alice Kelikian, *Town and Country under Fascism* (Oxford, 1986); and Anthony Cardoza, *Agrarian Elites and Italian Fascism* (Princeton, 1983).

3. On Lombroso and Positivism, see Pick, *Faces of Degeneration*.

4. Sighele, *Il nazionalismo e i partiti politici*, 100, 111; see also Enrico Corradini, *La vita nazionale* (Siena, 1905). On Corradini and Nationalism, see Alexander De Grand, *The Italian Nationalist Association* (Lincoln, 1978); on Corrado Gini's career and theories from liberalism to fascism, see Ipsen, *Dictating Demography;* and Claudio Pogliano, "Scienza e stirpe: Eugenica in Italia, 1912–39," *Passato e presente* (January–June 1984): 61–97.

5. Alfredo Rocco, "La dottrina politica del fascismo," *Scritti e discorsi politici* (Milan, 1925), 3:1103. On the evolution of Rocco's statist ideas, see Luca Farulli, "Alfredo Rocco: Politica e diritto fra guerra e fascismo," in *Tendenze*

della filosofia italiana nell'età del fascismo, ed. Ornella Faracovi (Livorno, 1985), 241–62; and Emilio Gentile, *Il mito dello Stato nuovo dal antigiolittismo al fascismo* (Bari, 1982), 167–204.

6. On the crackdown of these years, see Lyttleton, *Seizure of Power,* 269–332; and Alberto Acquarone, *L'organizzazione dello Stato totalitario* (Turin, 1965), 73–92. Quotation about ethnic minorities from police informer in Gorizia, July 1–September 30, 1930, in ACS, MI, DGPS, AGR, Cat. G1, b.227, f.467. On the curtailment of regional autonomy under fascism, see Sergio Salvi, *Le lingue tagliate* (Milan, 1975); and Sandro Fontana, *Il fascismo e le autonomie locali* (Bologna, 1973).

7. Benito Mussolini, introduction to *La civiltà fascista illustrata nelle dottrine e nelle opere,* ed. G. L. Pomba (Turin, 1928), 9, and *Opera Omnia,* ed. Edoardo and Duilio Susmel (Florence, 1951–63), 21:362. On the development of ISTAT, see Ipsen, *Dictating Demography.* Officials Enrico Beretta and Emilio Bodrero give the aims of the OND in Opera Nazionale Dopolavoro, *Costumi, musica, danze e feste popolari italiane* (Rome, 1931), 78 and 9–10.

8. Benito Mussolini, "Il discorso dell'Ascensione," 52, 53, 60, 73. A fine analysis of this speech is provided in Barbara Spackman, *Fascist Virilities: Rhetoric, Ideology, and Social Fantasy in Italy* (Minneapolis, 1996), 143–55.

9. Benito Mussolini, preface to Richard Kohrerr, *Regresso delle nascite: Morte dei popoli* (Rome, 1928), 10.

10. Benito Mussolini, "Decidersi!" *Il Popolo d'Italia* (January 12, 1932), in *Scritti e discorsi,* 8:11.

11. Benito Mussolini, "Forza e consenso," *Gerarchia* (March 1923).

12. Giuseppe Bottai, "Il problema delle riviste al convegno della stampa fascista," *Critica fascista* (January 15, 1925). Fascist patronage mechanisms in the arts are described in Stone, *The Patron State.*

13. Bruno Spampanato, "Rivedersi per vivere," *Critica fascista* (June 1, 1924); Benito Mussolini, "Nel solco delle grande filosofie: Relativismo e fascismo," *Il Popolo d'Italia* (November 22, 1922). For propaganda and press measures in this period, see Philip Cannistraro, *La fabbrica del consenso* (Bari, 1975); Frank Rosengarten, *The Italian Anti-Fascist Press, 1919–45* (Cleveland, 1968), 9–30; and Paolo Murialdi, *La stampa del regime fascista* (Bari, 1986), 1–9.

14. The writer Mario Moretti was denied a Mussolini Prize from the Italian Academy in 1932 because he had signed Croce's 1925 antifascist manifesto. See AAI, b.Verbali-Adunanze Generale, transcript of meeting of April 19, 1932, 4. On Pirandello's relations with the regime, see Gianfranco Vené, *Pirandello fascista* (Milan, 1977), 14–17. Croce's July 1924 pro-Mussolini interview with the *Giornale d'Italia* is excerpted in Emilio Papa, *Storia dei due manifesti* (Milan, 1958), 88, which also reprints both Croce and Gentile manifestos.

15. Giorgio Granata, "Residui e nuova cultura" *Oggi* (June 18, 1933); "Bonifica libraria."

16. The syndicate system did offer employment to those who did not receive patronage, since it spawned a new cultural bureaucracy that gave jobs to

many university graduates without footholds in the academic system. For figures on intellectuals' employment in public institutions under fascism, see Silvino Grussu, "Modificazione delle funzioni intellettuali dal 1936 ad oggi," *Critica marxista* (November-December 1977): 63–64. See Cannistraro, *La fabbrica del consenso*, 30–39, and Stone, *The Patron State*, on the development of the cultural bureaucracy. The Venice Biennale and the Quadriennale were headed respectively by Antonio Maraini and Cipriano Efisio Oppo, secretary and president of the Fascist Syndicate of Fine Arts; the Scuola Superiore di Architettura in Rome was directed by Alberto Calza-Bini, the head of the architects' syndicate; and the Fascist School of Journalism was directed by Ermanno Amicucci, head of the journalists' syndicate.

17. Giovanni Calendoli, quoted in Manlio Pompei, "Dialettica fascista," *Critica fascista* (February 1, 1931); Bottai, "Il problema delle riviste al convegno della stampa fascista"; editorial note, *Critica fascista* (June 15, 1924). On Bottai's career, which included stints as minister of corporations, minister of national education, and governor of Rome, see De Grand, *Bottai e la cultura fascista*. My point about fascist criticism is also made by Gentile, *Il mito dello Stato nuovo*, 209–13.

18. Giuseppe Bottai, "Totalità, perennità, universalità della rivoluzione fascista," *Quadrante* (December 1933).

19. My thinking on language, patronage, and cultural politics has been formed by the work of Arthur Herman Jr., "The Language of Fidelity in Early Modern France," *Journal of Modern History* 67 (March 1995): 1–24; Sharon Kettering, J. Russell Major, and Arlette Johnson, "Patronage, Language, and Political Culture," *French Historical Studies* (fall 1992), 839–81; Mario Biagioli, *Galileo Courtier* (Chicago, 1994); Jean-Pierre Faye, *Theorie du recit* (Paris, 1972); and Pierre Bourdieu, *Language and Symbolic Power* (Cambridge, Mass., 1991), and *The Field of Cultural Production* (Cambridge, 1993).

20. Benito Mussolini, "Il giornalismo come missione," speech of October 10, 1928, in *Scritti e discorsi*, 6:251.

21. Ardengo Soffici, "Spirito ed estetica del fascismo," *Lo Spettatore italiano* (May 1924). Obscure and coded discourse was a tradition in Italy, and it characterized the speech of intellectuals and public officials after 1945 as well. See Jader Jacobelli, ed., *La communicazione politica in Italia* (Bari, 1989). Matei Calinescu gives an insightful discussion of the mechanisms and uses of coded language in *Rereading* (New Haven, 1993), esp. 227–72. The phrase "habitual guilt" *(colpa abitudinaria)* is from Francesco Flora, "Dignità dello scrittore," *Corriere della sera* (August 26, 1943).

22. Decree of January 7, 1926, *Gazzetta Ufficiale del Regno d'Italia* (January 25, 1926): 356.

23. Report from Rome, November 18, 1930, in ACS, MI, DPP, Affari per materia, Pacco 153, f.15, K20; see also reports of March 12–13, 1930; March 22, 23 and 27, 1929; September 28, 1929; and March 22 and 23, 1932. Academy members are profiled in Marinella Ferrarotti, *L'accademia d'Italia* (Naples,

1979). For the establishment of a *Discoteca dello Stato,* see AAI, b.Verbali, Adunanze Generali, 1929–34, February 16, 1931, meeting.

24. Volt, "Necessità di un'accademia," *Critica fascista* 4 (1926): 64. Ada Negri won the L50,000 Mussolini Prize in 1931; Cecchi won it in 1936. In 1929, the Academy received 550 requests for encouragement prizes; and in 1931, 1,682 individuals applied for 108 grants. Numbers on grant requests are from an undated (but 1931) report in AAI, b.Verbali—Adunanze Generali 1929–34. In 1940, the encouragement prizes were replaced by four Academic Prizes of L10,000 each; recipients included Alvaro (1940), the historian Federico Chabod (1941), the architect Giovanni Michelucci (1941), and the writer Carlo Emilio Gadda (1942). Other awards included grants for scientists and inventors from the *Fondazione Alessandro Volta,* grants for architectural designs on "Christian-Catholic" themes from the *Fondazione Palanti,* and "commendations" *(encomi)* and donations *(erogazioni)* for scholars in all fields. For a complete list of prizes as they stood at the end of the regime, see the *Annuario della Reale Accademia d'Italia, 1940–41* (Rome, 1942), 402–7.

25. Mino Maccari, "Arte fascista," *Critica fascista* (November 1, 1926); Cipriano Efisio Oppo, "Arte fascista e arte di Stato," *Critica fascista* (February 1, 1927); Filippo Tommaso Marinetti, "L'arte fascista futurista," *Critica fascista* (January 1, 1927); Massimo Bontempelli, "Arte fascista," *Critica fascista* (November 15, 1926); Antonio Pagano, "Arte fascismo e popolo," *Critica fascista* (December 1, 1926); and Ardengo Soffici, "Arte fascista," *Critica fascista* (October 15, 1926).

26. Ardengo Soffici, "Arte fascista"; Giuseppe Bottai, "Risultanza dell'inchiesta sull'arte fascista," *Critica fascista* (February 15, 1927); and Alessandro Pavolini, "Dell'arte fascista," *Critica fascista* (November 1, 1926).

27. For attacks on the Jews with reference to modernism, see Mino Maccari, "L'agonia del modernismo," *Il Selvaggio* (April 20, 1934); and the editorial "Gazzettino: Perchè combattiamo il modernismo," *Il Selvaggio* (May 15, 1934).

28. Mino Maccari, "Addio del passato," *Il Selvaggio* (March 1–14, 1926).

29. On Strapaese, see Giorgio Luti, *La letteratura nel ventennio fascista* (Florence, 1972): 156–70; and Luisa Mangoni, *L'interventismo della cultura,* 93–195. On the movement as a protest against Americanization, see Walter Adamson, "The Culture of Italian Fascism and the Fascist Crisis of Modernity: The Case of *Il Selvaggio," Journal of Contemporary History* 30 (1995): 555–75. Anthony D. Smith discusses the relationship between ethnicity and nationalism in *The Ethnic Origins of Nations* (Oxford, 1986), and *National Identity* (Reno, 1991), 19–42. Cavazza, *Piccole patrie;* and Carl Levy, ed., *Italian Regionalism* (New York: Berg, 1996), offer insight into the specificities of the Italian case.

30. Novecentist architecture is examined in Richard Etlin, *Modernism in Italian Architecture, 1890–1940* (Cambridge, 1991), 165–224; and Dennis Doordan, *Building Modern Italy* (New York, 1988), 29–44. On painting, see Rossana Bossaglia, *Il "Novecento Italiano"* (Milan, 1979).

31. Curzio Malaparte, "La Voce," *Il Selvaggio* (April 16–30, 1926); and Massimo Bontempelli, "Lo stagno dei ranocchi" (1925), in *L'avventura novecentista (1926–38)* (Florence, 1938), 124. Quote from *L'Italiano* in Giuliano Manacorda, *Storia della letteratura italiana fra le due guerre* (Rome, 1977), 123. On literary Novecentism, also known as Stracittà, see Mangoni, *L'interventismo della cultura*, 121–36; see also Marino, *L'autarchia della cultura*, 99–105.

32. M. B., "Conseils," *'900* (Cahier de printemps 1927), and his "Caravane immobile," *'900* (Cahier d'automne 1926).

33. Gherardo Casini, "Integralismo," *Critica fascista* (March 1, 1931).

34. Berto Ricci, "Avvisi," *L'Universale* (April 3, 1932).

35. Vitaliano Brancati, *Singolare avventura di viaggio* (Milan, 1934), 70–71; and Nino Bertocchi, "Imposizione della sobrietà," *L'Orto* (April 1932).

36. See Bruno Wanrooj, "The Rise and Fall of Italian Fascism as a Generational Revolt," *Journal of Contemporary History* 22 (1987): 401–18; Laura Malvano, "Il mito della giovinezza attraverso l'immagine," in *Storia dei giovani*, ed. Giovanni Levi and Jean-Claude Schmitt (Rome, 1994), 311–48; and Koon, *Believe, Obey, Fight*. On Bottai's role in formulating this policy, see De Grand, *Bottai e la cultura fascista*; and Mario Sechi, *Il mito della nuova cultura* (Manduria, 1984), 9–62.

37. Mario Pannunzio, "Contributo all'inchiesta sulla nuova cultura," *Saggiatore* (August-October 1933): 348; and Antonio Anile, "Quesiti sulla nuova generazione," *Saggiatore* (July 1932). Circulation figures for these journals ranged from a few hundred to a few thousand copies, as compared with ten to twelve thousand for *Critica fascista* and around ninety thousand for a popular journal like *Rivista illustrata del Popolo d'Italia*. Initially, *Orpheus*, edited by Luciano Anceschi and Enzo Paci, had less than fifty subscribers but distributed hundreds of copies to bookstores per month. See AA, b.Orpheus; for other periodicals, see Albertina Vittoria, *Le riviste del Duce* (Milan, 1983), 181, n. 3. The Anceschi papers, which were kept in Professor Anceschi's home in Bologna when I consulted them, were given to the University of Bologna following the philosopher's death in 1995.

38. Luciano Anceschi, "Contributo alla nuova cultura," *Saggiatore* (August-October 1933): 267; Giorgio Granata, "Residui e nuova cultura"; and Attilio Riccio, "Arte e costruzione," *Critica fascista* (April 15, 1932).

39. Domenico Carella, "Crisi della cultura," *Saggiatore* (June 1932), and his "Punti fermi," *Saggiatore* (April 1933); and Pietro Cristiano Drago, "Inquietudine etica e cultura," *Saggiatore* (July 1930).

40. Libero Solaroli, "I giovani d'oggi: Vinicio Paladino," *L'Interplanetario* (March 1, 1928); Leo Longanesi, "La crisi e l'estetica," *L'Italiano* 11 (1932); and Giorgio Granata, "Residui e nuova cultura." See also Giannini Marescalchi, "Il nostro pessimismo," *L'Orto* (February-March 1932); and Domenico Carella, "Spade di carta," *Lavoro fascista* (October 11, 1932).

41. Adalberto Libera, "Introduzione alla esposizione," *Primo esposizione*

internazionale di architettura razionale (Rome, 1928), cited in Michele Cennamo, *Materiali per l'analisi dell'architettura moderna* (Naples, 1973), 1:105–6; Vinicio Paladini, "Cinematografia della vita vera," *Cinemateatro* (September 1928); Ettore Desideri, "Il manifesto musicale," *La Stampa* (December 21, 1932); Nino Bertocchi, "Imposizione della sobrietà," *L'Orto* (April 1932); and Delio Cantimori, "Chiarificazione di idee," *Vita nova* (July 1932).

42. Walter Gropius, cited in John Willett, *Art and Politics in the Weimar Period*, 121. On the *Sachlichkeit* ethos, see Peter Galison, "Aufbau/Bauhaus: Logical Positivism and Architectural Modernism," *Critical Inquiry* (summer 1990): 709–52; *Neue Sachlichkeit and German Realism of the 1920s* (London, 1979); and Henri R. Paucker, ed., *Neue Sachlichkeit im "Dritten Reich" und im Exil* (Stuttgart, 1974).

43. Emmanuel Mounier, 1932 *Esprit* article, quoted in *Mounier et sa génération*, ed. Paulette Mounier-Leclerq (Paris, 1956), 84; Thierry Maulnier, "Un regime ennemi des arts," *Combat* (April 1936); and, from within the left, Henri Poulaille, *Nouvel âge littéraire* (Paris, 1930), 113; and Georges Valois, "La Révolution culturelle," *Chantiers cooperatifs* (June 1932). On French youth culture in these years, see Jean-Louis Loubet del Bayle, *Les Non-conformistes des années trente* (Paris, 1969); and Sternhell, *Neither Right nor Left*.

44. For discussions of these realist positions, see the catalogs *Les réalismes entre révolution et réaction, 1919–39* (Paris: Centre Georges Pompidou, 1981); *Kunst und Diktatur*, 2 vols. (Baden, 1994); and Régine Robin, *Le réalisme socialiste* (Paris, 1986). On the internal contradictions of *Neue Sachlichkeit*, see Pierre Vaydat, "Neue Sachlichkeit als ethische Haltung," in "Die 'Neue Sachlichkeit': Lebensgefühl oder Markenzeichen?" special issue of *Germanica* 9 (1991), 37–54; and Jost Hernand, "*Neue Sachlichkeit:* Ideology, Lifestyle, or Artistic Movement?" in *Dancing on the Volcano*, ed. Thomas W. Kniesche and Stephen Brockman (Columbia, S.C., 1994), 57–68.

45. Renato Coniglia, *Il dramma di Tunisi* (Naples, 1930), 59.

46. "Introduzione," *Saggiatore* (August-October 1933): 242.

47. Alfredo Casella, "Fascismo e musica," *Educazione fascista* (November 1932); L'Interpellante, "Interpellanze," *Il Selvaggio* (May 15, 1933).

48. Carlo Enrico Rava, "Dell'Europeanismo in Architettura," *Rassegna italiana* (February 1928), in Cennamo, *Materiali*, 77–84. Rava was a member of the Group 7 architectural collective. For complaints about Rationalism from architects of the war generation, see Filippo Fichera, "L'Esposizione Internazionale di Architettura Moderna in Budapest," *L'Architettura* (January-February 1931); and Marcello Piacentini, "Prima Internazionale Architettonica," *L'Architettura* (August 1928). The debates over Rationalism are detailed in Etlin, *Modernism in Italian Architecture;* and Doordan, *Building Modern Italy*.

49. On the domestic and international effects of Mussolini's "Europeanism," see Giovanni Mira and Luigi Salvatorelli, *Storia d'Italia nel periodo fascista* (Turin, 1970), 2:180–96; on the universal fascist movement, see

Michael Ledeen, *L'internazionale fascista* (Bari, 1973). For Italy's tourism crisis, see Richard Bosworth, *Italy and the Wider World, 1860–1960* (New York, 1996), 173–75.

50. "Camminare," *Educazione fascista* (June 1932).

51. Luca Dei Sabelli, *Nazioni e minoranze etniche*, 2:v–vi; and Giuseppe Bottai, preface to *La crisi del capitalismo* (Florence, 1933), which contained essays by Gaetan Pirou, Werner Sombart, E. F. M. Durbin, Ernest Minor Patterson, Ugo Spirito, and Giuseppe Bruguier.

52. Plinio Marconi, review of *Costruzione razionale della casa*, by Enrico Griffini, *L'Architettura* (January 1932).

53. Mario Labroca, "Per la conoscenza dell'Italia nel mondo," *Critica fascista* (February 1, 1933). Head of the Corporation for New Music, Labroca became chief of the music section of the General Directorate of Entertainment (Direzione Generale dello Spettacolo) of the Ministry of Press and Propaganda in 1935. See also Pinna Berchet, "La funzione economica delle fiere campionarie," *La Fiera di Milano* (January-February 1933).

54. Ugo Ojetti, "Italia in mostra," *Pègaso* (May-June 1933).

55. July 23, 1930, letter from the prefect of Venice to the Presidenza Consiglio dei Ministri, in ACS, PCM (1928–30), 14.2.11763. On the expansion of the Biennale, see Antonio Maraini's February 11, 1931, letter to Benito Mussolini, in ACS, PCM (1931–33), 14.1.1543; see also Stone, *The Patron State*, on this and other fascist exhibitions. On music festivals in this period, see Fiamma Nicolodi, "Su alcuni aspetti dei festivals tra le due guerre," in *Musica italiana del primo novecento* (Florence, 1981), 161–166; and Harvey Sachs, *Music in Fascist Italy* (New York, 1987), 89–100. My thinking on exhibitions has also been shaped by Tony Bennett, "The Exhibitionary Complex," in *Culture/Power/History*, ed. Nicholas B. Dirks et al. (Princeton, 1994), 123–54; and the essays in Ivan Karp and Steven D. Levine, eds., *Exhibiting Cultures* (Washington, D.C., 1991).

56. For the Grape Festivals, see ACS, PCM, (1931–33), 14.2.2646. On the *Mostra della Rivoluzione Fascista*, see Jeffrey Schnapp, "Epic Demonstrations: Fascist Modernity and the 1932 Exhibition of the Fascist Revolution," in *Fascism, Aesthetics, and Culture*, ed. Richard Golsan (Hanover, N.H., 1992), 1–37. I discuss the Venice Biennale Film Show in chapter 3.

57. On the architectural congresses and the Triennale, see, respectively, Alberto Calza-Bini's speech in *L'Architettura* (October 1933); ACS, PCM (1931–33), 14.3.9785; Anty Pansera, "Le Triennali del regime: Un occhio aperto sull'oltralpe," in *Annitrenta* (Milan, 1983), 311–23.

58. Corrado Alvaro, *Quasi una vita* (Milan, 1950), 105.

59. Flora, "Dignità dello scrittore." Giuseppe Pagano, for example, became the consultant on architectural exhibitions in 1933, beginning a busy and prosperous official career that included the direction of many pavilions of the 1936 Triennale and commissions to work with Piacentini on the University of Rome complex (1935) and the exposition-city of EUR (1942). Albini also became a

fixture of fascist exhibition design teams; Gadda, who was trained as an engineer, provided texts for exhibitions on autarchy and minerals; and Mafai contributed frescos to the *Mostra del dopolavoro* in 1937.

60. Adriano Lualdi, quoted in Nicolodi, "Su alcuni aspetti dei festivals," 162.

61. Ugo Ojetti, "Il viaggio d'Italia," *Pègaso* (August 1929); "Lettera a Michele Barbi, pel suo Dante" *Pègaso* (September 1932); "Lettera a Giuseppe Bottai, sui vantaggi del dir di no," *Pègaso* (October 1932); and "Italianità e modernità (Lettera di Ojetti e risposta di Bottai)," *Critica fascista* (October 15, 1932).

62. "Al lettore," *Pan* (December 1933).

63. R. Bova Scoppa, *Russia rossa* (Rome, 1932), 23; and Gaetano Ciocca, preface to *Un fascista al paese dei Soviet*, by Pier Maria Bardi (Rome, 1933), 10.

64. On the travels of western Europeans to America and the Soviet Union, see Mary Nolan, *Visions of Modernity* (New York, 1994); Bernadette Galloux-Fournier, "Un Regard sur l'Amérique: Voyageurs français aux Etats-Unis, 1919–39," *Revue d'histoire moderne et contemporaine* (April-June 1990): 297–307; Marcello Flores, "Il mito dell'Urss negli anni trenta," in *L'estetica della politica*, ed. Maurizio Vaudagna (Rome, 1989), 129–50; and Fred Kupferman, *Au pays des soviets* (Paris, 1979). The attention that the English-speaking world gave to Italian fascism is detailed in John P. Diggins, *Mussolini and Fascism* (Princeton, 1972); and Marco Palla, *Fascismo e Stato corporativo* (Milan, 1991).

65. Gaetano Ciocca, *Giudizio sul bolscevismo* (Milan, 1934), 33. On Italian travelers to Soviet Russia, see Luciano Zani, "L'immagine dell'URSS nell'Italia degli anni trenta," *Storia contemporanea* (December 1990): 1197–1224.

66. Giulio Santangelo, "La Russia: Questione di civiltà," *Occidente* (July-September 1933); and "La Russia senza filo," *Educazione fascista* (March 20, 1932). See Pier Giorgio Zunino, *L'ideologia del fascismo* (Bologna, 1985), 332–44, for the evolution of attitudes toward the Soviets.

67. Ettore Lo Gatto, *Dall'epica alla cronaca nella Russia soviettista* (Rome, 1929), 195. At the time of these trips, Lo Gatto was president of the *Istituto per l'Europa Orientale*, professor of Slavic philology at the University of Padova, and director of the *Rivista di letteratura slava*. See also Ciocca, *Giudizio sul bolscevismo*, 227. On Ciocca's experiences in Russia, see Jeffrey Schnapp, "Between Fascism and Democracy: Gaetano Ciocca—Builder, Inventor, Farmer, Engineer," *Modernism/modernity* (September 1995): 117–58. See also Corrado Alvaro, *I maestri del diluvio* (Milano, 1935); and Enrico Emanuelli, *Racconti sovietici* (Rome, 1935).

68. Alvaro, *I maestri del diluvio*, 114; and Luigi Barzini, *L'impero del lavoro forzato* (Milan, 1932), 199.

69. Emanuelli, *Racconti sovietici*, 114; and Ettore Lo Gatto, *URSS 1931* (Rome, 1932), 77–83.

70. Alvaro, *I maestri del diluvio*, 134; see also Bardi, *Un fascist al paese dei soviet*, 158; Lo Gatto, *Dall'epica alla cronaca*, 166; and Giuseppe Lombrassa, "La gioventù nella Russia Sovietica" *Critica fascista* (February 1, 1934).

71. Pier Maria Bardi, "Isacco alleva i maiali," in *Un fascista al paese dei soviet*, 71–80; Lo Gatto, "Il problema ebraico," in *Dall'epica alla cronaca*, 145–56. On Russia as Asiatic, see Rodolfo Mosca, *Verso il secondo piano quinquennale* (Milan, 1932); and Barzini, *L'impero del lavoro forzato*, 195.

72. Ciocca, preface to *Un fascista al paese dei soviet*, 30; and Ciocca, *Giudizio sul bolscevismo*, 23.

73. Orco Bisorco, "Gazzettino ufficiale del Strapaese," *Il Selvaggio* (March 30, 1928).

74. Luigi Barzini, *Nuova York* (Milan, 1931), cited in Emilio Gentile, "Impending Modernity: Fascism and the Ambivalent Image of the United States," *Journal of Contemporary History* 28 (1993): 7–29.

75. For a measured view of America's strengths and weaknesses, see Romier, *Qui sera le maître, Europe ou Amérique?*; a more negative view is given by Robert Aron and Arnaud Dandieu, *Le Cancer américain* (Paris: Rieder, 1931). French attitudes toward America pre- and post-1945 are detailed in Richard Kuisel, *Seducing the French* (Berkeley and Los Angeles, 1993); Tony Judt, *Past Imperfect* (Berkeley and Los Angeles, 1992), 187–204; and Romy Golan, *Modernity and Nostalgia* (New Haven, 1995): 79–83. On the meanings of America under Hitler's rule, see Philipp Gassert, *Amerika im Dritten Reich* (Stuttgart, 1997). For Italian reactions to America, see Michela Nacci, *L'anti-americanismo in Italia negli anni trenta* (Turin, 1989); and Michel Beynet, *L'Image de l'Amérique dans la culture italienne de l'entre-deux-guerres* (Aix-en-Provence, 1990).

76. On the relationship between fascist Italy and America, see Diggins, *Mussolini and Fascism*; and Gian Piero Brunetta, "Il sogno a stelle e strisce di Mussolini," in *L'estetica della politica*, ed. Maurizio Vaudagna (Rome, 1989), 187–202. For Mussolini's pro-Americanism, see his "Messaggio al popolo americano," January 20, 1931, in *Scritti e discorsi* 7:277–78.

77. Margherita Sarfatti, *America, ricerca della felicità* (Milan, 1937), 20; and Barzini, *Nuova York*, 65.

78. Valentino Piccoli, "Babbit o l'uomo standard," *Critica fascista* (December 1, 1932).

79. Adriana Dottorelli, *Viaggio in America* (n.p., 1933), 15; and Renato Paresce, *L'Altra America* (Rome, 1935).

80. Emilio Cecchi, "Taccuino Americano," *Occidente* (April-June 1934); and Paresce, *L'Altra America*, 61.

81. Cecchi, "Taccuino Americano," and *America amara* (Florence, 1940), 89, 285; Paresce, *L'Altra America*, 102–8; and Mario Soldati, *America primo amore* (Florence, 1935), 95–96.

82. Lilli, "Americanismo ed europeanismo," *Critica fascista* (November 15, 1931); and Euno Poggiani, *Viaggio nel Far West* (Cremona, 1936), 34.

83. While commentators often cite Soldati's inability to find stable employment in America as a reason for his reentry, Soldati has admitted in interviews that he did not look very seriously. See Davide Lajolo, *Conversazione in una stanza chiusa con Mario Soldati* (Milan, 1983), 36.

84. Soldati, *America primo amore*, 195.

85. Soldati, "(Panorami) America," reprinted in revised form in *America primo amore*, 180.

86. Alberto Moravia, *Alberto Moravia-Giuseppe Prezzolini* (Milan, 1982), 1936 letter, 21.

87. Soldati, *America primo amore*, 101–4.

88. Ibid., 87. At the time he wrote this text, Soldati had also recently separated from his American wife, Marion Rieckelman, who had been his student at Columbia.

89. Corrado Alvaro, "Il clima intellettuale a Berlino," *Italia letteraria* (July 28, 1929); and Angioletti, "Sogni e storture della Germania."

90. Corrado Alvaro, *Itinerario italiano* (Rome, 1933), 102; and Angioletti, "Sogni e storture." Similar laments were expressed by other European intellectuals: Romier, *Qui sera le maître, Europe ou Amérique?* 86–105; Jaspers, *Die Geistige Situation der Zeit;* and José Ortega y Gasset, "Masculino o femenino?" *El Sol* (June 26 and July 3, 1927).

91. Corrado Alvaro, "Solitudine," in *Il Mare* (Milan, 1934), 74, 75, 80.

92. Lombrassa, "I giovani nella Russa Sovietica."

93. Corrado Alvaro, *Cronaca (o fantasia)* (Rome, 1933), 99; Paresce, *L'Altra America*, 49; and Soldati, *America primo amore*, 184.

CHAPTER 2

1. Giovanni Titta Rosa, "Invito al romanzo," *Corriere padano* (February 16, 1928).

2. Arrigo Benedetti, letter to Antonio Delfini, September 10, 1936, in *Antonio Delfini*, special issue of *Riga* 6 (1994): 214.

3. On the popularity of foreign popular fiction, see Forgacs, *Italian Culture*, 78–81; see also Gigliola De Donato and Vanna Gazzola, *I best-seller del ventennio* (Rome, 1991).

4. Alvaro, *Quasi una vita*, entry for July 1944, 339.

5. Pasquale Iaccio, "Il censore e il commediografo: Note sull'applicazione della revisione teatrale nel periodo fascista," *Storia contemporanea* (August 1994), and his "La censura teatrale durante il fascismo," *Storia contemporanea* (August 1986): 567–614. For similar relationships between censors and censored in other contexts, see Miklos Haraszti, *The Velvet Prison* (New York, 1987); and Robert Von Hallberg, ed., *Literary Intellectuals and the Dissolution of the State* (Chicago, 1996).

6. These works included Alvaro's *Gente in Aspromonte (The People of Aspromonte)* (Florence, 1930), which appeared in *Pègaso*, Carlo Emilio Gadda's

La cognizione del Dolore (Acquainted with Grief) (Turin: Einaudi, 1963), fragments of which were published in *Letteratura*, and Vittorini's *Conversazione in Sicilia (Conversation in Sicily)* (Milan, 1941), which appeared in *Letteratura*.

7. For the evolution of the Press Office of the Head of the Government, see Maurizio Cesari, *La censura del periodo fascista* (Naples, 1978), 26–45; and Cannistraro, *La fabbrica del consenso*, 75–127. For the 1932 list of monthly subsidies, see ACS, MCP, b.155, f.10.

8. The critic's role in shaping the meaning of literary texts and in legitimating discourses about national literatures is explored in Peter Uwe Hohendahl, *The Institution of Criticism* (Ithaca, N.Y., 1982), and his *Building a National Literature* (Ithaca, N.Y., 1989). See also Jusdanis, *Belated Modernity and Aesthetic Culture*; and Liu, *Translingual Practice*, esp. 183–213. On the issue of reception, see Wolfgang Iser, *The Act of Reading* (Baltimore, 1978); and Hans Robert Jauss, *Toward an Aesthetic of Reception*, trans. Timothy Bahti (Minneapolis, 1982).

9. Arnaldo Bocelli of *Corriere padano* wrote propaganda pamphlets for the PNF, while G. B. Angioletti, who directed *Fiera letteraria* for six years, worked for the Italian Cultural Institute abroad.

10. Alberto Moravia, "C'è una crisi del romanzo?" *Fiera letteraria* (October 9, 1927); "Per il programma," *La Libra* (November 1928); and Giorgio Napolitano, "Difesa di una generazione," *I Lupi* (February 10, 1928).

11. Salvatore Rosati, "Sulla letteratura contemporanea," *Giornale di letteratura e di politica* (January 1929); Corrado Alvaro, "La prosa," *'900* (August 1, 1928); and Alfredo De'Donno, "Il romanzo nazionale," *La Stirpe* (October 1932). The novel's role at crucial historical junctures in diffusing a more "national" consciousness has been described in Benedict Anderson, *Imagined Communities:* (London, 1990); and critiqued in Homi Bhabha, ed., *Nation and Narration* (London, 1990), and in the studies cited in n. 8.

12. Mario Pannunzio, "Necessità del romanzo," *Saggiatore* (May 1932); see also Bonaventura Tecchi, "Inchiesta sul romanzo," *Corriere padano* (October 27, 1932); and Alberto Moravia, "Appunti sul romanzo," *Italia letteraria* (March 30, 1930).

13. Attilio Riccio, "Arte e costruzione," *Critica fascista* (April 15, 1932); and Giorgio Granata, "Aspetti del nuovo scrittore," *Critica fascista* (April 15, 1932).

14. Sigfrido Wolfango, "Il realismo moderno," *Oggi* (December 31, 1933); and Mario Robertazzi, "Questo giornale," *Oggi* (October 22, 1933).

15. Massimo Bontempelli, "Corsivo no. 4," *Quadrante* (May 1933).

16. Arnaldo Bocelli, "Ritorno al romanzo," *Corriere padano* (August 28, 1930). The intersection between realist aesthetics and the campaign for the new novel is discussed by Giuseppe Langella, *Il secolo delle riviste* (Milan, 1982), 325–83; Cesare De Michelis, *Alle origini del neorealismo* (Cosenza, 1980); Bruno Falcetto, *Storia della narrativa neorealista* (Milan, 1992); Robin Pickering-Iazzi, *Politics of the Visible* (Minneapolis, 1997).

17. Giuseppe Bottai, "Verga politico," *Corriere padano* (October 9, 1929).

18. Bocelli, "Ritorno al romanzo"; Mario Pannunzio, "Precisazioni," *Oggi* (October 8, 1933); and Giovanni Titta Rosa, "Narrarsi," *Italia letteraria* (June 1, 1930).

19. Nicola Perrotti, "Perché la letteratura italiana non è popolare in Europa," *Saggiatore* (November 1930).

20. Elio Vittorini, "Scarico di coscienza," *Italia letteraria* (October 13, 1929): 1; and Vitaliano Brancati, "Chiuso mondo verghiano," *Lavoro fascista* (August 8, 1931). Alberto Moravia recalled his generation's repudiation of past literary models in "Assenza di maestri," in *L'uomo senza fine e altri saggi* (Milan, 1963), 58–62.

21. Barbaro translated authors such as Vladimir Mayakofsky, Mikhail Bulgakov, André Gide, and Hermann Kesten; Emanuelli translated Jakob Wassermann, and Moravia translated Hemingway. For recent reflections about translation as a conduit of cultural exchange, see Sanford Budick and Wolfgang Iser, eds., *The Translatability of Cultures* (Stanford, 1996).

22. *Espero's* foreign editorial committee included Ernst Robert Curtius and Valéry Larbaud.

23. Mondadori began its "Medusa" collection for foreign authors. See the company history *Editoria e cultura a Milano tra le due guerre (1920–40)* (Milan, 1983). On the publishing industry during fascism, see Forgacs, *Italian Culture in the Industrial Era*, 57–63.

24. The Ferrarese editor Schifanoia also had a series on Russian writers. *L'Italiano's* special issue presented samples of proletarian, fellow-traveler *(poputchiki)*, and Five-Year Plan literature.

25. Giuseppe Raimondi, "Giovani scrittori russi," *Italia letteraria* (May 4, 1930); Umberto Barbaro, "Lidia Sejfullina," *La rivista di letteratura slava* (August-December 1928).

26. See Lo Gatto, *Dall'epica alla cronaca nella Russia soviettista*, 213; and Tommaso Napolitano, "I problemi morali nella letteratura sovietica," *Critica fascista* (February 15, 1932). Polonski lost his editorial position at *Novy Mir* for opposing the new policy of "social command" promulgated by the Russian Association of Proletarian Writers after 1929. On Stalinist literary policy, see Gleb Struve, *Russian Literature under Lenin and Stalin, 1917–33* (Norman, Okla., 1971), 221–33.

27. Cesare Pavese, "Ieri e oggi," *L'Unità* (August 3, 1947). The influence of American literature on Pavese and other writers is discussed in Marco Santoro, "Pavese e la letteratura americana," in *La cultura italiana negli anni, 1930–45* (Naples, 1984), 1:643–56.

28. Valentino Piccoli, "Babbitt o l'uomo standard," *Critica fascista* (December 1, 1932); Aldo Sorani, "Sinclair Lewis," *Pègaso* (December 1930); and Giacomo Lumbroso, "Sinclair Lewis," *Lavoro fascista* (February 1, 1931).

29. Ugo Ojetti, "Lettera a Dos Passos sulla povera America," *Pègaso* (August 1932).

30. Anceschi, "Nuova obbiettività," *Orpheus* (July 9, 1933); Remo Cantoni, "Dos Passos' 42nd parallelo," *Cantiere* (April 21, 1934); and Carlo Izzo, " 'New York' di Dos Passos," *Corriere padano* (January 24, 1933).

31. Moravia, 1936 letters to Giuseppe Prezzolini, in Moravia, *Alberto Moravia–Giuseppe Prezzolini,* 19–20. Moravia's reportages from abroad are collected and discussed in Alberto Moravia, *Viaggi,* ed. Enzo Siciliano (Milan, 1994); and Louis Kibler, "Alberto Moravia as Journalist: 1930–35," in *Forum Italicum* (1993): 71–95. On the "myth of America" as an ally of antifascism, see Dominique Fernandez, *Il mito dell'America negli intellettuali italiani* (Caltanisetta, 1969); and Nicola Carducci, *Gli intellettuali e l'ideologia americana nell'Italia letteraria degli anni trenta* (Manduria, 1973). For more nuanced views, see Beynet, *L'Image de l'Amérique;* and Nacci, *L'anti-americanismo in Italia negli anni trenta.*

32. Bonaventura Tecchi, "Opinioni sul romanzo," *Corriere padano* (October 27, 1932); Francesco Bruno, "Realismo germanico," *Saggiatore* (July 1931); and Drago, "Inquietudine etica e cultura."

33. Enrico Rocca, "Tappe del romanzo tedesco e letteratura italiana," *Critica fascista* (September 1, 1929).

34. Giovanni Titta Rosa, review of Döblin and Dreiser in *La Stampa,* cited in "Notiziario," *Occidente* (January-March 1933); Bonaventura Tecchi, December 1931 review of Renn's *Nachkrieg,* in Bonaventura Tecchi, *Scrittori tedeschi del Novecento* (Florence, 1941), 37; and Enrico Rocca, review of Erich Kästner's works, in *Pègaso* (August 1932).

35. Enrico Rocca, "*Berlin Alexanderplatz,*" *Pègaso* (May 1930).

36. Corrado Alvaro, "Lineamenti letterari," and "Conclusioni sulla Germania letteraria," *Italia letteraria* (September 22 and 29, 1929); and Luigi De Crecchio, "Tre di tre millioni," *Oggi* (July 16, 1933).

37. Spackman discusses the relationship of biography, ideology, and language in *Fascist Virilities.*

38. For *Gli indifferenti* as an antifascist text, see Olga Lombardi, *La narrativa italiana nelle crisi del novecento* (Caltanisetta, 1971), 30; and Edward Reichl, "Literarischer Text und Politischer Kontext: Faschismuskritik in Narrativer Form: Moravias *Gli indifferenti,*" *Romanistische Zeitschrift für Literaturgeschichte* 1 (1980): 65–81. For *Gli indifferenti* as an existentialist work, see Cristina Benussi, "Moravia nell'esistenzialismo italiano," *Forum Italicum* 5 (1993): 3–20. My intent here is not to cast doubt on the latter interpretation but to point out another source of inspiration for the novel.

39. See, for example, the police report from August 1937, which tracked Moravia's movements and recommended continued "cautious and extremely discreet surveillance." ACS, MI, DGPS, Divisione Affari Generali e Riservati, H2, b.129, f.Roma—Complotti Giustizia e Libertà. I thank Joel Blatt for bringing this document to my attention.

40. Giorgio Napolitano, "Difesa di una generazione."

41. Moravia's name does not appear on the masthead, but he is named as an

editor in a note in the June 1, 1928, issue. His stories were entitled "Cinque sogni," *Interplanetario* (February 15, 1928); "Assunzione in cielo di Maria Luisa," *Interplanetario* (March 15, 1928); "Albergo di terz'ordine," *Interplanetario* (April 1, 1928); and "Villa Mercedes," *Interplanetario* (June 1, 1928). On the stories and their relation to the novel, see Umberto Carpi, "*Gli indifferenti* rimossi," *Belfagor* (November 30, 1981): 696–709.

42. Alberto Moravia, "Dialogo fra Amleto e il Principe di Danimarca," *I Lupi* (February 29, 1928); Moravia, "Villa Mercedes."

43. Alberto Moravia, *Gli indifferenti* (Milan, 1929; reprint, Milan, 1993), 7, 31.

44. Ibid., 11, 247.

45. Ibid., 310.

46. Nello Quilici, review in *Corriere padano* (November 5, 1929); Aristotele Campanile, review in *Antieuropa* (November 15, 1929); Giuseppe Lombrassa, "L'indifferenza: Male di moda," *Critica fascista* (January 1, 1930).

47. *Gli indifferenti* was named "one of the hundred best books" of contemporary letters and was listed as an example of the new national literature in the *Enciclopedia Italiana*. "Italia," *Enciclopedia Italiana*, 29:958; "I cento libri più belli della letteratura contemporanea," *Fiera letteraria* (November 2, 1929). For praise of the book, see Bonaventura Tecchi, "Quesiti sulla nuova generazione," *Saggiatore* (December 1932); Giorgio Granata, "Moravia o dell'indifferenza," *Saggiatore* (December 1931); Giovanni Titta Rosa, "*Gli indifferenti* o del moralismo," *Corriere padano* (November 5, 1929); and Enrico Rocca, "Gli indifferenti," *Critica fascista* (September 1, 1929). For Moravia's memory of his work's fate, see his "Ricordi di censura," *La Rassegna d'Italia* (December 1946).

48. Euralio De Michelis, *Adamo* (Vicenza: Jacchia, 1931); and Elio Talarico, *Tatuaggio* (Rome: Edizioni d'Italia, 1933).

49. The only full-length study of Barbaro is the valuable work of Gian Piero Brunetta, *Umberto Barbaro e l'idea del neorealismo* (Padua, 1969). See also Brunetta's introduction to his anthology of Barbaro's writings in Umberto Barbaro, *Neorealismo e realismo*, 2 vols. (Rome, 1976).

50. Brunetta mentions this ambiguity as a possible reason for Barbaro's neglect by postwar critics. "In Barbaro's language," he notes, "one find things very similar to those being said by intellectuals who were openly fascist." It is not Barbaro's language that creates such confusion, he maintains, but the context of his writings, which "distorts . . . and neutralizes his intentions," leaving him vulnerable to associations with fascism. Brunetta, in Barbaro, *Neorealismo e realismo*, 1:22.

51. The Ordine Nuovo group headed by Gramsci was among the few open to the possibility of an avant-garde communist art, but this door was firmly shut after the March on Rome. Barbaro's journal, *La Bilancia*, which he founded in 1923, continued this tradition of collaboration, hosting Marinetti and other fascist militants even as it championed left-wing movements such as Dadaism and Surrealism. Günter Berghaus, *Futurism and Politics* (Providence,

1996), esp. 172–217; and Umberto Carpi, *Bolscevico immaginista* (Naples, 1981), illuminate this complex world.

52. Barbaro, *Luce fredda*, 157.

53. Ibid., 219.

54. Ibid., 224, 11.

55. Antonio Bruers, "Cronache del pensiero filosofico," *Gerarchia* (January 1929).

56. Aldo Capasso, *"Luce fredda," Il Tevere* (July 15, 1931); and Domenico Carella, *"Luce fredda," Saggiatore* (November 1931).

57. Arnaldo Bocelli, *"Luce fredda," Corriere padano* (July 21, 1931).

58. G. B. Angioletti, "La prosa italiana d'oggi," cited in Enrico Rocca, "Cronache letterarie," *Lavoro fascista* (June 23, 1931); also Massimo Bontempelli, "Opinioni sul romanzo," *Corriere padano* (July 29, 1932).

59. Dos Passos and Döblin were acknowledged by Emanuelli as influences on his book in a postwar interview. See Anco Marzio Mutterle, *Emanuelli* (Florence, 1968), 3. At the same time Emanuelli was writing *X-Ray of a Night*, he was translating New Objectivity writer Jacob Wassermann's *Die Juden von Zirndorf* for the Milan editorial house Corbaccio.

60. Enrico Emanuelli, *Radiografia di una notte* (Lanciano, 1932), 21, 24.

61. Ibid., 212.

62. Elio Vittorini, *"Radiografia di una notte," Il Lavoro* (August 31, 1932); and Mario Bonfantini, "Prose di romanzi 1932," *Rivista di sintesi letteraria* (January-March 1934).

63. *Annuario della Reale Accademia d'Italia, 1932–33* (Rome, 1933), 336; AAI, b.Verbali—Adunanze Generali, 1929–34, April 21, 1932 report.

64. Guglielmo Serafini, *"Uomo del '700 e Radiografia di una notte," Oggi* (July 20, 1933); Luigi Tonelli, "Introspezioni," *Il Marzocco* (September 25, 1932); Pier Maria Pasinetti, review in *Il Ventuno* (August 28, 1932).

65. Carlo Villani, "Attraverso il romanzo italiano," *Convivium* (May-June 1933); Arnaldo Mussolini, "Coscienza e Dovere," speech of November 30, 1931, to the Scuola di Mistica Fascista, copy in ACS, PCM (1931–33), 14.2.3861; Luigi Chiarini, "Fatti vecchi e idee nuove," *Educazione fascista* (January 20–February 20, 1932); Felice Benuzzi, "Disfacitori," *Frontespizio* (January 1934).

66. Alberto Moravia, "Ancora sul romanzo," *Italia letteraria* (March 8, 1931); and Pannunzio, "Necessità del romanzo."

67. Giuseppe Bottai, "La tessera e l'ingegno," *Critica fascista* (April 15, 1931), and his "Italianità e modernità," *Critical fascista* (October 15, 1932).

68. Academy awards went to the writer De Michelis as well as Emanuelli, and these two writers also began to contribute articles to *Critica fascista*. Vittorini came under the patronage of Ciano and Alessandro Pavolini, who invited him to write for *Il Bargello*. On Moravia's new social standing, see Alain Elkann, *Vita di Moravia* (Milan, 1990), 44.

69. Luigi Chiarini, "A proposito di una polemica," *Educazione fascista* (July 1932).

70. G. B. Angioletti, "Funzione della letteratura," and Chiarini's reply, both in *Educazione fascista* (September-October 1932); see also Luigi Chiarini, "Arte e vita," *Educazione fascista* (December 1932).

71. Gherardo Casini, "Per una letteratura: Appello al coraggio," *Critica fascista* (October 15, 1932), and his "Elementi politici di una letteratura," *Critica fascista* (May 1933).

72. Benito Mussolini, speech of April 28, 1933, in *Opera Omnia*, ed. Edoardo and Duilio Susmel (Florence, 1951– 63), 35:51.

73. See the following articles by Barbaro: "Considerazioni sul romanzo," *Occidente* (October-December 1932), "Opinioni sul romanzo di Umberto Barbaro," *Roma* (July 29, 1932), "La mia fede," *Giornale d'Italia* (February 3, 1933), and L'arte e il tempo," *Italia vivente* (June 15, 1933). For Chiarini's statement, see his introduction to Barbaro, *Film e il risarcimento marxista dell'arte* (Rome, 1960), xiii.

74. Bottai, "La tessera e l'ingegno."

75. Alberto Moravia, " 'Gli indifferenti' giudicato dall'autore," *Il Tevere* (January 8, 1933).

76. In one discussion on style and the Italian novel, Moravia recommended that writers "trace the most essential themes of fascism and concretize them in one protagonist, rather than photographically reproducing insignificant details of everyday reality." "La moda del collettivismo," *Oggi* (February 1934).

77. Corrado Sofia, "Il nostro tempo," *Critica fascista* (May 15, 1933). That Moravia harbored little sympathy for fascism at this time may be gathered from a 1932 letter he wrote to the exiled antifascist Nicola Chiaromonte. In it, he stated that, although the presence of fascism made things difficult, he felt it was his duty to stay in Italy and try to work for the betterment of Italian culture. See Enzo Siciliano, "Due amici: Moravia e Chiaromonte," *Nuovi Argomenti* (April-June 1996): 50.

78. Francesco Bruno, "Impopularità del romanzo," *Italia che scrive* (February 1934); see also Angelo Silvio Novaro, "Inchiesta sull'arte del nostro tempo," *Italia vivente* (June 15, 1933).

79. Novaro, "Inchiesta sull'arte del nostro tempo." I thank Jeffrey Schnapp for providing me with a copy of this survey.

80. Corrado Alvaro, "Opinioni sul romanzo," and his "La solita polemica," *La Stampa* (February 8, 1933), and *Cronaca (o fantasia)* (Rome, 1933), 115– 16.

81. Corrado Alvaro, "Presentimento del diluvio," *L'Orizzonte italiano* (October 1923).

82. Franco Ciarlantini to Bontempelli, October 25, 1926, in GRI, BP, Correspondence files, Box 4, folder C. The Bontempelli Papers have been recataloged since I viewed them in 1994.

83. Alvaro, *Quasi una vita*, 34.

84. Corrado Alvaro, "Il clima intellettuale a Berlino," *Italia letteraria* (July 28, 1929); see also his "Lineamenti letterari," and "Conclusioni sulla

Germania letteraria," *Italia letteraria* (September 22 and 29, 1929), and 1928 diary entry, in *Quasi una vita*, 31.

85. Corrado Alvaro, cited in Walter Mauro, *Invito alla lettura di Alvaro* (Milan, 1973), 47; and autobiographical note of 1928–29, cited in Gaetano Cingari, "Alvaro tra Storia e Politica," in *La "Politica" di Alvaro*, ed. Cingari et al. (Rome, n.d. [1977]), 30.

86. Corrado Alvaro, "Paese e città," *Italia letteraria* (January 28, 1930).

87. As Antonio Palermo points out in his excellent study *Solitudine del moralista* (Naples, 1986), Alvaro based his account of Calabria's social conditions on a study by Vincenzo Padula, *Stato delle persone in Calabria*, which appeared in 1864–65 in the paper *Il Bruzio*.

88. Alvaro, *Gente in Aspromonte*, 3.

89. This strategy was even more evident in Alvaro's *Calabria* (Florence, 1931).

90. See the ad in *Pègaso* (June 1930).

91. Enrico Rocca, *"Gente in Aspromonte," Lavoro fascista* (April 2, 1931); Bonaventura Tecchi, *"Gente in Aspromonte," Italia letteraria* (December 21, 1930); Alfonso Silipo, "Lettura di Alvaro," *Circoli* (November-December 1931); and Alberto Consiglio, "Corrado Alvaro," *Solaria* (April 1931).

92. Fernando Palazzi, "Notizie Bibliografiche," *L'Italia che scrive* (September 1930).

93. Alvaro, *Quasi una vita*, 123.

94. Corrado Alvaro, "Impressioni del premiato," *Italia letteraria* (April 5, 1931). The interview included a biographical note that omitted his antifascist activities and played up his war experience. For Alvaro's involvement with Sarfatti, see Philip Cannistraro and Brian J. Sullivan, *The Duce's Other Woman* (New York, 1993), 337–39.

95. Corrado Alvaro, "Roma nuova," *Educazione fascista* 6 (1933), and *Cronaca (o Fantasia)*, 99, 118.

96. Corrado Alvaro, *Turchia* (Milan: Mondadori, 1932), *I maestri del diluvio, Itinerario italiano* (Rome, 1933), *Cronaca (o fantasia)*, and *Terra nuova* (Rome, 1934).

97. Corrado Alvaro, "Quesiti sulla nuova generazione," *Saggiatore* (July 1932).

98. Giovanni Titta Rosa, "Il romanzo," *Corriere padano* (September 19, 1936); and Eligio Possenti, "Volontà costruttiva e realtà nazionale nella letteratura fascista dell'anno XIII," *Corriere della sera* (October 27, 1935).

99. Arnaldo Bocelli, "Aspetti della letteratura d'oggi: Realismo," *Corriere della sera* (April 26, 1934), and his "Crepuscolarismo e letteratura d'oggi," *Corriere della sera* (April 18, 1935).

100. Arrigo Cajumi, *"I Villatauri," Il Lavoro* (December 28, 1935); and Alfredo Galletti, *Storia letteraria d'Italia* (Milan, 1935), 506, 501–2.

101. In July 1934, Ciano commissioned a study on the Nazi Ministry for Propaganda; see Cornelio Di Marzio's resulting report in ACS, PCM (1934–36), f.1.1.2.2219, sf.1.

102. March 2, 1935, order, in Francesco Flora, *Stampa dell'era fascista* (Rome, 1945), 83.

103. Ciano procured Bilenchi a job with the Florentine newspaper *La Nazione*. Romano Bilenchi, *Amici* (Milan, 1988), 70–73.

CHAPTER 3

1. Leo Longanesi, "Film italiano," *L'Italiano* (January-February 1933).

2. Francesco Flora, "Il cinema come arte civilizzatrice," *Rivista internazionale del cinema educatore* (June 1933). For Barbaro's decision to leave literature for the cinema, see his article "Per diventare critici cinematografici," *Vie nuove* (February 1, 1958).

3. On the relations of writers with the cinema, see Gian Piero Brunetta, *Storia del cinema italiano, 1896–1945* (Rome, 1993), 178–96; and Micciché, "Cinema italiano sotto il fascismo: elementi per un ripensamento possibile."

4. Alberto Consiglio, "Funzione sociale del cinema," *Rivista internazionale del cinema educatore* (November 1933).

5. Giacomo Debenedetti, "Inchiesta sul cinema," *Solaria* (March 1927), cited in Gian Piero Brunetta, *Buio in sala* (Venice, 1989), 153.

6. Ibid., 70–74; Giuliana Bruno, *Streetwalking on a Ruined Map* (Princeton, 1993), 52–53; and Miriam Hansen, *Babel and Babylon* (Cambridge, Mass., 1991).

7. Bruno, *Streetwalking on a Ruined Map*, 49–53; Hansen, *Babel and Babylon*. On the growth of cinema as a manifestation of the development of consumer and spectator society, see Leo Charney and Vanessa Schwartz, eds., *Cinema and the Invention of Modern Life* (Berkeley and Los Angeles, 1995). The gendering of mass culture is analyzed by Andreas Huyssen, *After the Great Divide* (Bloomington, Ind., 1986), 44–62.

8. On fascist film censorship, see Jean Gili, *Stato fascista e cinematografia* (Rome, 1981); and Mino Argentieri, *La censura nel cinema italiano* (Rome, 1974).

9. See Brunetta, *Storia del cinema italiano*, 52–75, on Catholic attitudes toward cinema in the fascist period.

10. Piero Solari, "Per una rinascita del cinematografo," *Fiera letteraria* (March 6, 1927).

11. Corrado Pavolini, "Dare all'Italia una coscienza nazionale cinematografica," *Il Tevere* (May 1, 1930); Massimo Bontempelli, "Nous et le theâtre," *'900* (Cahier d'hiver 1926–27); Mario Serandrei, "Corriere dell'Urbe," *Il Corriere cinematografico* (January 26, 1929).

12. See the general observations on national cinemas in Andrew Higson, *Waving the Flag* (Oxford, 1995), 4–25, and Darrell William Davis, *Picturing Japaneseness* (New York, 1995), 11–36. See also Marcia Kinder, *Blood Cinema* (Berkeley and Los Angeles, 1993); Heide Fehrenbach, *Cinema in Democratizing Germany* (Chapel Hill, 1995); Eric Rentschler, *The Ministry of Illusion* (Cambridge, Mass., 1996); Sumita S. Chakravarty, *National Identity in Indian*

Popular Cinema, 1947–87 (Austin, 1993); and de Grazia's comparative assessment of German, French, and Italian film policies in "Mass Culture and Sovereignty."

13. Umberto Masetti, "La ragione di un successo," *Cinematografo* (August 27, 1927).

14. Mario Gromo, "La II Biennale del film," *Pan* (October 1934). The exception here is communist Russia, which was primarily interested in domestic indoctrination rather than making films that would compete with Hollywood abroad. See David A. Cook, *A History of Narrative Film* (New York, 1990), 141.

15. On this issue with regard to Nazi Germany, see Linda Schulte-Sasse, *Entertaining the Third Reich* (Durham, 1996); and especially, Rentschler, *The Ministry of Illusion*.

16. Italy's law was passed in June 1931; Germany's "Aryan Clause," which was probably modeled on the Italian legislation, took effect in June 1933 and served to exclude Jews from the film industry.

17. Hungarian texts proved popular sources for French, German, and Italian movies through the World War II years. For Italy, see Ernesto Laura, "Il mito di Budapest e i modelli ungheresi nel cinema italiano dal 1930 al 1945," in *Telefoni bianchi: Realtà e finzione nella società e nel cinema italiano degli anni quaranta*, ed. Gianfranco Casadei and Ernesto Laura (Ravenna, 1991), 31–49; and Mino Argentieri, *L'asse cinematografico Roma-Berlino* (Naples, 1986), 105–9. On internationalization in Nazi Germany, see Rentschler, *Ministry of Illusion*.

18. Before World War I, Italian films had 20 percent of the German market, as opposed to 25 percent and 30 percent for American and French films respectively. German films filled 15 percent; the remaining percentage of the market was made up of Danish and English imports. (Figures in Fehrenbach, *Cinema in Democratizing Germany*, 24.) On the successes of Italy's early film industry, see Aldo Bernardini, *Cinema muto italiano*, 3 vols. (Rome, 1980–82); Bruno, *Streetwalking on a Ruined Map*.

19. Anton Giulio Bragaglia, *Il film sonoro* (Rome: Corbaccio, 1929), 189. Paris, Berlin, London, Vienna, and Hollywood were common destinations. On Italians abroad, see Elaine Mancini, "The Free Years of the Fascist Film Industry: 1930–35" (Ph.D. diss., New York University, 1981), 31–32; and Vittorio Martinelli, "I *Gastarbeiter* tra le due guerre," *Bianco e nero* (May-June 1978). Figures on Italian film production vary from source to source. This statistic is from Pierre Leprohon, *The Italian Cinema*, trans. Roger Greaves and Oliver Stallybrass (New York, 1972), 51.

20. Riccardo Redi, *La Cines* (Rome, 1991).

21. Benito Mussolini, quoted in Giuseppe Rossi, "La propaganda agraria cinematografica svolta dall'Opera Nazionale Combattenti," *La Conquista della terra* (February 1930).

22. On Blasetti's role in the creation of a fascist film culture, see Gianfranco Gori, *Alessandro Blasetti* (Florence, 1983); and Mancini, *Free Years*, 99–101.

23. Alessandro Blasetti, "Dopo i primi films LUCE," *Lo Schermo* (November 6, 1926); see also "Guerra nostra," *Cinematografo* (June 12, 1927).

24. Alessandro Blasetti, "Non confondiamo," *Cinematografo* (October 2, 1927); editorial note, *Lo Schermo* (January 15, 1927); and Alessandro Blasetti, "S.O.S.," *Lo Spettacolo d'Italia* (February 5, 1928). Articles that detailed the supposedly negative reception of Soviet films abroad supported this view. See Bruno Quaiot, "Sergei Eisenstein," *Cinematografo* (July 8, 1928); see also the editorial note "Eisenstein allontanato dalla Francia," *Il Tevere* (March 30, 1930).

25. Alessandro Blasetti, "Augustus," *Cinematografo* (December 11, 1927).

26. *Sole*'s scenario, script, and director's notes are reproduced in Adriano Aprà and Riccardo Redi, eds., *Sole* (Rome, 1985).

27. On *Kif Tebbi*, see Alberto Farassino, "Camerini, au-delà du cinéma italien," in Alberto Farassino, ed., *Mario Camerini* (Locarno, 1992), 17–18; Camerini gives notice of the government award in an interview with Sergio Grmek Germani, in Farassino, ed., *Mario Camerini*, 103.

28. Francesco Caretti, "Nascita della critica," in Riccardo Redi, ed., *Cinema italiano sotto il fascismo* (Venice, 1979), 145–64; and Brunetta, *Storia del cinema italiano*, 197–230.

29. Pavolini, "Dare all'Italia una coscienza nazionale cinematografica"; Mario Serandrei, "Funzione antieuropea della cinematografia italiana," *Cinematografo* (September 8, 1929), and his "Corriere dell'Urbe." See also Mario Baffico, "Il cinematografo," *Il Popolo d'Italia* (May 17, 1933); and Raffaello Matarazzo, "Il teleobbiettivo puntato sulla cinematografia italiana," *Il Tevere* (May 6 and June 24, 1929). Antiliberal prejudices prohibited the mention of pre–World War I realist films such as those Elvira Notari directed on the streets of Naples with nonprofessional actors and natural lighting. On these films *dal vero*, see Bruno, *Streetwalking on a Ruined Map*.

30. Corrado Alvaro, "Del cinematografo," *Italia letteraria* (September 8, 1929); A. G. Bragaglia, "Per un'estetica cinematografica," *Cinematografo* (March 17, 1929).

31. Raffaello Matarazzo, "Roma avrà un suo centro di cultura e di studi cinematografici," *Il Tevere* (March 20, 1930); Baffico, "Il cinematografo"; also Corrado Sofia, "Il cinematografo affare di Stato," *Critica fascista* (April 1, 1934).

32. Genealogies of this hybrid aesthetic from fascism through Neorealism are traced in Peter Bondanella, *The Films of Roberto Rossellini* (Cambridge, 1993), 3–11; and Ruth Ben-Ghiat, "Roberto Rossellini's Fascist War Trilogy," in *Roberto Rossellini*, ed. David Forgacs, Sarah Lutton, and Geoffrey Nowell-Smith (London, 2000).

33. On the spread of American film culture in fascist Italy, see Nacci, *L'antiamericanismo in Italia negli anni trenta*, 159–67; and James Hay, *Popular Film Culture in Fascist Italy* (Bloomington, Ind., 1987), 64–96.

34. Soldati, *America primo amore*, 185–86; Serandrei, "Funzione antieuropea della cinematografia italiana"; and Matarazzo, "Il teleobbiettivo puntato sulla cinematografia italiana."

35. Luigi Chiarini, *Il cinematografo* (Rome, 1935), 79; and Soldati, *America primo amore*, 184.

36. Soldati, *America primo amore*, 181, 175.

37. See Mussolini's comment of "nothing doing" scrawled across the Soviet embassy's proposal for an exhibition that would commemorate "the progress made by film and photography in the fifteen years since the Russian Revolution," in ACS, PCM (1931–33), 14.1.4699.

38. Pavolini, "Dare all'Italia una coscienza nazionale cinematografica"; Vinicio Paladini, "Cinematografia della vita vera," *Cinemateatro* (September 1928); Serandrei, "Funzione antieuropea della cinematografia italiana"; and Raffaello Matarazzo, "Il cadavere vivente di Oziep," *Italia letteraria* (February 1, 1931). On the influence of Russian films in fascist Italy, see Brunetta, *Storia del cinema italiano*, 167–74; and Vito Zagarrio, "Il modello sovietico: Tra piano culturale e piano economico," in *Cinema italiano sotto il fascismo*, ed. Riccardo Redi (Venice, 1979), 185–200.

39. Sofia, "Il cinematografo affare di Stato"; Libero Solaroli, "Il cinema italiano deve imitare quello Russo?" *Cinematografo* (March 3, 1929); and Giacomo Debenedetti, "Risorse del cinema," *Il Convegno* (June 1931).

40. Eugenio Giovannetti, cited in Mancini, *Free Years*, 38.

41. Guglielmo Alberti, "Cronaca del cinematografo," *Pègaso* (April 1932); Mario Pannunzio, "Del cinema italiano," *Saggiatore* (November 1932). The fascists objected to the airing of foreign languages to mass audiences; until dubbing practices improved in 1932, they required films to be shown silent with subtitles in Italian projected over the images.

42. These included Poland, Palestine, Holland, Hungary, France, Germany, England, and America. For programming information and critical reactions, see Giulio Cesare Castello and Claudio Bertieri, eds., *Venezia, 1932–39* (Rome, 1959). On the Film Show throughout the thirties, see Francesco Bono, "La Mostra del Cinema di Venezia: Nascita e sviluppo nell'anteguerra (1932–39)," *Storia contemporanea* (June 1991): 513–49: and Stone, *The Patron State*, 100–110.

43. Raffaello Matarazzo, "Commento inaugurale," *Il Tevere* (August 8, 1932); Mario Gromo, "La Biennale del cinema," *La Stampa* (September 3, 1932). The figure of ten thousand spectators is contained in an August 17, 1932, letter from Maraini to Benito Mussolini, in ACS, PCM (1934–37), 14.1.4677.

44. See the February 1, 1933, letter from Maraini to Guido Beer, who was on the administrative council of the Biennale, in ACS, PCM (1934–37), 14.3.8592, and memos in this file that show that the festivals associated with the trade fairs of Sorrento, Bari, and Milan had been prohibited from showing uncensored films by 1934.

45. The funds came in part from Confindustria. The law also increased protectionist measures; now one of three films shown in Italy had to be Italian. Taxes were also increased on dubbing rights. Figure on Italian film output from Brunetta, *Storia del cinema italiano*, 6.

46. Quotation in Brunetta, *Storia del cinema italiano*, 36; but see Alberto

Calza-Bini and A. Olivetti, "I provvedimenti a favore della cinematografia nazionale," *Lo Spettacolo italiano* (June 1931), for a complete description.

47. Giuseppe Bottai, "Dichiarazioni a favore della legge," *Lo Spettacolo italiano* (July-August 1931).

48. The Rationalist architect Vinicio Paladini's designs for *La Segretaria privata* (Alessandrini, 1931), for example, featured a living room modeled on that of the ultramodernist *Casa Elettrica*, which had been shown at the 1930 *Monza Biennale* architectural exhibition. Carlo Levi and Enrico Paolucci were the scenographers for the film *Patratac* (Gennaro Righelli, 1931). On Cines in these years, see Mancini, *Free Years*, 56–98; and Redi, ed., *La Cines*.

49. On Cecchi's self-professed apoliticism, see Mancini, *Free Years*, 73; for similar beliefs among German film professionals, see Rentschler, *Ministry of Illusion*, 122. In fact, the eighteen feature films made during Cecchi's short tenure are perfectly representative of the production of the fascist regime. They included romantic comedies of central European inspiration; nationalistic historical dramas; and several openly political films, among them Righelli's 1931 *L'armata azzura (The Blue Army)*, on the Italian air force, and Blasetti's *1860*, a Risorgimento epic that Cecchi personally produced.

50. Lelio Melani, "Battaglia del grano e psicologia rurale," *La Conquista della terra* (October 1930).

51. Mancini analyzes *Terra madre* in the context of Blasetti's career in *Free Years*, 99–120; see also Luca Verdone, *I film di Alessandro Blasetti* (Rome, 1989).

52. Daisy is described in the film's scenario as "a woman who dominates arrogantly through the allure of her French-perfumed femininity." "Richiamo alla terra," script by Foerster, Alessandrini, and Blasetti. Archivio Blasetti (AB), box "Terra Madre," (TM).

53. Press releases played up the film's "authenticity" and its national resonance by noting that it was set in the Roman countryside and featured music by a famous chorus from Emilia-Romagna. Advertisements and publicity stills can be found in AB, TM.

54. See Blasetti's statements on these scenes in Ugo Ugoletti, "Quattro parole con Alessandro Blasetti," *Cinema-Illustrazione* (March 4, 1931); also see his notes in the shooting script, in AB, TM.

55. For interpretations of the film as defending patriarchy and property and as promoting a new model of modernization, see, respectively, Marcia Landy, *Fascism in Film* (Princeton, 1986), 123–26; and Hay, *Popular Film Culture in Fascist Italy*, 137–40.

56. The establishing shot of *Terra madre*, a Soviet-style close-up of picks tilling the soil, is accompanied by a peasant choir, as are Soviet-influenced close shots of peasants' faces. On this point, see Vito Zagarrio, "Ideology Elsewhere: Contradictory Models of Italian Fascist Cinema," in *Resisting Images*, ed. Robert Sklar and Charles Musser (Philadelphia, 1990), 149–72.

57. See reviews in *Il Lavoro* (March 7, 1931); *Il Mattino* (March 5, 1931); *L'Ambrosiano* (March 4, 1931); see also Ubaldo Magnaghi, "*Terra Madre*," in

Corriere cinematografico (March 7, 1931). For negative reactions, see *Il Messaggero* (March 3, 1931); and *Il Giornale d'Italia* (March 4, 1931). All of the above reviews, most of which do not list the critic's name, are from the clip file in AB, TM.

58. Notice in *Gazzetta di Venezia* (December 16, 1931).

59. Reviews by Filippo Sacchi in *Corriere della sera* (August 12, 1932); Manlio Maserocchi in *L'Illustrazione italiana* (August 28, 1932); Mario Gromo in *La Stampa* (August 12, 1932).

60. The initial segment of *Gli uomini, che mascalzoni!*, which was shot on the streets of Milan, borrows from experimental "city films" of the 1920s, such as Ruttmann's *Berlin*. On Camerini's European formation, see Farassino, "Camerini, au-delà du cinéma italien," and Jean Gili, "Les horizons européens de Mario Camerini," in *Mario Camerini*, ed. Alberto Farassino (Locarno, 1992), 47–54.

61. The film can be compared with Soldati's attitudes in the articles collected in *America primo amore*, some of which were written while the film was being made.

62. The fair included an international cinema competition that, in 1932, showed foreign films such as Alexander Dovzhenko's *Earth*. On the fair's propagandistic potential among foreign and domestic audiences, see Berchet, "La funzione economica delle fiere campioniere."

63. On this point, see Landy, *Fascism in Film*, 241–45.

64. On the popular trains, see de Grazia, *Culture of Consent*, 180–81.

65. Review by Enrico Roma, in *Cinema Illustrazione* (November 29, 1933).

66. Opera Nazionale Dopolavoro, "Disposizioni per escursionisti," *Bollettino mensile* 11–12 (November-December 1927), cited in de Grazia, *Culture of Consent*, 183.

67. Artieri, "Natura magnetica della tradizione," *I Lupi* (February 10, 1928).

68. On Matarazzo, see Hay, *Popular Film Culture in Fascist Italy*, 213–14; Angela Prudenzi, *Raffaello Matarazzo* (Florence, 1991). For Matarazzo's opinions, see his articles cited in notes 29 and 31 of this chapter.

69. For this point, see Hay, *Popular Film Culture in Fascist Italy*, 145–48.

70. Filippo Sacchi, review in *Corriere della sera* (November 15, 1933); Enrico Roma, review in *Cinema Illustrazione* (November 29, 1933); and Dino Falconi, review in *Il Popolo d'Italia* (November 17, 1933).

71. Brunetta, *Storia del cinema italiano*, 4.

72. Longanesi, "Film italiano."

73. Giulio Santangelo, "Via Vejo," *Quadrante* (May 1933); Pannunzio, "Del cinema italiano"; and Fabio Marina, "Il cinematografo in Italia," *Orpheus* (November 1933).

74. On Freddi's trip to Hollywood, see Luigi Freddi, *Il cinema* (Rome, 1949), 1:61. Goebbels publicized his plans for the Reichsfilmkammer in Italy in 1933. See Giuseppe Goebbels, "Come riorganizzo la cinematografia tedesca," *Quadrante* (August 1933).

75. The law also mandated the dubbing of foreign films, which opened the way for the regime to further censor movies by omitting or changing questionable dialogue without most spectators being any the wiser. See Gili, *Stato fascista e cinematografia*, 131–35.

76. Freddi, February 28, 1934, report to Benito Mussolini, in ACS, PCM (1934–36), 3.2.2.1397.

77. The September 1934 report is not in the ACS file but is reproduced, together with the February 28, 1934, report, in Freddi, *Il cinema*, 1:80–85.

78. The other initial appointees to the Direzione Generale were Esodo Pratelli, a painter who directed the Scuola Superiore d'Arte in Milan, and the film historian Jacopo Comin, who had long served on state censorship commissions. Riccio would join the office after 1936.

79. As the screenwriter Cesare Zavattini later recalled, "The censors actually intervened very little. There was no need for them to bang their fists on the table; an allusion was enough." Zavattini, interviewed by Jean Gili, in *Nuovi materali sul cinema italiano*, 138; see also the interviews with the producer Alfredo Guarini and the journalist Mino Doletti, in Francesco Savio, *Cinecittà anni trenta* (Rome, 1979), 2:494 and 646.

80. Gili, *Stato fascista e cinematografia*, 135–47. A film credit bureau modeled on the one set up by Goebbels in Germany was also established at the *Banco Nazionale del Lavoro*. It gave money for production and anticipated funds from government prizes. For contemporary reflections on the creative contributions of writers versus directors, see Ugo Magnaghi, "Consigli ai giovani cineasti," *Libro e moschetto* (January 31, 1935); and Eugenio Giovannetti, "Gli scenaristi cinematografici possono considerarsi autori?" *Comoedia* 5 (1934).

81. See Ben-Ghiat, "Roberto Rossellini's Fascist War Trilogy," for the documentary's appeal as a site of aesthetic experimentation.

82. Galeazzo Ciano, "Discorso al Senato" (May 22, 1936), in Claudio Carabba, *Il cinema del ventennio nero* (Florence, 1974), 123–25.

83. The Scuola Nazionale di Cinematografia is discussed in Gian Piero Brunetta, *Intellettuali, cinema propaganda tra le due guerre* (Bologna, 1972), 83–85.

84. Luigi Chiarini, "Speranza ed esperienza," *Lo Schermo* (December 1935).

85. On the Centro Sperimentale, see the essays in "Il Centro Sperimentale tra tradizione e riforma," special issue of *Bianco e nero* (May-June 1976); and Gili, *Stato fascista e cinematografia*, 94–99.

86. Chiarini, "Speranza ed esperienza."

87. A complete list of CSC students and teachers can be found in *Vivere il cinema* (Rome, 1985), 98–106. For those who worked in the fascist film industry, see Elsa Avanzini et al., eds., *Almanacco del cinema italiano, 1942–43* (Rome, 1943), which does not, however, list assistant directors (or Jewish film professionals, due to the racial laws). Luisa Alessandrini was assistant director on *Frenesia* (Mario Bonnard, 1939); *Rose scarlatte* (De Sica, 1940), and *Piccolo*

alpino (Oreste Biancoli, 1940). Marisa Romano made the documentary *Il seme,* which was shown at the Biennale; political shorts; and a LUCE documentary, *Sinfonia in bianco,* on Sicily's salt mines. See G., "Marisa Romano," *Lo Schermo* (May 1940).

88. Quotation from Luigi Freddi, "Per il cinema italiano," *Intercine* (August 1935). Information on CSC routines from *Vivere il cinema,* 10.

89. Luigi Chiarini, "Il cinema e i giovani," *Lo Schermo* (August 1935); Freddi, "Per il cinema italiano."

CHAPTER 4

1. Few comparative studies exist of the youth policies followed by dictatorships. An initial and still valuable essay is by Gino Germani, "La socializzazione politica dei giovani nei regimi fascisti: Italia e Spagna," *Quaderni di sociologia* (January-June 1966): 11–58. See Koon, *Believe, Obey, Fight,* for a comprehensive analysis of Italian fascist youth policies; for Nazi Germany, see Arno Klönne, *Jugend im Dritten Reich* (Dusseldorf, 1982); and Detlev Peukert, *Inside Nazi Germany* (New Haven, 1987), 145–74. On Franco's Spain, see Marín Sáez, *El Frente de Juventudes: Política de juventud en la España de la postguerra (1937–1960)* (Madrid, 1988).

2. Wohl, *Generation of 1914,* 204–37; Wanrooj, "Rise and Fall of Italian Fascism"; and Mark Roseman, introduction to *Generations in Conflict,* ed. Mark Roseman (Cambridge, 1995), 15–20.

3. Adamson, *Avant-Garde Florence;* and Giovanni Lazzari, "Linguaggio, ideologia, politica culturale del fascismo," *Movimento operaio e socialista* (January-April 1984): 49–56.

4. Roland Alix, *La nouvelle jeunesse* (Paris: Valois, 1930), 154; "L'Enquête auprès des étudiants d'aujourd'hui," *Les Nouvelles littéraires* (November 17, 1928, through February 2, 1929); also the Italian version, which appeared in *Italia letteraria* (December 2, 1928, through February 17, 1929). For Germany, see Günther Gründel, *Die Sendung der Jungen Generation* (Munich: Beck, 1932); and Franz Matke, *Jugend bekennt: So sind wir!* (Leipzig: P. Reclam, 1930). Generational conflicts were also central to many Italian and German realist novels and to the international film genre of the schoolgirl comedy.

5. By the end of 1921, students made up over 13 percent of fascist supporters. Numbers in Wanrooj, "Rise and Fall of Italian Fascism," 406.

6. "Disciplina," *Critica fascista* (July 15, 1923); and "Un regime di giovani," *Critica fascista* (June 1, 1928).

7. Carlo Scorza, "Relazione sui FGC, sui GUF, sui Milizia universitaria," July 11, 1931, in ACS, SPCR, Carteggio Riservato, b31, f.242/R, sf.2; report from Turin, May 30, 1931, in ACS, MI, DGPS, AGR (1927–33), Cat. C2, b.1; report from Naples, April 20, 1931, in ACS, MI, DPP, Affari per materia, pacco 149, f.21, K112 (1929–31). This last file also contains reports from Parma, Modena, Milan, and Bologna, as well as the original order from the fascist chief

of police, which asked informers to find out "what students are doing and if bad feelings are brewing."

8. Giuseppe Bottai, "Funzione della gioventù," *Critica fascista* (March 15, 1933).

9. Dagmar Reese makes a similar point for the German case, arguing that women's experiences in the youth groups of Hitler's regime left them with a generational identity that often overrode gender consciousness. See her essay, "The BDM Generation: A Female Generation in Transition from Dictatorship to Democracy," in *Generations in Conflict*, ed. Mark Roseman (Cambridge, 1995), 227–46. On the situation of young female intellectuals and professionals under fascism, see de Grazia, *How Fascism Ruled Women*; and Emma Scaramuzza, "Professioni intellettuali e fascismo: L'ambivalenza dell'Alleanza muliebre culturale italiana," *Italia contemporanea* (September 1983): 111–33.

10. Alfredo Panzini, in AAI, b.Verbali—lettere, meeting of January 28, 1930; see also the PNF directive of January 20, 1930. On fascism's cult of youth, see Malvano, "Il mito della giovinezza," 311–48; and Koon, *Believe, Obey, Fight*.

11. "Giovani vecchi e educatori maleducatori," *Critica fascista* (January 15, 1932). On the place of youth in Bottai's vision of fascism, see De Grand, *Bottai e la cultura fascista*, 131–74.

12. Between 1928 and 1932, over 120,000 Italians were expelled from the PNF and only young people were admitted. Acquarone, *L'organizzazione dello Stato totalitario*, 177–88.

13. Camillo Pellizzi, "Terza lettera," *Il Selvaggio* (March 31, 1932); Massimo Bontempelli, "Scuola dell'ottimismo," *Occidente* (November-December 1932).

14. Alvaro, "Opinioni sul romanzo"; Alfredo Casella, "Fascismo e musica," *Educazione fascista* (November 1932); and Luigi Chiarini, "Fatti vecchi e idee nuove," *Educazione fascista* (January 20-February 20, 1932); for the youth side, see Domenico Carella, "Crisi della cultura," *Saggiatore* (May 1932); and Berto Ricci, "Avvisi," *L'Universale* (April 3, 1932).

15. Agostino Nasti, "Classe dirigente," *Critica fascista* (March 15, 1931); Eduardo Persico, "Tendenze d'oggi," *Italia letteraria* (March 23, 1930).

16. Mario Tinti, "La fine di un'epoca," *L'Orto* (December 1931).

17. Mario Zagari, "Realismo rivoluzionario," *Camminare* (February 28, 1934).

18. For the first position, which is associated with the trope of the "long voyage," see Ruggiero Zangrandi, *Il lungo viaggio attraverso il fascismo* (Turin, 1962); see also Alessandro Bonsanti, "La cultura degli anni trenta dai Littoriali all'antifascismo," *Terzo programma* 4 (1963): 183–217; and Paolo Alatri, "Cultura e politica: Gli studenti romani dal 1936 al 1943," *Incontri meridionali* 3–4 (1979): 7–17. The second reaction, which is more common in those born around 1920, runs through the interviews collected in Renato Palmeri et al., eds., *La generazione degli anni difficili* (Bari, 1962); see also

Ugoberto Alfassio Grimaldi, "La generazione sedotta e abbandonata," *Tempo presente* (January 1963). Essays by Alexander von Plato, Michael Buddrus, and Dagmar Reese in Roseman, ed., *Generations in Conflict*, highlight parallel feelings among German men and women after 1945.

19. On the cult of the Duce, see Luisa Passerini, *Mussolini immaginario* (Rome, 1991); and Koon, *Believe, Obey, Fight*, 14–19.

20. This notion of power is best explicated in Michel Foucault's *History of Sexuality*, vol. 1: *An Introduction*, trans. Richard Hurley (New York, 1978), esp. 17–49, and in his *Power/Knowledge*, ed. and trans. Colin Gordon (New York, 1980); see also Gerald Graff, "Co-optation," in Aram Veeser, *The New Historicism* (New York, 1989), 168–81. Carlo Cartiglia also comes to this conclusion in his study of "*frondist* fascism": see "Il 'fascismo di fronda': Appunti e ipotesi di lavoro," *Italia contemporanea*, 122 (1976): 5–22.

21. Nino Bertocchi, "Imposizione della sobrietà," *L'Orto* (April 1932).

22. Dino Garrone to Berto Ricci, letter of May 3, 1929, quoted in Paolo Buchignani, *Un fascismo impossible* (Bologna, 1994), 105–6; Persico, "Tendenze d'oggi."

23. "Autobiografismo," *Oggi* (October 15, 1933). On the youth reviews of this period, see Mangoni, *L'interventismo della cultura*, 197–238; and Sechi, *Il mito della nuova cultura*, 63–214; for sample texts, see Alberto Folin, *Le riviste giovanile del period fascista* (Treviso, 1977).

24. Massimo Cimino, "Dal concetto di classe a quello di funzione," *Saggiatore* (December 1932); "Posizione," *Orpheus* (April 1933); compare with Stefan Zweig, "Lettera," *Saggiatore* (February 1933); and Karl Mannheim, *Ideology and Utopia* (New York, 1936).

25. Benito Mussolini, cited in Mariani, *Fascismo e "città nuove,"* 54; Benito Mussolini "La dottrina del fascismo," *Enciclopedia Italiana*, 9:850.

26. Document cited in Falasca-Zamponi, *Fascist Spectacle*, 130.

27. Bruno Brunello, "Capitalismo e corporativismo," *La Stirpe* (March 1934); Ugo Spirito, "L'iniziativa individuale," *Critica fascista* (December 15, 1932); and Benito Mussolini, "Per lo Stato corporativo," November 4, 1933, in *Scritti e discorsi*, 8:257–73; see also Giuseppe Bottai, "Statismo corporativo," *Critica fascista* (February 1, 1933); and Ciocca, *Giudizio sul bolscevismo*, 271. The range of positions on corporativism is surveyed in Gianpasquale Santomassimo, "Aspetti della politica culturale del fascismo: Il dibattito sul corporativismo e l'economia politica," *Italia contemporanea* (October-December 1975): 3–26.

28. On the itineraries of Sergio Panunzio and other syndicalists from socialism to fascism, see Zeev Sternhell, with Mario Szrajder and Maia Asheri, *The Birth of Fascist Ideology* (Princeton, 1994); and David Roberts, *The Syndicalist Tradition and Italian Fascism* (Chapel Hill, 1979).

29. Maier, *Recasting Bourgeois Europe*; Kelikian, *Town and Country under Fascism*, provides a case study. Franklin Hugh Adler, *Italian Industrialists from Liberalism to Fascism* (Cambridge, 1996), emphasizes industrialists' attempts to make corporativism serve their own needs.

30. De Grand, *Bottai e la cultura fascista,* 71–132; and Sabino Cassese, "Un programmatore degli anni trenta: Giuseppe Bottai," in *La formazione dello Stato amministrativo* (Milan, 1974), 187–210. Bottai's ideas are summarized in his writings *Esperienza corporativa* (Rome, 1929), and *Il cammino delle corporazioni* (Florence, 1935).

31. "Sviluppo dell'azione sindacale," *Cantiere* (May 12, 1934); and Giuseppe Bianchini, "Funzione del sindacato," *L'Universale* (August 1934).

32. On foreign interest in corporativism, see Palla, *Fascismo e Stato corporativo;* Diggins, *Mussolini and Fascism;* and Maurizio Vaudagna, *New Deal e corporativismo* (Turin, 1981). On the place of corporativist doctrine in fascist ideology, see Zunino, *L'ideologia del fascismo,* 245–310.

33. *La crisi del capitalismo; L'economia programmatica* (Florence: Sansoni, 1933); and *Bolscevismo e capitalismo* (Florence: Sansoni, 1935) all featured prefaces by Bottai. On the fascist attention to communist thinkers, see Roberto Romani, "Il piano quinquennale sovietico nel dibattito corporativo italiano, 1928–36," *Italia contemporanea* (June 1984): 27–41.

34. Giuseppe Bottai, "Ripresa rivoluzionaria," *Critica fascista* (April 1, 1931).

35. "Rivoluzione di popolo," *Cantiere* (March 10, 1934).

36. Alexandre Marc, "L'homme nouveau," *Esprit* (December 1933). On this generation of French radicals, see Loubet del Bayle, *Les non-conformistes des années trente;* Sternhell, *Neither Right nor Left,* chapter 4; and Nacci, "I rivoluzionari dell'apocalisse."

37. Riccio, "Arte e costruzione."

38. Francesco Orlando, "Fuori della metafisica," *Saggiatore* (May-June 1930); Nicola Perotti, "La crisi attuale della spirito," *Saggiatore* (March-April 1930); and Domenico Carella, "Riflessioni sul pragmatismo," *Saggiatore* (May-June 1930). Five out of eight founders of the review (Nicola Chiaromonte, Attilio Riccio, Giorgio Granata, Luigi De Crecchio, and Nicola Perotti) were associated with the Italian Psychoanalytic Society, which was suppressed by the government in 1934. See Michel David, *La psicoanalisi nella cultura italiana* (Turin, 1966), 312–14. On the review in general, see Sechi, *Il mito della nuova cultura,* 63–108; and Pasquale Voza, "Il problema del realismo negli anni trenta: 'Il Saggiatore' e 'Il Cantiere,'" *Lavoro critico* (January-June 1981): 65–105. This generation's reaction against Idealism is well analyzed by Arcangelo Leone de Castris, *Egemonia e fascismo* (Bologna, 1981), 57–132.

39. In the early thirties Gentile retained control of many cultural institutions, including the *Fondazione Leonardo,* the *Istituto Interuniversitario Italiano,* the *Istituto Nazionale di Cultura Fascista,* the *Istituto Italo-Germanico,* the *Istituto per Medio e Basso Oriente,* and the *Istituto Treccani,* and headed the Sansoni publishing house. For his role in fascist culture, see Albertina Vittoria, "Gentile e gli istituti culturali," in *Tendenze della filosofia italiana,* ed. Ornella Pompeo Faracovi (Livorno, 1985), 115–44.

40. The survey "Quesiti sulla nuova generazione" took place from April

1932 to January 1933; respondents included Father Agostino Gemelli and Pietro De Francisci, rectors of the *Università Sacro Cuore* and the University of Rome, as well as members of the Italian Academy.

41. "Conclusioni ai quesiti sulla nuova generazione," *Saggiatore* (January 1933). After following the polemic from his prison cell, Gramsci concluded that the *Saggiatore* youth had become misguided and "servile" propagators of credos handed them by the regime. Gramsci, *Quaderni del carcere*, 3:1814.

42. Enzo Paci, "Cenni per una nuova clima," *Orpheus* (February 1933).

43. "Posizione," *Orpheus* (April 1933); and Enzo Paci, "In margine di un'inchiesta," *Orpheus* (July-September 1933). Banfi's 1932–33 University of Milan lectures, which Paci and Anceschi attended, are the basis for Antonio Banfi, *La crisi* (Milan, 1967); see also Eugenio Garin, *Intellettuali italiani del XX secolo* (Rome, 1974), 215–39, on Banfi's thought. Information on Banfi's influence is from my interviews with Anceschi, Bologna, June 22 and July 2, 1990; Luciano Anceschi, "L'insegnamento di Antonio Banfi," *Belfagor* (May-June 1978): 335–42; and Paci's recollections in *Antonio Banfi e il pensiero contemporaneo* (Florence, 1967), 34–45.

44. Jean-Paul Sartre, "Une idée fondamentale de la phénoménologie de Husserl: L'Intentionalité," in *Situations* (Paris: Gallinard, 1947), 1:32–33.

45. Pietro Tronchi, "La Scuola Superiore di cultura e d'arte," *Orpheus* (January 1933); Tronchi, "Intenzioni," *Orpheus* (February 1933). The school's teachers included the artist Raffaele Giolli and the architects Eduardo Persico and Agnoldomenico Pica.

46. Carlo Marchetti, review of *Es ist Zeit*, by Otto Flake, *Orpheus* (February 1933); on the Otto Dix show, see Tronchi to Anceschi, February 2, 1934, in AA, b.Orpheus.

47. Enzo Paci, "Appunti per la definizione di un nuovo atteggiamento," *Orpheus* (November 1933).

48. "I giovani e la nuova cultura," *Orpheus* (December 1933); Granata, "Aspetti del nuovo scrittore"; and Giannini Marescalchi, "Poeti in piazza," *L'Orto* (October 1933).

49. "Per la formazione dell'Italiano nuovo: Per un rinnovata etica sessuale," *Orpheus* (January-March 1934); "Risposta alla polemica del 'Secolo-Sera' contro la donna negli uffici," *Orpheus* (December 1933). Besides Grete Aberle, the correspondent from Berlin, female contributors included Eva Rande, Federica Vecchietti, Lorenza Maranini, Käte Bernhardt, Maria Albini, Clara Albini, and Clara Valente, many of whom were university students.

50. Daria Banfi Malaguzzi, *Femminilità contemporanea* (Milan, 1928), 15, 131. De Grazia, *How Fascism Ruled Women*, 116–65, explores the dilemmas and possibilities of educated young women in fascist Italy.

51. Mario M. Morandi, "Classe 1908," *Educazione fascista* (1933).

52. Clara Valente, "Esiste una questione femminile?" *Orpheus* (May-June 1933); and the responses to the same survey by F. Koren (July-September 1933), Sara Scalzi, and Federica Vecchietti (January-March 1934). On the "fas-

cist feminist" positions of older women, such as Teresa Labriola, who had participated in earlier suffragist movements, see Spackman, *Fascist Virilities*, 41–48; and de Grazia, *How Fascism Ruled Women*, 249–55.

53. "Risposta alla polemica del 'Secolo-Sera,'" responses of A. M. Mazzucchelli, C. Albini, A. Dossi, C. di Pinerolo, and G. Libani, from whom the quotation is taken; see also Maria Albini, "Il lavoro femminile e l'indipendenza della donna," *Orpheus* (November 1933).

54. Ricci had begun his journalistic career writing for *Il Selvaggio* and had remained a follower of Maccari and the artist Ottone Rosai, a former squadrist. On Ricci and *L'Universale*, see Buchignani, *Un fascismo impossibile*.

55. "L'Universale," *L'Universale* (January 1931); see also Indro Montanelli, "Noi giovani."

56. Berto Ricci, *Lo scrittore italiano* (Rome, 1931), 114–15; see also *L'Universale*'s March 10, 1933 issue, which is entirely devoted to the cause of Rationalist architecture.

57. "Manifesto realista," *L'Universale* (January 1933); see also "Risposta alla santità di Papa Pio XI sull'ultima enciclica," *L'Universale* (July 1931).

58. "Amice Lector," *L'Universale* (February 1931); and Berto Ricci, "Avvisi," *L'Universale* (June 3, 1932, and February 10, 1933).

59. Berto Ricci, *Errori del nazionalismo italico* (Florence, 1931), 20–21; and "Manifesto realista."

60. "Manifesto realista." *L'Universale*'s critique of the Church separated it from the universal fascist ideology of the Action Committees for the Universality of Rome, which were founded by Mussolini in 1933. See Ledeen, *L'internazionale fascista*, and Mira and Salvatorelli, *Storia d'Italia nel periodo fascista*, 2:181–83, for official support for universal fascism.

61. Granata to Anceschi, May 2, 1934; Mino Castellani to Anceschi, August 19, 1933, in AA, b.Orpheus. This file also contains information on the advertising agreements *Orpheus* had with other youth journals; with modernist forums like *Domus, Case d'oggi, Occidente,* and *Quadrante;* and with the French journals *Les Nouvelles littéraires* and *La Nouvelle revue française.*

62. Granata to Anceschi, July 7, 1933, in AA, b.Orpheus.

63. See the issue entitled "Contributo alla nuova cultura," *Saggiatore* (August-October 1933). Fifty-five men and two women (Marise Ferro and Lorenza Maranini of *Orpheus*) participated.

64. Chiarini, "Fatti vecchi e idee nuove"; and Giuseppe Bottai, "Quesiti sulla nuova generazione," *Saggiatore* (August-September 1932), and "Questo tempo," *Critica fascista* (September 15, 1932).

65. Press directive of January 17, 1933, in ACS, Carte Morgagni, b.3, f.7. The phrase "generational mobilization without generational conflict," is from Roseman, introduction to *Generations in Conflict*, 31.

66. Luigi Chiarini, "Effimere," *Educazione fascista* (March 1933).

67. Gherardo Casini, "Necessità dell'umano," *Critica fascista* (March 15, 1933); and Casini's reply to Domenico Carella, "Nostro realismo," *Critica fascista* (April 1933).

68. *Saggiatore*, *Orpheus*, and *Camminare* were started with family funds, and like *L'Universale* and *Oggi*, depended on donations from the editors and their friends and associates. *Camminare* had fewer financial concerns, as its editor was the publishing scion Arnaldo Mondadori. Information on the first two journals is from interviews with Maria Granata, Rome, July 10, 1987, and Luciano Anceschi, Bologna, June 22 and July 2, 1990. On *Oggi*, see Pannunzio's letters in *Antonio Delfini*, special issue of *Riga* 6 (1993): 146–73. *Saggiatore* won a L3,000 "encouragement prize" from the Italian Academy in 1932; *L'Universale* was aided privately by Ciano, Giorgio Pini, Enrico Vallecchi, and Bottai. See Buchignani, *Un fascismo impossibile*, 170–71.

69. Alberto Calza-Bini to Benito Mussolini, March 1, 1928, and November 12, 1930, also Bottai to Mussolini, March 12, 1928, in ACS, PCM (1931–33), 14.1.128. Pagano became a consultant on architectural exhibitions, Griffini on international competitions, and Piccinato on urbanistic matters. Notice of their *incarichi speciali* is given in "Pagina di vita sindacale," *L'Architettura* (October 1933). On the Rationalists changing relationship with the regime, see Diane Ghirardo, "Italian Architects and Fascist Politics," *Journal of the Society of Architectural Historians* (May 1980): 109–27.

70. Bilenchi, *Amici*, 71–74; Domenico Carella, *Fascismo primo, fascismo dopo* (Rome, 1973), 134.

71. On Spinetti's ideas, see Ledeen, *L'internazionale fascista*, 59–76; Langella, *Il secolo delle riviste*, 296–99.

72. Gaetano Polverelli to Benito Mussolini, March 23, 1933, in ACS, PCM (1934–36), f.1.1.11997, sf.2.

73. Editorial from *La Sapienza* (June-July 1933), reproduced in Folin, *Le riviste giovanile del periodo fascista*, 222–23. Police informer's reports of June 18 and August 21, 1933, in ACS, MI, DGPS, DPP (1927–43), Affari per materia, b.142, f.K96.

74. See Spinetti's October 1933 letter to Benito Mussolini, in ACS, SPCO, CO, b.1373, f.512629; his government subsidies are listed in NA, PPBM, job 26, neg.012640. Spinetti gives his own account of his career trajectory in his *Difesa di una generazione* (Rome, 1948).

75. GUF membership grew from 55,000 in 1931 to 75,000 in 1936. Koon, *Believe, Obey, Fight*, 196–216; and Enzo Santarelli, *Storia del movimento e del regime fascista* (Rome, 1967), 2:279–84. On GUF radio programs, see ACS, PCM, Gabinetto, Atti (1931–33), f. 13/1 and 14.3/4528; Franco Monteleone, *La radio italiano nel periodo fascista* (Venice, 1976), 115–17. Italians could remain members of the GUF organizations until the age of twenty-eight, so new graduates often continued to frequent the university and contribute to student publications.

76. Giuseppe Bottai, "Significato dei Littoriali," *Critica fascista* (May 15, 1934). On the Littoriali as a place of antifascist organizing, see Bonsanti, "La cultura degli anni trenta dai Littoriali all'antifascismo"; Koon, *Believe, Obey, Fight*, 202–7. Marina Addis Saba and Ugoberto Alfassio Grimaldi, *Cultura a passo romano* (Milan, 1983); and Zangrandi, *Il lungo viaggio*, 641–715,

list prizewinners. For parallel observations about the emancipatory effects of Hitler Youth organizations, see Alexander von Plato, "The Hitler Youth Generation and Its Role in the Two Post-War Germanies," in *Generations in Conflict*, ed. Mark Roseman (Cambridge, 1995), 212.

77. Valente, "Esiste una questione femminile?"; and Partito Nazionale Fascista, *I gruppi dei fascist universitari* (Rome, 1941), 50–51.

78. "Le sezioni cinematografiche dei GUF," *Gioventù fascista* (February 1, 1935); and Giuseppe Bottai, "Il regno della noia," *Critica fascista* (August 15, 1928).

79. Soldati was assistant director but played a large role in setting up shots due to Ruttmann's inability to speak or understand Italian.

80. Cecchi's summary of the film in *L'Illustrazione italiana* (March 12, 1933), reproduced in Claudio Camerini, ed., *Acciaio: Un film degli anni Trenta* (Rome, 1990), 205.

81. "Cinema puro," *Oggi* (June 18, 1933). Ruttmann also draws numerous analogies between the realms of work and spectacle by crosscutting from the factory to the activities of a local circus. Skyrocketing unemployment in Italy (from three hundred thousand in 1929 to over a million in 1933) had devastating effects in industrial centers like Terni; many of the laborers shown in the film had lost their jobs. See Camerini, *Acciaio*, 18, 40.

82. Reviews by Lea Schiavi in *L'Impero* (April 15, 1933); L. F. Chiarelli in *Il Giornale d'Italia* (April 16, 1933); and Guglielmo Alberti in *Scenario* (April 1933), in Camerini, *Acciaio*, 218, 219, 231.

83. Interview with Mario Soldati, in Camerini, ed., *Acciaio*, 193. On Ruttmann's career path from Weimar to the Nazis, see Barry Fuchs, "Walter Ruttmann, the Avant-Garde Film, and Nazi Modernism," *Film and History* (May 1984): 26–35.

84. "Il significato dei Littoriali," *Il Popolo d'Italia* (April 28, 1934).

85. Benito Mussolini, "Per lo Stato corporativo," speeches of November 14, 1933, and January 13, 1934, in *Scritti e discorsi*, 8:259 and 9:13–22; and Benito Mussolini, "Sintesi del regime," speech of March 18, 1934, and "Discorso agli operai di Milano," speech of October 6, 1934, both in *Scritti e discorsi*, 9:33 and 128–29.

86. Benito Mussolini, "Sintesi del regime"; March 1934 memo on *Saggiatore* stationery, AA, b.Cantiere; and "Fronte Unico," *Orpheus* (January-March 1934).

87. Ermete De Grazia, "Condizioni degli zolfatori in Sicilia," *Cantiere* (September 29 and November 3, 1934); Guglielmo Serafini, "Case ai rurali," *Cantiere* (April 14, 1934); Mario Champ, "Inchiesta sulla vita dei lavoratori," *Cantiere* (April 21 and December 15, 1934); and "In tema di salari," *Cantiere* (March 24, 1934).

88. Giuseppe Bianchini, "Denuncia," *L'Universale* (May 25, 1935); Romano Bilenchi, "Indicatore," *L'Universale* (August 1934); and Diano Brocchi's column "Osservatorio corporativo," in *L'Universale*, which began in January 1935.

89. Zagari, "Realismo rivoluzionario."

90. Pietro Nenni, "Mussolini a décapité la solidisante aile gauche du fascisme," *Le Peuple* (July 23, 1935).

91. Luciano Anceschi, "Nuova obbiettività estetica e moralità," *Cantiere* (March 31, 1934); and Enzo Paci, "Cultura e rivoluzione," *Camminare* (March 31, 1934).

92. Luciano Anceschi, "Socialità del romanzo," *Quadrivio* (January 14, 1934); "Fatti e argomenti," *Cantiere* (March 24, 1934); "Romanzo collettivo," *Cantiere* (May 19, 1934); and Valentino Bompiani, "Romanzo collettivo," *La Gazzetta del Popolo* (March 14, 1934).

93. Domenico Carella, "Collettivismo e personalità," *Saggiatore* (July 1933).

94. Massimo Scaligero, "Pericolo di un mito contemporaneo," *Critica fascista* (July 15, 1931).

95. "Manifesto realista"; letter from Ricci to Bilenchi, March 27, 1934, quoted in Buchignani, *Un fascismo impossibile*, 259; Berto Ricci, "Avvisi," *L'Universale* (June 25, 1934). Adriano Ghiron, "Rivoluzionari di Francia," *L'Universale* (June 25, 1934), points out similarities with the program of the French youth journal *L'Ordre nouveau*.

96. For Pannunzio, see "Senso della personalità," *Oggi* (February 1934); letter to Antonio Delfini, March 10, 1934, in *Antonio Delfini*, 171. For Moravia, see letter to Pannunzio, March 11, 1934, in *Antonio Delfini*, 175; "Il parere di un romanziere," *La Gazzetta del Popolo* (April 25, 1934); "La moda del collettivismo," *Oggi* (February 1934); "Irrazionalità delle masse," *La Gazzetta del Popolo* (May 31, 1934).

97. "Ragione del titolo," *Caratteri* (March 1, 1935). Pannunzio makes reference to the accusations against him in a letter to Delfini, April 27–28, 1934, in *Antonio Delfini*, 175.

98. Umberto Barbaro, "Come si diventa scrittori," *Quadrivio* (August 1934).

99. Elio Vittorini, *Il garofano rosso* (Milan, 1989), 37; and Benito Mussolini, "1934," *Il Popolo d'Italia* (January 2, 1934).

100. Vitaliano Brancati, *Singolare avventura di viaggio* (Milan, 1934), 93; see also Romano Bilenchi *Vita di Pisto* (Turin: Il Selvaggio, 1931). The memoirs and fiction published in those years by Marcello Gallian and Ottone Rosai linked fascist squadrism with an antidisciplinarian body politics (clubbings, random sexual encounters, the ambiguous homosociality of combat life). See Gallian, *Comando di Tappa* (Rome, 1934), especially the story "Donna di camicie nere," and Rosai, *Dentro la guerra*. Bilenchi praised Gallian's books on the squadrist years (*Comando di Tappa* and *Il soldato postumo*) as testaments to "aspirations that have remained unsatisfied or repressed" in *Il Popolo d'Italia* (August 20, 1935).

101. Vittorini, *Il garofano rosso*, 37.

102. Ibid., 181–82, 185.

103. On the book's censorship, see Lorenzo Greco, *Scrittura e censura*

(Rome, 1983), 99–132. Vittorini discusses the vicissitudes of the novel in a preface to the first edition, which did not appear until 1948. The preface is reproduced as an appendix to the 1989 edition cited in n. 99 above.

104. Camillo Pellizzi, "Considerazioni intorno alla classe 1910," *Critica fascista* (March 15, 1934); and Giuseppe Bottai, "Mussolini e le nuove generazioni fasciste," *Critica fascista* (April 15, 1934); see also Ugo D'Andrea, "Individuo e collettivo: Lettera aperta a Cantiere," *Critica fascista* (May 1, 1934); and Carmelo Sgroi, *Tormento di due generazioni* (Catania: Studio editoriale moderno, 1935), 87.

105. "Rivoluzione," *Critica fascista* (June 15, 1934); and Giuseppe Bottai, "Appunti sui rapporti tra lingua e rivoluzione," *L'Orto* (May-June 1934).

106. Reports on Mondadori and his collaborators in Milan of May 3 and 5 and June 30, 1935, in MI, DGPS, DPP, b.132, K11; information on Anceschi and *Cantiere* is from my interview with Anceschi, Bologna, June 22, 1990, and NA, PPBM, job 31, neg.014964. Ciano's suggestions with regard to National Socialism and the family are mentioned in an April 11, 1934, letter of Granata to Anceschi, in AA, b.Orpheus. The resulting articles include Federico Curato, "Pangermanesimo e Hitler," *Cantiere* (April 14, 1934); and "Che cos'è l'Africa Orientale," *Cantiere* (March 16 and 23, 1935).

107. On the troubles of Ricci and *L'Universale*, see Buchignani, *Un fascismo impossibile*, 171–75. The group's audience with the Duce took place on July 5, 1934; see ACS, SPCO, Carteggio ordinario, 514829/1 and 514829/2. Icilio Petrone, Edgardo Sulis, Mario Tinti, Gioacchino Contri, Ottone Rosai, Giorgio Bertolini, and Bilenchi received government funds: See NA, PPBM, job 26, negs.012384–012738.

108. Report from Ancona, July 26, 1934, ACS, MI, DGPS, DPP, b.132, K11.

109. Reports of May 10 and June 13, 1935, in ibid.

110. Arnaldo Fioretti, quoted in Albertina Vittoria and Michela Nacci, "Convegno italo-francese di studi corporativi, Roma, 20–24 maggio, 1935" *Dimensioni* 40–41 (1986): 30–119; Emmanuel Mounier, "'Esprit' au congrès franco-italien," *Esprit* (June 1935); and Indro Montanelli, "Il convegno corporativo italo-francese," *L'Universale* (June 10, 1935). French participants included Mounier, Dandieu, Aron, Pierre Ganivet of *L'Homme réel*, and representatives from the Fronte Paysan, Jeunesses Patriotes, Federation Nationale Catholique, and Fronte Social.

111. "Avvisi," *L'Universale* (August 25, 1935); Nenni, "Mussolini a décapité la solidisante aile gauche du fascisme"; and Ruggero Grieco, "Largo ai giovani," *Lo Stato operaio* (October 1936).

112. On the suppression of *L'Universale* and *Cantiere*, see Bilenchi, *Amici*, 83; and Carella, *Fascismo prima, fascismo dopo*, 12. See Ricci's protests to officials in ACS, SPCO, 514829/2.

113. Giuseppe Bottai, "Funzione della scienza nell'economia moderna," *Critica fascista* (November 15, 1932).

114. Bottai, quoted in "Il pensiero del corporativismo dalla Carta di Lavoro ad oggi," *Critica fascista* (April 15, 1937).

115. C. B. [Carlo Bernard], "Colloquio con Alvaro," *Italia letteraria* (November 16, 1935).

116. Barbaro praised the *Direzione Generale di Cinematografia* in "Milioni per il cinematografo," *Quadrivio* (April 7, 1935).

117. Pannunzio to Delfini, September 22, 1934, in *Antonio Delfini*, 182.

118. 1936 letter from Moravia to Prezzolini, in Moravia, *Alberto Moravia–Giuseppe Prezzolini*, 16; Elkann, *Vita di Moravia*, 117, and Moravia's 1932 letter to Nicola Chiaromonte, quoted in Siciliano, "Due amici."

119. Soldati, *America primo amore*, 87, 15, 18.

120. Cesare Pavese, entry of October 16, 1935, in *Il mestiere di vivere, 1935–50*, ed. Marziano Guglielminetti and Laura Nay (Turin, 1990), 13.

CHAPTER 5

1. Orestano, "Adunanza inaugurale"; Giuseppe Bottai, "Soldato fascista," *Critica fascista* (December 1, 1935).

2. "Elementi per una nuova geografia italiana," *Critica fascista* (September 1, 1937).

3. Ciro Poggiali, *Diario A.O.I.* (Milan, 1971), entry for December 5, 1936, 126; and Bottai, cited in Ipsen, *Dictating Demography*, 185.

4. Benito Mussolini to Ciano, quoted in Galeazzo Ciano, *Diario, 1937–43* (Milan, 1990), 156.

5. Ferrante Azzali, "La cultura e la vita," *Critica fascista* (April 15, 1938).

6. Benito Mussolini, "Al Consiglio Nazionale del PNF," October 25, 1938, in *Opera Omnia*, 29:185–91.

7. Akira Iriye, *Cultural Internationalism and World Order* (Baltimore, 1997).

8. Prizes included the Italian Academy's *Premio Mussolini*, the city of Bologna's *Premio al poeta originale*, the Milan Cultural Institute's *Concorso di poesia su tema dettato dal Duce*, and the *Concorso per un'opera sull'Estremo Oriente* of the Institute for the Study of the Middle and Far East. A full list is in "I premi letterari approvati," *Il Resto del Carlino* (November 17, 1938).

9. A detailed analysis of literary-filmic collaborations is given in Micciché, "Cinema italiano sotto il fascismo."

10. See Giorgio Rochat, "La repressione della resistenza araba in Cirenaica nel 1930–31," in Rochat, *Guerre italiane in Libia e in Etiopia* (Treviso, 1991), 29–98; and Gustavo Ottolenghi, *Gli italiani e il colonialismo* (Milan, 1997). On the fascist colonization of Libya, see Claudio Segrè, *Fourth Shore* (Chicago, 1974); on colonial urban planning schemes, consult Maria Gubiena Fuller, *Colonial Constructions* (Routledge, forthcoming).

11. Giuseppe Lombrassa, "Il senno dei Tigrini," *Lo Schermo* (November 1935); Prospector, "La colonizzazione nell'Impero," *Africa italiana* (November 1938); and Dante Benedetti, "L'Italia e la schiavitù in Abissinia," *Gioventù fascista* (January 15, 1936). The best overall work on the fascist con-

quest of Ethiopia is Angelo Del Boca, *Gli Italiani in Africa Orientale*, 4 vols. (Bari, 1976–84); see also Alberto Sbacchi, *La colonizzazione italiana in Etiopia, 1936–40* (Milan, 1983).

12. Enrico Emanuelli, "Scontri di pattuglie e cammelli disgraziati," *Il Lavoro* (January 5, 1936).

13. Angelo Del Boca, ed., *I gas di Mussolini* (Rome, 1996), 152; and Ottolenghi, *Gli italiani e il colonialismo*, esp. 177–82.

14. Benito Mussolini, speech of October 2, 1935, in *Scritti e discorsi*, 9:218, and speech of December 2, 1935, in 10:13–14. On the idea that the 1919 treaty dishonored Italy, see James H. Burgwyn, *The Legend of the Mutilated Victory* (Westport, Conn., 1993). The phrase "virtuous victim," and my analysis of Italy's reaction to the sanctions, is drawn from Falasca-Zamponi, *Fascist Spectacle*, 171–82.

15. Soldati, interview with Jean Gili in Gili, *Le Cinéma italien à l'ombre des faisceax* (Perpignan, 1990), 86.

16. On the Universitarian's Battalion, see Zangrandi, *Il lungo viaggio*, 66. On Vittorini and Visconti, see the former's letter of September 19, 1935, in *Lettere, 1933–43*, ed. Carlo Minoia (Turin, 1985), 57; and Lino Micciché, *Visconti e il neorealismo* (Venice, 1990), 16.

17. Elio Vittorini, "Ragioni dell'Azienda Collettiva in Africa Orientale," *Il Bargello* (July 19, 1936); Vasco Pratolini, "Il soldato torna contadino," *Il Bargello* (July 12 and September 6, 1936); Berto Ricci, "Avvisi," *L'Universale* (August 25, 1935); and Ruggiero Zangrandi, "Rivoluzione continua," manifesto of December 1935, in his *Il lungo viaggio*, 474–75.

18. Benito Mussolini, cited in Preti, *Impero fascista, africani ed ebrei*, 68; G. A. Fanelli, "Fine del volontarismo romantico," *Critica fascista* (February 1, 1936); Gianni Granzotto, "La vita d'Africa e il costume degli italiani," *Critica fascista* (June 1, 1938). For press directives, see the order of July 11, 1935, in ACS, MCP, b.185, f.34, and that of May 26, 1936, cited in Cesari, *La censura nel periodo fascista*, 51.

19. Benito Mussolini, "Decidersi!" and "La razza bianca muore?" *Il Popolo d'Italia* (September 4, 1934); and Carlo Curcio, "La decadenza demografica della razza bianca," in *Populazione e fascismo*, ed. Luigi Lojacno (Rome, 1934), 32–35.

20. The aims of this "demographic colonization" are described in Prospector, "La colonizzazione nell'Impero"; and Turco, "Colonizzazione positiva," *Gioventù fascista* (July 31, 1936). On land policies, see Haile Larebo, *The Building of an Empire* (New York, 1994); Ipsen, *Dictating Demography*, examines the links between domestic and colonial demographic concerns.

21. Emilio Canevari, in "La guerra è finita," *Critica fascista* (May 15, 1936); and Orestano, "Adunanza inaugurale."

22. Raffaele Di Lauro, *Il governo delle genti di colore* (Milan, 1940), 89.

23. Mario Moreno, "Politica di razza e politica coloniale italiana," *Gli Annali dell'Africa italiana* (June 1939); Di Lauro, *Il governo delle genti di colore*,

32–38. On the regulation of racial relations, see Sbacchi, *La colonizzazione italiana,* 217–41. The importance of race in colonial city planning is addressed by Fuller, "Colonial Constructions."

24. Guido Guidi, "Razze e popoli dell'A.O.," *Etiopia* (April 1940); Angelo Piccioli, "La razza e l'impero," *Etiopia* (April 1939); A. Mordini, "Stato attuale delle ricerche ethnografiche (cultura materiale)," *Etiopia* (March 1938); and Raffaele Corso, "Conoscenze etnografiche dell'impero," *Africa italiana* (May 1939). On ethnography and fascist colonialism, see the essays in Nicola Labanca, ed., *L'Africa in Vetrina* (Treviso, 1992); and Fulvio Suvich, "Le spedizioni scientifiche italiane in Africa Orientale e in Libia durante il periodo fascista," in *Le guerre coloniali del fascismo,* ed. Angelo Del Boca (Bari, 1991), 443–68.

25. Bottai, "Soldato fascista."

26. Adolfo Dolmetta, "La funzione della donna nella politica razziale," *Critica fascista* (May 15, 1939); Istituto Coloniale Fascista, *Corso di preparazione coloniale per la donna* (Naples, 1937), 18 and 22. Four hundred thousand women were enrolled in colonial preparation courses by the end of 1937. On *Sotto la croce del sud,* see Ruth Ben-Ghiat, "Envisioning Modernity," *Critical Inquiry* (autumn 1996): 135–44. For warnings against miscegenation, see Carlo Bellafiore, "I problemi razziali dell'Impero," *Etiopia* (April 1939); Mario Baccigalupi, "I delitti contro il prestigio di razza," *Difesa della razza* (December 20, 1939); and Angiolo Mori, in Accademia Reale d'Italia, *Convegno di scienze morali e storiche: L'Africa* (Rome, 1939), 1:902–8.

27. Marinetti's 1909 colonial novel *Mafarka le futuriste* is an example of the literary manifestations and antecedents of this specific imperial fantasy. See Spackman, *Fascist Virilities,* 49–76; and Pinkus, *Bodily Regimes,* 33–41, who also addresses the fetishization of the black body and its use in consumer culture.

28. Luigi Barzini, "Ethiopia: Enter Madam," *Esquire* (June 1936). Colonial officials also cohabited with indigenous women or kept pied-à-terres in indigenous quarters. On racial legislation in Italian Africa, see Sbacchi, *La colonizzazione italiana,* 224–41; Preti, *Impero fascista, africani ed ebrei,* 87–121; Richard Pankhurst, "Lo sviluppo del razzismo nell'impero coloniale italiano, 1935–41," *Studi piacentini* 3 (1988): 175–95.

29. On class considerations as articulated in colonial ideologies, see Ann Laura Stoler, "Rethinking Colonial Categories: European Communities and the Boundaries of Rule," in *Colonialism and Culture,* ed. Nicholas B. Dirks (Ann Arbor, 1992), 319–52. On the colonies as destinations for independent-minded Italian women, see Cristina Lombardi-Diop, "Writing the Female Frontier" (Ph.D. diss., New York University, 1999).

30. Farinacci to Benito Mussolini, April 1938, in De Felice, *Storia degli ebrei sotto il fascismo,* 238, n. 1; Ciano, *Diario,* entry of January 8, 1938, 86; Benito Mussolini, "Al Consiglio Nazionale del PNF." For similar concerns about southern colonists in the context of the Italian Dodecanese, see Nicholas Doumanis, *Myth and Memory in the Mediterranean* (London, 1997), 185–90.

31. Di Lauro, *Il governo delle genti di colore*, 86.

32. Alessandro Lessona, *Scritti e discorsi coloniali* (Milan: Instituto coloniale fascista, 1935), 149. On the reflexive quality of Italian colonialism, see Fuller, "Colonial Constructions."

33. In 1936, the Ministry of Press and Propaganda had 183 employees, but Alfieri wished to increase it to almost 800. On the MCP's expansion, see Philip Cannistraro, "Burocrazia e politica culturale nello Stato fascista: Il Ministero della Cultura Popolare," *Storia contemporanea* (June 1970): 273–98. Cesari, *La censura del periodo fascista*, 52–58, covers changes in Casini's press directorate.

34. Documentation in Cesari, *La censura del periodo fascista*, 56.

35. In 1939, the Society for Italian Authors and Editors set up a Reading Committee to review treatments *before* they were submitted to the government. The committee looked at twenty-page story summaries "of living authors of Italian nationality" and decided which stories should be sent to the Ministry of Popular Culture for an additional "artistic and technical examination" that determined whether a script could be written. On post-1936 film censorship, see Gili, *Stato fascista e cinematografia*, 33–80.

36. Alvaro, *Quasi una vita*, 260, entry of 1941.

37. Vero Roberti, "Le corrazzate con le rotelle," *Lo Schermo* (April 1938); Maurizio Rava, "I popoli africani dinanzi al schermo," *Cinema* (July 10, 1936); Vittorio Mussolini, "Cinema per gli indigeni," *Cinema* (January 10, 1939); Lombrassa, "Il senno dei Tigrini"; and "Il cinema per l'Impero," *Lo Schermo* (June 1936).

38. Giuseppe Longo, "La cultura sul piano imperiale," *Critica fascista* (May 15, 1937).

39. See Corrado D'Errico, "Luce A.O.," *Critica fascista* (April 1936). On *Il cammino degli eroi*, see Gili, *Stato fascista e cinematografia*, 86–87; Mancini, *Free Years of the Italian Film Industry*, 140–42; and Ben-Ghiat, "Envisioning Modernity," 130–35. On the transformation of the *Neue Sachlichkeit* under Nazism, see Anson G. Rabinbach, "The Aesthetics of Production in the Third Reich," *Journal of Contemporary History* (October 1976): 43–74.

40. In the 1920s, D'Errico was associated with A. G. Bragaglia's experimental Teatro degli Indipendenti in Rome, and wrote for periodicals such as *2000* and *Interplanetario*.

41. Soldati, interview in Gili, *Le cinéma italien*, 68 (see also Camerini's assessment in ibid., 77), and interview in *"Il Grande appello," Lo Schermo* (November 1936); and Soldati, "Con spirito nuovo 'si gira' nei luoghi dell'Impero," *Cinema* (August 25, 1936). Freddi uses identical language to describe the project in "Guerre e guerrieri sullo schermo," *Lo Schermo* (June 1936). On this film, see Gian Piero Brunetta and Jean Gili, *L'ora d'Africa del cinema italiano, 1911–89* (Rovereto, 1990), 50–58; and Hay, *Popular Film Culture in Fascist Italy*, 185–88.

42. Azzali, "La cultura e la vita."

43. Luigi Chiarini, *Fascismo e letteratura* (Rome, 1936), 21, 22, 13; and

Partito Nazionale Fascista, *La cultura fascista* (Rome, 1936), 27. I have named Bocelli as author since this book reprints his earlier articles in the daily and periodical press. See also Eugenio Donadoni, *Breve storia della letteratura italiana* (Milan, 1939), 354–57.

44. Giuseppe Pagano, *Architettura rurale italiana* (Milan, 1936); and Jacopo Comin, "Appunti sul cinema d'avanguardia," *Bianco e nero* (January 31, 1938). Comin made an exception for the documentarism of Ruttmann and Vertov, which he claimed found an echo in the films of Blasetti, Barbaro, and Matarazzo.

45. Carlo Formichi, Carlo Carrà, and Gino Severini, in Accademia Reale d'Italia, *Convegno di arti*, 17, 37, 52. The 1936 Triennale featured exhibitions on Italian decorative arts and art schools in Italy. See Giuseppe Pagano, *Arte decorativa italiano* (Milan, 1938), which celebrated traditional "Italian" arts such as mosaic, ceramics, embroidery, tile work, glass, gold- and silversmithing, and marble work.

46. Different aspects of these trends within 1930s modernism in France and Germany are explored by Alan Colquhoun, *Modernity and the Classical Tradition* (Cambridge, Mass., 1989), esp. 175–78; Golan, *Modernity and Nostalgia*; Helmut Frank, "Avanguardia e moderno nella Germania nazista," in *L'Europa dei razionalisti*, ed. Luciano Caramel (Milan, 1989), 302–13; and George Mosse, "L'autorappresentazione nazionale negli anni Trenta negli Stati Uniti e in Europa," in *L'estetica della politica*, ed. Maurizio Vaudagna (Rome, 1989), 3–24.

47. Albert Laprade, cited in Golan, *Modernity and Nostalgia*, 120.

48. Formichi, in Accademia Reale d'Italia, *Convegno di arti*, 12; OND official Emma Bono, in *Atti del IV Congresso Nazionale di arti e tradizioni popolari* (Rome, 1940), 2:613.

49. *Atti del IV Congresso Nazionale di arti e tradizioni popolari*, 87 and 609; also Giuseppe Bottai, *La politica degli arti*, ed. Alessandro Masi (Rome, 1992).

50. Luigi Freddi, "Dei dialetti," *Il Popolo d'Italia* (August 14, 1929). See statistics on Italian and dialect speakers in Gabriella Klein, *La politica linguistica del fascismo* (Bologna, 1986), 34–35. On government antidialect policies, see Klein, *La politica linguistica del fascismo*; and Lorenzo Coveri, "Mussolini e il dialetto: Notizie sulla campagna antidialettale del fascismo," *Parlare fascista*, special issue of *Movimento operaio e socialista* (January-April 1984): 117–32. The contradictions of this policy are explored by Ruth Ben-Ghiat, "Language and the Construction of National Identity in Fascist Italy," *European Legacy* (fall 1997): 438–43.

51. On measures against ethnic minorities, see Salvi, *Le lingue tagliate*; and ACS, PCM (1931–33), 16.1.6002.

52. The work of the Commissione per l'Italianità della Lingua can be traced in AAI, b.Commissione per l'Italianità della Lingua. Lists of substitutes, together with banned words *(forestierismi)* were to be submitted to the MCP and then to the press. See, for example, "Altri forestierismi," *La Nazione* (July 20,

1941). On linguistic autarchy, see Giacomo Devoto, "Appunti sull'autarchia della lingua," *Lingua nostra* (January 1943); and Carlo Formichi, "Per la difesa dell'italianità della lingua," *Radiocorriere* (March 13–14, 1938). On purist campaigns under fascism, see Sergio Raffaelli, *Le parole proibite* (Bologna, 1983); and Klein, *La politica linguistica del fascismo*, 113–41.

53. "Elementi per una nuova geografia italiana," *Critica fascista* (September 1, 1937); and Luigi Chiarini, "Incontro di civiltà cinematografica a Venezia," *Lo Schermo* (August 1937); see also Luciano De Feo, "Elementi del film nazionale," *Lo Schermo* (January 1937).

54. Umberto De Francisci, "Scenografia vera," *Cinema* (February 25, 1940); see also De Feo, "Elementi del film nazionale"; Ciano, May 1936 speech reprinted in Carabba, *Il cinema del ventennio nero*, 123–25; and Luigi Freddi, "Rapporto sul cinema italiano," *Lo Schermo* (January 1936), which announced the creation of a state-supported production company (Etrusca Film) that would specialize in films shot entirely outside the studio.

55. Ernesto Cauda, "Cinema autarchico," *Bianco e nero* (January 1939); Francesco Pasinetti, "Il monopolio dei film stranieri e la produzione italiana," *Bianco e nero* (January 1939); and G. V. Sampieri, "Autarchia del cinema," *Lo Schermo* (November 1937). Ministries and production companies sponsored numerous story competitions; Pannunzio and Ugo Betti won top honors in one held by Era Films in 1939. For writers' views of the situation, see Mario Puccini, "Gli scrittori nel cinema," *Bianco e nero* (January 1938); G. B. Angioletti, "La parte dello scrittore," *Bianco e nero* (September 1939); and Corrado Alvaro, "Il diario d'una donna amata," *Lo Schermo* (March 1936).

56. Vittorio Mussolini, "Un momento critico," *Cinema* (November 25, 1938); and Luigi Chiarini, "Prefazione," *Bianco e nero* (February 1939).

57. In 1938, Italy made forty-four films, which took in L54,281,426 in profits, as opposed to L293,019,032 for the Americans, L20,110,437 for the French, L18,852,561 for the Germans, and L11,109,637 for the British. In 1939, Italy made seventy-seven films, which took in L104,524,974 in profits, as opposed to L125,371,483 for the Americans, L66,176,145 for the French, L32,554,174 for the British, and L27,658,261 for German films. Figures on film production and profits are in Brunetta, *Storia del cinema italiano;* and Argentieri, *L'asse cinematografico*, 7.

58. Jacopo Comin, "Lanciare il cinema italiano," *Cinema* (June 10, 1937); and G. V. Sampieri, "Divismo," *Lo Schermo* (July 1939). In 1939, 58 American films from minor houses were shown in Italy; this dropped to 34 in 1941, and 8 in 1942.

59. Guido Aristarco, review in *La Voce di Mantova* (August 26, 1939); and Alberto Barbieri, review in *La Tribuna* (August 26, 1939).

60. See the essays in Gianfranco Casadei and Ernesto Laura, eds., *Telefoni bianchi: Realta e finzione nella societa e nel cinema italiano degli anni quaranta* (Ravenna: Longo, 1991), on the use of central European texts in fascist films.

61. Giuseppe Gabetti, "Italia e Germania: Gli accordi culturali," *Primato*

(May 15, 1940). On the Italian-German alliance, see Frederick Deakin, *The Brutal Friendship* (London, 1962); on its cultural relations, see Ruth Ben-Ghiat, "Fascist Italy and Nazi Germany: The Dynamics of an Uneasy Relationship," in *Culture and the Nazis*, ed. Richard Etlin (Chicago, forthcoming); and Jens Petersen, "Vorspiel zu 'Stahlpakt' und Kriegsallianz: Das deutsche italienische Kulturabkommen vom 23. November 1938," *Vierteljahreshefte für Zeitgeschichte* 36 (1989): 41–77.

62. Journalistic exchanges were common; Bontempelli was invited to Germany in April 1937 for a ten-day junket. See letter from Casini to Bontempelli, April 5, 1937, in GRI, BP, Correspondence Files, box 4, folder C. Details about Axis-inspired film collaborations can be found in Argentieri's valuable book, *L'asse cinematografico Roma-Berlino*.

63. Gherardo Casini, "Premessa," in *Italia e Germania, maggio XVI* (Rome, 1938), 9. Corrado Alvaro gives notice of a 1939 lunch that Italian writers gave to honor the German poet Hans-Friedrich Blunck, in Alvaro, *Quasi una vita*, 218. The folklore review *Lares* had an exchange agreement with the *Zeitschrift für Volkskunde* that resulted in special issues on recent Italian-German research; other scholarly journals and organizations had similar arrangements.

64. Jacopo Comin, "Documentario di sette giornate," *Cinema* (May 25, 1938). On the events surrounding Hitler's 1938 visit, see Etlin, *Modernism in Italian Architecture*, 571–75. Notice of Hitler's gifts, which included a vase from the fourth century B.C., is given in Jonathan Petropoulos, *Art as Politics in the Third Reich* (Chapel Hill, 1996), 271.

65. Critics lauded Barbaro's focus on colonial medicine: see the note on the film in *Lo Schermo* (June 1936); and Chiarini, "Incontro di civiltà cinematografica a Venezia."

66. Vinicio Paladini, "La scenografia ne *L'Ultima nemica*," *Cinema* (August 25, 1937).

67. Umberto Barbaro, "Potenza del cinema," *Lo Schermo* (December 1937); see also his lectures collected in *Soggetto e sceneggiatura* (Rome, 1947).

68. Corrado Alvaro, *L'uomo è forte* (Milan, 1938; reprint, Milan, 1989), 7, 109, 54.

69. Ibid., 77.

70. Excerpts from reviews by Bontempelli, Ugo Dettore, and other critics are given in a 1938 ad for the novel, which is reproduced in the 1989 edition of *L'uomo è forte* between vi and vii and in figure 12.

71. Alvaro, *Quasi una vita*, 1936 entry, 161, 171–72.

72. Corrado Alvaro, "Avvertenza," *L'uomo è forte*, n.p. The critic Benjamin Crémieux highlighted the ambiguity of the novel in his review, noting that Alvaro's depiction of the individual under a dictatorship was written with "an implacable acuity and, it seems, not without some intimate knowledge of the subject." Crémieux, "Lettres Etrangères," *La Nouvelle revue française* (November 1, 1938). The publication of the novel did make Alvaro a spokesman of anticommunist concerns; see his "Il pubblico sovietico," *Cinema* (December 10, 1939). He also worked on anticommunist films such as the two-part

Alessandrini movie, *Noi vivi,* and *Addio Kira!* (1942), adapted from Ayn Rand's novel *We the Living;* and his volume of Russian reportage was reissued as *Viaggio in Russia* in 1943.

73. The continued importance of local and regional identities within the Italian state also contributed to a climate of tolerance by hindering the individuation of a shared internal enemy, as did the virtual absence of Jews in southern Italy and Sicily following the mass expulsions of 1492. Useful overviews of the position of Jews in liberal Italy can be found in Andrew Canepa, "Christian-Jewish Relations in Italy from Unification to Fascism," in *The Italian Refuge,* ed. Ivo Herzer (Washington, D.C., 1989), 13–33; see also Mario Toscano, "Gli ebrei in Italia dall'emancipazione alle persecuzioni," *Storia contemporanea* (October 1986): 905–54.

74. "Gazzettino," *Il Selvaggio* (November 30, 1934, and January 31, 1935); the special issue of *L'Italiano* on National Socialism (November 1934); Partito Nazionale Fascista, *Il cittadino soldato* (Rome, 1935), 24; and Mario Rivoire, "La razza contro la storia," *Il Popolo di Lombardia* (September 1, 1934). For Mussolini's own declarations, see Emil Ludwig, *Colloqui con Mussolini* (Milan, 1932), 73.

75. Mussolini's changing attitudes on Jewish issues are analyzed thoroughly by De Felice, *Storia degli ebrei sotto il fascismo* (Turin, 1993); Meir Michaelis, *Mussolini and the Jews* (Oxford, 1978), and Michaelis, "Fascist Policy toward the Italian Jews: Tolerance and Persecution," in *The Italian Refuge,* ed. Ivo Herzer (Washington, D.C., 1989), 34–72; and Michele Sarfatti, *Mussolini contro gli ebrei,* which concentrates on the period surrounding the 1938 laws.

76. "Il troppo storpia," *Il Popolo d'Italia* (December 31, 1936), in *Opera Omnia,* 28:98. The anonymous article, which has been universally attributed to him, formed part of a diatribe against Léon Blum and the Popular Front.

77. Meir Michaelis, *Mussolini and the Jews,* touches on differences between Italian fascist and Nazi German racial ideas, as does Aaron Gillette's "La Difesa della Razza: Racial Theories in Fascist Italy" (manuscript). I thank Aaron Gillette for allowing me to consult portions of his work. In 1941, before the start of German deportations and after almost six thousand Italian Jews (about 12 percent of the Jewish community) had converted to Catholicism and baptized offspring of mixed marriages, Mussolini commented happily that the high rate of intermarriage meant that the "Jewish characteristics" of Italian Jews would be absorbed by the Aryan bloodline within a generation. Mussolini, interview with Yves De Begnac, October 1941, in Yves De Begnac, *Palazzo Venezia* (Rome, 1950), 643. On abjurations and conversions among Jews in 1938–39, see De Felice, *Storia degli ebrei sotto il fascismo,* 334.

78. Ipsen, *Dictating Demography,* 185–94.

79. "Il Manifesto degli scienzati razziale," *Il Giornale d'Italia* (July 14, 1938), reprinted in Alberto Cavaglion and Gian Paolo Romagnani, *Le interdizioni del Duce* (Turin, 1988), 24–26.

80. "Scoperta!" *Il Popolo d'Italia* (July 26, 1938); and "Anche nella ques-

tione di razza noi tireremo diritto!" *Il Popolo d'Italia* (July 31, 1938), both in *Opera Omnia*, 29:125–26; see also the anonymous note in *Informazione diplomatica* (the bulletin of the Ministry of Foreign Affairs) (August 5, 1938), which most scholars have attributed to Ciano and Mussolini.

81. "Come coprire i vuoti," *Vita universitaria* (October 5, 1938). On the impact of the decrees for students and educators, see Roberto Finzi, *L'università italiana e le leggi antiebraiche* (Rome, 1997); and on scientists, see Giorgio Israel and Piero Nastasi, *Scienza e razza nell'Italia fascista* (Bologna, 1998).

82. The November 1938 law is reproduced in Michele Sarfatti, *Mussolini contro gli ebrei*, 190–94. It defined as Jews all individuals with two Jewish parents (even if they did not profess Judaism themselves), or one foreign Jewish parent, or a Jewish mother (regardless of the father's religion), or Jewish parents who might profess another faith but were members of a Jewish congregation or engaged in "any kind of demonstration of Hebraism." In March 1939 the government established an *Ente di Gestione e Liquidazione Immobiliare* to accelerate the expropriation of Jewish assets.

83. The fascist racial bureaucracy still awaits a detailed analysis of personnel and policies, but see Michele Sarfatti, *Mussolini contro gli ebrei*, 129–76, on the organization of the 1938 Jewish census; and Ipsen, *Dictating Demography*, 184–94, which details the convergence of demographic and racial concerns at the administrative level.

84. Exempt categories of persons included families of victims, heroes, and volunteers of World War I and fascist wars; families of fascist martyrs; families of those who joined the PNF before the March on Rome or during the Matteotti crisis; and families of Jews who demonstrated "exceptional merit" in civic matters. By the fall of 1942, of 9,647 requests for "racial certification," 3,371 Italians had been declared Aryan and 3,839 Jewish, and almost 400 Jews had submitted separate Aryanization requests to the General Directorate of Demography and Race. De Felice, *Storia degli ebrei sotto il fascismo*, 346–49.

85. The circumstances of Sarfatti's emigration are related in Cannistraro and Sullivan, *The Duce's Other Woman*, 518–33. See Harvey Sachs, *Music in Fascist Italy*, on the fate of Renzo Massarani, Mario Castelnuovo-Tedesco, and other Jewish musicians.

86. Planning memorandum for the *Commission per la bonifica libraria* from Casini to Alfieri, April 8, 1938, cited in Cavaglion and Romagnani, *Le interdizioni del Duce*, 33; Starace, cited in De Felice, *Storia degli ebrei sotto il fascismo*, 336. Cannistraro, *La fabbrica del Duce*, 117–119, reprints the list of 900 "Autori non graditi in Italia," found in ACS, MCP, b.130, f. "Scrittori ebrei." This list was given to prefects, who then put pressure on booksellers and publishers to purge their stocks. On the name changes of Jewish publishers, see Casini's memo to Alfieri, October 17, 1939, in Cavaglion and Romagnani, *Le interdizioni del Duce*, 34–35.

87. Alvaro, *Quasi una vita*, 1938 entry, 211–12. Alvaro's abandonment of Sarfatti is recounted in Cannistraro and Sullivan, *The Duce's Other Woman*, 617, n. 42. The writers Emilio Cecchi, Ada Negri, and Giuseppe Ungaretti and

the architect Giovanni Muzio were among the others who accepted Italian Academy memberships in the years when the Academy was among the biggest producers of anti-Jewish propaganda.

88. In "Come coprire i vuoti," the Minister of National Education journal *Vita universitaria* tried to allay the stream of requests by informing Italians that chairs and permanent positions would be replaced with year-to-year contracts. For Bontempelli's expulsion and reinstatement, see Alfieri to Bontempelli, October 2, 1939, in GRI, BP, CF, box 4, folder A, and PNF vice-secretary Vincenzo Zangrara to Bontempelli, August 17, 1939, in ibid., folder U-Z. Bottai intervened to give the poets Giuseppe Ungaretti and Alfonso Gatto and the artist Ottone Rosai state teaching jobs after 1938 (at the University of Rome, the University of Bologna, and the Liceo Artistico of Florence, respectively), although there is no evidence that these men took over posts that had been occupied by Jews. On Rosai's appointment, see ACS, MI, DGPS, AGR, Cat.AI, 1942, b.99.

89. Zangrandi, *Il lungo viaggio*, 403–29, reproduces racist statements in the press from intellectuals in various fields. In the *Corriere della sera*, see the editorials "Razzismo fascista" (October 8, 1938), and "Difesa della razza" (November 11, 1938). Anti-Semitic radio programming began in 1938 and intensified with the 1940 Italian-German radio accord. The Ispettorato per la Radiodiffusione had anti-Semitic "conversations" on topics such as "Judaism against Western Culture." The INFC's lectures included "Racial Hygiene" and "Colonization and Racial Consciousness." On the emergence of a culture of race, see De Felice, *Storia degli ebrei sotto il fascismo*, 379–401; Etlin, *Modernism in Italian Architecture*; Israel and Nastasi, *Scienza e razza*; Sachs, *Music in Fascist Italy*; and Gabriele Turi, "Ruolo e destino degli intellettuali nella politica razziale del fascismo," in *La legislazione antiebraica in Europa* (Rome, 1989), 98–121.

90. *Difesa della razza* was directed by Interlandi, whose close links with Mussolini have been documented in Meir Michaelis, "Mussolini's Unofficial Spokesman." Its editors were Guido Landra, an assistant in anthropology at the University of Rome and head of the Racial Studies Office at the Ministry of Popular Culture; Lidio Cipriani, director of the National Museum of Anthropology and Ethnology in Florence, who was heavily involved in ethnographic missions in Ethiopia; Leone Franzi, an assistant in pediatric medicine at the University of Milan; Marcello Ricci, an assistant in zoology at the University of Rome; and Lino Businco, an assistant in general pathology at the University of Rome.

91. Pius XI's antiracist speech was summarized in the *L'Osservatorio romano* of July 30, 1938. Other protests included a September 1938 address on Catholic Belgian Radio and the 1937 Papal Encyclical *Mit brennender Sorge*, delivered in German to reach its target audience of National Socialist racists.

92. P. Francesco Capponi, "Gli Ebrei ed il Concilio," *L'Osservatore romano* (August 14, 1938). Catholic attitudes about Jewish conversion and assimilation are explored in Lynn M. Gunzberg, *Strangers at Home* (Berkeley and Los An-

geles, 1992); and De Felice, *Storia degli ebrei sotto il fascismo,* 36–40. The Vatican's attitudes with regard to pre–World War II fascist racial laws are explored in G. Miccoli, "Santa Sede e Chiesa italiana di fronte alle legge antiebraiche del 1938," in *La legislazione antiebraica in Italia e in Europa* (Rome, 1989), 163–274.

93. Ipsen, *Dictating Demography,* 185, also makes this point. The intertwining of the concepts of race and stock is especially evident in the review *Razza e civiltà,* published by the General Directorate of Demography and Race. On the differences between Italian and German racial theories, see Meir Michaelis, *Mussolini and the Jews;* see also Gentile, "La nazione del fascismo," 100–107. Michele A. Cortelazzo analyzes Mussolini's evolving use of the term *race* in "Il lessico del razzismo fascista," in *Parlare fascista,* special issue of *Movimento operaio e socialista* (April-June 1984): 57–66.

94. Giovanni Papini, "La tradizione italiana," 77.

95. Dei Sabelli, *Nazioni e minoranze etniche,* 1:52 and 275; see also Ojetti, "Il viaggio d'Italia"; and Napolitano, "Difesa di una generazione."

96. "Il manifesto degli scienzati razziale," in Cavaglion and Romagnani, *Le interdizioni del Duce,* 25–26; Edgardo Sulis, "L'ebreo contro la nuova Europa," *Razza e civiltà* (July-September 1940); and Giovanni Schiavi, "Idee chiare sul razzismo," *Corriere padano* (May 26, 1943). German questions about Italian racial purity are mentioned in Meir Michaelis, *Mussolini and the Jews,* 177.

97. Positivists such as Alfredo Niceforo and Lombroso had included criminals, prostitutes, and southerners in their classifications of "atavistic beings" who obstructed Italian modernization, and Lombroso added Jews to the list. See Alfredo Niceforo, *L'Italia barbara contemporanea* (Milan: Remo Sandron, 1898), and his *Italiani del nord e italiani del sud* (Turin: Fratelli Bocca, 1901); and Cesare Lombroso, *L'antisemitismo e le scienze moderne* (Turin, 1894). Lombroso (himself a Jew) argued that the Jews' refusal to give up circumcision and other ancient practices that differentiated them from Christians was a prime cause of anti-Semitism. See Nancy Harrowitz, *Antisemitism, Misogyny, and the Logic of Cultural Difference* (Lincoln, 1994), 41–62. The genealogy of the southerner as an internal Other is traced in Nelson Moe, "'Altro che Italia!' Il Sud dei piemontesi (1860–61)," *Meridiana,* 15 (1992): 53–89; and Mary Gibson, "Biology or Environment? Race and Southern 'Deviancy' in the Writings of Italian Criminologists, 1880–1920," in *The Southern Question: Orientalism in One Country,* ed. Jane Schneider (New York, 1998), 99–115; see also Pick, *Faces of Degeneration,* 109–52; and John Dickie, *Darkest Italy* (New York, 1999).

98. Giulio Cogni, "Preliminari sul cinema in difesa della razza," *Bianco e nero* (January 31, 1938). Cogni was a leading disseminator of the Nordicist school of racial theory that found minor acceptance in Italian circles. For assertions of Jewish criminality, see Tancredi Gatti, "Ferocia astuzia ponderazione degli ebrei," *Difesa della razza* (January 5, 1939); and Giuseppe Pensabene, "Psicologia dei semiti e dei camiti," *Difesa della razza* (February 5, 1939). Under fascism, Italians from the Trieste border area were also regarded with

suspicion, and became emblems of Slavic primitivity. On this see Glenda Sluga, "Italian National Memory, National Identity, and Fascism," in *Italian Fascism*, ed. Richard Bosworth and Patrizia Dogliani (New York, 1999), 178–80.

99. "Il manifesto degli scienzati razziale"; Benito Mussolini, "Discorso di Trieste," and "Le dichiarazioni del Gran Consiglio," in Cavaglion and Romagnani, *Le interdizioni del Duce*, 36–43.

100. "Razza italiana e cinema italiana," *Cinema* (September 10, 1938); and Gherardo Casini, "Bonifica della cultura italiana," *L'Orto* (January 1938); for race as a repository of national traditions, see the folklorist Raffaele Corso, "La civiltà italiana e le tradizioni popolari," *Razza e civiltà* (March 23, 1940); and the biological racist Guido Landra, "Razza italiana oltre confine," *Difesa della razza* (November 20, 1938).

101. Filippo Tommaso Marinetti, "L'Italianità dell'arte moderna," *Il Giornale d'Italia* (November 24, 1938); Berto Ricci, "Arte e razza," *Origini* (November 1938); Giuseppe Bottai, "L'Arte Moderna," *Critica fascista* (December 1, 1938); and "Bonifica libraria." Buchignani explains Ricci's anti-Semitism as a "necessary" maneuver to save the cause of modern art. See his *Il fascismo impossibile*, 302–8. On these debates, see Etlin, *Modernism in Italian Architecture*, 585–97.

102. Luigi Fontanelli, in *Lavoro fascista* (September 4, 1938), cited in De Felice, *Storia degli ebrei sotto il fascismo*, 395.

103. Bilenchi, "Piccola guardia," *Critica fascista* (April 1, 1937).

104. Alberto Luchini, "Arte borghese and anti-borghese," *Arte mediterranea* (September-October 1939). The anti-Semitic Edgardo Sulis (then one of Mussolini's speechwriters) edited the book *Processo alla borghesia* (Rome: Edizioni Roma, 1939), to which Ricci, Luchini, and other *L'Universale* alumni contributed.

105. "Le dichiarazioni del Gran Consiglio."

106. ACS, MI, DGPS, DPP, b.132, K11, report from Genoa, June 13, 1937; Gino Barbero, in *Il Popolo Biellese* (August 30, 1937), cited in Zangrandi, *Il lungo viaggio*; Fidia Gambetti, *Il controveleno* (Osimo, 1942), 281.

107. Reports from Milan, January 12, 1938; April 7, 1938, which contains informers' findings from ten Italian cities; reports of April 9, May 8, and May 31, 1938, all in ACS, MI, DGPS, DPP, b.132, f.K11. On changing youth attitudes, see Koon, *Believe, Obey, Fight*, 237–46; Vito Zagarrio, "Giovani e apparati culturali a Firenze nella crisi del regime fascista," *Studi storici* (July-September 1980): 609–35.

108. Giulia Veronesi, "Chi siamo," *Campo di Marte* (September 1, 1938).

109. Vasco Pratolini, "Tempo culturale per la politica," *Il Bargello* (April 1937). Compare with his "Vita e ricerca," *Campo di Marte* (October 15, 1938), and "Diario," *Campo di Marte* (May 15, 1939).

110. Moravia, *La mascherata* (Milan, 1941; reprint, Milan, 1997), 128, 9, 10.

111. Ibid., 31, 13.

112. Ibid., 13, 24, 34, 54, 125. Moravia identifies Saverio's books as "old socialist and anarchist propaganda" (29).

113. Ibid., 38–39. Compare with Moravia's statements on mass society cited in chapter 4.

114. Alvaro, *L'uomo è forte*, 13. Alvaro specifies that Dale is of the "middle generation" rather than of a cohort raised under the new regime (21); see also Moravia, *La mascherata*, 39.

115. Renzo Paris, *Moravia* (Florence, 1996), 135–36. For examples of attacks after 1938 on Moravia as a Jew, see "Manomissione ebraica della nazione italiana," *Difesa della razza* (July 5, 1939); and Francesco Biondolillo, "Giudaismo letterario," *L'Unione sarda* (April 14, 1939).

116. Moravia, *La mascherata*, 22, 39. Jewish internalization of anti-Jewish images and prejudice is explored in Sander Gilman, *Jewish Self-Hatred* (Baltimore, 1986).

117. The figure of Quadri in *Il conformista* presents many similarities to Saverio; see also Moravia's declarations about the Rossellis in Elkann, *Vita di Moravia*, 19. On Carlo Rosselli, see Stanislao Pugliese, *Carlo Rosselli* (Cambridge, Mass., 2000). Joel Blatt, "The Battle of Turin, 1933–36," *Journal of Modern Italian Studies* (fall 1995): 22–57, examines the anti-Semitic sentiments occasioned by the arrests of members of Rosselli's *Giustizia e Libertà* movement (many of whom were Jewish) in the early 1930s.

118. Crémieux, "Lettres Etrangères."

119. Paola Masino, *Nascita e morte della massaia* (Milan, 1945; reprint, Milan 1982), 13–14.

120. Ibid., 60, 63, 84.

121. Ibid., 65, 199. See Lucia Re, "Fascist Theories of 'Woman' and the Construction of Gender," in *Mothers of Invention*, ed. Robin Pickering-Iazzi (Minneapolis, 1995), 93.

122. Masino, *Nascita e morte*, 212, 226.

123. Information on Masino is from Re, "Fascist Theories of 'Woman,'" 95; information on Moravia is from Elkann, *Vita di Moravia*, 122–23. Francesco Flora, *Stampa dell'era fascista* (Milan, 1945), 83, reprints the MCP order to the press of February 13, 1941, to "ignore Moravia and his publications."

124. See ACS, SPCO, 514829/2 for *L'Universale*; and Bilenchi, *Amici*, 83.

125. See Elena Banfi, "Attività del Cineguf-Milano," *Communicazione sociali* (July-December 1988): 304–29; interview with Renato Castellani, in Francesco Savio, *Cinecittà anni trenta* (Rome: Bulzoni, 1979), 1:252; Brunetta, *Storia del cinema italiano*, 76–97.

126. Names of Littoriali winners are from Alfassio Grimaldi and Addis Saba, *Cultura a passo romano*, 199–229. Moro came in seventh in 1937 with an essay on fascist doctrine, Alicata took eighth place in literature in 1938, Sottsass took third in set design, Taviani placed sixth in corporativism in 1935 and ninth in the same subject in 1940. Lattuada took third place in screenwriting in 1938, Paci placed ninth in fascist doctrine in 1938, and Guttuso came in second in figurative art in 1937.

127. After the final competitions in April 1941, the Bolognese student Lu-

ciana Pastino complained of the "curious vetoes" of families and male teachers
that had kept away many women. Pastino, "I Littoriali Femminili della Cultura," *Il Bò* (April 15, 1941); for opposition to women's participation, see Remo
Valianti, "La donna oggi," *Architrave* (March 1, 1941). Ortese won first place
for poetry, second for narrative in 1939, and first in narrative in 1940; Guidacci
won first prize for poetry in 1940, and Milani took first place in poetry in 1941.
See Addis Saba and Alfassio Grimaldi, *Cultura a passo romano,* 230–39, for
listings.

128. Antonio Ghirelli, "Il GUF di Largo Ferrandina," in *La Campania dal
fascismo alla repubblica,* ed. Giovanna Percopo and Sergio Riccio (Naples,
1977), 2:142.

129. Giuseppe Melis Bassu, quoted in Koon, *Believe, Obey, Fight,* 207. Lattuada, quoted in Gili, *Le cinéma italien,* 109. There is a rich literature on the
use of official forums by antifascist students. For memoiristic accounts, see
Bonsanti, "La cultura degli anni trenta dai Littoriali all'antifascismo"; Giorgio
Caputo, "L'opposizione antifascista degli studenti romani alla vigilia della seconda guerra mondiale," *Mondo operaio* (March and April-May 1970): 34–42
and 62–73; and Alatri, "Cultura e politica." See also Koon's overview in *Believe, Obey, Fight,* 223–52.

130. [Curiel,] "Futura di un problema," *Il Bò* (April 23, 1938), and "Tendenze e aspirazioni della gioventù intellettuale," *Lo Stato operaio* (December 1,
1938); see also "Littoriali a porte chiuse" (April 23, 1938) and "Che cosa
significa il 'largo ai giovani'" (August 1, 1937), both in *Il Bò*. On Curiel and the
issue of double discourse, see Ivano Paccagnella, "Stampa di fronda: 'Il Bò' tra
GUF e Curiel," in *La lingua italiana e il fascismo* (Bologna, 1977), 83–110. The
PCI's "entrist" strategy of these years is discussed in Paolo Spriano, *Storia del
Partito Communista* (Turin, 1990), 3:196–201.

131. Editorial note, *Vita giovanile* (original name of *Corrente* from Janu-
ary 15 through October 1938) (February 1, 1938). The journal's antifascist
politics have often been overstated, as in Mario De Micheli, *Consenso, Fronde,
Opposizione* (Milan, 1977), 80–95. Bette Talvacchia's analysis focuses on the
antifascist artistic line: see her "Politics Considered as a Category of Culture:
The Anti-Fascist *Corrente* Group," *Art History* (September 1985): 336–55.
The journal's transformation from fascism to antifascism is discussed in Ruth
Ben-Ghiat, "The Politics of Realism: *Corrente di Vita Giovanile* and the Youth
Culture of the 1930s," *Stanford Italian Review* 8, nos. 1–2 (1990): 139–64. A
good overall presentation is given by Alfredo Luzi in his introduction to the
anthology *Corrente di Vita giovanile* (Rome, 1975).

132. Pietro Nuvolone, "La Germania, nuova forza storica," *Corrente* (June
30, 1938); Claudio Belingardi, "Il nostro razzismo," *Corrente* (December 31,
1938); Enzo Paci, "Orientamenti del pensiero contemporaneo," *Corrente* (May
31, 1938); Antonio Bruni, "Il riconoscimento di Franco," *Corrente* (January 15,
1938); and Roggia Battista, "Il communismo nel Medio Oriente," *Corrente*
(May 15, 1938). On the influence of Alfieri, see the interviews with Alberto

Lattuada and Ernesto Treccani in Giovanella Desideri, *Antologia della rivista "Corrente"* (Naples, 1979), 35; information also drawn from my interview with Treccani, Milan, June 21, 1990.

133. Raffaelle De Grada, "La mostra prelittoriale dell'arte a Milano," *Corrente* (March 31, 1938); "Continuità," *Corrente* (December 15, 1939); see also Lodovico Barbiano di Belgioioso, "Il canto del gallo," *Corrente* (January 1, 1939). On the causes and enterprises of *Corrente*, see *Corrente: Il movimento di arte e cultura di opposizione, 1930–45* (Milan, 1985).

134. Renato Birolli, "Aspetti non privati dell'artista," *Corrente* (May 31, 1940); and Raffaelle De Grada, "Invito alla discussione," *Corrente* (January 31, 1940), "Filippo De Pisis," *Corrente* (January 31, 1939), and "Tranquillo Cremona e gli artisti lombardi del suo tempo," *Corrente* (May 15, 1938). De Grada and Birolli were detained by the fascist police during their affiliation with the journal. Birolli had been harassed by the police since 1937. He was arrested in 1942 and confined to the island of Ventotene; De Grada was incarcerated in 1943. On Birolli, see ACS, CPC, MI, DGPS, Div. AAGGRR, b.661; also Domenico Zucarò, *Cospirazione operaia: Resistenza al fascismo in Torino-Genova-Milano, 1927–43* (Turin, 1965), 150–51. For De Grada's postwar Realist positions, see his journal *Realismo*, especially the initial editorial "Presentazione" (June 1952).

135. Enzo Paci, "Esistenzialismo gnoseologico," *Corrente* (January 31, 1940), also "Orientamento del pensiero contemporaneo," *Corrente* (May 31, 1938). On Paci's philosophical trajectory from fascism to the republic, see Amedeo Vigorelli, *L'esistenzialismo positivo di Enzo Paci* (Rome, 1992).

136. Giorgio Vecchietti, in *La Stampa* (December 28, 1938), quoted in Zangrandi, *Il lungo viaggio,* 418; Amintore Fanfani, "Impulso politico all'economia," *Rivista internazionale di scienze sociali* (May 1939); and Giampaolo Callegari, *Il cuore a destra* (Milan, 1939). Callegari won the Biella literary prize for *La terra e il sangue.* See Gunzberg, *Strangers at Home,* 263–68.

137. Castellani, in *Nuovi materali,* 2:110; and Ugo Alfassio Grimaldi, *Autobiografie di una generazione* (Brescia, 1946), 40.

CHAPTER 6

1. Benito Mussolini, cited in Knox, *Mussolini Unleashed,* 89–90; Benito Mussolini, speech of June 10, 1940, in *Opera Omnia,* 29:404–5. On these points, see P. J. Morgan, "The Italian Fascist New Order in Europe," in *Making the New Europe,* ed. M. L. Smith and Peter Stirk (London, 1990), 29–30.

2. Ciano, *Diario,* entry of October 13, 1941, 544–45; and Edgardo Sulis, ed., *Nuova civiltà per la Nuova Europa* (Rome, 1942). Enzo Collotti charts the vicissitudes of the Italian-German alliance in "L'alleanza italo-tedesca, 1941–43," in *Gli italiani sul fronte russo* (Bari, 1982), 3–62.

3. Angelo Michele Imbriani, *Gli italiani e il Duce* (Naples, 1982), 82–97.

4. "Gerarchia di popoli," *Critica fascista* (August 1, 1940); Manlio Lupi-

nacci, "Nozione di Europa," *Primato* (March 15, 1940); and Fantasio Piccoli, "La Nazione e l'ordine nuovo," *Gerarchia* (July 1942). The New Order is discussed by Gentile, "La Nazione del fascismo," 108–14; and Morgan, "The Italian Fascist New Order."

5. "Vincere," *Critica fascista* (June 15, 1940); "Potenza e cultura," *Critica fascista* (August 15, 1940); Ferdinando Loffredo, "Nuovi caratteri del soldato italiano," *Critica fascista* (September 15, 1940); Arrigo Ghiara, "Letteratura di Domani," *Critica fascista* (August 1, 1940); Gambetti, *Il controveleno*, 104.

6. Benito Mussolini, cited in Ciano, *Diario*, entry of April 11, 1940, 418.

7. Giorgio Pasquali, "Neologismi di guerra," *Primato* (September 1, 1940); Salv. [sic], "'Tempo nostro' e ambientazione dei film," *Lo Schermo* (April 1942); Loffredo, "Nuovi caratteri del soldato italiano"; "Dell'attitudine degli Italiani a organizzare," *Critica fascista* (March 1, 1942); and Gambetti, *Il controveleno*, 103–9.

8. Gambetti, *Il controveleno*, 21; Cesare Zavoli, "Spirito della modernità fascista," *Critica fascista* (January 1, 1941); "Noi, popolo italiano" *Critica fascista* (January 15, 1941); Giuseppe Maggiore, "Odiare il nemico," *Critica fascista* (March 1, 1942); and Benito Mussolini, speech of December 2, 1942, in *Opera Omnia*, 21:118–33.

9. Emmanuel Artom, entries of October 16, 17, and 18, 1941, in Artom, *Diari:* (Milan, 1966), 27–36; and Domenico Vanelli, "Rivoluzione totalitaria," *Critica fascista* (March 1, 1941).

10. Karl Löwith, *My Life in Germany before and after 1933* (Chicago, 1994), 86–88. On the fates of foreign Jews in fascist Italy, see Klaus Voigt, "Jewish Refugees and Immigrants in Italy, 1933–45," in *The Italian Refuge*, ed. Ivo Herzer (Washington, D.C., 1990), 141–58. Italian fascist policy toward the Jews during World War II is detailed in Jonathan Steinberg, *All or Nothing* (London, 1990); and Susan Zuccotti, *The Italians and the Holocaust* (New York, 1987).

11. On changes in press directives after 1940, see Cesari, *La censura*, 81–84; and Cannistraro, *La fabbrica del consenso*, 162–221.

12. February 15, 1943, note from Fernando Mezzasoma to Polverelli, in ACS, MCP, b.29, f.426.

13. "Oltre il muro di casa," *Primato* (January 15, 1941); Ghiara, "Letteratura di domani"; "Cultura e spazio vitale," *Primato* (May 15, 1941); and Gambetti, *Il controveleno*, 108.

14. Mezzasoma to Pavolini, note of February 15, 1943. See Carlo Bordoni, *Cultura e propaganda nell'Italia fascista* (Messina, 1974), 82–83, on the imbalances between imports and exports in wartime Italy.

15. Vittorio Mussolini, "Nuova situazione," *Cinema* (December 25, 1941); and Sisto Favre, "Cinematografia e nuova Europa," *Lo Schermo* (July 1941).

16. Giame Pintor, "Americana," in *Il sangue d'Europa, 1939–43* (Turin, 1950), 148–57. On this point, see Lorenzo Quaglietti, "Cinema americano, vecchio amore," in *Schermi di guerra*, ed. Mino Argentieri (Rome, 1995), 307–

28; and Mino Argentieri, *Il cinema in guerra* (Rome, 1998), which is essential reading for all aspects of Italian cinema between 1940 and 1944.

17. Sisto Favre, "Film di guerra," *Lo Schermo* (June 1943); "Come il popolo italiano ha visto la sua guerra attraverso il cinema," *Lo Schermo* (June 1941); and Fernando Cerchio, "Servizio di guerra," *Cinema* (July 10, 1940). The military had first right of approval on material that would be included in news-reels, documentaries, and some commercial films. On the role of LUCE news-reels in shaping public opinion during World War II, see Simona Rinaldi, "I cinegiornali LUCE e la 'non belligeranza'"; and Giampaolo Bernagozzi, "La 'campagna' di Russia: Finzioni e realtà," both in Argentieri, *Schermi di guerra*, 19–134.

18. "Il cinema strumento di lotta e di vittoria," *Lo Schermo* (May 1941); and Guglielmo Ceroni, "Nove film di guerra," *Lo Schermo* (June 1943), which revises this initial plan. The anti-Jewish film was never made. See Gianni Ron-dolino, "Italian Propaganda Films, 1940–43," in *Film and Radio Propaganda in World War Two*, ed. K. R. M. Short (Knoxville, 1983), 220–29.

19. See Maria Adriana Prolo, *Storia del cinema muto italiano* (Milan, 1951), 82–88, on the use of cinema during World War I.

20. Giuseppe Isani, review of *La nave bianca* in *Cinema* (October 10, 1941). I am here referring to Rossellini's *La nave bianca* (1941), which blends documentary footage of the activities of an Italian hospital ship with a love story between a navy man and a nurse. The term *documentario romanzato* is used in reference to Rossellini's and De Robertis's films by Domenico Meccoli, "I nuovi registi," *Cinema* (December 25, 1941). On these experimentations, see Mino Argentieri, *Il cinema in guerra*, 120–32; Ben-Ghiat, "Roberto Rossellini's Fascist War Trilogy."

21. Glauco Viazzi and Ugo Casiraghi, "Presentazione postuma di un classico," *Bianco e nero* (April 1942); and Giuseppe Isani, "Film di questi giorni," *Cinema* (February 25, 1941).

22. Glauco Pellegrini, "Il documentario: Ieri, oggi, domani," *Bianco e nero* (September 1942). On the radio as agent of state authority in wartime Nazi Germany, see Kate Lacey, *Feminine Frequencies* (Ann Arbor, 1996), esp. 127–46.

23. Alfieri, report of March 31, 1942, in ACS, MCP, b.19, f.269; Joseph Goebbels, *Die Tagebücher von Josef Goebbels*, ed. Elke Fröhlich, 14 vols. (Munich, 1993–98), entry for June 28, 1941, 9:409–410; and Sisto Favre, "Cinematografia 'nazionale' ed 'europea,'" *Lo Schermo* (March 1942). Wartime competition and collaboration between Italy and Germany is examined in Ben-Ghiat, "Fascist Italy and Nazi Germany."

24. On the International Film Chamber and Nazi film policies in occupied Europe, see Argentieri, *L'asse cinematografica*. The chamber's members as of 1941 included Italy, Hungary, Bohemia, Moravia, Belgium, Bulgaria, Croatia, Denmark, Finland, Holland, Norway, Rumania, Slovakia, and the "neutral" countries of Spain, Sweden, Turkey, Switzerland, and Portugal.

25. Goebbels, *Die Tagebücher von Josef Goebbels,* entry for June 13, 1941, 9:369–70. Film export figures in Pavolini's June 1942 report on the Italian cinema industry, reproduced in *Bianco e nero* (August 1942). See Argentieri, *L'asse cinematografico,* 111–49, on fascist expansion into the film markets of Eastern Europe; and Morgan, "The Italian Fascist New Order in Europe," on the parallel geography of fascist economic expansion.

26. Alfieri, report of March 31, 1942, in ACS, MCP, b.19, f.269.

27. Papini, speech of March 25, 1942, in ACS, MCP, b.19, f.269.

28. Giame Pintor, "Scrittori tedeschi," *Primato* (December 1, 1941), "Commento da un soldato tedesco," *Primato* (February 1, 1941), "Un'antologia tedesca," *Primato* (April 15, 1940), and "Scrittori a Weimar," in Pintor, *Il sangue d'Europa,* 133–36. The Italian delegation to Weimar was approved by Mussolini and included Emilio Cecchi, Antonio Baldini, Alfredo Acito, Giulio Cogni, Mario Sertoli, Enrico Falqui, Arturo Farinelli, and Elio Vittorini. Corrado Alvaro and Eugenio Montale were approved for participation but did not attend. The Ministry of National Education vetoed Vittorini's participation, but since the invitation had come from the German Embassy he was allowed to attend. ACS, MCP, b.19, f.269; PCM (1940–41), 14.3.54689.

29. Enzo Paci, "Il pensiero italiano contemporaneo," *Primato* (December 15, 1940); Milena Milani, "Femminilità armata," *Roma fascista* (December 11, 1941); Giuseppe Bottai, "La giovinezza come ordine nuovo," *Critica fascista* (July 15, 1942); Bruno Romani, "Funzione della gioventù: Per la continuità della rivoluzione," *Critica fascista* (June 15, 1941); and "Ringraziamento a Bottai," *Intervento* (April 1942). On youth enthusiasm for the war, see De Grand, *Bottai e la cultura fascista,* 241–42; Nazario Onofri, *I giornali bolognesi nel ventennio fascista* (Bologna, 1972), 198–203; and Marina Addis Saba, *Gioventù italiana del Littorio*(Milan, 1973).

30. Knox, *Mussolini Unleashed,* 289 and passim. The three categories of support that Alexander von Plato uses to characterize German youth under Hitler are more or less applicable to Italian youth as well: a large group of pragmatists and opportunists whose support was personally motivated and fluctuating, a medium-sized group of enthusiasts who supported their leaders to the end, and a minuscule group of anti-Hitler activists. Von Plato, "The Hitler Youth Generation," 211.

31. Ricci, cited in Buchignani, *Un fascismo impossibile,* 313; and Berto Ricci, "Diagramma della vigilia," *Rivoluzione* (June 5, 1940).

32. Gambetti, *Il controveleno,* 63.

33. Claudio Pavone, *Una guerra civile* (Turin, 1991), 77–78; and Giampaolo Bernagozzi, "La 'campagna' di Russia," in Argentieri, *Schermi di guerra.*

34. Spinetti, report of February 21, 1940, in ACS, MCP, b.84, f.1; also Giuseppe Bottai, *Vent'anni e un giorno* (Milan, 1949), 163. On the fracturing effects of internal rivalries, see De Grand, "Cracks in the Facade: The Failure of Fascist Totalitarianism in Italy, 1935–39," *European History Quarterly* 4

(1991): 515–35. Youth disillusionment during World War II is covered in Koon, *Believe, Obey, Fight,* 246–50; Pavone, *Una guerra civile,* 63–123, expertly analyzes the dilemmas posed by the war for Italians of all ages.

35. Piccoli, "La Nazione e l'ordine nuovo"; Ugo Spirito, "La guerra rivoluzionaria" (1941), cited in Gentile, "La nazione del fascismo," 116–17; "Umanità della nostra guerra," *Critica fascista* (January 1, 1942).

36. Bottai, *Diario,* entry of August 12, 1940, 221.

37. Contributors included Carlo Emilio Gadda, Salvatore Quasimodo, Cesare Pavese, Pratolini, Renato Guttuso, Corrado Alvaro, Giovanni Gentile, Eugenio Montale, Antonio Banfi, Gianfranco Contini, and Giuseppe Ungaretti. Sibilla Aleramo was the sole female collaborator. On *Primato,* see Mangoni, *L'interventismo della cultura,* 333–66; De Grand, *Bottai e la cultura fascista,* 273–85; and Luti, *La letteratura del ventennio nero,* 229–73.

38. "Il coraggio della concordia," *Primato* (March 1, 1940).

39. "Giustizia nella storia," *Primato* (August 15, 1942). For expansionist writings, see Enrico Emanuelli, "Una miseria di quei giorni," *Primato* (April 1, 1941); Alfredo Schiaffini, "L'Italianità linguistica della Dalmazia," *Primato* (June 1, 1941); and Carlo Morandi, "Preludio al Mediterraneo italiano," *Primato* (August 15, 1940). For historians' warnings about Germany, see Ernesto Sestan, "Risorgimento italiano e unità tedesca," *Primato* (December 15, 1942); and Carlo Morandi, "L'unità di Europa," *Primato* (September 15, 1942).

40. Galvano Della Volpe, "Antiromanticismo," *Primato* (May 15, 1941).

41. Pintor, "Commento da un soldato tedesco."

42. On the so-called humanism debate and the elaboration of rival genealogies of Western civilization, see Anson Rabinbach, *In the Shadow of Catastrophe* (Berkeley and Los Angeles, 1997), 107–10; and Ben-Ghiat, "Fascist Italy and Nazi Germany."

43. Manlio Lupinacci, "Un nuovo romanticismo," *Primato* (March 15, 1941).

44. Enzo Paci, "Romanticismo e antiromanticismo," *Architrave* (July 1, 1941), and his "Il pensiero italiano contemporaneo," *Primato* (December 15, 1940); and Della Volpe, "Antiromanticismo." On the "new Romanticism" debate, see Vigorelli, *L'esistenzialismo positivo di Enzo Paci,* 145–52.

45. Lupinacci, "Un nuovo romanticismo," *Primato* (March 15, 1941); and Mario Alicata, "Del nuovo romanticismo," *Primato* (June 1, 1941). For similar sentiments among antifascist artists, see the July 1943 "Manifesto of Painters and Sculptors" reproduced in Treccani, *L'arte per amore* (Milan, 1978), 34.

46. Manlio Lupinacci, "Romantici e antiromantici," *Primato* (June 15, 1941).

47. Ugo Spirito, "Romanticismo e ordine nuovo," *Primato* (July 1, 1941); and Giame Pintor, "Il nuovo romanticismo," *Primato* (August 15, 1941).

48. Paci, "Il pensiero italiano contemporaneo."

49. First and final quotations from Alfonso Gatto, "Itinerario italiano"; also G. B. Angioletti and Giacomo Antonini, *Narratori italiani d'oggi* (Florence: Vallecchi, 1943), 19 and 11; Giancarlo Vigorelli, "Verso il romanzo,"

Corrente (February 28, 1939); Giorgio Cabella, "Narratori tra due guerre," *Critica fascista* (October 1, 1941); Arrigo Ghiara, "Tempo di attesa," *Critica fascista* (January 15, 1940); and "Oltre il silenzio," *Primato* (March 15, 1940). For Alvaro's prize, see *Annuario della Reale Accademia d'Italia, 1940–41,* 470.

50. Alba De Céspedes, *Nessuno torna indietro* (Milan, 1938), 12.

51. Ibid., 442, 125. On *Nessuno torna indietro,* see Carole Gallucci, "Alba De Céspedes' 'There's No Turning Back': Challenging the New Woman's Future," in *Mothers of Invention,* ed. Robin Pickering-Iazzi (Minneapolis, 1995), 200–219; Robin Pickering-Iazzi, *Politics of the Visible,* 164–88; and Ellen Nerenberg, "'Donna proprio . . . proprio donna': The Social Construction of Femininity in *Nessuno torna indietro,*" *Romance Languages Annual* 3 (1991), 267–73.

52. De Céspedes, *Nessuno torna indietro,* 162. In *Politics of the Visible,* Pickering-Iazzi places De Céspedes's novel within the context of interwar experiments with realist aesthetics.

53. De Céspedes, *Nessuno torna indietro,* 434, 228.

54. Ibid., 261, 361, 430.

55. Ibid., 433–34.

56. Vittorini, *Conversazione in Sicilia,* 131–32, 285.

57. Ibid., 156, 285.

58. Ibid., 309.

59. Ibid., 249–50. On *Conversazione in Sicilia,* see Wilkinson, *The Intellectual Resistance in Europe,* 207–13.

60. Giame Pintor, "Nome e lagrime," *Prospettive* (April 15–May 15, 1941); Alicata, review in *Oggi,* reprinted in Mario Alicata, *Scritti letterari* (Milan, 1968), 80–83; and G. Marchi [Giorgio Bassani], "Situazione di Elio Vittorini," *Emporium* (May 1942). *Nome e lagrime* was the title of the first edition published in 1941, by Parenti; later that year Bompiani brought out another edition under its final name.

61. Don Ferrante, "Corriere della letteratura," *Primato* (June 1, 1941); Enrico Falqui, "Conversazione in Sicilia," *La Gazzetta del Popolo* (June 19, 1941); and "Una sporca conversazione," *Il Popolo d'Italia* (July 30, 1942).

62. Pannunzio, "Del romanzo." See the editors' explanation of the survey, which was undertaken between January and February 1942, in "Opinioni sul romanzo," *Corriere padano* (January 8, 1942). Contributors included Antonio Baldini and Luigi Bartolini (January 8, 1942), Beniamino Del Fabbro and Corrado Pavolini (January 29, 1942), and Montale (February 1, 1942).

63. "Avvertimento," *La Ruota* (April 1940); Carlo Muscetta, "De Sanctis o la letteratura come vita morale," *La Ruota* (April 1940). Compare with post-1945 explications of De Sanctis by Carlo Salinari, "Il ritorno di De Sanctis," *Rinascita* (May 1952): 289–92. On the PCI's cultural platform in the Resistance and Reconstruction years, see Nello Ajello, *Intellettuali e PCI, 1944–58* (Bari, 1979); Nicoletta Misler, *La via italiana al realismo* (Milan, 1973); and Stephen Gundle, *The Italian Communists and the Challenge of Mass Culture, 1943–1991* (Durham, N.C., forthcoming). On Alicata's own formation, see

Sergio Bertelli, *Il gruppo* (Milan, 1980), 116–34; Enzo Frustaci, *Un'episodio letterario dell'Italia fascista* (Rome, 1980).

64. Mario Alicata and Giuseppe De Santis, "Verità e poesia: Verga e il cinema italiano," *Cinema* (October 10, 1941); and "Ancora di Verga e del cinema italiano," *Cinema* (November 25, 1941).

65. Giuseppe De Santis, "Il linguaggio dei rapporti," *Cinema* (December 25, 1941); see also De Santis, "Per un paesaggio italiano," *Cinema* (April 25, 1941); and Mario Alicata, "Ambiente e società nel racconto cinematografico," *Cinema* (February 10, 1942).

66. De Santis was also assistant director. Gianni Puccini collaborated on the script, which eventually received the assistance of Antonio Pietrangeli and Moravia as well. On *Ossessione,* see the superb essay by Lino Micciché in Micciché, *Visconti e il neorealismo,* 21–68. In English, see Mira Liehm, *Passion and Defiance* (Berkeley and Los Angeles, 1984), 41–59.

67. Antonio Pietrangeli, "Verso un cinema italiano," *Bianco e nero* (August 1942), and his "Analisi spettrale del film realistico," *Cinema* (July 25, 1942); and Aldo Scagnetti, "Personaggi e paesaggio in 'Ossessione,'" *Lo Schermo* (August 1942). *Ossessione* received funding from the cinema credit section of the *Banco Nazionale del Lavoro,* which had been set up by the *Direzione Generale della Cinematografia* in 1935. Visconti's friend Eitel Monaco, who headed the *Direzione Generale* after April 1941, shepherded the film through the censorship process. See Gili, *Stato fascista e cinematografia,* 66–68.

68. Guido Aristarco, "Ossessione," *Corriere padano* (June 8, 1943); Umberto Barbaro, "Neo-realismo," *Film* (June 12, 1943); and Massimo Mida Puccini, "A proposito di 'Ossessione,'" *Cinema* (July 10, 1943). Brunetta, *Storia del cinema italiano,* 72, discusses Catholic aversion to the film.

69. Renato Guttuso, "Pensieri sulla pittura," *Primato* (August 15, 1941); Treccani, diary entry of June 28, 1943, in *L'arte per amore,* 21.

70. Corrado Pavolini, "Rapporto sul cinema," ACS, MCP, b.11, f. 154.

71. Alberto Lattuada, *Occhio quadrato* (Milan, 1941), xiii–xv. Published by the *Corrente* imprint, the book was released only after a ceiling was placed on the number of copies that would circulate. See Lattuada's interviews with Savio, *Cinecittà anni trenta,* 2:664–65, and with Jean Gili in *Nuovi materiali,* 2:126–27.

72. Polverelli, speech reprinted in *Cinema* (May 25, 1943); "Vie del nostro cinema," *Cinema* (July 10, 1943).

73. Primo Levi, *Il sistema periodico* (Turin, 1975), 66; see also Bottai, *Diario,* entry of June 13, 1942, 311, in which he describes his meeting with Alberto Mondadori as the latter was bound for the Russian front. Both Gentile, "La nazione del fascismo," and Ernesto Galli della Loggia, *La morte della Patria* (Rome, 1996), trace the crisis of national identity in these years.

74. Imbriani, *Gli italiani e il Duce,* 144.

75. See the essays in *Gli italiani sul fronte russo;* Bottai, *Diario,* 311, and Ciano, *Diario,* entry of May 27, 1942, report Italian impressions of Russia and German conduct there.

76. Treccani, *L'arte per amore*, 26.
77. Artom, *Diari*, 76.

EPILOGUE

1. Giovanni Gentile, "Ripresa," *Nuova Antologia* (January 1, 1944).
2. General accounts of the Resistance include Roberto Battaglia, *Storia della Resistenza Italiana* (Turin, 1964); and, in English, Charles Delzell, *Mussolini's Enemies* (Princeton, 1961). For women's roles in the Resistance, see Jane Slaughter, *Women and the Italian Resistance, 1943–45* (Denver, 1997); and Annamaria Bruzzone and Rachele Farina, *La resistenza taciuta* (Florence, 1976).
3. Ada Gobetti, *Diario partigiano* (Turin, 1996), 15. In *Una guerra civile*, the historian Claudio Pavone has identified three different and overlapping struggles within the Resistance—a class war against the bourgeoisie, a patriotic war against a foreign invader, and a civil war against a domestic enemy.
4. Mario Pannunzio, "Una generazione tra le due guerre," *Risorgimento liberale* (August 1944).
5. "La figura del caduto," *Avanti!* (December 30, 1943), in Pavone, *Una guerra civile*, 555.
6. "Cursor" [Teresio Olivelli], in the clandestine journal *Il Ribelle* (March 1944), cited in Addis Saba and Alfassio Grimaldi, *Cultura a passo romano*, 76–77.
7. Pintor, letter to his brother Luigi Pintor, November 28, 1943, in *Il sangue d'Europa*, 185–88; Franco Calamandrei, *La vita indivisibile:* (Rome, 1984), 130, February 1944 entry. Calmandrei's missions in this period included the attack on a German command post on Rome's Via Rasella in March 1944.
8. On the Servizio Ausiliario Femminile, see Maria Fraddosio, "La donna e la guerra," *Storia contemporanea* (December 1989), 1105–81. Police forces included the Republican National Guard, the Italian African Police, the carabinieri, fascist militia units, the Ministry of Interior police, and the Racial Inspectorate's own Jew-hunting force. Another seventy thousand men were in paramilitary bands. Figures on enlistments in Salò military bodies are from Martin Clark, *Modern Italy, 1871–1982* (London, 1995), 308–10.
9. See the testimonies in Miriam Mafai, *Pane nero* (Milan, 1988), 230–31, and Pavone, *Una guerra civile*, 682.
10. On this subject, see Liliana Picciotto Fargion, "The Jews during the German Occupation and the Italian Social Republic," in *The Italian Refuge*, ed. Ivo Herzer (Washington, D.C., 1990), 109–38. In *Il mito del bravo italiano* (Milan, 1993), 65, David Bidussa notes that of 7,013 Italian Jews arrested, 1,898 were caught by Italians, 2,489 were taken by Germans, 312 were taken in combined Italian-German actions, and 2,314 were arrested in "unknown circumstances."
11. Italian Catholic aid to Jews is discussed in Zuccotti, *Italians and the Holocaust*.

12. See Pavone, *Una guerra civile*, 262, on the evolution of the term "fascism" into "Nazifascism." My thinking here about the relation between bureaucracy and the evasion of moral responsibility draws on Zygmunt Bauman, *Modernity and the Holocaust* (Ithaca, 1989).

13. Corrado Alvaro, *Italia rinunzia?* (1944; reprint, Palermo, 1986), 40. Alfassio Grimaldi, in Addis Saba and Alfassio Grimaldi, *Cultura a passo romano*, 167, recalled that he and other Italians "did not know whether to consider themselves guilty or victims" in the aftermath of World War II.

14. See Elena Aga Rossi, *Una nazione allo sbando* (Bologna, 1993); and "1943: Crisi di regime, crisi di nazione," special issue of *Storia contemporanea* 24, no. 6 (1993). On Italian deportations to Germany, see Gerhard Schreiber, *I militari italiani internati nei campi di concentramento del Terzo Reich, 1943–45* (Rome, 1992); Paci's experience in Germany is mentioned in Vigorelli, *L'esistenzialismo positivo*, 191.

15. Alvaro, *Quasi una vita*, entry of 1944, 353; Moravia, letter to Prezzolini of autumn 1946, in *Alberto Moravia–Giuseppe Prezzolini*, 33; and Elkann, *Vita di Moravia*, 139–51; Bottai, *Diario, 1944–48*.

16. Enrico Emanuelli, *Teatro personale* (Milan, 1945), 70, October 1943 entry; Emanuelli, *Dei Sentimenti* (Milan, 1944), cited in Enrico Falqui, *La letteratura del ventennio nero* (Rome, 1948), 236.

17. Alvaro, *Italia rinunzia?* 11, 40, 80, 82, 92; Pannunzio, "Una generazione tra le due guerre." The theme of betrayal by older Germans runs through the testimonies collected by von Plato, Buddries, and Reese in Roseman, ed., *Generations in Conflict.*

18. For Croce's ideas on fascism as a parenthesis, see his *Scritti e discorsi, 1943–47* (Bari, 1963), 1:7–16, 56; and 2:46–50, 361–62, and his articles in *Risorgimento liberale* (April 7, 1945, and September 22, 1945). On Croce's theory of fascism, see Pier Giorgio Zunino, *Interpretazione e memoria del fascismo* (Rome, 1991), 111–42.

19. Giame Pintor, "Colpo di Stato," in *Il sangue d'Europa*, 180–81; Carlo Levi, in *Italia liberale* (February 3, 1946). On the Action Party's analyses of fascism, see David Ward, *Antifascisms: Cultural Politics in Italy, 1943–46* (Madison, N.J., 1996).

20. Hans Woller, *Die Abrechnung mit dem Faschismus in Italien 1943 bis 1948* (Munich, 1996); and Gian Enrico Rusconi, *Resistenza e postfascismo* (Bologna, 1995), argue that the purges were effective given the constraints placed on all parties by domestic exigencies such as the need for votes and legitimation as well as by the international situation.

21. On Gallian's fate, see Paolo Buchignani, *Marcello Gallian* (Rome, 1982); documentation on Bontempelli's continued payments for service to the Confederation of Professionals and Artists in GRI, BP, Correspondence files, box 3, folder B. On the manipulation of the memory of fascist literary culture after 1945, see Ruth Ben-Ghiat, "Fascism, Writing, and Memory," *Journal of Modern History* (September 1995): 627–65; for the gender politics of those manipulations, see Pickering-Iazzi, *Politics of the Visible.*

22. On the purges, see the analyses of Woller, *Die Abrechnung mit dem Faschismus in Italien;* Roy Domenico, *Italian Fascists on Trial, 1943–48* (Chapel Hill, 1991); Lamberto Mercuri, *L'epurazione in Italia, 1943–48* (Cuneo, 1988).

23. Salvatore Ambrosino, "Il cinema ricomincia: Attori e registi fra 'continuità' e 'frattura,'" in *Il neorealismo italiano,* ed. Alberto Farassino (Rome, 1989), 63; see also Farassino, ed., *Mario Camerini,* 134.

24. Lorenzo Quaglietti, *Storia economica-politica del cinema italiano, 1945–80* (Rome, 1980), 37–38, covers the conditions of the film industry in 1944–45.

25. Chiarini, interview by Gili in *Nuovi materali,* 2:116.

26. I am referring here to works such as Roland Sarti, *Fascism and the Industrial Leadership in Italy* (Berkeley and Los Angeles, 1971); Ipsen, *Dictating Demography;* de Grazia, *How Fascism Ruled Women;* and Luisa Passerini, *Fascism in Popular Memory,* trans. Robert Lumley and Jude Bloomfield (Cambridge, 1987). Dau Novelli, *Famiglia e modernizzazione,* 10–12, cautions that the argument that modernization occurred "despite" or "against" fascist goals presumes that no "unity of intention" existed between the Italian people and the regime. On the question of fascism and modernization, see also the reflections of Enzo Collotti and Lutz Klinkhammer, *Il fascismo e l'Italia in guerra* (Rome, 1996), 108–13.

27. Mario Sechi has examined the philosopher Luciano Anceschi's itinerary from the years of *Orpheus* to his participation in the Group 63 neo-avant-garde movement. See Sechi, "Ideologia urbana tra 'crisi' e sviluppo: La generazione del 'Verri'" *Lavoro critico* (January-March 1975): 61–89; on the 1930s as a crucible of postwar literary attitudes and trends, see Antonio Palermo, "Gli anni trenta: Per una nuova periodizzazione della storiografia letteraria," *La cultura italiana negli anni, 1930–45* (Naples, 1984), 159–70.

28. Enzo Paci, "Contributo," *Saggiatore* (August-October 1933).

29. On this point, see Gundle, *The Italian Communists and the Challenge of Mass Culture, 1943–1991.* Zagarrio, in "Giovani e apparati culturali a Firenze nella crisi del regime fascista," 622, observes that the regime's wish to achieve a "daily encounter of young people with politics" instilled an interest in ideology and a habit of close study of political texts that would carry over to postwar Italian intellectual life as well.

Bibliography

MANUSCRIPT SOURCES AND ABBREVIATIONS

ACS Archivio Centrale dello Stato, Rome
   CM Carte Morgagni
   DGPS Direzione Generale di Pubblica Sicurezza
   MCP Ministero della Cultura Popolare
   MI Ministero dell'Interno
     AD Atti Diversi (1903–49)
     AGR Affari Generali e Riservati
     DPP Divisione Polizia Politica (1927–43)
   PCM Presidenza del Consiglio dei Ministri, Gabinetto
   PNF Partito Nazionale Fascista
   SPCO Segretaria Particolare del Duce, Carteggio Ordinario
   SPCR Segretaria Particolare del Duce, Carteggio Riservato

NA National Archives, Washington, D.C.
   PPBM The Personal Papers of Benito Mussolini

GRI The Getty Research Institute, Los Angeles
   BP Massimo Bontempelli papers

AA Archivio Luciano Anceschi, Bologna

AAI Archivio della Reale Accademia d'Italia, Rome

AB Archivio Alessandro Blasetti, Rome

INTERVIEWS

Anceschi, Luciano. Bologna, June 22 and July 2, 1990.
Granata, Maria. Rome, July 10, 1987.
Treccani, Ernesto. Milan, June 21, 1990.

BOOKS AND ARTICLES

Absalom, Roger. *A Strange Alliance*. Florence: Olschki, 1991.

Abse, Tobias. "Italian Workers and Italian Fascism." In *Fascist Italy and Nazi Germany: Comparisons and Contrasts*, ed. Richard Bessel, 40–60. Cambridge: Cambridge University Press, 1996.

Accademia Reale d'Italia. *Convegno di arti: Rapporti dell'architettura con le arti figurative*. Rome: Accademia Reale d'Italia, 1937.

———. *Convegno di scienze morali e storiche: L'Africa*. 2 vols. Rome: Accademia Reale d'Italia, 1939.

Acquarone, Alberto. *L'organizzazione dello Stato totalitario*. Turin: Einaudi, 1965.

Adamson, Walter. *Avant-Garde Florence: From Modernism to Fascism*. Cambridge: Harvard University Press, 1993.

———. "The Culture of Italian Fascism and the Fascist Crisis of Modernity: The Case of *Il Selvaggio*." *Journal of Contemporary History* 30 (1995): 555–75.

Addis Saba, Marina. *Gioventù italiana del Littorio: La stampa dei giovani nella guerra fascista*. Milan: Feltrinelli, 1973.

Addis Saba, Marina, and Ugoberto Alfassio Grimaldi. *Cultura a passo romano*. Milan: Feltrinelli, 1983.

Adler, Franklin Hugh. *Italian Industrialists from Liberalism to Fascism*. Cambridge: Cambridge University Press, 1996.

Aga Rossi, Elena. *Una nazione allo sbando: L'armistizio italiano del settembre 1943*. Bologna: Il Mulino, 1993.

Agosto, Paolo. "Mussolini: Strumentalizzazione e desemantizazzione di lessemi marxisti." In *La lingua italiana e il fascismo*, 15–23. Bologna: Consorzio provinciale pubblica lettura, 1977.

Ajello, Nello. *Intellettuali e PCI, 1944–58*. Bari: Laterza, 1979.

Alatri, Paolo. "Cultura e politica: Gli studenti romani dal 1936 al 1943." *Incontri meridionali*, nos. 3–4 (1979): 7–17.

Albertoni, Ettore, et al., eds. *La generazione degli anni difficili*. Bari: Laterza, 1962.

Alfassio Grimaldi, Ugoberto. *Autobiografie di una generazione*. Brescia: Morcellano, 1946.

———. "La generazione sedotta e abbandonata." *Tempo presente* (January 1963).

Alicata, Mario. *Scritti letterari*. Milan: Mondadori, 1968.

Alvaro, Corrado. *Cronaca (o fantasia)*. Rome: Le Edizioni d'Italia, 1933.

———. *Gente in Aspromonte*. Florence: Le Monnier, 1930.

———. *Italia rinunzia?* 1944. Reprint, Palermo: Sellerio, 1986.

———. *Itinerario italiano*. Rome: Novissima, 1933.

———. *I maestri del diluvio*. Milan: Mondadori, 1935.

———. *Il mare*. Milan: Mondadori, 1934.

―――. *Quasi una vita: Giornale di uno scrittore, 1927–47*. Milan: Bompiani, 1959.

―――. *Terra nuova: Prima cronaca dell'Agro Pontina*. Rome: Istituto Nazionale di Cultura Fascista, 1934.

―――. *L'uomo è forte*. 1938. Reprint, Milan: Bompiani, 1989.

―――. *Vent'anni*. Milan: Treves, 1931.

Ambrosino, Salvatore. "Il cinema ricomincia: Attori e registi fra 'continuita' e 'frattura.'" In *Il neorealismo italiano*, ed. Alberto Farassino, 60–77. Rome: 1989.

Anceschi, Luciano. "L'insegnamento di Antonio Banfi." *Belfagor* 33 (May–June 1978): 335–42.

Anderson, Benedict. *Imagined Communities: Reflections on the Origin and Spread of Nationalism*. London: Verso, 1990.

Les années 30: L'architecture et les arts de l'espace entre industrie et nostalgie, sous le direction de Jean-Louis Cohen. Paris: Editions du Patrimoine, 1997.

Annitrenta: Arte e cultura in Italia. Milan: Mazzotta, 1983.

Annuario della Reale Accademia d'Italia, 1932–33. Rome: Reale Accademia d'Italia, 1933.

Annuario della Reale Accademia d'Italia, 1934–37. Rome: Reale Accademia d'Italia, 1938.

Annuario della Reale Accademia d'Italia, 1940–41. Rome: Reale Accademia d'Italia, 1942.

Antonio Banfi e il pensiero contemporaneo. Florence: La Nuova Italia, 1969.

Antonio Delfini. Special issue of *Riga* 6 (1994).

Aprà, Adriano, and Riccardo Redi, eds. *Sole: Soggetto, sceneggiatura, note per la realizzazione*. Rome: Di Giacomo, 1985.

Argentieri, Mino. *L'asse cinematografico Roma-Berlino*. Naples: Sapere, 1986.

―――. *La censura nel cinema italiano*. Rome: Riuniti, 1974.

―――. *L'occhio del regime: Informazioni e propaganda nel cinema del fascismo*. Florence: Vallecchi, 1979.

―――, ed. *Il cinema in guerra: Arte, comunicazione, e propaganda in Italia, 1940–44*. Rome: Riuniti, 1998.

―――, ed. *Schermi di guerra: Cinema italiano, 1939–45*. Rome: Riuniti, 1995.

Arte decorativa italiana. Milan: Hoepli, 1938.

Artom, Emanuelle. *Diari: Gennaio 1940–febbraio 1944*. Milan: Centro di documentazione ebraica contemporanea, 1966.

Asor Rosa, Alberto. *Scrittori e popolo*. Rome: Samona e Savelli, 1964.

Atti del IV congresso nazionale di arti e tradizioni popolari. 2 vols. Rome: Edizioni dell'O.N.D., 1940.

Avanzini, Elsa, et al., eds. *Almanacco del cinema italiano, 1942–43*. Rome: Societa Editrice Anonima Cinema, 1943.

Banfi, Antonio. *La crisi*. Milan: All'insegna del pesce d'oro, 1967.

Banfi, Elena. "Attività del Cineguf-Milano." *Communicazione sociali* (July–December 1988): 305–29.

Banfi Malaguzzi, Daria. *Femminilità contemporanea.* Milan: Alpes, 1928.

Barbagli, Marzio. *Disoccupazione intellettuale e sistema scolastico in Italia, 1859–1973.* Bologna: Il Mulino, 1974.

Barbaro, Umberto. *Film e il risarcimento marxista dell'arte.* Rome: Riuniti, 1960.

———. *Luce fredda.* Lanciano: Carabba, 1931.

———. *Neorealismo e realismo.* Ed. Gian Piero Brunetta. 2 vols. Rome: Riuniti, 1976.

———. *Soggetto e sceneggiatura.* Rome: Riuniti, 1947.

Barbian, Jan-Pieter. "Literary Policy in the Third Reich." In *National Socialist Cultural Policy,* ed. Glenn R. Cuomo, 155–96. New York: St. Martin's Press, 1995.

Bardi, Pier Maria. *Un fascista al paese dei Soviet.* Rome: Le Edizioni d'Italia, 1933.

Barnouw, Dagmar. *Weimar Intellectuals and the Threat of Modernity.* Bloomington: Indiana University Press, 1988.

Barrows, Susanna. *Distorting Mirrors: Visions of the Crowd in Late Nineteenth-Century France.* New Haven: Yale University Press, 1981.

Bartov, Omer. *Murder in Our Midst: The Holocaust, Industrial Killing, and Representation.* New York: Oxford University Press, 1996.

Barzini, Luigi. *L'impero del lavoro forzato.* Milan: Hoepli, 1932.

———. *Nuova York.* Milan: Agnelli, 1931.

Battaglia, Roberto. *Storia della Resistenza italiana.* Turin: Einaudi, 1964.

Bauman, Zygmunt. *Modernity and the Holocaust.* Ithaca, N.Y.: Cornell University Press, 1989.

Ben-Ghiat, Ruth. "Envisioning Modernity: Desire and Discipline in the Italian Fascist Film." *Critical Inquiry* (autumn 1996): 109–44.

———. "Fascism, Writing, and Memory: The Realist Aesthetic in Italy, 1930–50." *Journal of Modern History* 67 (September 1995): 627–65.

———. "Fascist Italy and Nazi Germany: The Dynamics of an Uneasy Relationship." In *Culture and the Nazis,* ed. Richard Etlin. Chicago: University of Chicago Press, forthcoming.

———. "Italian Fascism and the Aesthetics of the 'Third Way.'" *Journal of Contemporary History* (April 1996).

———. "Language and the Construction of National Identity in Fascist Italy." *The European Legacy* (fall 1997): 438–43.

———. "The Politics of Realism: *Corrente di Vita Giovanile* and the Culture of the 1930s." *Stanford Italian Review* 8, nos. 1–2 (1990): 139–64.

———. "Roberto Rossellini's Fascist War Trilogy." In *Roberto Rossellini,* ed. David Forgacs, Sarah Lutton, and Geoffrey Nowell-Smith. London: British Film Institute, 2000.

Bennett, Tony. "The Exhibitionary Complex." In *Culture/Power/History,* ed. Nicholas B. Dirks et al., 123–54. Princeton: Princeton University Press, 1994.

Benussi, Cristina. "Moravia nell'esistenzialismo italiano." In *Homage to Moravia*, ed. Rocco Capozzi and Mario B. Mignone, supplement to *Forum Italicum* 5 (1993): 3–20.

Berezin, Mabel. *Making the Fascist Self: The Political Culture of Interwar Italy*. Ithaca, N.Y.: Cornell University Press, 1996.

Berghaus, Günter. *Futurism and Politics*. Providence: Berghahn, 1996.

Bernagozzi, Giampaolo. "La 'campagna' di Russia: Finzioni e realtà." In *Schermi di guerra: Cinema italiano, 1939–45*, ed. Mino Argentieri, 135–76. Rome: Riuniti, 1995.

Bernardini, Aldo. *Cinema muto italiano*. 3 vols. Rome: Laterza, 1980–82.

Bertelli, Sergio. *Il gruppo: La formazione del gruppo dirigente del PCI, 1936–48*. Milan: Rizzoli, 1980.

Beynet, Michel. *L'Image de l'Amérique dans la culture italienne de l'entre-deux-guerres*. 3 vols. Aix-en-Provence: Université de Provence, 1990.

Bhabha, Homi K., ed. *Nation and Narration*. London: Routledge, 1990.

Biagioli, Mario. *Galileo Courtier*. Chicago: University of Chicago Press, 1994.

Bidussa, David. *Il mito del bravo italiano*. Milan: Il Saggiatore, 1993.

Bilenchi, Romano. *Amici: Vittorini, Rosai ed altri incontri*. Turin: Einaudi, 1976.

———. *Il capofabbrica*. Florence: Vallecchi, 1972.

Blatt, Joel. "The Battle of Turin, 1931–36: Carlo Rosselli, Giustizia e Libertà, OVRA, and the Origins of Mussolini's Anti-Semitic Campaign." *Journal of Modern Italian Studies* (fall 1995): 22–57.

Bondanella, Peter. *The Films of Roberto Rossellini*. Cambridge: Cambridge University Press, 1993.

———. *Italian Cinema: From Neorealism to the Present*. New York: Frederick Ungar, 1983.

Bongiovanni, Bruno. *L'Università di Torino durante il fascismo*. Turin: G. Chiappichelli, 1976.

Bono, Francesco. "La Mostra del Cinema di Venezia: Nascita e sviluppo nell'anteguerra (1932–39)." *Storia contemporanea* (June 1991): 513–49.

Bonsanti, Alessandro. "La cultura degli anni trenta dai Littoriali all'antifascismo." *Terzo Programma* 4 (1963): 183–217.

Bontempelli, Massimo. *L'avventura novecentista (1926–38)*. Florence: Vallecchi, 1938.

Bordoni, Carlo. *Cultura e propaganda nell'Italia fascista*. Messina: G. D'Anna, 1974.

Bossaglia, Rossana. *Il "Novecento Italiano": Storia, documenti, iconografia*. Milan: Feltrinelli, 1979.

Bosworth, Richard. *Italy and the Wider World, 1860–1960*. New York: Routledge, 1996.

———. *Italy: Least of the Great Powers*. Cambridge: Cambridge University Press, 1980.

Bottai, Giuseppe. *Il cammino delle corporazioni*. Florence: Vallecchi, 1935.

———. *Diario, 1935–44*. Milan: Rizzoli, 1982.

———. *Diario, 1944–58.* Milan: Rizzoli, 1988.

———. *Esperienza corporativa.* Rome: Edizioni del Diritto del Lavoro, 1929.

———. *La politica degli arti.* Ed. Alessandro Masi. Rome: Editalia, 1992.

———. *Vent'anni e un giorno.* Milan: Garzanti, 1949.

Bourdieu, Pierre. *The Field of Cultural Production.* Cambridge: Polity Press, 1993.

———. *Language and Symbolic Power.* Cambridge: Harvard University Press, 1991.

Brancati, Vitaliano. *Singolare avventura di viaggio.* Milan: Mondadori, 1934.

Brantlinger, Patrick. *Bread and Circuses: Theories of Mass Culture as Social Decay.* Ithaca, N.Y.: Cornell University Press, 1983.

Braun, Emily. *Mario Sironi and Italian Modernism: Art and Politics in Fascist Italy.* Cambridge: Cambridge University Press, 2000.

———. "Mario Sironi's *Urban Landscapes:* The Futurist/Fascist Nexus." In *Fascist Visions,* ed. Matthew Affron and Mark Antliff. Princeton: Princeton University Press, 1996.

Brunetta, Gian Piero. *Buio in sala: Cent'anni di passione dello spettatore cinematografico.* Venice: Marsilio, 1989.

———. *Cinema italiano tra le due guerre.* Milan: Mursia, 1975.

———. *Intellettuali, cinema e propaganda tra le due guerre.* Bologna: Patron, 1972.

———. "Il sogno a stelle e strisce di Mussolini." In *L'estetica della politica,* ed. Maurizio Vaudagna, 187–202. Rome: Laterza, 1989.

———. *Storia del cinema italiano, 1896–1945.* Rome: Laterza, 1993.

———. *Umberto Barbaro e l'idea di neorealismo.* Padua: Liviana, 1969.

Brunetta, Gian Piero, and Jean Gili. *L'ora d'Africa del cinema italiano, 1911–1989,* 187–202. Rovereto: Rivista di studi storici, 1990.

Bruno, Giuliana. *Streetwalking on a Ruined Map: Cultural Theory and the Films of Elvira Notari.* Princeton: Princeton University Press, 1993.

Bruzzone, Annamaria, and Rachele Farina. *La Resistenza taciuta: Dodici vite di partigiane piemontesi.* Florence: La Pietra, 1976.

Buchignani, Paolo. *Un fascismo impossibile: L'eresia di Berto Ricci nella cultura del ventennio.* Bologna: Il Mulino, 1994.

———. *Marcello Gallian: La battaglia antiborghese di un fascista anarchico.* Rome: Bonacci, 1982.

Budick, Sanford, and Wolfgang Iser, eds. *The Translatability of Cultures: Figurations of the Space Inbetween.* Stanford: Stanford University Press, 1996.

Bullivant, Keith, ed. *Culture and Society in the Weimar Republic.* Manchester: University of Manchester Press, 1979.

Burgwyn, James H. *The Legend of the Mutilated Victory.* Westport, Conn.: Greenwood Press, 1993.

Burke, Joanna. *Dismembering the Male: Men's Bodies, Britain, and the Great War.* Chicago: University of Chicago Press, 1996.

Burleigh, Michael, and Wolfgang Wipperman. *The Racial State.* Cambridge: Cambridge University Press, 1991.

Busini, Renato. "'Il Selvaggio' squadrista: Le radici di un corrente del cosidetto 'fascismo di sinistra.'" *Quaderno '70 sul Novecento* (1970): 37–88.

Calamandrei, Franco. *La vita indivisibile: Diario, 1941–47*. Rome: Riuniti, 1984.

Calinescu, Matei. *Rereading*. New Haven: Yale University Press, 1993.

Calzini, Raffaelle, ed. *Ventennio: Italia, 1914–34*. Special issue of *Domus* (December 1933).

Camerini, Claudio, ed. *Acciaio: Un film degli anni trenta*. Rome: Edizioni RAI, 1990.

Canepa, Andrew. "Christian-Jewish Relations in Italy from Unification to Fascism." In *The Italian Refuge: The Rescue of Jews during the Holocaust*, ed. Ivo Herzer. Washington, D.C.: Catholic University of America Press, 1989, 13–33.

Cannistraro, Philip. "Burocrazia e politica culturale nello Stato fascista: Il Ministero della Cultura Popolare." *Storia contemporanea* (June 1970): 273–98.

———. *La fabbrica del consenso: Fascismo e mass media*. Bari: Laterza, 1975.

Cannistraro, Philip, and Brian Sullivan. *The Duce's Other Woman*. New York: William Morrow, 1993.

Caputo, Giorgio. "L'opposizione antifascista degli studenti romani alla vigilia della seconda guerra mondiale." *Mondo operaio* 3 (March 1970): 34–42; and 4 (April-May 1970): 62–73.

Carabba, Claudio. *Il cinema del ventennio nero*. Florence: Vallecchi, 1974.

Cardoza, Anthony. *Agrarian Elites and Italian Fascism: The Province of Bologna, 1901–1926*. Princeton: Princeton University Press, 1983.

Carducci, Nicola. *Gli intellettuali e l'ideologia americana nell'Italia letteraria degli anni trenta*. Manduria: Lacaita, 1973.

Carella, Domenico. *Fascismo prima, fascismo dopo*. Rome: A. Armando, 1973.

Carpi, Umberto. *Bolscevico immaginista*. Naples: Liguori, 1981.

———. "*Gli indifferenti* 'rimossi.'" *Belfagor* (November 30, 1981): 696–709.

Cartiglia, Carlo. "Il 'fascismo di fronda': Appunti e ipotesi di lavoro." *Italia contemporanea* 122 (1976): 1–22.

Casadei, Gianfranco. "Il cinema dei telefoni bianchi." In *Telefoni bianchi: Realta e finzione nella societa e nel cinema italiano degli anni quaranta*, ed. Gianfranco Casadei and Ernesto Laura, 8–30. Ravenna: Longo, 1991.

Cassese, Sabino. "Un programmatore degli anni trenta: Giuseppe Bottai." In *La formazione dello Stato amministrativo*, 187–210. Milan: Giuffre, 1974.

Castello, Giulio Cesare, and Claudio Bertieri, eds. *Venezia, 1932–39: Filmografia critica*. Rome: Bianco e nero, 1959.

Catalano, Franco. *La generazione degli anni '40*. Milan: Contemporanea, 1975.

Cavaglion, Alberto, and Gian Paolo Romagnani. *Le interdizioni del Duce*. Turin: Albert Meynier, 1988.

Cavallo, Pietro. *Italiani in guerra: Sentimenti e immagini dal 1940 al 1943*. Bologna: Il Mulino, 1997.

Cavazza, Stefano. "La folkloristica italiana e il fascismo." *La ricerca folkloristica* (April 1987).

————. *Piccole patrie: Feste popolari tra regione e nazione durante il fascismo.* Bologna: Il Mulino, 1997.

Cecchi, Emilio. *America amara.* Florence: Sansoni, 1940.

Cennamo, Michele. *Materiali per l'analisi dell'architettura moderna.* 2 vols. Naples: Fausto Fiorentino, 1973 and 1977.

Cesari, Maurizio. *La censura nel periodo fascista.* Naples: Liguori, 1978.

Chakravarty, Sumita S. *National Identity in Indian Popular Cinema, 1947–87.* Austin: University of Texas, 1993.

Charney, Leo, and Vanessa Schwartz, eds. *Cinema and the Invention of Modern Life.* Berkeley and Los Angeles: University of California Press, 1995.

Chiarini, Luigi. *Il cinematografo.* Rome: Cremonese, 1935.

————. *Fascismo e letteratura.* Rome: Istituto nazionale di cultura fascista, 1936.

Ciano, Galeazzo. *Diario, 1937–43.* Milan: Rizzoli, 1990.

Cingari, Gaetano, et al., eds. *La "politica" di Alvaro.* Cosenza: Lerici, n.d. [1977].

Ciocca, Gaetano. *Giudizio sul bolscevismo: Com'è finito il piano quinquennale.* Milan: Bompiani, 1933.

Clair, Jean. *The 1920s: Age of Metropolis.* Montreal: Montreal Museum of Fine Arts, 1991.

Clark, Katerina. "Little Heros and Big Deeds: Literature Responds to the Five-Year Plan." In *Cultural Revolution in Russia, 1928–31,* ed. Sheila Fitzpatrick, 189–206. Bloomington: University of Indiana Press, 1984.

Clark, Martin. *Modern Italy, 1871–1995.* London: Longman, 1995.

Clayton, Jay, and Eric Rothstein, eds. *Influence and Intertextuality in Literary History.* Madison: University of Wisconsin Press, 1991.

Colajanni, Napoleone. *Latini e anglosassoni: Razze inferiori e razze superiori.* Rome: Rivista popolare, 1906.

Collotti, Enzo. "L'alleanza italo-tedesca, 1941–43." In *Gli italiani sul fronte russo,* 3–62. Bari: De Donato, 1982.

Collotti, Enzo, and Lutz Klinkhammer. *Il fascismo e l'Italia in guerra: Una conversazione fra storia e storiografia.* Rome: Ediesse, 1996.

Colquhoun, Alan. *Modernity and the Classical Tradition.* Cambridge: Harvard University Press, 1989.

Cook, David A. *A History of Narrative Film.* New York: W. W. Norton, 1990.

Corrente: Il movimento di arte e cultura di opposizione, 1930–45. Milan: Vangelista, 1985.

Cortelazzo, Michele A. "Il lessico del razzismo fascista." In *Parlare fascista,* special issue of *Movimento operaio e socialista* (April-June 1984): 57–66.

Coveri, Lorenzo. "Mussolini e il dialetto: Notizie sulla campagna antidialettale del fascismo." In *Parlare fascista,* special issue of *Movimento operaio e socialista* (January-April 1984): 117–32.

La crisi del capitalismo. Florence: Sansoni, 1933.

Croce, Benedetto. *Scritti e discorsi politici (1943–47).* 2 vols. Bari: Laterza, 1963.

Dalle Vacche, Angela. *The Body in the Mirror.* Princeton: Princeton University Press, 1992.

Daniel-Rops, Henri. *Le Monde sans âme.* Paris: Plon, 1932.

Dau Novelli, Cecilia. *Famiglia e modernizzazione in Italia tra le due guerre.* Rome: Studium, 1994.

David, Michel. *La psicoanalisi nella cultura italiana.* Turin: Boringhieri, 1966.

Davis, Darrell William. *Picturing Japaneseness: Monumental Style, National Identity, and Japanese Film.* New York: Columbia University Press, 1995.

Deakin, Frederick. *The Brutal Friendship.* London: Harper and Row, 1962.

De Antonellis, Giacomo. *Napoli sotto il regime.* Milan: Donati, 1972.

De Begnac, Yves. *Palazzo Venezia: Storia di un regime.* Rome: La Rocca, 1950.

De Céspedes, Alba. *Nessuno torna indietro.* Milan: Mondadori, 1938.

De Donato, Gigliola, and Vanna Gazzola. *I best-seller del ventennio: Il regime e il libro di massa.* Rome: Riuniti, 1991.

De Felice, Renzo. *Le interpretazioni del fascismo.* Bari: Laterza, 1983.

———. *Mussolini il Duce.* 2 vols. Turin: Einaudi, 1974–81.

———. *Mussolini il fascista.* 2 vols. Turin: Einaudi, 1966–68.

———. *Storia degli ebrei sotto il fascismo.* Turin: Einaudi, 1993.

De Grada, Raffaelle. *Il movimento di Corrente.* Milan: Edizioni di cultura popolare, 1952.

De Grand, Alexander. *Bottai e la cultura fascista.* Bari: Laterza, 1978.

———. "Cracks in the Facade: The Failure of Fascist Totalitarianism in Italy, 1935–39." *European History Quarterly* 4 (1991): 515–35.

———. *Fascist Italy and Nazi Germany: The "Fascist" Style of Rule.* New York: Routledge, 1995.

———. "Giuseppe Bottai e il fallimento del revisionismo." *Storia contemporanea* (December 1975): 697–731.

———. *Italian Fascism: Its Origins and Development.* Lincoln: University of Nebraska Press, 1982.

———. *The Italian Nationalist Association.* Lincoln: University of Nebraska Press, 1978.

de Grazia, Victoria. "The Arts of Purchase: How American Publicity Subverted the European Poster, 1920–40." In *Remaking History,* ed. Barbara Kruger and Phil Mariani, 221–57. Seattle: Bay Press, 1989.

———. *Culture of Consent.* Cambridge: Cambridge University Press, 1981.

———. *How Fascism Ruled Women: Italy, 1922–45.* Berkeley and Los Angeles: University of California Press, 1992.

———. "Mass Culture and Sovereignty: The American Challenge to European Cinemas, 1920–60." *Journal of Modern History* (March 1989): 53–87.

———. "Nationalizing Women: Competition between Fascist and Commercial Cultural Models in Mussolini's Italy." In *The Sex of Things,* ed. Victoria de Grazia, 337–58. Berkeley and Los Angeles: University of California Press, 1996.

Dei Sabelli, Luca. *Nazioni e minoranze etniche.* 2 vols. Bologna: Zanichelli, 1929.

Del Boca, Angelo. *Gli Italiani in Africa Orientale.* 4 vols. Bari: Laterza, 1976–84.

———, ed. *I gas di Mussolini: Il fascismo e la guerra d'Etiopia.* Rome: Riuniti, 1996.

Delzell, Charles. *Mussolini's Enemies: The Italian Anti-Fascist Resistance.* Princeton: Princeton University Press, 1961.

De Micheli, Mario. *Consenso, Fronda, Opposizione.* Milan: Cooperativa libreria universitaria del politecnico, 1977.

De Michelis, Cesare. *Alle origini del neorealismo.* Cosenza: Lerici, 1980.

De Sanctis, Francesco. *Storia della letteratura italiana (1870–71).* 2 vols. Turin: Einaudi, 1966.

Desideri, Giovanella. *Antologia della rivista "Corrente."* Naples: Guida, 1979.

Detragiache, Denise. "Il fascismo femminile da San Sepolcro all'affare Matteotti, 1919–24." *Storia contemporanea* (April 1983): 211–51.

Dickie, John. *Darkest Italy: The Nation and Stereotypes of the Mezzogiorno, 1860–1900.* New York: St. Martin's Press, 1999.

Diggins, John. *Mussolini and Fascism: The View from America.* Princeton: Princeton University Press, 1972.

Di Lauro, Raffaele. *Il governo delle genti di colore.* Milan: Fratelli Bocca, 1940.

Dombroski, Robert. "Brancati and Fascism: A Profile." *Italian Quarterly* (summer 1969): 41–63.

Domenico, Roy. *Italian Fascists on Trial, 1943–48.* Chapel Hill: University of North Carolina Press, 1991.

Donadoni, Eugenio. *Breve storia della letteratura italiana.* Milan: C. Signorelli, 1939.

Doordan, Dennis. *Building Modern Italy: Italian Architecture, 1914–36.* Princeton: Princeton University Press, 1988.

Dottorelli, Adriana. *Viaggio in America.* N.p.: L'Eroica, 1933.

Doumanis, Nicholas. *Myth and Memory in the Mediterranean: Remembering Fascism's Empire.* London: St. Martin's, 1997.

Dow, James, and Hannjost Lixfeld. *The Nazification of an Academic Discipline: Folklore and the Third Reich.* Bloomington: Indiana University Press, 1994.

Drieu la Rochelle, Pierre. *Le Jeune Européen.* Paris: Gallimard, 1927.

Editoria e cultura a Milano tra le due guerre (1920–40). Milan: Mondadori, 1983.

Eksteins, Modris. *The Rites of Spring: The Great War and the Birth of the Modern Age.* Boston: Houghton Mifflin, 1989.

Elkann, Alain. *Vita di Moravia.* Ed. G. B. Guerri. Milan: Bompiani, 1990.

Emanuelli, Enrico. *Racconti sovietici.* Rome: Ceschina, 1935.

———. *Radiografia di una notte.* Lanciano: Carabba, 1932.

———. *Storie crudele.* Lanciano: Carabba, 1934.

———. *Teatro personale.* Milan: Muggioni, 1945.

Etlin, Richard. *Modernism in Italian Architecture, 1890–1940.* Cambridge: Cambridge University Press, 1991.

Falasca-Zamponi, Simonetta. *Fascist Spectacle: The Aesthetics of Power in*

Mussolini's Italy. Berkeley and Los Angeles: University of California Press, 1997.

Falcetto, Bruno, *Storia della narrativa neorealista.* Milan: Mursia, 1992.

Falqui, Enrico. *La letteratura del ventennio nero.* Rome: La Bussola, 1948.

Farassino, Alberto. "Camerini, au-delà du cinéma italien." In *Mario Camerini,* ed. Alberto Farassino. Locarno: Edizioni Festival, 1992.

Fargion, Liliana Picciotto. "The Jews during the German Occupation and the Italian Social Republic." In *The Italian Refuge,* ed Ivo Herzer, 109–38. Washington, D.C.: Catholic University Press of America, 1990.

Farulli, Luca. "Alfredo Rocco: Politica e diritto fra guerra e fascismo." In *Tendenze della filosofia italiana nellíeta del fascismo,* ed. Ornella Faracovi, 241–62. Livorno: Belforte, 1985.

Faure, Christian. *Le project culturel de Vichy: Folklore et révolution nationale, 1940–44.* Lyon: Presses Universitaires de Lyon, 1989.

Faye, Jean-Pierre. *Théorie du recit: Introduction aux "langages totalitaires."* Paris: Hermann, 1972.

Fehrenbach, Heide. *Cinema in Democratizing Germany: Reconstructing National Identity after Hitler.* Chapel Hill: University of North Carolina Press, 1995.

Fernandez, Dominique. *Il mito dell'America negli intellettuali italiani.* Caltanisetta: Sciasica, 1969.

Ferrarotti, Marinella. *L'accademia d'Italia.* Naples: Liguori, 1977.

Finzi, Roberto. *L'università italiana e le leggi antiebraiche.* Rome: Riuniti, 1997.

Flora, Francesco. *Ritratto di un ventennio.* Naples: Gaetano Macchiaroli, 1944.

———. *Stampa dell'era fascista: Note di servizio.* Milan: Mondadori, 1945.

Flores, Marcello. "Il mito dell'Urss negli anni trenta." In *L'estetica della politica,* ed. Maurizio Vaudagna, 129–50. Rome: Laterza, 1989.

Folin, Alberto. *Le riviste giovanile del periodo fascista.* Treviso: Canova, 1977.

Folli, Anna. *Vent'anni di cultura ferrarese: Antologia del "Corriere padano."* 2 vols. Bologna: Patron, 1978.

Fontana, Sandro. *Il fascismo e le autonomie locali.* Bologna: Il Mulino, 1973.

Forgacs, David. *Italian Culture in the Industrial Era, 1880–1980.* Manchester: University of Manchester Press, 1990.

Foucault, Michel. *History of Sexuality.* Vol. 1: *An Introduction,* trans. Richard Hurley. New York: Pantheon, 1978.

———. *Power/Knowledge: Selected Interviews and Other Writings, 1972–77.* Ed. and trans. Colin Gordon. New York: Pantheon, 1980.

Fraddosio, Maria. "La donna e la guerra: Aspetti della militanza femminile nel fascismo–dalla mobilitazione civile alle origini del Saf nella Repubblica Sociale Italiana." *Storia contemporanea* (December 1989): 1105–81.

Frank, Helmut. "Avanguardia e moderno nella Germania nazista." In *L'Europa dei razionalisti,* ed. Luciano Caramel, 302–13. Milan: Electa, 1989.

Freddi, Luigi. *Il cinema.* 2 vols. Rome: L'Arnia, 1949.

Fritzsche, Peter. "Nazi Modern." *Modernism/Modernity* (January 1996): 1–21.

Frustaci, Enzo. *Un'episodio letterario dell'Italia fascista: "La Ruota."* Rome: Bulzoni, 1980.

Fuchs, Barry. "Walter Ruttmann, the Avant-Garde Film, and Nazi Modernism." *Film and History* (May 1984): 26–35.

Fuller, Maria Gubiena. *Colonial Constructions: Architecture, Cities, and Italian Colonialism.* London: Routledge, forthcoming.

Galison, Peter. "Aufbau/Bauhaus: Logical Positivism and Architectural Modernism." *Critical Inquiry* (summer 1990): 709–52.

Gallavotti, Eugenio. *La scuola fascista del giornalismo.* Milan: SugarCo, 1982.

Gallerano, Nicola. "Gli italiani in guerra, 1940–43: Appunti per una ricerca." In *L'Italia nella seconda guerra mondiale e nella resistenza,* ed. Francesca Ferratini Tosi et al., 307–24. Milan: Franco Angeli, 1988.

Galletti, Alfredo. *Storia letteraria d'Italia.* Milan: Franco Vallardi, 1935.

Gallian, Marcello. *Comando di tappa.* Rome: Cabala, 1934.

Galli della Loggia, Ernesto. *Morte della patria: La crisi dell'idea di nazione tra resistenza, antifascismo, e repubblica.* Rome: Laterza, 1996.

Galloux-Fournier, Bernadette. "Un Régard sur l'Amérique: Voyageurs français aux États-Unis, 1919–39." *Revue d'histoire moderne et contemporaine* (April-June 1990): 297–307.

Gallucci, Carole. "Alba De Céspedes' 'There's No Turning Back': Challenging the New Woman's Future." In *Mothers of Invention,* ed. Robin Pickering-Iazzi, 200–219. Minneapolis: University of Minnesota Press, 1995.

Gambetti, Fidia. *Il controveleno.* Osimo: n.p., 1942.

Garin, Eugenio. *Intellettuali italiani del XX secolo.* Rome: Riuniti, 1974.

———. "Gli italiani e la crisi d'Europa." *Terzo Programma* 3 (1962): 168–76.

Gassert, Philipp. *Amerika im Dritten Reich: Ideologie, Propaganda und Volksmeinung, 1933–45.* Stuttgart: F. Steiner, 1997.

Gellner, Ernst. *Nations and Nationalism.* Ithaca, N.Y.: Cornell University Press, 1983.

Gentile, Emilio. "Un'apocalisse della modernità: La grande guerra e il mito della rigenerazione della politica." *Storia contemporanea* (October 1995): 773–87.

———."The Conquest of Modernity: From Modernist Nationalism to Fascism." *Modernism/modernity* 1, no. 3 (1994): 55–87.

———. *Il culto del littorio: La sacralizzazione della politica nell'italia fascista.* Bari: Laterza, 1993.

———. "Impending Modernity: Fascism and the Ambivalent Image of the United States." *Journal of Contemporary History* 28 (1993): 7–29.

———. *Il mito dello nuovo Stato dall'antigiolittismo al fascismo.* Bari: Laterza, 1982.

———. "La nazione del fascismo: Alle origini del declino dello Stato nazionale." *Nazione e nazionalità in Italia,* ed. Giovanni Spadolini. Bari: Laterza, 1994.

———. *La via italiana al totalitarianismo: Il partito e lo Stato nel regime fascista.* Rome: La Nuova Italia, 1995.

—————. *Le origini dell'ideologia fascista.* Bari: Laterza, 1974.

Germani, Gino. "La socializzazione politica dei giovani nei regimi fascisti: Italia e Spagna." *Quaderni di sociologia* (January-June 1966): 11–58.

Ghirardo, Diane. *Building New Communities: New Deal America and Fascist Italy.* Princeton: Princeton University Press, 1989.

—————. "*Città fascista:* Surveillance and Spectacle." *Journal of Contemporary History* (April 1996): 347–72.

—————. "Italian Architects and Fascist Politics: An Evaluation of the Rationalists' Role in Regime Building." *Journal of the Society of Architectural Historians* (May 1980): 109–27.

Ghirelli, Antonio. "Il GUF di Largo Ferrandina." In *La Campania dal fascismo alla repubblica,* ed. Giovanna Percopo and Sergio Riccio, 7–19. Naples: Storia, 1977.

Gibson, Mary. "Biology or Environment? Race and Southern 'Deviancy' in the Writings of Italian Criminologists, 1880–1920." In *The Southern Question: Orientalism in One Country,* ed. Jane Schneider. New York: Berg, 1998.

Gili, Jean. *Le Cinéma italien à l'ombre des faisceaux.* Perpignan: Institut Jean Vigo, 1990.

—————. "Les horizons européens de Mario Camerini." In *Mario Camerini,* ed. Alberto Farassino, 47–54. Locarno: Edizioni Festival, 1992.

—————. *Stato fascista e cinematografia: Repressione e promozione.* Rome: Bulzoni, 1981.

Gilman, Sander. *Jewish Self-Hatred: Anti-Semitism and the Hidden Language of Jews.* Baltimore: Johns Hopkins University Press, 1986.

Giocondi, Michele. *Lettori in camicia nera: Narrativa di successo in Italia fascista.* Messina: G. D'Anna, 1978.

Giuntella, Cristina. "I gruppi universitari fascisti nel primo decennio del regime." *Movimento di liberazione in Italia* 107 (April-June 1972): 3–38.

Gli italiani sul fronte russo. Bari: De Donato, 1982.

Gobetti, Ada. *Diario partigiano.* Turin: Einaudi, 1996.

Goebbels, Joseph. *Die Tagebücher von Joseph Goebbels.* Ed. Elke Fröhlich. 14 vols. Munich: Saur, 1993–1998.

Golan, Romy. *Modernity and Nostalgia: Art and Politics in France between the Wars.* New Haven: Yale University Press, 1995.

Gori, Gianfranco. *Alessandro Blasetti.* Florence: La Nuova Italia, 1984.

Graff, Gerald. "Co-optation." In *The New Historicism,* ed. Aram Veeser, 168–81. New York: Routledge, 1989.

Gramsci, Antonio. *Passato e presente.* Rome: Einaudi, 1971.

—————. *Quaderni del carcere.* Ed. V. Gerratana. 4 vols. Turin: Einaudi, 1975.

Greco, Lorenzo. *Scrittura e censura.* Milan: Il Saggiatore, 1983.

Griffin, Roger. *The Nature of Fascism.* London: Routledge, 1993.

—————. "The Sacred Synthesis: The Ideological Cohesion of Fascist Cultural Policy." *Modern Italy* (May 1998): 3–24.

Grossmann, Atina. "*Girlkultur*, or Thoroughly Rationalized Female: A New Woman in Weimar Germany?" In *Women in Culture and Politics*, ed. Judith Friedlander et al., 62–80. Bloomington: Indiana University Press, 1986.

Groys, Boris. *The Total Art of Stalinism: Avant-Garde, Aesthetic Dictatorship, and Beyond*. Trans. Charles Rougle. Princeton: Princeton University Press, 1992.

Grussu, Silvino. "Modificazione delle funzioni intellettuali dal 1936 a oggi: Una analisi." *Critica marxista* 6 (1977): 37–72.

Guerri, Giordano Bruno. *Giuseppe Bottai: Un fascista critico*. Milan: Feltrinelli, 1977; reprint, Milan: Mondadori, 1996.

Gundle, Stephen. *The Italian Communists and the Challenge of Mass Culture, 1943–1991*. Durham: Duke University Press, forthcoming.

Gunzberg, Lynn. *Strangers at Home: Jews in the Italian Literary Imagination*. Berkeley and Los Angeles: University of California Press, 1992.

Hansen, Miriam. *Babel and Babylon: Spectatorship in American Silent Film*. Cambridge: Harvard University Press, 1991.

Haraszti, Miklos. *The Velvet Prison: Artists under State Socialism*. Trans. Katalin and Stephen Landesmann. New York: Basic Books, 1987.

Harrowitz, Nancy. *Antisemitism, Misogyny, and the Logic of Cultural Difference*. Lincoln: University of Nebraska Press, 1994.

Hay, James. *Popular Film Culture in Fascist Italy*. Bloomington: Indiana University Press, 1987.

Hellman, John. *Emmanuel Mounier and the New Catholic Left, 1930–50*. Toronto: University of Toronto Press, 1981.

Herf, Jeffrey. *Reactionary Modernism*. Cambridge: Cambridge University Press, 1984.

Herman, Arthur, Jr. "The Language of Fidelity in Early Modern France." *Journal of Modern History* 67 (March 1995): 1–24.

Hernand, Jost. "*Neue Sachlichkeit*": Ideology, Lifestyle, or Artistic Movement?" In *Dancing on the Volcano: Essays on the Culture of the Weimar Republic*, ed. Thomas W. Kniesche and Stephen Brockman, 57–68. Columbia, S.C.: Camden House, 1994.

Higson, Andrew. *Waving the Flag: Constructing a National Cinema in Britain*. Oxford: Oxford University Press, 1995.

Hoffman, Hilmar. *The Triumph of Propaganda: Film and National Socialism, 1933–45*. Providence: Berghahn, 1996.

Hohendahl, Peter Uwe. *Building a National Literature: The Case of Germany, 1830–70*. Ithaca, N.Y.: Cornell University Press, 1989.

———. *The Institution of Criticism*. Ithaca, N.Y.: Cornell University Press, 1982.

Horn, David. *Social Bodies: Science, Reproduction, and Italian Modernity*. Princeton: Princeton University Press, 1994.

Huyssen, Andreas. *After the Great Divide: Modernism, Mass Culture, Postmodernism*. Bloomington: University of Indiana Press, 1986.

Iaccio, Pasquale. "Il censore e il commediografo: Note sull'applicazione della revisione teatrale nel periodo fascista." *Storia contemporanea* (August 1994): 15–32.

―――. "La censura teatrale durante il fascismo." *Storia contemporanea* (August 1986): 567–614.

Imbriani, Angelo Michele. *Gli italiani e il Duce.* Naples: Liguori, 1992.

Ipsen, Carl. *Dictating Demography: The Problem of Population in Fascist Italy.* Cambridge: Cambridge University Press, 1996.

Iriye, Akira. *Cultural Internationalism and World Order.* Baltimore: Johns Hopkins University Press, 1997.

Iser, Wolfang. *The Act of Reading.* Baltimore: Johns Hopkins University Press, 1978.

Isnenghi, Mario. *Il mito della grande guerra da Marinetti a Malaparte.* Bari: Laterza, 1971.

Israel, Giorgio, and Piero Nastasi. *Scienza e razza nell'Italia fascista.* Bologna: Il Mulino, 1998.

Istituto Coloniale Fascista. *Corso di preparazione coloniale per la donna.* Naples: Istituto Coloniale Fascista, 1937.

Italia e Germania, maggio XVI. Rome: Agenzia Stefani, 1938.

Jacobelli, Jader, ed. *La communicazione politica in Italia.* Bari: Laterza, 1989.

James, Harold. *A German Identity, 1770–1990.* New York: Routledge, 1989.

Jardine, Alice. *Gynesis: Configurations of Woman and Modernity.* Ithaca, N.Y.: Cornell University, 1985.

Jaspers, Karl. *Die Geistige Situation der Zeit.* Berlin: William de Gruyter, 1931.

Jauss, Hans Robert. *Toward an Aesthetic of Reception.* Trans. Timothy Bahti. Minneapolis: University of Minnesota Press, 1982.

Judt, Tony. *Past Imperfect: French Intellectuals, 1944–56.* Berkeley and Los Angeles: University of California Press, 1992.

Jusdanis, Gregory. *Belated Modernity and Aesthetic Culture: Inventing National Literature.* Minneapolis: University of Minnesota Press, 1991.

Karp, Ivan, and Stephen D. Levin. *Exhibiting Cultures: The Politics and Poetics of Museum Display.* Washington, D.C.: Smithsonian Institute Press, 1991.

Kelikian, Alice. *Town and Country under Fascism: The Transformation of Brescia, 1915–26.* Oxford: Clarendon Press, 1986.

Kern, Stephen. *The Culture of Time and Space, 1880–1918.* Cambridge: Harvard University Press, 1983.

Kettering, Sharon, Russell J. Major, and Arlette Johnson. "Patronage, Language, and Political Culture." *French Historical Studies* (fall 1992): 839–81.

Kibler, Louis. "Alberto Moravia as Journalist: 1930–35." Supplement to *Forum Italicum* 5 (1993): 71–95.

Kinder, Marsha. *Blood Cinema: The Reconstruction of National Identity in Spain.* Berkeley and Los Angeles: University of California Press, 1993.

Klein, Gabriella. *La politica linguistica del fascismo.* Bologna: Il Mulino, 1986.

Klönne, Arno. *Jugend im Dritten Reich.* Dusseldorf: Diedrichs, 1982.

Knox, MacGregor. "Expansionist Zeal, Fighting Power, and Staying Power in the Italian and German Dictatorships." In *Fascist Italy and Nazi Germany:*

Comparisons and Contrasts, ed. Richard Bessel, 113–33. Cambridge: Cambridge University Press, 1996.

———. *Mussolini Unleashed: Politics and Strategy in Italy's Last War, 1939–1941*. Cambridge: Cambridge University Press, 1982.

Kohrerr, Richard. *Regresso delle nascite: Morte dei popoli*. Rome: Libreria del Littorio, 1928.

Koon, Tracy. *Believe, Obey, Fight: The Political Socialization of Youth in Italy, 1922–43*. Chapel Hill: University of North Carolina Press, 1985.

Kuisel, Richard. *Seducing the French: The Dilemma of Americanization*. Berkeley and Los Angeles: University of California Press, 1993.

Kunst und Diktatur: Architektur, Bildhauerei und Malerei in Österreich, Deutschland, Italien und der Sowjetunion, 1922–56. 2 vols. Baden: Verlag Grasl, 1994.

Kupferman, Fred. *Au pays des soviets: Le voyage français en Union Sovietique, 1917–39*. Paris: Gallimard, 1979.

Labanca, Nicola, ed. *L'Africa in Vetrina: Storie di musei e di esposizioni coloniali in Italia*. Treviso: Pagus, 1992.

Lacey, Kate. *Feminine Frequencies: Gender, German Radio, and the Public Sphere 1923–45*. Ann Arbor: University of Michigan Press, 1996.

Lajolo, Davide. *Conversazione in una stanza chiusa con Mario Soldati*. Milan: Frassinelli, 1983.

Lanaro, Silvio. *Nazione e lavoro: Saggio sulla cultura borghese in Italia, 1870–1925*. Venice: Marsilio, 1979.

Landy, Marcia. *Fascism in Film: The Italian Commercial Cinema, 1931–43*. Princeton: Princeton University Press, 1986.

Langella, Giuseppe. *Il secolo delle riviste*. Milan: Vita e pensiero, 1982.

Larebo, Haile M. *The Building of an Empire: Italian Land Policy and Practice in Ethiopia, 1935–41*. New York: Oxford University Press, 1994.

Lattuada, Alberto. *Occhio quadrato*. Milan: Edizioni Corrente, 1941.

Laura, Ernesto. "Il Centro Sperimentale di Cinematografia fra tradizione e riforma." *Bianco e nero* 5–6 (May-June 1976): 4–29.

———, ed. "Il mito di Budapest e i modelli ungheresi nel cinema italiano dal 1930 al 1945." In *Telefoni bianchi: Realtà e finzione nella società e nel cinema italiano degli anni quaranta*, ed. Laura and Gianfranco Casadei. Ravenna: Longo, 1991.

———. *Tutti i film di Venezia, 1932–84*. Venice: La Biennale, 1985.

Lazzari, Giovanni. "Linguaggio, ideologia, e politica culturale del fascismo." *Movimento operaio e socialista* (January-April 1984): 49–56.

Le Bon, Gustave. *The Crowd: A Study of the Popular Mind*. Trans. and ed. Robert Nye. 1895. Reprint, New Brunswick, N.J.: Transaction, 1995.

Lebovics, Herman. *True France: The Wars over Cultural Identity, 1900–1945*. Ithaca, N.Y.: Cornell University Press, 1992.

Ledeen, Michael. *L'internazionale fascista*. Bari: Laterza, 1973.

Leone de Castris, Arcangelo. *Egemonia e fascismo*. Bologna: Il Mulino, 1981.

Leprohon, Pierre. *The Italian Cinema.* Trans. Roger Greaves and Oliver Stally-brass. New York: Praeger, 1972.

Lethen, Helmut. *Neue Sachlichkeit, 1924–32.* Stuttgart: Metzler, 1975.

Levi, Primo. *Il sistema periodico.* Turin: Einaudi, 1975.

Levy, Carl, ed. *Italian Regionalism: History, Identity, and Politics.* New York: Berg, 1996.

Leyda, Jay. *Kino: A History of Russian and Soviet Film.* New York: Collier's, 1973.

Liehm, Mira. *Passion and Defiance: Italian Film from 1942 to the Present.* Berkeley and Los Angeles: University of California Press, 1984.

Liu, Lydia. *Translingual Practice: Literature, National Culture, and Translated Modernity — China, 1900–1937.* Stanford: Stanford University Press, 1995.

Lo Gatto, Ettore. *Dall'epica alla cronaca nella Russia soviettista.* Rome: Istituto per l'Europa Orientale, 1929.

———. *Letteratura soviettista.* Rome: Istituto per l'Europa Orientale, 1928.

———. *URSS 1931: Vita quotidiana-piano quinquennale.* Rome: Anonima romana editoriale, 1932.

Lombardi, Olga. *La narrative italiana nelle crisi del novecento.* Caltanisetta: Sciascia, 1971.

Lombardi-Diop, Cristina. "Writing the Female Frontier: Italian Women in Africa, 1890–1940." Ph.D. diss., New York University, 1999.

Lombardo-Radice, Lucio. "L'università di Roma tra il '35 e il '40." *Incontri oggi* (April 1955): 17–21.

Longhitano, Rino. *La Russia di fronte all'Europa.* Catania: Edizioni Rinnovamento, 1933.

Loubet del Bayle, Jean-Louis. *Les Non-conformistes des années trente.* Paris: Éditions du Seuil, 1969.

Löwith, Karl. *My Life in Germany before and after 1933.* Chicago: University of Illinois Press, 1994.

Ludwig, Emil. *Colloqui con Mussolini.* Milan: Mondadori, 1932.

Luti, Giorgio. *La letteratura del ventennio fascista: Cronache letterarie tra le due guerre, 1920–40.* Florence: La Nuova Italia, 1972.

Luzi, Alfredo, ed. *Corrente di Vita giovanile.* Rome: Edizioni dell'Ateneo, 1975.

Lyttleton, Adrian. *The Seizure of Power: Fascism in Italy, 1919–29.* London: Weidenfeld and Nicolson, 1973.

Mack Smith, Denis. *Mussolini.* New York: Vintage, 1982.

Mafai, Miriam. *Pane nero.* Milan: Mondadori, 1988.

Magnani, Valdo, and Aldo Cucchi. *Crisi di una generazione.* Florence: La Nuova Italia, 1952.

Maier, Charles. *Recasting Bourgeois Europe.* Princeton: Princeton University Press, 1975.

Malvano, Laura. *Fascismo e politica dell'immagine.* Turin: Boringhieri, 1988.

———. "Il mito della giovinezza attraverso l'immagine: Il fascismo italiano."

In *Storia dei giovani: L'età contemporanea,* ed. Giovanni Levi and Jean-Claude Schmitt, 311–48. Rome: Laterza, 1994.

Manacorda, Giuliano. *Letteratura e cultura del periodo fascista.* Milan: Principato, 1974.

———. *Storia della letteratura italiana tra le due guerre, 1919–43.* Rome: Riuniti, 1980.

Mancini, Elaine. *The Free Years of the Fascist Film Industry, 1930–35.* Ann Arbor: UMI, 1985.

Mangoni, Luisa. *L'interventismo della cultura: Intellettuali e riviste del fascismo.* Bari: Laterza, 1974.

Mannheim, Karl. *Ideology and Utopia.* New York: Harcourt, Brace, 1936.

Marchesini, Daniele. *La scuola dei gerarchi.* Milan: Feltrinelli, 1980.

Marcus, Millicent. *Filmmaking by the Book: Italian Cinema and Literary Adaptation.* Baltimore: Johns Hopkins University Press, 1993.

Mariani, Riccardo. *Fascismo e "città nuove."* Milan: Feltrinelli, 1976.

Marino, Giuseppe Carlo. *L'autarchia della cultura: Intellettuali e fascismo negli anni trenta.* Rome: Riuniti, 1983.

Martinelli, Vittorio. "I *Gastarbeiter* tra le due guerre." *Bianco e nero* (May-June 1978).

Masino, Paola. *Nascita e morte della massaia.* 1945. Reprint, Milan: Bompiani, 1982.

Mason, Tim. "Italy and Modernization: A Montage." *History Workshop* (spring 1983): 127–47.

Maulnier, Thierry. *La Crise est dans l'homme.* Paris: Librairie de la Revue Française, 1932.

Mauro, Walter. *Invito alla lettura di Alvaro.* Milan: Mursia, 1973.

Maxence, Jean-Paul. *Histoire de dix ans, 1927–37.* Paris: Gallimard, 1939.

McClintock, Anne. *Imperial Leather: Race, Gender, and Sexuality in Colonial Conquest.* New York: Routledge, 1995.

Mercuri, Lamberto. *L'epurazione in Italia, 1943–48.* Cuneo: L'Arciere, 1988.

Miccichè, Lino. "Cinema italiano sotto il fascismo: Elementi per un ripensamento possibile." In *Modelli culturali e Stato sociale negli anni trenta,* ed. Carlo Vallauri and Giuseppina Grassiccia. Florence: Le Monnier, 1988.

———. *Visconti e il neorealismo.* Venice: Marsilio, 1990.

Miccoli, G. "Santa Sede e Chiesa italiana di fronte alle legge antiebraiche del 1938." In *La legislazione antiebraica in Europa: Atti del convegno nel cinquantenario delle leggi razziali,* 163–274. Rome: Camera dei Deputati, 1989.

Michaelis, Meir. "The Current Debate over Fascist Racial Policy." In *Fascist Antisemitism and the Italian Jews,* ed. Robert Wistrich and Sergio Della Pergola, 48–96. Jerusalem: Vidal Sassoon International Center for the Study of Antisemitism, 1995.

———. "Fascist Policy toward the Italian Jews: Tolerance and Persecution." In *The Italian Refuge: The Rescue of Jews during the Holocaust,* ed. Ivo Herzer. Washington, D.C.: Catholic University of America Press, 1989.

————. *Mussolini and the Jews: German-Italian Relations and the Jewish Question in Italy, 1922–45.* Oxford: Clarendon Press, 1978.

————. "Mussolini's Unofficial Spokesman: Telesio Interlandi." *Journal of Modern Italian Studies* (fall 1998): 217–40.

Michaud, Guy, ed. *Identités collectives et relations inter-culturelles.* Brussels: Éditions Complex, 1978.

Mida, Massimo, and Lorenzo Quaglietti. *Dai telefoni bianchi al neorealismo.* Bari: Laterza, 1980.

Mira, Giovanni, and Luigi Salvatorelli. *Storia d'Italia nel periodo fascista.* 2 vols. Turin: Einaudi, 1970.

Misler, Nicoletta. *La via italiana al realismo: La politica culturale artistica del PCI dal 1944 al 1956.* Milan: Mazzotta, 1973.

Moe, Nelson. " 'Altro che Italia!' Il Sud dei piemontesi (1860–61)." *Meridiana* 15 (1992): 53–89.

Monteleone, Franco. *La radio italiana nel periodo fascista.* Venice: Marsilio, 1976.

Moravia, Alberto. *Alberto Moravia–Giuseppe Prezzolini: Lettere.* Milan: Rusconi, 1982.

————. *Gli indifferenti.* 1929. Reprint, Milan: Bompiani, 1993.

————. *La mascherata.* 1941. Reprint, Milan: Bompiani, 1997.

————. *L'uomo come fine e altri saggi.* Milan: Bompiani, 1963.

————. *Viaggi: Articoli, 1930–1990.* Ed. Enzo Siciliano. Milan: Bompiani, 1994.

Morgan, Philip. *Italian Fascism, 1919–45.* New York: St. Martin's Press, 1995.

————. "The Italian Fascist New Order in Europe." In *Making the New Europe,* ed. M. L. Smith and Peter Stirk. London: Pinter, 1990.

Mosca, Rodolfo. *Verso il secondo piano quinquennale.* Milan: Agnelli, 1932.

Mosse, George. "L'autorappresentazione nazionale negli anni trenta negli Stati Uniti e Europa." In *L'estetica della politica,* ed. Maurizio Vaudagna, 3–24. Rome: Laterza, 1989.

————. *Masses and Man: Nationalist and Fascist Perceptions of Reality.* New York: Transaction Books, 1980.

————. *Nationalism and Sexuality: Respectability and Abnormality in Modern Europe.* New York: Howard Fertig, 1985.

Mounier-Leclerq, Paulette, ed. *Mounier et sa génération.* Paris: Éditions du Seuil, 1956.

Murialdi, Paolo. *La stampa del regime fascista.* Bari: Laterza, 1986.

Mussolini, Benito. *Opera Omnia.* Ed. Edoardo and Duilio Susmel. 35 vols. Florence: La Fenice, 1951–63.

————. *Scritti e discorsi.* Ed. Valentino Piccoli. Vols. 1–9. Milan: Hoepli, 1934–35.

Mutterle, Anco Marzio. *Emanuelli.* Florence: La Nuova Italia, 1968.

Nacci, Michela. *L'anti-americanismo in Italia negli anni trenta.* Turin: Boringhieri, 1989.

————. "La crisi della civiltà: Fascismo e cultura europea." In *Tendenze della* filosofia italiana nell'età di fascismo, ed. Ornella Faracovi, 41–72. Livorno: Belforte, 1985.

―――. "I rivoluzionari dell'apocalisse: Società e politica nella cultura francese fra le due guerre." Intersezioni (April 1984): 85–123.

―――. Tecnica e cultura della crisi, 1914–39. Turin: Loescher, 1982.

Natta, Alessandro. "Una scuola di antifascismo." Incontri oggi (February 1955): 11–16.

Nello, Paolo. L'avanguardismo giovanile alle origini del fascismo. Bari: Laterza, 1978.

―――. "Mussolini e Bottai: Due modi diversi di concepire l'educazione fascista della gioventù." Storia contemporanea 2 (June 1977): 335–66.

Nerenberg, Ellen. " 'Donna proprio . . . proprio donna': The Social Construction of Femininity in Nessuno torna indietro." Romance Languages Annual 3 (1991): 267–73.

Neue Sachlichkeit and German Realism of the 1920s. London: Arts Council, 1979.

Nicolodi, Fiamma. Musica e musicisti nel ventennio fascista. Firenze: Nuova Italia, 1984.

―――. "Su alcuni aspetti dei festivals tra le due guerre." In Musica italiana del primo novecento, 161–66. Florence: L. S. Olschki, 1981.

Nolan, Mary. Visions of Modernity: American Business and the Modernization of Germany. New York: Oxford University Press, 1994.

Nuovi materali sul cinema italiano, 1929–43. Ancona: Mostra del nuova cinema, 1976.

Nye, Robert. The Origins of Crowd Psychology: Gustave Le Bon and the Crisis of Mass Democracy in the Third Republic. London: Sage, 1975.

Onofri, Nazario. I giornali bolognesi nel ventennio fascista. Bologna: Moderna, 1972.

Opera Nazionale Dopolavoro. Costumi, musica, danze e feste popolari italiane. Rome: Edizioni O.N.D., 1935.

―――. I primi cinque anni. Rome: Novissima, 1930.

Orestano, Francesco. "Adunanza inaugurale." In Convegno di scienze morali e storiche: L'Africa. Rome: Reale Accademia d'Italia, 1939.

Ortega y Gasset, José. The Revolt of the Masses. 1930. Reprint, Madrid: Revista de Occidente, 1964.

Ostenc, Michel. "Les étudiants fascistes italiens des années trente." Le mouvement social 120 (July-September 1982): 95–106.

―――. Intellectuels italiens et fascisme, 1915–29. Paris: Payot, 1983.

―――. La scuola italiana durante il fascismo. Bari: Laterza, 1981.

Ottolenghi, Gustavo. Gli italiani e il colonialismo: I campi di detenzione italiani in Africa. Milan: SugarCo, 1997.

Paccagnella, Ivano. "Stampa di fronda: Il Bò tra GUF e Curiel." In La lingua italiana e il fascismo, 83–100. Bologna: Consorzio provinciale pubblica lettura, 1977.

Pagano, Giuseppe. Architettura rurale italiana. Milan: Hoepli, 1936.

————. *Arte decorativa italiana.* Milan: Hoepli, 1938.

Palermo, Antonio. "Gli anni trenta: Per una nuova periodizzazione della storiografia letteraria." In *La cultura italiana negli anni, 1930–45,* 159–70. Naples: Edizioni scientifiche italiane, 1984.

————. *Solitudine del moralista.* Naples: Liguori, 1986.

Palla, Marco. *Fascismo e Stato corporativo: Un'inchiesta della diplomazia brittanica.* Milan: Franco Angeli, 1991.

Palmeri, Renato, et al., eds. *La generazione degli anni difficili.* Bari: Laterza, 1962.

Pankhurst, Richard. "Lo sviluppo del razzismo nell'impero coloniale italiano, 1935–41." *Studi piacentini* 3 (1988): 175–95.

Pansera, Anty. "Le Triennali del regime: Un occhio aperto sull'oltralpe." In *Annitrenta: Arte e cultura in Italia,* 311–23. Milan: Mazzotta, 1983.

Papa, Emilio. *Storia dei due manifesti.* Milan: Feltrinelli, 1958.

Paresce, Renato. *L'Altra America.* Rome: Quadrante, 1935.

Paris, Renzo. *Moravia: Una vita controvoglia.* Florence: Giunti, 1996.

Partito Nazionale Fascista. *Il cittadino soldato.* Rome: Libreria dello Stato, 1935.

————. *La cultura fascista.* Rome: Libreria dello Stato, 1936.

————. *Dizionario di politica.* 5 vols. Rome: Istituto dell'Enciclopedia Italiana, 1940.

————. *I gruppi dei fascist universitari.* Rome: Centro studenti stranieri dei GUF, 1941.

Passerini Luisa. *Fascism in Popular Memory.* Trans. Robert Lumley and Jude Bloomfield. Cambridge: Cambridge University Press, 1987.

————. *Mussolini immaginario.* Rome: Laterza, 1991.

Paucker, Henri R., ed. *Neue Sachlichkeit im "Dritten Reich" und im Exil.* Stuttgart: Reclam, 1974.

Pavese, Cesare. *La letteratura americana e altri saggi.* Turin: Einaudi, 1962.

————. *Il mestiere di vivere, 1935–50.* Ed. Marziano Guglielminetti and Laura Nay. Turin: Einaudi, 1990.

Pavone, Claudio. *Una guerra civile: Saggio sulla moralità della Resistenza.* Turin: Boringhieri, 1991.

Pende, Nicola. *Bonifica umana razionale e biologia politica.* Bologna: Cappelli, 1933.

Petersen, Jens. "Vorspiel zu 'Stahlpakt' und Kriegsallianz: Das deutsche italienische Kulturabkommen vom 23. November 1938." *Vierteljahreshefte für Zeitgeschichte* 36 (1989): 41–77.

Petropoulos, Jonathan. *Art as Politics in the Third Reich.* Chapel Hill: University of North Carolina Press, 1996.

Peukert, Detlev. *Inside Nazi Germany: Conformism, Opposition, and Racism in Everyday Life.* New Haven: Yale University Press, 1987.

Piacentini, Marcello. *Architettura d'oggi.* Rome: Cremonese, 1930.

Pick, Daniel. *Faces of Degeneration: A European Disorder, c. 1848–c. 1918.* Cambridge: Cambridge University Press, 1989.

Pickering-Iazzi, Robin. *Politics of the Visible: Writing Women, Culture, and Fascism*. Minneapolis: University of Minnesota, 1997.

————, ed. *Mothers of Invention: Women, Italian Fascism, and Culture*. Minneapolis: University of Minnesota Press, 1995.

Pinkus, Karen. *Bodily Regimes: Advertising under Italian Fascism*. Minneapolis: University of Minnesota, 1995.

Pintor, Giame. *Il sangue d'Europa, 1939–43*. Turin: Einaudi, 1950.

Poggiali, Ciro. *Diario A.O.I. 15 giugno 1936–4 ottobre 1937*. Milan: Longanesi, 1971.

Poggiani, Euno. *Viaggio nel Far West*. Cremona: Cremona Nuova, 1936.

Pogliano, Claudio. "Scienza e stirpe: Eugenica in Italia, 1912–39." *Passato e presente* (January-June 1984): 61–97.

Pomba, G. L., ed. *La civiltà fascista illustrata nelle dottrine e nelle opere*. Turin: Unione tipografica editrice torinese, 1928.

Poulaille, Henri. *Nouvel âge littéraire*. Paris: Valois, 1930.

Preti, Luigi. *Impero fascista, africani ed ebrei*. Milan: Mursia, 1968.

Prolo, Maria Adriana. *Storia del cinema muto italiano*. Milan: Mondadori, 1951.

Prudenzi, Angela. *Raffaello Matarazzo*. Florence: La Nuova Italia, 1991.

Pugliese, Stanislao. *Carlo Rosselli: Socialist Heretic and Anti-Fascist Exile*. Cambridge: Harvard University Press, 2000.

Quaglietti, Lorenzo. "Cinema americano, vecchio amore." In *Schermi di guerra: Cinema italiano, 1939–45*, ed. Mino Argentieri, 307–27. Rome: Riuniti, 1995.

————. *Storia economica-politica del cinema italiano, 1945–80*. Rome: Bulzoni, 1980.

Rabinbach, Anson G. "The Aesthetics of Production in the Third Reich." *Journal of Contemporary History* (October 1976): 43–74.

————. *In the Shadow of Catastrophe: German Intellectuals between Apocalypse and Enlightenment*. Berkeley and Los Angeles: University of California Press, 1997.

Raffaelli, Sergio. *Le parole proibite: Purismo di Stato e regolamentazione della pubblicità in Italia, 1812–1945*. Bologna: Il Mulino, 1983.

Rava, Carlo Enrico. *Nove anni di architettura vissuta*. Rome: Cremonese, 1935.

Re, Lucia. "Fascist Theories of 'Woman' and the Construction of Gender." In *Mothers of Invention*, ed. Robin Pickering-Iazzi, 76–99. Minneapolis: University of Minnesota Press, 1995.

Les réalismes entre révolution et réaction, 1919–39. Paris: Centre Georges Pompidou, 1981.

Redi, Riccardo. *La Cines: Storia di una casa di produzione italiana*. Rome: CNC Edizioni, 1991.

————, ed. *Cinema italiano sotto il fascismo*. Venice: Marsilio, 1979.

Reese, Dagmar. "The BDM Generation: A Female Generation in Transition from Dictatorship to Democracy." In *Generations in Conflict*, ed. Mark Roseman, 227–46. Cambridge: Cambridge University Press, 1995.

Reichl, Edward. "Literarischer Text und Politischer Kontext: Faschismuskritik in Narrativer Form: Moravias *Gli indifferenti.*" *Romanistische Zeitschrift für Literaturgeschichte* 1 (1980): 65–81.

Reichl, Peter. *Der Schöne Schein des Dritten Reiches.* Munich: Carl Hanser Verlag, 1993.

Rentschler, Eric. *The Ministry of Illusion: Nazi Cinema and Its Afterlife.* Cambridge: Harvard University Press, 1996.

Ricci, Berto. *Errori del nazionalismo italico.* Florence: Edizioni fiorentine, 1931.

———. *Lo scrittore italiano.* 1931. Reprint, Rome: Ciarapico, 1984.

Rinaldi, Simona. "I cinegiornali LUCE e la 'non-belligeranza.'" In *Schermi di guerra: Cinema italiano, 1939–45,* ed. Mino Argentieri, 19–134. Rome: Riuniti, 1995.

Roberts, David. *The Syndicalist Tradition and Italian Fascism.* Chapel Hill: University of North Carolina Press, 1979.

Roberts, Mary Louise. *Civilization without Sexes: Reconstructing Gender in France, 1917–1927.* Chicago: University of Chicago Press, 1994.

Robin, Régine. *Le réalisme socialiste: Une esthétique impossible.* Paris: Payot, 1986.

Rocco, Alfredo. *Scritti e discorsi politici.* 3 vols. Milan: Giuffre, 1938.

Rochat, Giorgio. *Guerre italiane in Libia e in Etiopia.* Treviso: Pagus, 1991.

Rodondi, Raffaella. *Il presente vince sempre.* Palermo: Sellerio, 1985.

Romani, Roberto. "Il piano quinquennale sovietico nel dibattito corporativo italiano, 1928–36." *Italia contemporanea* 155 (June 1984): 27–41.

Romier, Lucien. *Qui sera le maître, Europe ou Amérique?* Paris: Hachette, 1927.

Rondolino, Gianni. "Italian Propaganda Films, 1940–43." In *Film and Radio Propaganda in World War Two,* ed. K. R. M. Short, 220–29. Knoxville: University of Tennessee Press, 1983.

Rosai, Ottone. *Dentro la guerra.* Rome: Quaderni di Novissima, 1934.

Roseman, Mark, ed. *Generations in Conflict: Youth Revolt and Generation Formation in Germany, 1770–1968,* Cambridge: Cambridge University Press, 1995.

Rosen, Philip. "History, Textuality, Nation: Kracauer, Burch, and Some Problems in the Study of National Cinemas." *Iris* 2 (1984): 69–84.

Rosengarten, Frank. *The Italian Antifascist Press, 1919–45.* Cleveland: Case Western Reserve Press, 1968.

Rosselli, Aldo. *La famiglia Rosselli: Una tragedia italiana.* Milan: Bompiani, 1983.

Rusconi, Gian Enrico. *Resistenza e postfascismo.* Bologna: Il Mulino, 1995.

Sachs, Harvey. *Music in Fascist Italy.* New York: W. W. Norton, 1987.

Sáez, Marín. *El Frente de Juventudes: Politica de juventud en la España de la postguerra (1937–1960).* Madrid: Siglo veintuno de España, 1988.

Salvi, Sergio. *Le lingue tagliate.* Milan: Rizzoli, 1975.

Santarelli, Enzo. *Storia del movimento e del regime fascista.* 3 vols. Rome: Riuniti, 1967.

Santomassimo, Gianpasquale. "Aspetti della politica culturale del fascismo: Il dibattito sul corporativismo e l'economia politica." *Italia contemporanea* 121 (October-December 1975): 3–26.

Saraceno, Chiara. "Redefining Maternity and Paternity: Gender, Pronatalism, and Social Policies in Fascist Italy." In *Maternity and Gender Policies: Women and the Rise of the European Welfare States, 1880s–1950s*, ed. Gisela Bock and Pat Thane, 196–212. New York: Routledge 1991.

Sarfatti, Margherita. *America, ricerca della felicità*. Milan: Mondadori, 1937.

Sarfatti, Michele. *Mussolini contro gli ebrei*. Turin: Silvio Ramorani, 1994.

Sarti, Roland. *Fascism and the Industrial Leadership in Italy*. Berkeley and Los Angeles: University of California Press, 1971.

Savio, Francesco. *Cinecittà anni trenta*. 3 vols. Rome: Bulzoni, 1979.

———. *Ma l'amore no*. Milan: Sonzogno, 1975.

Sbacchi, Alberto. *La colonizzazione italiana in Etiopia, 1936–40*. Milan: Mursia, 1983.

Scaramuzza, Emma. "Professioni intellettuali e fascismo: L'ambivalenza dell'Alleanza muliebre culturale italiana." *Italia contemporanea* (September 1983), 111–33.

Schnapp, Jeffrey. "Between Fascism and Democracy: Gaetano Ciocca—Builder, Inventor, Farmer, Engineer." *Modernism/modernity* (September 1995): 117–58.

———. "Epic Demonstrations: Fascist Modernity and the 1932 Exhibition of the Fascist Revolution." In *Fascism, Aesthetics, and Culture*, ed. Richard Golsan, 1–37. Hanover, N.H.: University Press of New England, 1992.

———. *Staging Fascism: 18BL and the Theater of Masses for Masses*. Stanford: Stanford University Press, 1996.

Schnapp, Jeffrey, and Barbara Spackman. "Selections from the Great Debate on Fascism and Culture: *Critica Fascista*, 1926–27." In *Fascism and Culture*, special issue of *Stanford Italian Review* 8, nos. 1–2 (1990): 235–72.

Schreiber, Gerhard. *I militari italiani internati nei campi di concentramento del Terzo Reich, 1943–45*. Rome: Stato maggiore dell'esercito, Ufficio storico, 1992.

Schulte-Sasse, Linda. *Entertaining the Third Reich*. Durham: Duke University Press, 1996.

Sechi, Mario. "Ideologia urbana tra 'crisi' e sviluppo: La generazione del 'Verri.'" *Lavoro critico* (January-March 1975): 61–89.

———. *Il mito della nuova cultura: Giovani, realismo e politica negli anni trenta*. Manduria: Lacaita, 1984.

Segrè, Claudio. *Fourth Shore: The Italian Colonization of Libya*. Chicago: University of Chicago Press, 1974.

Siciliano, Enzo. "Due amici: Moravia e Chiaromonte." *Nuovi Argomenti* (April-June 1996).

Sighele, Scipio. *L'intelligenza della folla*. Turin: Fratelli Bocca, 1903.

———. *Il nazionalismo e i partiti politici*. Milan: Treves, 1911.

Slaughter, Jane. *Women and the Italian Resistance, 1943–45.* Denver, Colo.: Arden Press, 1997.

Sluga, Glenda. "Italian National Memory, National Identity, and Fascism." In *Italian Fascism: History, Memory, and Representation,* ed. Richard Bosworth and Patrizia Dogliani, 178–94. New York: St. Martin's Press, 1999.

Smith, Anthony D. *The Ethic Origins of Nations.* Oxford: Blackwell, 1986.

——. *National Identity.* Reno: University of Nevada Press, 1991.

Soldati, Mario. *America primo amore.* Florence: Bemporad, 1935.

Spackman, Barbara. *Fascist Virilities: Rhetoric, Ideology, and Social Fantasy in Italy.* Minneapolis: University of Minnesota Press, 1996.

Spengler, Oswald. *Der Mensch und die Technik.* Munich: Beck, 1931.

Spinetti, Gastone. *Difesa di una generazione.* Rome: Edizione Polilibreria, 1948.

Spriano, Paolo. *Storia del Partito Comunista Italiano.* 8 vols. Turin: Einaudi, 1990.

Steinberg, Jonathan. *All or Nothing: The Axis and the Holocaust, 1941–43.* London: Routledge, 1990.

Sternhell, Zeev. *Neither Right nor Left: Fascist Ideology in France.* Berkeley and Los Angeles: University of California Press, 1986.

Sternhell, Zeev, with Mario Szrajder and Maia Asheri. *The Birth of Fascist Ideology: From Cultural Rebellion to Political Revolution.* Princeton: Princeton University Press, 1994.

Stille, Alexander. *Benevolence and Betrayal.* New York: Summit Books, 1991.

Stirk, Peter. "Introduction: Crisis and Continuity in Interwar Europe." In *European Unity in Context,* ed. Peter Stirk, 1–23. London: Pinter, 1989.

Stites, Richard. *Revolutionary Dreams: Utopian Vision and Experimental Life in the Russian Revolution.* New York: Oxford University Press, 1989.

Stoler, Laura Ann. *Race and the Education of Desire.* Durham: Duke University Press, 1995.

——. "Rethinking Colonial Categories: European Communities and the Boundaries of Rule." In *Colonialism and Culture,* ed. Nicholas B. Dirks, 319–52. Ann Arbor: University of Michigan Press, 1992.

Stone, Marla Susan. *The Patron State: Culture and Politics in Fascist Italy.* Princeton: Princeton University Press, 1998.

Struve, Gleb. *Russian Literature under Lenin and Stalin.* Norman: University of Oklahoma Press, 1971.

Sulis, Edgardo, ed. *Nuova civiltà per la nuova Europa.* Rome: Edizioni Roma, 1942.

Suvich, Fulvio. "Le spedizioni scientifiche italiane in Africa Orientale e in Libia durante il periodo fascista." In *Le guerre coloniali del fascismo,* ed. Angelo Del Boca, 443–68. Bari: Laterza, 1991.

Talvacchia, Bette. "Politics Considered as a Category of Culture: The Anti-Fascist *Corrente* Group." *Art History* 8, no. 3 (September 1985): 336–55.

Tecchi, Bonaventura. *Scrittori tedeschi del novecento.* Florence: Garzanti, 1941.

Theweleit, Klaus. *Male Fantasies.* 2 vols. Minneapolis: University of Minnesota, 1987 and 1989.

Thongchai, Winichakul. *Siam Mapped: A History of the Geo-Body of the Nation.* Honolulu: University of Hawaii Press, 1994.

Titta Rosa, Giovanni. *Invito al romanzo.* Milan: Crippa, 1930.

Toscano, Mario. "Gli ebrei in Italia dall'emancipazione alle persecuzioni." *Storia contemporanea* (October 1986): 905–54.

Traniello, Francesco. "La storiografia italiana del dopoguerra e il concetto di nazione." In *Nazione Etnia Cittadinanza,* ed. Gian Enrico Rusconi, 37–48. Brescia: La Scuola, 1993.

Treccani, Ernesto. *L'arte per amore.* Milan: Feltrinelli, 1978.

Turi, Gabriele. *Il fascismo e il consenso degli intellettuali.* Bologna: Il Mulino, 1980.

———. "Ruolo e destino degli intellettuali nella politica razziale del fascismo." In *La legislazione antiebracia in Italia e in Europa,* 95–121. Rome: Camera dei Deputati, 1989.

Vaudagna, Maurizio. *New Deal e corporativismo: Integrazione e conflitto sociale negli Stati Uniti, 1933–41.* Turin: Rosenberg and Sellier, 1981.

Vaydat, Pierre. "Neue Sachlichkeit als ethische Haltung." In *Die "Neue Sachlichkeit": Lebensgefühl oder Markenzeichen?* special issue of *Germanica* 9 (1991): 37–54.

Vené, Gianfranco. *Pirandello fascista.* Milan: SugarCo, 1977.

Veneruso, Danilo. *Gentile e il primato della tradizione culturale italiana.* Rome: Studium, 1984.

Vento, Luigi. *La personalità e l'opera di Corrado Alvaro.* Chiaravalle Centrale: Frama Sud, 1979.

Verdone, Luca. *I film di Alessandro Blasetti.* Rome: Gremese, 1989.

Vigorelli, Amedeo. *L'esistenzialismo positivo di Enzo Paci.* Rome: Franco Angeli, 1992.

Vittoria, Albertina. "Gentile e gli istituti culturali." In *Tendenze della filosofia italiana nell'eta del fascismo,* ed. Ornella Pompeo Faracovi, 115–44. Livorno: Belfore, 1985.

———. *Le riviste del Duce: Politica e cultura del regime.* Milan: Guanda, 1983.

———. "Totalitarianismo e intellettuali: L'Istituto Nazionale Fascista di Cultura dal 1925 al 1937." *Studi storici* (October-December 1982): 897–918.

Vittoria, Albertina, and Michela Nacci. "Convegno italo-francese di studi corporativi, Roma, 20-24 maggio 1935." *Dimensioni,* nos. 40–41 (1986): 30–119.

Vittorini, Elio. *Conversazione in Sicilia.* Milan: Bompiani, 1941.

———. *Il garofano rosso.* Milan: Mondadori, 1948.

———. *Letteratura arte società.* Ed. Raffaella Rodondi. Turin: Einaudi, 1997.

———. *Lettere, 1933–43.* Ed. Carlo Minoia. Turin: Einaudi, 1985.

Vivere il cinema: Cinquant'anni del Centro Sperimentale di Cinematografia. Rome: CSC, 1985.

Voigt, Klaus. "Jewish Refugees and Immigrants in Italy, 1933 – 45." In *The Italian Refuge,* ed. Ivo Herzer, 141–58. Washington, D.C.: Catholic University Press of America, 1990.

Von Hallberg, Robert, ed. *Literary Intellectuals and the Dissolution of the State: Professionalism and Conformity in the GDR.* Chicago: University of Chicago Press, 1996.

von Plato, Alexander. "The Hitler Youth Generation and Its Role in the Two Post-War Germanies." In *Generations in Conflict,* ed. Mark Roseman. Cambridge: Cambridge University Press, 1995.

Voza, Pasquale. "Il problema del realismo negli anni trenta: 'Il Saggiatore,' e 'Il Cantiere.'" *Lavoro critico* (January-June 1981): 65–105.

Wanrooj, Bruno. "The Rise and Fall of Italian Fascism as a Generational Revolt." *Journal of Contemporary History* 22 (1987): 401–18.

Ward, David. *Antifascisms: Cultural Politics in Italy, 1943 – 46.* Madison, N.J.: Farleigh Dickinson, 1996.

Weisgerber, Jean, ed. *Le Réalisme magique: Roman, peinture, et cinéma.* Lausanne: L'Age d'homme, 1987.

Wilkinson, James. *The Intellectual Resistance in Europe.* Cambridge: Harvard University Press, 1981.

Willett, John. *Art and Politics of the Weimar Period.* New York: Pantheon, 1978.

Winter, Jay. "War, Family, and Fertility in Twentieth Century Europe." In *The European Experience of Declining Fertility,* ed. John Gillis, Louise Tilly, and David Levine, 291–309. Cambridge: Blackwell, 1982.

Wohl, Robert. *The Generation of 1914.* Cambridge: Harvard University Press, 1979.

Wollen, Peter. "Cinema/Americanism/The Robot." In *Modernity and Mass Culture,* ed. James Naremore and Patrick Brantlinger, 23 – 40. Bloomington: Indiana University Press, 1991.

Woller, Hans. *Die Abrechnung mit dem Faschismus in Italien 1943 bis 1948.* Munich: Oldenbourg, 1996.

Zagarrio, Vito. "Giovani e apparati culturali a Firenze nella crisi del regime fascista." *Studi storici* (July-September 1980): 609–35.

———. "Ideology Elsewhere: Contradictory Models of Italian Fascist Cinema." In *Resisting Images: Essays on Cinema and History,* ed. Robert Sklar and Charles Musser, 149–72. Philadelphia: Temple University Press, 1990.

———. "Il modello sovietico: Tra piano culturale e piano economico." In *Cinema italiano sotto il fascismo,* ed. Riccardo Redi, 185–200. Venice: Marsilio, 1979.

Zangrandi, Ruggiero. *Il lungo viaggio attraverso il fascismo: Contributo alla storia di una generazione.* Turin: Einaudi, 1948.

Zani, Luciano. "L'immagine dell'URSS nell'Italia degli anni trenta." *Storia contemporanea* (December 1990): 1197–1224.

Zapponi, Niccolò. *Cultura e società, 1870–1975* Naples: Edizioni scientifiche italiane, 1983.

Zucarò, Domenico. *Cospirazione operaia: Resistenza al fascismo in Torino-Genova-Milano, 1927–43.* Turin: Einaudi, 1965.

Zuccotti, Susan. *The Italians and the Holocaust.* New York: Basic Books, 1987.

Zunino, Pier Giorgio. *L'ideologia del fascismo.* Bologna: Il Mulino, 1985.

———. *Interpretazione e memoria del fascismo.* Rome: Laterza, 1991.

Index

2000 (journal), 255n40
'900 (journal), 27–28, 65
IX Maggio (journal), 166

Aberle, Grete, 104, 246n49
Acito, Alfredo, 269n28
Action Committees for the Universality of Rome, 247n60
Action Party, 202, 207, 208
Africa italiana (journal), 128
Aggiornamento (becoming up-to-date): 33–36, 51, 78–79, 120
Alberti, Guglielmo, 78, 111
Albini, Clara, 105, 246n49
Albini, Franco, 36, 224n59
Albini, Maria, 246n49
Aleramo, Sibilla, 270n37
Alessandrini, Goffredo, 208; *Addio Kira!*, 259n72; *Noi viv*, 259n72; *La Segretaria privata*, 239n48
Alessandrini, Luisa, 91
Alfassio Grimaldi, Ugoberto, 170
Alfieri, Dino, 131, 167, 168, 175, 179, 255n33
Alicata, Mario, 167, 186, 187, 194–97, 199, 211, 264n126
Alleanza muliebre culturale italiana, 96
Alpes publishing house, 57
Alvaro, Corrado, 36, 68, 80, 97, 142, 187–88, 205–7, 221n24, 258n63,

270n37; in Berlin, 44–45, 53–54, 269n28; and film, 70, 76; and public commitment to fascism, 121; self-censorship of, 47, 131; in Soviet Union, 39. Works: *L'amata alla finestra (The Loved One at the Window)*, 66; *Gente in Aspromonte (The People of Aspromonte)*, 66, 67, 227n6; *Itinerario italiano (Italian Itinerary)*, 188; "Solitudine," 44, 65; *L'uomo è forte (Man Is Strong)*, 141, 143–47, 151, 160–61; *Vent'anni*, 67; *Viaggio in Russia*, 259n72
Amendola, Giovanni, 65
America, 39–44, 52–53, 194
American cinema, 77, 139, 175
Americanization, cultural, 26, 39–41
Amicucci, Ermanno, 220n16
Anceschi, Luciano, 30–31, 106–7, 112, 113, 118, 190, 222n37, 275n27; on American literature, 52–53; in Littoriali competitions, 109; philosophical interests of, 52, 103, 167; retreat from political involvement of, 121; on sexual equality, 104
Andreotti, Giuliano, 209
Angioletti, Giovanni Battista, 59, 62, 228n9
Anschluss, 158, 169
Anti-Comintern Pact, 135, 145
Anti-Idealist Congress, 109

STUDIES ON THE HISTORY OF SOCIETY AND CULTURE

Victoria E. Bonnell and Lynn Hunt, Editors

Text:	10/13 Aldus
Display:	Aldus
Composition:	G & S Typesetters, Inc.
Printing and binding:	Thomson-Shore, Inc.
Index:	Ruth Elwell